INTERNATIONAL SOCIAL MOVEMENT RESEARCH

Volume 1 • 1988

FROM STRUCTURE TO ACTION:
COMPARING SOCIAL MOVEMENT
RESEARCH ACROSS CULTURES

Supplement Series to RESEARCH IN SOCIAL MOVEMENTS,
CONFLICTS AND CHANGE

This volume is the result of the activities of the Research Planning Group on Participation in Social Movements sponsored by the Council for European Studies. The work of the Planning Group was also assisted by the Dutch National Science Foundation and by Cornell University's Western Societies Program. We are grateful to these organizations for their support and encouragement.

INTERNATIONAL SOCIAL MOVEMENT RESEARCH

A Research Annual

FROM STRUCTURE TO ACTION:
COMPARING SOCIAL MOVEMENT RESEARCH ACROSS CULTURES

Edited by: BERT KLANDERMANS
Department of Social Psychology
Free University of Amsterdam

HANSPETER KRIESI
Department of Political Science
University of Amsterdam

SIDNEY TARROW
Department of Government
Cornell University

VOLUME 1 • 1988

 JAI PRESS INC.

Greenwich, Connecticut   *London, England*

CONTENTS

PART II.   CONSENSUS MOBILIZATION OR THE CONSTRUCTION OF MEANING

PART III.   THE CREATION AND CAREERS OF COLLECTIVE ACTORS

LIST OF CONTRIBUTORS

Robert D. Benford

Department of Sociology
University of Nebraska

Donatella della Porta

European University Institute
Florence, Italy

Mario Diani

Department of Sociology
Bocconi University of Milan

William A. Gamson

Department of Sociology
Boston College

Bert Klandermans

Department of Social Psychology
Free University of Amsterdam

Hanspeter Kriesi

Department of Political Science
University of Amsterdam

Giovanni Lodi

Department of Sociology
State Univesity of Milan

Doug McAdam

Department of Sociology
University of Arizona

Alberto Melucci

Department of Sociology
University of Trento

Karl-Dieter Opp

Department of Sociology
University of Hamburg

Dieter Rucht

Department of Political Science
University of Munich

Ben Schennink

Peace Research Institute
University of Nijmegen
The Netherlands

David A. Snow

Department of Sociology
University of Arizona

Sidney Tarrow

Department of Government
Cornell University

PREFACE FROM
THE SERIES EDITOR

This volume is the first in a new series on *International Social Movement Research*. It is my objective to bring together in this series social movement research written from a comparative perspective. Each volume will be organized around some specific theme, whether it be a movement, a theoretical approach, or an issue in the social movement field. Although all would agree to its relevance, comparative social movement research is rare. By creating this specific outlet for it, I hope to stimulate the study of social movements from a comparative perspective.

From Structure to Action is not only an attempt to synthesize the European and American approaches to the study of contemporary social movements. It also focuses on the processes which mediate between macrostructural and social psychological determinants of movement participation. In demonstrating the importance of these intermediate processes in different countries and within different movements, it directs our attention to the formation and mobilization of consensus, a theme neglected until recently in the social movement literature.

Bert Klandermans
Series Editor

PREFACE

From Structure to Action is an attempt to bridge several gaps in the literature on social movements. Coming from different cultural and scientific backgrounds, we were surprised by the similarities we saw between contemporary movements across cultures and the different directions taken by the European and American approaches to studying them. More important, we were struck by the lack of comparative work in the social movement field. Struggling through the mass of American and European writings on social movements since the 1960s, we became more and more convinced that there was a blind spot between the two areas: in the dynamics that transform macro-structural developments into individual decisions to participate in social movement activities. The focal point of our interest became the formation and mobilization of consensus around social movement goals, and the networks, structures and subcultures supporting individuals' participation in movements.

Taking contemporary social movements like the environmental movement, the women's movement and the peace movement as our empirical points of reference, we wanted to bring together scholars familiar with the two predominant theoretical currents on each continent—resource mobilization in the United States and new social movements in Europe. We did so in two meetings, the first in Ithaca and the second in Amsterdam.

This anthology is the end-product of those two meetings. Klandermans and Tarrow brought together a core group of six students of social movements (McAdam, Melucci, Klandermans, Kriesi, Snow, and Tarrow) at a planning meeting in Ithaca in August 1985. Two days of extremely intense, creative and stimulating discussions set the theoretical stage for the second conference in

Amsterdam in June 1986, at which Kriesi joined in the planning and a larger group of scholars took part, representing the Netherlands, West Germany, Italy and the United States.

This volume is the collective product of the Ithaca and Amsterdam meetings. Though for reasons of cohesiveness and space, a selection from among the papers presented at the two conferences had to be made, the contributions of all the participants were fundamental to our collective enterprise. We hope they will remember with as much pleasure as we do riding the waves of our "real" social movement in Amsterdam.

Our efforts were supported at various times by a number of institutions and organizations. First, Klandermans and Tarrow were awarded a Research Planning Group grant by the Council of European Studies, whose Executive Director, Ioannis Sinanoglou, showed comprehension and encouragement at all times. Second, Klandermans was awarded a grant from The Netherlands Organization for the Advancement of Pure Scientific Research for the organization of the Amsterdam conference. Cornell University's Western Societies Program provided logistical and financial support for the Ithaca meeting, while the Free University of Amsterdam did the same for the Amsterdam conference. Both the Free University and the University of Amsterdam helped to support the costs of editing this book.

Many individuals helped us to organize these activities, of whom we wish to single out three whose contributions were particularly important. Diarmuid Maguire's thorough summary of the Ithaca meeting helped the editors to plan the Amsterdam Conference. Gerrita van der Veen's on-the-spot organizing did a great deal to help the Amsterdam conference to succeed. Martha Linke worked on all the papers, checked the references and deserves particular praise for editing the English of our foreign contributors. We owe her a special debt for the care and resourcefulness with which she faced an arduous and apparently endless task. Finally, we thank our contributors, who wrote and turned in their papers with dispatch and showed a willingness to submit to suggestions for revision with patience and forbearance.

Bert Klandermans, Hanspeter Kriesi and Sidney Tarrow
Ithaca, New York, August 1987.

MOBILIZATION INTO SOCIAL MOVEMENTS:
SYNTHESIZING EUROPEAN AND AMERICAN APPROACHES

Bert Klandermans and Sidney Tarrow

INTRODUCTION

When in the late 1960s the calm of the postwar decades was shattered by worker, student, and general discontent, political and scholarly certitudes were challenged as well. In government, elites could no longer assume that they enjoyed the unquestioning consent of compliant publics; in the party system, activists rebelled against established leaders and ideologies; and in the mass public, participation burst the bounds of inherited institutions. A host of new vehicles of participation were created, from citizen's movements to neighborhood committees to factory councils to the public interest lobby.

At first, the dissidents seemed to come mainly from the fringes of society, from among students, marginal workers, ethnic and linguistic minorities, blacks. But it was soon clear that insurgency had spread to organized workers,

International Social Movement Research, Vol. 1, pages 1-38.
Supplement to Research in Social Movements, Conflicts and Change
Copyright © 1988 by JAI Press Inc.
All rights of reproduction in any form reserved.
ISBN: 0-89232-955-6

1

to staid middle class neighborhoods, and to the heart of the party system. Even voter surveys demonstrated that the new demands had infiltrated older channels; when voters in seven countries were asked about their participation preferences, it was discovered that the active voter was frequently sympathetic to protest actions as well (Barnes, Kaase, and Allerbeck 1979).

Scholars were quick to perceive that changes were afoot in what some would call "postindustrial society." Though some had once assured us that ideology and militance were dead, others now concluded that mass politics had run amok and that democratic institutions were threatened by hypermobilization (Crozier et al. 1975). Other writers, moved less by fear than by enthusiasm, inferred that the revolutionary models of the past had been reborn. Still others saw the emergence of an "antipolitics" that rejected the politics of consensus inherited from the postwar settlement (Berger 1979).

Students of social movements were more circumspect, but on both sides of the Atlantic they too questioned whether inherited models of participation would endure. On the European side, the most obvious casualty was the notion that the working class was a radical social movement's necessary basis, and material benefits its goal (Touraine 1971); on the American side, it was the fixation on the idea that movement participation was caused by personal alienation, for militants were often found to be integrated members of their communities (Oberschall 1973). Some (McAdam 1982; Piven and Cloward 1977) stressed the political structuring of the new movements, while others emphasized their cultural content (Melucci 1980) and their relation to the formation of new class identities (Pizzorno 1978).

Whatever their approach, these scholars perceived the contentious politics of the late 1960s and early 1970s as a revitalizing force for a subject that had too long remained on the edge of scholarly and political legitimacy. Some scholars focused on the cultural meaning of the new movements (Melucci 1980); others saw a new political paradigm replacing the postwar political settlement (Offe 1983), while others (Pizzorno 1978; Tarrow 1983) discussed the period as part of a recurring cycle of protest.

In the wake of the developments of those years, even as it was becoming clear that both the "end of ideology" paradigm and its "crisis of democracy" successor were exaggerated stereotypes, serious research on social movements has continued to evolve. Two major new paradigms emerged: in the United States, what has been called "resource mobilization" and, in Western Europe, the "new social movement" approach. Although both paradigms reflect the common surge of mass mobilization in Europe and America, the two nevertheless differ significantly. By no means were all the Europeans advocates of the new social movements approach or all the Americans "resource mobilizationists," but, in Europe, many focused on larger structural issues— the structural causes of social movements, their ideologies, and their relation to the culture of advanced capitalist society—whereas Americans developed their research mainly at the group and individual level, looking systematically at the groups that organized mass protest, at their forms of action, and at the motivations of individuals who joined them.

Only recently have some scholars begun to attempt to integrate European and American approaches (cf. Kitschelt 1985). It is our hope to advance that integration in this volume. We have assembled contributions from within the emerging American and European traditions and have highlighted some of the typical movements that emerged during and after the 1960s: from the early student and (in the United States) civil rights movements of the 1960s, to the ecological and women's movements that appeared in the early 1970s, to the peace movements that developed in the late 1970s to the more radical, and sometimes violent, forms of action that have appeared at every stage in the four countries we shall examine—Italy, West Germany, the Netherlands, and the United States.

In this book we do not attempt to "cover" two decades of social unrest on two continents, nor do we explore in any depth the ideologies and programs of the individual movements. Rather, we emphasize the process of mobilization—that is, how the potential for social movements which emerges from the social and political structure of advanced capitalist democracies is *translated* into social and political action. We argue that this process occurs through the social and political networks in which individuals and groups come together around common goals; through the political opportunities that provide them with outlets for collective action; and through the construction of new meanings out of which new collective actors emerge.

In part one of this chapter, we review the two major paradigms that have emerged from the past two decades in Western Europe and the United States. In part two, we sketch some tentative lines for a bridge between the two paradigms. Part three argues for the importance of a comparative approach and points to some of its benefits for the study of social movements; part four introduces the major movements examined in the book. And in part five, we survey the types of social movements that have been notable in the four countries from which our collaborators have drawn their examples and their conclusions. Finally, we provide brief introductions to the essays included in the volume.[1]

I. RESOURCE MOBILIZATION AND NEW SOCIAL MOVEMENTS[2]

Though the recent history of social movements in Europe is in many ways similar to parallel developments in the United States, resource mobilization theory and new social movements approaches represent rather different appraisals of contemporary social movements. A brief review of the two paradigms will underscore this difference, as well as the place of each in the future of social movement studies.

A. Resource Mobilization

Resource mobilization theory departed from the traditional social movement approach, according to which the origins of social movements are explained by the existence of grievances in a society. Research mobilization theorists argued that grievances are ubiquitous in every society and that, as a consequence, grievances alone cannot be sufficient conditions for the rise of social movements. The availability of resources and opportunities for collective action were considered more important than grievances in triggering social movement formation (McCarthy and Zald 1973, 1977; Jenkins 1983). Although McAdam (1982) distinguished between those aspects of resource mobilization theory that focus on internal resources and those that focus on political opportunities, we discuss the two at the same time.

The resource mobilization approach has been most fruitful in analyzing mobilization processes and in emphasizing the role of existing organizations and networks in laying the groundwork for social movement formation (Oberschall 1973). This emphasis was reinforced by the healthy flowering of mass mobilization of the 1960s and 1970s, which shifted the study of social movements from the arcane to the normal. The "normalization" of social movement studies can be illustrated by three key elements of the theory.

1. The costs and benefits of participation. The costs and benefits of participation play an important role in the analysis of mobilization processes (Oberschall 1973, 1980; Klandermans 1984). This component of resource mobilization theory leans heavily on Olson's (1968) logic of collective action, and particularly on his distinction between collective and selective incentives. Incentives differ in the way they are related to participation; since collective incentives are characterized by jointness of supply, obtaining collective incentives is not contingent upon participation, while obtaining selective incentives is contingent upon participation. The core argument of Olson's theory is that rational individuals will not participate in collective action unless selective incentives encourage them to do so.

Olson's theory is attractive because it offers an explanation for the fact that people often *do not* take part in collective action, despite their interest in the collective goals. This explanation is consistent with the initial assumption that grievances are not a sufficient condition for the rise of a social movement. In building on Olson's theory, resource mobilization theorists introduced a different problem: Olson can indeed explain why individuals *do not* participate in collective action; but why they sometimes *do* participate, even in the absence of selective incentives, remained a vexing problem.[3]

Various solutions have been suggested to this problem. Oliver (1984) asserted that individuals participate in more active forms of participation because they realize that the collective good would never be achieved if everyone reasoned as Olson's rational individual did. Oberschall (1980) explained that, given the multiplicative relationship between the value of the collective goal and its possible realization, for some people the goal is so valuable that even a slight chance of success is enough to motivate participation, especially if selective incentives are associated with participation. Klandermans and Oegema (1987b) showed that this was indeed true for participation in one of the large peace demonstrations in the Netherlands. Carde (1978) pointed to the ideological incentives people receive by working for a cause they believe to be just. Gamson and Fireman (1979) argued that the two main reasons for participation are loyalty to the larger collectivity engaged in collective action, and the felt obligation to participate in order to maintain one's self-respect.

The introduction of the costs and benefits of participation made possible a more sophisticated approach to the study of recruitment into social movements. Collective (or purposive) incentives were distinguished from selective incentives, and selective incentives were in turn divided into social and nonsocial incentives (Wilson 1973; Oberschall 1980; Klandermans 1984). Olson's thesis that collective incentives make no difference is no longer taken seriously except by a minority of social movement students; instead, in recent work the two types of incentives are seen as reinforcing or compensating for one another. A distinction is made between willingness to participate in different forms of action, in moderate and militant action (Klandermans 1984), and in low- and high-risk activities (McAdam 1986), because of divergent cost-benefit ratios.

2. *Organization.* According to resource mobilization theory, organization is an important resource for a social movement, but it is not equivalent to movements as a whole, which theorists have tended to identify with mobilized sentiment pools (McCarthy and Zald 1977) or with continuing confrontations between challengers and authorities (Tilly 1984). Organization decreases the costs of participation (Morris 1984); it is important in the recruitment of participants (Oberschall 1973, 1980); and, in the opinion of most students, it increases the chances of success (Gamson 1975; but see Piven and Cloward 1979 for a different view). Resource mobilization theory's emphasis on organization as a resource was a departure from the traditional approach, which deemed a low level of organization characteristic of social movements.

Resource mobilization theorists did not, however, confuse movement organizations with interest groups. They were clearly aware that movements frequently produced forms of organization that differ fundamentally from traditional bureaucratic organizations. For example, they wrote of the "transitory teams" (McCarthy and Zald 1973) of militants who, using the new mobility and means of communication of advanced industrial society, could come together and separate around issues as they arose. They observed the importance of the media as a substitute for conventional organization in producing movement successes—and eventually failures (Oberschall 1978). And they innovated in looking at the development of social movements *within* organizations (Zald and Berger 1978) and at what they called social movement sectors (Garner and Zald 1985).

3. Expectations of success play an important role in the collective incentives of participation for resource mobilization theorists (Oberschall 1980; Pinard 1983; Klandermans 1984; Oliver, Marwell, and Teixeira 1985). This factor is related to several others noted in the literature: political opportunity structure (Eisinger 1973; McAdam 1982; Tarrow 1983), the influence of sympathetic third parties (Pinard 1971; Jenkins and Perrow 1977), and influential allies available to challengers (Gamson 1975; Lipsky 1968; Tilly 1979). A favorable political opportunity structure, the presence of third parties, and allies considerably increase the chances of success of a social movement (Fireman and Gamson 1979).

Theorists attention to these factors began to move resource mobilization theory closer to the analysis of politics and political interaction (Piven and Cloward 1977; McAdam 1982) and toward the concerns of political scientists. It was observed, for example, that the discovery of a new tactic sometimes inaugurates a protest cycle or shifts it to a new level of interaction with authorities (McAdam 1983; Tarrow 1983). As long as the opponent does not know how to respond to the tactic, the protesters chances of success remain high. Eventually this advantage dissipates because the opponent learns how to react to the new tactic.

Tilly (1978) has devoted much of his work to the development of a concept of "repertoires" of collective action, and to the relation between such repertoires and political crises and regime changes (Snyder and Tilly 1972). Piven and Cloward (1977) emphasized the importance of electoral realignments in triggering social movements. Tarrow (1983) argued that a reform cycle runs parallel to the protest cycle and is thus an indicator of how the government responds to the new protest tactic. These authors shifted attention from movements as emergent and unstructured forms of collective action to movements as a form of mass politics.

Oberschall (1980) and Klandermans (1984) linked expectations of success to the number of people participating in a movement. Klandermans stipulated that people have to decide to participate at a point when they do not know whether others will participate or not, and argued that, accordingly, their decisions must be based on expectations about the behavior of others. This argument, albeit emerging from the assumptions of resource mobilization theory, re-emphasized the collective life of social movements (but in a far more empirical way than the arguments of the older collective behavior school). It thus proposed a bridge toward the "new social movement" approach, some of whose proponents, particularly Melucci (1980), have made the collective life of the movement a cardinal issue, as we shall see.

B.   New Social Movements

In contrast to the resource mobilization orientation, the new social movement approach seeks explanation for the rise of the social movements of the past two decades in the appearance of new grievances. It stresses that the new movements (the environmental movement, the women's movement, and the peace movement) differ from old movements (generally characterized as the labor movement) in values, action forms, and constituency. New social movements are thought to be a reaction to structural changes in western industrialized societies.

Though interpretations differ, the following characteristics appear to typify new social movements, according to the authors we have surveyed:[4]

1.   *Values.* New social movements are antimodernistic. They do not accept the premises of a society based on economic growth. They have broken with the traditional values of capitalistic society. They seek a new relationship to nature, to one's own body, to the opposite sex, to work, and to consumption.

2.   *Action forms.* New social movements make extensive use of unconventional forms of action. They take a dissociative attitude toward society, as witnessed by their antagonism to politics. They prefer small-scale, decentralized organizations, are antihierarchical, and favor direct democracy.

3.   *Constituency.* Two population groups are particularly predisposed to participate in new social movements. The first group includes people who are paying the costs of problems resulting from modernization, primarily those who have been marginalized by societal developments. This group cannot be defined by social classes or ranks, because the problems it confronts are not limited to particular social strata. The second group consists of those who, because of more general shifts in values and needs, have become particularly sensitive to problems resulting from modernization. Members of this group are found primarily in the new middle class and among the well-educated young people working in the civil service. Brand et al. (1983) state that the new social movements recruit primarily from the latter category. The values and needs of these people determines to a large extent the dynamics of the new social movements.

The new social movement literature seeks to answer the question of where these new values, action forms, and constituencies come from. The answer has been sought in various sources, although all explanations link the new developments to modernization and economic growth. Brand (1982) classifies the various explanations as theories focusing either on rising demands or on need defense. The former seek an explanation in the new values, needs, and wishes that are rooted in the modernization process and clash with the traditional system; the latter seek it in the negative consequences of modernization for the individual.

4. *New aspirations.* One group of authors, drawing on Inglehart's theory about postmaterial values, ascribes the rise of new social movements to changed values. Inglehart (1971, 1977) described a "silent revolution" in Europe: a dramatic change from materialist to postmaterialist values. Postwar youth, assured of the satisfaction of material needs, developed nonmaterial needs such as self-actualization and participation. Other observers discerned changes in other values as well: conventional middle-class values appeared to be eroding, the traditional work ethic was declining, and attitudes toward work and career were changing (see Brand 1980 for research on West German; Oudijk 1983 for research on the Netherlands). Proponents of these new values were coming into conflict with an essentially materialist political and social system.

Another group of authors describes new social movements as a reaction to the welfare state. The welfare state has created new entitlement needs with respect to government services, these authors argue (Klages 1980; de Geest 1984). Increased prosperity has caused an increased demand for scarce goods. Many of these are positional goods (pleasant living surroundings, a car, good education). When these goods become widespread, they become an obstruction to the satisfaction of other needs, leading to, for example, suburbs, traffic jams, the devaluation of degrees. The general result is increased competition, which in turn produces more grievances (F. Hirsch 1980).

5. *Satisfaction of needs endangered.* Some of those who seek to explain the rise of new social movements attribute the phenomenon not to an "explosion of aspirations" (Klages 1980) but to increased social strain related to industrialization and bureaucratization. These two processes, it is argued, have resulted in a *loss of identity,* leading to the loss of traditional ties and loyalties. As a consequence, people become receptive to visions of new utopias and to new commitments. Young people in the 1960s and 1970s are supposed to be particularly vulnerable to this (Horn 1973; Berger et al. 1975; Lowenthal 1979; Narr 1979), but its resemblance to an older collective behavior approach should be noted (Kornhauser 1959).

Industrialization has had many negative consequences for the satisfaction of important needs (Raschke 1980). Self-destructive aspects of western society (e.g., the exhaustion of resources, conflicts between industrialized countries, rising economic, social, psychological, and ecological costs of production), together with a decreased problem-solving capacity have generated tremendous social problems. Having become accustomed to new services, people then become dissatisfied with the level at which services are performed (Hirschman

1982). These dissatisfactions provide the breeding ground for new social movements.

Yet other theorists consider the intervention of the state and capitalistic economy into new reaches of life as the chief explanation for the rise of new social movements (Habermas 1973; J. Hirsch 1980; Melucci 1980, 1981). The state took upon itself the responsibility for satisfying needs that the market economy could no longer meet. The restructuring of the capitalistic economy in the wake of recession led to the exclusion of a growing number of unemployed or otherwise disqualified persons. To a greater and greater extent, the state was given the task of alleviating the consequences of this process of restructuring. Thus a network of regulatory, ministering, supervisory, and controlling institutions developed and increased the danger of loss of legitimacy.

The significance of new social movements must, as Melucci argues, be determined within the context of these changes. The new social movements fight for the "reappropriation of time, of space, and of relationships in the individual's daily experience" (Melucci 1980, p. 219). The members "negotiate" new collective identities as part of the process of responding to new problems. How these problems, values, and identities are activated is a problem of the translation of structure into action.

C.   Resource Mobilization and New Social Movements

Resource mobilization theory has been criticized for focusing too much on organization, politics, and resources while neglecting the structural precondition of movements—that is, for focusing too much on the "how" of social movements and not enough on their "why." This charge has led to another critical observation: that the theory directs attention to movements that are "acceptable" to elites but does not apply to those that challenge essentials of the system (McAdam 1982). And critics have claimed that in its insistence on the invariant character of grievances, resource mobilization theory ignores the social-psychological bases of social movements (Jenkins 1983) and how new resources emerge in the production of collective action (Tarrow 1983).

The new social movement approach has stimulated the opposite criticisms. Some contend that it focuses in a reductionist way on the structural origins of strain and does not pay enough attention to the "how" of mobilization. Others say an insistence on the antimodernist character of movements leads to ignoring a number of groups that have been important products of the recent cycle of protest. And still others claim that it diverts attention from the political preconditions and the political processing of movements.[5]

These criticisms and and counter-criticisms are a healthy part of a cultural encounter between the two main paradigms. But they will concern us less than the gap left by both paradigms between the structural determinants of social movements and the psychological dynamics of individual participation in such movements. For what we mainly lack are detailed theoretical and empirical analyses of the mobilization processes that intervene between the structural transformations of advanced industrial society and the new actors, the new forms of action and the new grievances observed by recent students of social movements.

What we need, in other words, is a better understanding of how structural change is transformed into collective action. The contributions to this volume are for the most part intended to bridge that gap between structure and participation. But in order to understand its character, we need a theoretical elaboration of mobilization as a process linking the structural and individual levels and "transforming" structure into action. The following section proposes such an elaboration.

II.   TRANSFORMING STRUCTURE INTO ACTION

A.   The Context of Participation

Mobilization has sometimes been conceived in such a global way that it is difficult to study empirically.[6] We think it is best studied if it can be broken down into its constituent phases: the formation of mobilization potentials, the formation and activation of recruitment networks, the arousal of the motivation to participate, and the removal of barriers to participation (Klandermans and Oegema 1987b).

In the formation of mobilization potentials, movement organizations must win attitudinal and ideological support. In the formation and activation of recruitment networks, they must increase the probability that people who "belong" to their mobilization potential are reached. In arousing motivations to participate, they must favorably influence the decisions of people who are reached by a mobilization attempt. In removing barriers, they must increase the probability that people who are motivated will eventually participate.

It is important to distinguish these processes because each is likely to be influenced by different factors and different theories are needed to analyze each one. Moreover, to exert influence on them, social movement organizations must tailor their activities to each process. The formation of mobilization potentials entails grievance interpretation; the formation and activation of recruitment networks requires coalition formation and linking movement organizations to existing formal and informal networks. Arousing the motivation to participate requires control of the costs and benefits of participation. The removal of barriers requires control of the situation participants are in.

These distinctions will be examined in much greater detail, in particular in Bert Klandermans's chapter on consensus mobilization, so a brief introduction suffices for our present objectives.

1. The mobilization potential of a society refers to the set of individuals who could theoretically be mobilized by a social movement. It excludes people with attitudes that place a social movement in the 'latitude of rejection' (Sherif, Sherif, and Nebergall 1965). Attitudes toward a movement concern its means and/or its goals. With respect to attitudes toward the means, the concept of mobilization potential is related to Barnes and Kaase's concept of protest potential (1979), which these authors define as the willingness to participate in unconventional forms of political behavior. But this definition is too uniformly behavioral: it should be broadened to include the willingness to identify with collective actors that challenge constituted authority, even when unconventional action is unlikely to result. Alberto Melucci makes this point in his contribution to this volume.

Identification with collective actors leads to attitudes toward goals, relating the concept of mobilization potential to that of political potential (Kriesi 1982). In Kriesi's definition, the political potential of a movement refers to a group of people in a common structural situation who share certain "objective" interests. Mobilization potential sets the limits within which a mobilization campaign can be successful. People who do not belong to the mobilization potential will not consider participating in activities of the movement, even if they are reached by a mobilization attempt.

2. Recruitment networks. However successful a movement may be in the formation of a mobilization potential, if it does not have access to a network through which to reach people, its mobilization potential cannot be put to use. That part of the mobilization potential which becomes the target of mobilization attempts tells us something about a movement's strategy and organization and the networks to which it has access. The more extensive a movement's branchings, and the more interwoven with other organizations they are, the greater the number of people who will be reached by a mobilization attempt.

Recruitment networks are made up of linkages within and between formal organizations, the strong and weak ties within informal networks, and formal and informal communication networks, as indicated in Garner and Zald's concept of the "social movement sector," in which relations are both cooperative and competitive (1985, p. 120). Consequently, a typical type of case study in the social movement field—of individual recruitment into a single movement organization—may be inadequate for explaining a movement's potential recruitment basis. Donatella della Porta's contribution to this volume, for example, shows that joining an Italian terrorist organization was seldom an individual act; recruitment usually depended upon networks within non-terrorist organizations in the social movement sector.

The formation of recruitment networks involves both extending the reach of the organization—particularly at a local level—and forming coalitions with other organizations (Wilson and Orum 1976; Klandermans and Oegema 1987a;

Ferree and Miller 1985). During a mobilization campaign, a movement organization will first have to mobilize those within the recruitment network before it can reach broader sectors of its mobilization potential. If these people back out, recruitment efforts come to a dead end.

The density of the recruitment network also influences the method of recruitment. A social movement using face-to-face methods can reach many people only if it has a dense network; if it does not have this network, it can turn to indirect methods such as mass communication or direct mail (McCarthy 1983; Mitchell 1984b). There is evidence, however, that such indirect methods work well only in cases of low risk or low-threshold participation (McAdam 1986; Briet et al. 1987). At the other extreme of the risk dimension—the secret terrorist organizations studied by della Porta—recruitment is almost always direct and personal.

3. *The motivation to participate* is a function of the perceived costs and benefits of participation (Oberschall 1980; Klandermans 1984; Muller and Opp 1986). Both collective and selective incentives vary as a function of the kind of activity a person is participating in. Movement organizations—but also competing and opposing organizations and authorities—control the costs and benefits of participation to a varying extent.

Individuals decide whether or not to participate in complex situations about which they have very imperfect information concerning the costs and benefits of participation. The variance in information explains why people objectively in the same situation may arrive at very different appraisals of costs and benefits, depending on the cues they are selecting. Perceptions can be manipulated, and opponents will try to do so. Thus mobilization campaigns are to a large extent struggles to win over people's minds.

4. *Barriers to participation.* Motivation can predict willingness to participate. Willingness alone, however, is an insufficient condition for participation; it can simply predict participation in so far as intentions can be carried out. Participation itself is a function of the interrelation of motivation and barriers. The more highly motivated people are, the higher the barriers they can overcome. This relation opens up two possible strategies for a movement organization: maintaining or increasing motivation and removing barriers. The former strategy is of course closely related to the arousal of motivation and the mobilization of internal resources; the latter to legitimation, alliance-building, and the mobilization of external resources.

B.   Consensus Mobilization and Action Mobilization

Through the four aspects of mobilization distinguished above runs the distinction between consensus mobilization and action mobilization (Klandermans 1984). The former involves the propagation of the views of the movement, the latter the activation of individuals. From our initial elaboration above, it should be clear that the formation of a mobilization potential is primarily a matter of consensus mobilization, whereas the remaining stages entail both consensus and action mobilization. Consensus mobilization is the major conceptual tool that we propose for linking the "macro" and "micro" approaches, respectively, of the new social movement and the resource mobilization schools of thought.

In this case too the traditional emphasis on movement organizations is inadequate. For an important factor in consensus mobilization is the interplay between the organization attempting to carry out the mobilization and other elements in the social movement sector, which may be responsible for the initial consensus mobilization of which that organization takes advantage. This interplay is well illustrated by the role of the student movements of the late 1960s in preparing the terrain that other new movements—the environmental, women's, and peace movements—could cultivate. Similarly, *non*social movement organizations, such as trade unions and political parties, may either knowingly or unwittingly mobilize consensus among their members or sympathizers and so predispose them to action mobilization by others.

An advantage of investigating consensus mobilization is that consensus mobilization provides a bridge between the internal actions of social movement organizations and the larger political system. By investigating this phase in the process of mobilization, we may perceive links between the organizations that carry out the actions at the end of the mobilization process and the alignments and realignments in opinion that provide new interpretive frames for movement leaders to use in stimulating action mobilization. These points become particularly clear in the essays by William Gamson and by David Snow and Robert Benford, in the final section of this volume.

C. Synthesizing and Amending the Two Approaches

To return to the European and American literatures on social movements; it is obvious that theorists on each side of the Atlantic have tended to concentrate on different aspects of mobilization. The more "structural" new social movement approaches have concentrated on the factors that determine the mobilization potential of contemporary social movements, specifically the deprivations of the societal groups most immediately affected by the unfavorable consequences of postindustrial developments, and the aspirations of those most sensitive to those developments. The original resource mobilization approach reveals the reverse emphasis: a great concentration on the mobilization of resources and the costs and benefits of participation but only brief consideration given to the formation of the mobilization potentials that movements draw from in mobilization campaigns. If carefully examined and selectively used, each perspective can help correct the relative bias of the other.

One thing both approaches overlook is the importance of consensus mobilization. The structural approach too easily assumes that mobilization potentials form spontaneously through societal developments. It overlooks the fact that social networks and social movement organizations themselves have an important share in defining the situation which can lead to action. Since resource mobilization theory does not concern itself with the formation of mobilization potentials at all, it too largely disregards the importance of consensus mobilization in the creation of mobilization potentials.

In general, theorists pay insufficient attention to movements' attempts to influence the perceptions of potential participants. More specifically, neither the new social movement approach nor resource mobilization theory studies an important link between mobilization potentials and the motivation to participate: the legitimization of action goals in relation to the problems that define the mobilization potential of a movement and its mobilization of consensus. It is mainly this intermediate level between structural factors and individual motivation to participate that is examined in this volume.

Can the synthesis we propose between the primarily structural approach of the new social movement school and the primarily motivational approach of American researchers "fit" the broad range of movements studied by scholars on both sides of the Atlantic? Although it is reasonable to suppose that each body of theory is easiest to apply to its own "home ground," a truly integrated approach can be tested only through comparative analysis. It is to this that we shall turn.

III. COMPARING SOCIAL MOVEMENTS[7]

Until quite recently, social movements have been regarded as such rare and unusual phenomena that more energy has gone into describing their individual contours than into comparing their incidence and correlates. The 1960s, with their broad explosion of discontent, led to a widespread perception that movements were a "normal" part of mass politics. That perception leads logically to the need for systematic comparison. Yet comparative studies of social movements have been slow to develop. A survey of English language texts in comparative politics turns up a remarkable finding: in this field, few of the authors surveyed gave more than passing attention to either social or political movements.[8]

Although comparison is not a magic answer to the problems of any field, given the differences between the dominant paradigms in the Western European and American branches of this field, comparing European and American movements—which few have done until now—may yield a number of aids to better definition, more consistent operationalization, and greater synthesis than has been possible until now. At the very least, comparison can help scholars on both sides of the Atlantic know whether they are studying examples of the same phenomena, and, if so, to what they can attribute the differences among the movements they study.

The first and most obvious benefit of comparison is that it is a corrective to the theoretically inclusive but in practice narrowly tested structural models that have dominated the study of social movements in the past. Movements, being unusual phenomena, produce actions that may be classified as rare events. Consequently the study of social movements, unlike other fields of sociology or political science, has favored one-variable explanations and structural paradigms (e.g., "mass society," "postmaterialism"). Comparison can reveal that similar outcomes can produce different structural conditions, thereby forcing the analyst to adopt a more complicated or more clearly specified model. Recent European studies manifest an increasing comparative consciousness that is far less evident than in most research in the United States.

Second, comparison can serve as a check upon premature support for what seems to the observer to be "obvious" causal patterns that have emerged from narrowly drawn observations of individuals and groups. When analysis of the same movement or behavior in another system shows little relationship between commonly paired variables, the analyst is forced to specify the posited relationship more precisely in his own system or to translate it into more general terms that will cover the variety of conditions with which it is associated in different countries.

Particularly in the U.S., many studies have used individual motivation or group environment to provide plausible explanations for people's willingness to participate in social movements. But few researchers in this tradition have attempted to combine, or even compare, explanations based on individual and group factors with structural explanations of such participation, primarily because of the absence of sufficient variance in structural variables within the system to enable us to relate structural to motivational explanations of participation. Doug McAdam's contribution to this volume is a relatively rare attempt to fill this lacuna.

A third benefit of comparison is that it can sensitize observers to the theoretical possibilities of social movements even when these are not evident on their home ground. For example, comparison is almost the only way to delimit the potential range of participation in social movements among groups at different "distances" from the movement's epicenter. This is important because social movements, unlike formal organizations, frequently lack observable boundaries. If movement M attracts support from social group G in country A, but not in country B, then the range of attraction in each country can be related to features of social structure, movement strategy, or political opportunities. If we have looked at the movement only in country B, we may never perceive that its appeal or lack of appeal to group G is theoretically interesting and needs explanation.

One version of this problem is the tendency to regard social movement participation as coterminous with membership in organizations, a too frequent practice in American studies. But conventional membership is not characteristic of many of these movements, as Melucci argues in his contribution to this volume. The most reasonable solution is to focus on both organizational members and external participants, leaving as an empirical question the importance of the two in each movement and the relationship between them. In comparative research, this approach could draw attention to the factors that explain a greater or lesser attraction of social movement organizations under different conditions.

Fourth, comparison can help to overcome the fact that the countries that produce the most research on social movements may not be those in which such movements are either most important or most typical. Funding patterns, political concerns, sunk costs in expertise, or research traditions may, more than its quantitative importance or innovative tendencies, explain scholars' attention to a particular movement. The existence of a large "reserve army" of current or former movement members in a country may also play a determining role.[9]

Much of the European work on new social movements comes from the more advanced capitalist democracies of northern Europe, particularly from West Germany. Does this prove that such movements are either quantitatively or qualitatively more important in West Germany than in, say, Italy or Spain? Or, rather, that West German scholars produce more research on the subject than do their Spanish or Italian colleagues, who are more preoccupied with, respectively, their countries' regional problems and party system?

The answer to this question is relevant to one of the most basic assumptions of the German school of social movement studies: that there is a causal link between advanced industrialism and "new" social movements. Of course, if the same movements, centered around similar themes, were to appear just as often in the less advanced countries of southern Europe, the German school's assumption would need to be questioned. And, indeed, Mario Diani and Giovanni Lodi's contribution to this volume, on environmental groups in Milan, provides much evidence of a "northern European" movement flourishing in the heart of southern Europe.[10]

Fifth, comparing similar movements across national lines can sensitize us to the variety of outcomes that movements experience under different conditions, and can check gross generalizations about Iron Laws of Oligarchy or the inevitable cooptation of radical movements. Take the question of repression: although repression is a constant of state response to social movements, the form it takes, the extent to which it is imposed, and the measure of reform and accommodation that accompany it vary from country to country, thereby affecting the strategic and organizational development of the movements. Comparison is the only method that can give us a sense of how to link state responses to movement development in a non-deterministic way.

For example, American researchers have long held to a "career" model of movement evolution, which sees a movement progress from insurgency to incorporation according to what has generally been seen as a logic of internal development. But comparative research shows that movements arise in great numbers during cycles of protest (Tarrow 1983) or in periods of crisis (Goldstone 1977), but tend to die out or become senescent in periods of demobilization. These findings suggest that it may be primarily the conditions of national politics and not factors internal to social movements which determine their "careers."

Finally, comparison can demonstrate whether the innovations that scholars have seen in "new"—as opposed to "old"—social movements are really as significant as has been claimed. The characteristics that students of today's "new" social movements regard as innovative may have been characteristic of older movements when they were new, or may simply be equivalents of earlier forms in the specific conditions of late twentieth-century capitalism. Only by comparing old and new movements can we discover empirically whether the "newness" in the latter is inherent, developmental, or situational.

The best way to demonstrate the newness of new social movements is to compare similar movements in different countries, beginning with their structural preconditions and forms of organization, examining closely the themes around which they organize and the types of people who associate with them, and comparing their characteristic forms of action and demands. This is what we shall attempt to do in this book by looking mainly at four core movements and at a number of others that share at least some of the characteristics that have been attributed to new movements in either Western Europe or the United States.

IV. THE FOUR CORE MOVEMENTS

Though a number of types of social movement have gained attention over the past two decades in the democratic capitalist countries of the West, there are four movements that most scholars would agree are important in all four countries. Beginning with the student movement of the 1960s, "new" movements developed on both continents around the issues of the environment, women's rights, and peace and nuclear arms.

The dynamic of these four movements is remarkably similar in the four countries.[11] The student movement grew up in all four in the mid-1960s. By the end of the decade, the women's movement and environmental movements had arisen, and early in the 1980s, the peace movement appeared. The student movement is the only one of the four that no longer exists as such, but the women's movement has declined almost everywhere in its original forms.[12] The environmental and peace movements are still very much alive.

The interrelations among different types of movements are equally striking. In the U.S., the student movement was preceded by the civil rights movement, which greatly influenced both it and the women's movement. The environmental movement was partly a result of the growth and radicalization of already existing organizations; the women's and peace movements were revivals of movements that were started around the turn of the century and left important organizational legacies. In our terminology, part of the function of consensus mobilization for the later movements was carried out by the earlier ones.

The student movement and (in the United States) the civil rights movement were the starting points for the others, not only because many people joined them but also because they invented forms of action that later movements employed (e.g., sit-ins, teach-ins, occupations, etc.). In West Germany, the women's and the peace movements were modeled on the environmental movement, particularly the citizens' initiatives *(Burgerinitiative)* of the early 1970s. The women's movement and the environmental movement contributed greatly to the peace movement, as their overlapping activities and membership make clear.

These four movements exhibit many of the main themes identified by the new social movement approach: new social actors, the presence of radical forms of action and the themes of antimodernism. The movements also reveal shifting and decentralized organizational forms—another characteristic noted by new social movement theorists—and an avoidance of formal traditional leftwing ideologies.

But these characteristics are not all they reveal: as Dieter Rucht's contribution to this book illustrates, there are important differences among the movements in their internal "logics" and in their tendency to become institutionalized. Further, some of the four movements reveal the presence of older social actors, of more conventional forms of action, and of familiar economic and policy demands that have nothing to do with antimodernism, for example, greater rights for women. Indeed, throughout, we see a deep interpenetration of "old" and "new" and a progressive politicization that has led several of the movements into the area of the party system.

1. The student movement was a fundamentally antiauthoritarian movement aimed at achieving university reforms that would give students more power. But this was never its sole aim; it was also a movement against developments in our postindustrial age. It opposed the war in Vietnam, the university as a knowledge factory, and the University's connections with business. Though it rapidly produced radical forms of action, its leaders also became skilled at using the media and other conventional resources to mobilize allies, and parts of this movement soon merged with older protest traditions.

In the United States, the student movement brought the action techniques of the civil rights movement to the campus and also invented new ones (teach-ins, happenings, the occupation of university buildings). More generally, it contributed to the "esthetification of protest" by surrounding its protest meetings with all sorts of artistic expressions and demonstrating that American students were shrewd users of the media—at least until the media got tired of them (Gitlin 1980; Oberschall 1979).

From the United States, the student movement crossed the Atlantic to Europe, largely through the anti-Vietnam War movement. There, the student movement was more successful than in the United States in achieving its demands for university reforms. Why this should be true is an interesting question and probably had more to do with the presence of allies in the traditional party system than with the greater strength of the student movement in Europe.

Although European students stressed activities on the campus, the movement spread beyond the campuses more rapidly than it had across the Atlantic. In the United States, despite the presence of coordinating organizations such as the SDS which played a key role for a certain period, the campus movement petered out as the Vietnam War ended. In Europe it rapidly spread elsewhere: in Italy, a large and often violent movement in the high schools quickly followed the university agitations, but no single national organization developed to coordinate them. In West Germany, the Socialist Student Union, and in the Netherlands, the Student Union Movement helped to diffuse the movement. But in all four countries internal ideological conflicts and, in the United States, government infiltration, as we now know, soon put an end to the movement as such.

2.   *The environmental movement* in all four countries embraces groups ranging from conservative or at least moderate conservation organizations to radical organizations that are not averse to direct confrontations with the government (see Diani and Lodi's contribution to this volume and Kitschelt 1986). Parts of the movement have been in existence for quite some time but have taken advantage of growing public interest to become bolder and gain more members. And the movement not only accommodates several organizations, it teems with single issue initiatives: against the construction of a particular road, a runway or a pipeline, against large-scale urban development projects, and against soil or water pollution.

Antinuclear energy protests have been quite prominent in all the countries, with the exception of Italy, and they have been lacking there only because of the government's slowness in adopting nuclear energy. In the United States, antinuclear protests were intitially highly legalistic, involving court cases, referenda, and appeals. Success could be measured not in actual victories but in terms of delays: the construction of nuclear plants would be deferred so long that they became uneconomical and new information would cast doubt upon their safety. After the Three Mile Island disaster, utility companies throughout the country encountered financial trouble and state legislatures began to refuse licenses for the construction of new plants.

Radical tactics were frequently used by some elements of the ecological movement. Encouraged by the successful occupation of a construction site in West Germany, the American movement occasionally used occupations as well. But it was in West Germany (and France) that the strategy of occupation was most commonly used. Protest against nuclear energy soon became more radical in the Netherlands too, where it focused on the issue of waste disposal.

But occupations and blockades of construction sites or plants ultimately proved to be a dead end in all the countries, for governments could muster much more violence than the activists. Nevertheless, the movement succeeded in delaying or even preventing the construction of nuclear sites in both the Netherlands and West Germany. Although the destruction tactic was not successful in the United States, legal tactics, state licensing requirements, and the Three Mile Island accident provided some de facto assistance in achieving the same results obtained in West Germany and the Netherlands.

An important development in all four countries was the involvement of experts and technicians in the environmental movements (Nelkin and Pollak 1982). This involvement was stimulated by the highly technical nature of the issues, but it was also a function of the kind of constituency to which environmental issues appeal, one composed mainly of members of the new middle class. Even in Italy, and despite the weakness of the movement there, architects, lawyers, and doctors were important actors in many of the health and environmental movements of the 1970s.

3. *The women's movement.*[13] Ferree (1987) distinguishes between radical feminists, who take the oppression of women to be the root and symbol of all oppression; socialist feminists, who attempt to combine feminist insights with socialist programs, and liberal feminists, who stress self-affirmation and individual rights. All these elements are present in all four countries but in different proportions.

In the United States, where the women's movement has existed the longest, liberal feminists constitute the mainstream, and the key organization is the National Organization for Women (NOW). It is "autonomous" in the sense that it is not dependent on a party, but much of its effort has gone into supporting candidates who favor abortion rights. Neither West Germany, Italy, nor the Netherlands has a similar coordinating organization, and their women's movements are divided between autonomous and party-connected, socialist and radical feminist organizations. In West Germany and Italy, the term "feminist" refers only to the radical element of the women's movement.

The greater part of the women's movement in West Germany is autonomous, antihierarchical, and highly decentralized. To a much greater extent than in the United States, the movement works outside the system and its members cultivate the politics of cultural difference. Consequently it has not been very influential and has only a weak grasp of politics.

The Dutch movement occupies an intermediate position in terms of autonomy. On the one hand, its autonomous wing is well represented; on the other, thanks to their ties with political parties, important segments of the movement are capable of and willing to work within the system.

In Italy, where traditional women's groups existed in the Communist-Socialist UDI and Christian Democratic CID, the 1970s saw an increased influence of autonomous radical feminism, which had the effect of shifting the UDI markedly away from its ties with traditional socialist feminism. Feminists were also strongly represented in the extra-parliamentary groups; indeed, as in the radical wing of the U.S. women's movement, their formation into a distinct movement was a reaction against their subaltern position in the male-dominated formations of the New Left (Ergas 1982). With the collapse of the New Left in the late 1970s, it was within institutions—notably in Parliament and the trade unions—that women would bear the major burden of the movement (Beckwith 1987; Hellman 1987).

Despite their differences, the four movements use many similar action forms. The American movement has been taken as an example in many respects in Europe. Consciousness-raising groups, women's networks and collectives, shelters, and rape crisis centers are some of the practical measures Europeans have adopted from the American movement. Lobbying and electoral campaigns have become more important than the radically expressive forms of action which have, in any case, always been exaggerated in the media. Katzenstein (1987) argues forcefully that the "invisible" diffusion of feminist ideas makes this movement far more powerful than its organizational presence reveals.

A major outcome of the women's movement has been the prominence women have attained in related movements. The women of Greenham Common and the charismatic Petra Kelly are only the most visible examples of this development. In the U.S., groups such as MADD (Mothers Against Drunk Driving) have been one of the social movement successes of the last decade, and in both Europe and the United States, women are heavily represented at the leadership levels in environmental, antinuclear, and antidrug movements. Further, in the United States during the last decade the number of women elected to state legislatures has more than doubled.

4. *The peace movement* had several of the same predecessors in all four countries: the ban-the-bomb movement and the anti-Vietnam War movement

on the one hand, and the environmental movement on the other. More specific to West Germany were protests against German rearmament, and to the United States, the test ban movement. The new peace movement that arose in the late 1970s and 1980s now concentrates most of its energies on nuclear disarmament, though in Italy and West Germany the movement also agitates for the evacuation of American bases.

We may speak of grass-roots peace movements in all four countries, each movement exhibiting greater or lesser levels of institutionalization. These movements are, for the most part, unstructured, decentralized, and extraparliamentary, with strong internal organizations, rather than unified bureaucratic structures. The Dutch movement deviates somewhat from this pattern, but only in part. It has a centralized organization, though a modest one; the movement's real strength lies in the organization at the base, and it depends heavily on campaigns that draw on the efforts of allied groups, as Hanspeter Kriesi's and Ben Schennink's essays in this volume make clear. The Italian movement is deeply intertwined with the party system, especially the PCI, but there are Catholic and autonomous currents that appear during major campaigns.

The American movement is also independent of the party system, but its greatest strength lies in its moderate "freeze" wing, not in its radical disarmament fringe. In the other three countries, disarmament—unilateral or multilateral—is the predominant demand. The conservatism of the American administration may be one reason for the moderation of the U.S. peace movement, but a more basic reason lies in the absence of *any* support in the European party system for America's withdrawal from its hegemonic world role, a withdrawal implicit in nuclear disarmament.

The NATO decision to locate cruise missiles in Western Europe considerably accelerated the growth of all three European movements, and this growth manifested itself in the unprecedented demonstrations of 1981 and 1983. The American peace movement expanded around the same time but was aimed more at a general reduction of armaments and was reinforced by the simultaneous fear of involvement in Nicaragua, an issue with far less resonance in Europe. The Reagan administration's bellicose rhetoric stimulated the movement's rebirth in all four countries.

The most unusual aspect of the American movement is the significant role professionals play, professionals such as the "Physicians for Social Responsibility" and the scientists who have publicized the "nuclear winter" and opposed the Star Wars initiative. The freeze campaign had a strong grass-roots appeal: freeze resolutions and initiatives began to appear in local constituencies across the country during the 1980 election campaign. And in the United States, as in Western Europe, the personnel and themes of the peace movement overlap to a great extent those of the women's and environmental movements.

These are the four "core" movements of the past two decades. These movements all derived from a period of generalized insurgency and discontent—the 1960s (Jenkins 1985). Few would disagree that the general features of advanced industrial society in some way shaped the particular movements that developed. But it is a long way from the structural changes of advanced capitalism to the decisions of individuals and groups to participate in social movements. In this process of "transforming structure into action," national institutions and national traditions of protest and politics play an important role in shaping both the level of mobilization and forms of action, as the following section shows.

V. SOCIAL MOVEMENTS AND NATIONAL POLITICS

Karl Marx was perhaps the first social scientist to predict that national traditions of protest would impinge on the international social movement that he saw gathering across the map of Europe. In an early essay he observed the change in the nature of revolutionary activity as it crossed the Rhine from France to Germany:

> We are about to begin in Germany where France and England are about to end. The old rotton condition against which these countries are revolting in theory and which they bear as chains is greeted in Germany as the dawn of a glorious future (1966, p. 254).

We do not have to accept all the specifics of Marx's polemic against "German conditions" to agree that politics and national political traditions affect the character of the "new" movements in different countries. In no country did the movements find a total void in social and political organizations; everywhere they took their place alongside traditional lobbies and interest associations, parties, and elites, thus stimulating conflict and competition, and sometimes cooperation between existing and new actors and organizations. Were it true that social movements appear as thunderbolts out of the blue, then analysts could afford to ignore national variations. But since we believe that mobilization into action is constrained by the necessity to mobilize consensus and gain allies and legitimacy, the political and cultural contexts in which movements operate are crucial to understanding their strategies, their successes, and their failures.

It is often pointed out that new social movements reject politics and engage in forms of interaction outside the political arena (e.g., consciousness raising, networking, squatting). Melucci and his collaborators (1985) have done more than any other commentators to underscore the importance of the extrapolitical networks and interactions of many of these groups. Our point, however, is a different one: that national political traditions and alignments condition the formation, the strategies, and outcomes of the new movements, however much they operate outside of politics.

Consider the interaction between the student movements of the late 1960s and preexisting student and political associations. All these movements arose in opposition to government policies (e.g., Vietnam, university fees) and in reaction to traditional student politics. Almost everywhere, they radicalized, and, in some cases, led to the destruction of, traditional student associations. In Italy, for example, the student movement was strongly conditioned by the "communist heresies" that had developed in preexisting youth groups and the little journals of the Left (Lumley 1983). In West Germany, much of the controversy took place within the Young Socialist organization, leading to the group's radicalization and opposition to the SPD.

The feminist and environmental movements likewise challenged, and to some degree radicalized, existing women's and conservation organizations (Costain and Costain 1987). The peace movement renewed and expanded the appeal of traditional groups such as Britain's CND. The new movements have different styles, objectives, and personnel than did their predecessors, but they developed through interaction with the older groups, within the same movement "industries." The "new" movements would have been far less effective had they not had these older groups to compete with and to catalyze into new modes of action and more aggressive programs.

The same relations existed between the new movements and the party system. In some countries—France, for example—there were violent confrontations between the student movement and the dominant party on the Left. But in others, objective or even open coalitions developed between the new movements and the old party system.

In some cases, elements of the new left entered the traditional party system. The Dutch political parties proved rather open to new social movements. As a consequence, movements were relatively successful in infiltrating the parties and thus influencing government policy. In Italy, this absorption of the movement occurred in part through the opposition, as thousands of students who were radicalized in the movements of the 1960s joined and became grass-roots militants of the Communist party (Ercole, Lange, and Tarrow 1986).

In other cases, the relations between new and old left were conflictual but symbolic: in the Italian women's movement, for example, where an autonomous feminist movement helped to radicalize the PCI-oriented UDI, or in the SPD, where the movements could penetrate the Social Democrats only by radicalizing their youth branch. In the United States, the new movements did not penetrate the established parties directly, but the new convention rules of the Democratic party made it easier to affect its platforms. In many of these new-old relationships, then, conventional politics became the continuation (by other means) of nonconventional politics.

It was not only through the major parties that the new movements entered the political system. For example, in the Netherlands, small leftist parties drew many members and voters from the ranks of the new movements. In Italy, the *Manifesto,* followed by *Democrazia proletaria* and then the *Partito radicale,* drew much of their support from student and extraparliamentary groups. In the United States, where the electoral system discourages the formation of small parties, movements set up lobbies that proved to be more than minor parties. Of the four countries, only in West Germany did such movements lead to the formation of a successful new political party, the *Grunen* (Greens), a rainbow coalition of environmentalists, feminists, pacifists, and other anti-establishment groups.

Political institutions also have a strong influence on the forms and focus of the new movements. If it was the centralization of the French university system that helped the French May to paralyze the country, it was the decentralization of the American system that hindered the student movement from coordinating a national strategy after the Port Huron statement. And if the resistance of West Germany's political institutions to women's issues led to the radicalization of the women's movement there, it was the localism of American institutions that led to the success of the movement at the state and local levels in that country.

Consider the effect of institutional traditions on the environmental movement. Lobbying has long been an important part of American politics, and this fact was reflected in the rapid formation of a strong environmental lobby, with national organizations that conduct direct mail campaigns and make presentations to Congress. There is a powerful environmental lobby in the "open" Dutch political system as well, but through a different route, as environmental groups have found their way inside the governmental machinery.

The West German movement, on the other hand, is an anti-establishment movement. It is nowhere near as institutionalized as the Dutch or American movements. The Italian movement is deeply divided among traditional conservationists, radical environmental groups, and the ecological wings of the political parties. These differences reflect the structure and culture of the national political traditions within which the individual movements operate.

National traditions of social protest have firmly conditioned the "nationalization" of the new movements of the past two decades, not because of any "iron law" of cooptation but because the movement's need for consensus, allies, and legitimation lead them to use existing traditions of social movement organization and existing reservoirs of sentiment and expectation as raw materials.

For example, the strength of the Lockian consensus in America assured the predominance of liberal over socialist and radical feminist elements in that country. In the Netherlands, the traditions of religious association, however attenuated now, have affected the shape of the peace movement. In Germany, some have seen a resurgent, if reshaped nationalism combining with postindustrial concerns to produce the *Grunen.*[14] And in Italy, a persistent workerism in the ideology of the Left rapidly turned the attention of the student movement away from the universities and toward the factory (Tarrow 1988, chap. 7).

Some of the ways in which national protest traditions have affected the new movements since the 1960s become apparent if, turning from the four "core" movements, we briefly consider specific movements in particular countries: the civil rights movement in the United States, the Dutch and Italian labor movements, and the "radical" groups that have appeared in various countries throughout the period.

1. *The civil rights movement in the United States* is probably the movement most marked by national particularism. While all students of social movements in the United States inevitably look to the civil rights movement as the harbinger of the "1960s" and regard it as the original recruitment pool for subsequent movements, European scholars often doubt that it is a "new" social movement at all. After all, it was not motivated by a rejection of modernity, and among its members one finds little evidence of the professionals found in the women's, environmental, and peace movements in Western Europe.

Yet the civil rights movement did resemble a "new" social movement in the European sense, in several ways: it drew upon an emerging social group—the black middle class that evolved as a result of black mobility after World War II (Piven and Cloward 1977, pp. 189ff.), it placed a strong emphasis on emergent collective identity (Killian 1984), also thought to be typical of new movements in Europe (Melucci 1980; Pizzorno 1978); and it led to, indeed invented, some of the radical forms of action that were later taken up in Europe.

Yet the civil rights movement also substantiates the insights of resource mobilization theory. Most American scholars agree on several issues: that the black churches were major resources for the mobilization of the black population (Morris 1981; Oberschall 1973); that the media and white "conscience constituents" were important external resources (McCarthy and Zald 1977); and that recent electoral realignments favored the success of the movement (Piven and Cloward, pp. 195ff.). Thus the civil rights movement illustrates the usefulness of combining European and American perspectives.

2. *The labor movement in Italy and the Netherlands.*[15] The cycle of protest that began in the late 1960s affected not only the new movements described above but also the major "old" movement in Western Europe and the United States, the labor movement. Although the labor movement has many characteristics that new social movements lack (e.g., formal, bureaucratic organization, hierarchial structure, top-down management), drawing too stark a contrast with the new movements conceals the fact that unions have been part of the same protest cycle from which the new movements emerged in the 1960s and indeed share some of the new movements' characteristics.

New action repertoires, decentralized structures, and new actors and demands appeared within organized labor in several countries (Dubois 1978;

Pizzorno 1978). Action forms first seen among the new movements (e.g., occupations, sit-ins, demonstrations, and the "practice of the objective") were adopted by workers and others; new shopfloor organizations developed and, as a result, strike activity increased (Teulings and Leynse 1978; Regalia 1986). But rather than replacing old repertoires and structures with new ones, the old organizations adapted the tactics and themes of their competitors: in Italy, the unions adopted the factory councils as their own grass-roots units, and the Netherlands experienced a rapid growth of the civil servants' union (Visser 1985).

Moreover, unions and new social movements formed numerous links through overlapping membership in the new social movements and in movement networks within unions (e.g., women's groups in unions) or through formal coalitions with new social movements such as the peace movement, or through ex-student activists becoming involved in unions as professionals, researchers, and organizers. We have already mentioned the role of scientists in the antinuclear movement; equally striking is the case of former medical school activists who provided Italian unions with the scientific expertise they needed to investigate factory hazards (Reich 1984).

In summary, in both Italy and the Netherlands, "old" movements such as unions renewed themselves, redefined some of their goals, and adopted some of the new values and organizing principles of the new social movements. As a consequence, they were successful in organizing some parts of the new protest potentials on which new social movements are said to draw—especially among workers in the public sector. But they have been less successful in other sectors, for example, among those workers made redundant by industrialization or those who work in the informal sector.

As the generalized protest of the 1960s declined, unions worked to institutionalize the new themes and new forms of action, took control of factory committees, and recentralized bargaining. But some of those—both workers and students—who had been radicalized in the course of the factory struggles joined in the new and more radical struggles that developed in the course of the 1970s. Let us take a brief look at these more radical forms of protest.

3. *The radicalization of protest.*[16] The 1960s brought a radicalization of protest forms, as evidenced by numerous blockades, occupations, direct actions, and violent confrontations with the police. Several authors have seen this radicalization as a general feature of the new social movements (cf. Brand 1982) and as one of the main contrasts with existing political formations. Offe goes so far as to posit a "new political paradigm" developing in competition with the old politics of the immediate postwar settlement (1983).

A more disaggregated analysis, however, suggests that radicalism, rather than being a central feature of the movements themselves, is simply a current running through all the movements. Dalton reports from a survey of European environmental organizations that few of them ever engage in radical action (1986). Van der Loo and his collaborators (1984) go even further, arguing that the description of new social movements in the literature is in fact valid only for the radical currents of the movements.

Participants in the radical segments of new movements are usually young and, unlike the majority of participants in new social movements in general, are *not* exclusively middle class. Contrasting these radicals with participants in the student movements of the 1960s, Brand et al. (1983) characterize them as marginal and without much hope for the future. Marginality was also a factor in the revived Italian student movement of 1977, when the prospect of unemployment after graduation was a dominant theme among the activists.

Radical groups were widespread within the squatters' movement, where they are literally "sheltered" within a broader movement. The squatter world, which in many places reaches the proportions of a subculture, has had strategic importance in activating more policy-based movements. Here again, by no means all the squatters are radicals; rather, consensus mobilization occurs within the intensely communitarian squatter world.

The squatters' movement has been particularly significant in West Germany and the Netherlands, where building speculation had made it difficult for young people to obtain adequate housing. Thousands of these young people occupied empty buildings and converted them into living spaces. Larger buildings served as centers for youth culture and recreation and as meeting places for all kinds of groups and organizations. Squatters shaped loose, overarching structures to facilitate contacts with other groups and negotiations with authorities. Radical sectors of other movements were linked to the squatters through overlapping membership, through the use of occupied facilities for their meetings and activities, and through the effective recruitment networks that the squatters had built up in defense against attacks by the police.

We believe that the squatter's movement was susceptible to radicalization not because squatting is inherently radical, but because the squatters faced repeated conflicts with local authorities and police. Gradually, the ideologies of the squatters became increasingly antigovernment, antistate, and anarchistic (van Noort 1984). The radicalization of the movement and the decreasing willingness of local authorities to give into its demands resulted in extremely violent confrontations.

The squatters cannot be said to have had a radical project for the transformation of society, but they exhibited a version of that "radical pragmatism" that has been observed by many students of new social movements (Lumley 1983). Their aims seldom went beyond defending their own living space and supporting the goals of those radicals in more policy-oriented movements (peace, environment) who lived and recruited among them. The same cannot be said of another offshoot of the movements of the 1960s and 1970s which no survey of new social movements can ignore—the terrorists.

It has often been observed that terrorism is a phenomenon of the decline of protest cycles, and not of the phase of mass mobilization. Italy, the country in which terrorism came closest to being a mass phenomenon, illustrates this point well, for until the mid-1970s most of the violence arose from clashes between opposing groups and between groups and the police, rather than from attacks of groups on individuals or institutions (della Porta and Tarrow 1987). Toward the middle of the decade, as the flood of mass mobilization declined to a trickle, the more radical elements that were socialized during the protest cycle began to use tactics of organized violence.

In Germany, where terrorism reached almost the proportions it assumed in Italy, violence has sometimes been blamed on the fact that the West German government has a closed political opportunity structure—for example, civil servants can be fired because of their political opinions. The "closed" nature of the West German system has also been held responsible for the radical means adopted by the environmental movement there (Kitschelt 1986), which Kitschelt compares unfavorably to the "open" nature of the American and Swedish systems and the moderate tactics they are said to have encouraged.

But if West Germany's repression of mass protest was savage and its political system closed to legitimate dissent, the same certainly cannot be said of Italy, where terrorism was stronger, and this difference argues against the thesis that closed political systems beget violent tactics. On the contrary, in Italy, strikers seldom had to fear police interruption of their picket lines, and restraints on the civil rights of radicals were both slow in coming and moderate. Indeed, conservatives have argued that Italy's toleration of protest was itself responsible for allowing mass-based political violence to develop.

The rise of the similar phenomena of organized terrorism in both the "closed" German system and in the more "open" Italian one leads to a paradox if we want to derive protest strategies from national political structures. Since both causal inferences cannot be true, they point to the need to include categories more specific than the abstract "structures" used by Kitschelt and others (categories that acknowledge subnational and movement characteristics, e.g., protest potential and movement strategies, in analyzing patterns of mobilization. We must, in other words, give systematic attention to how structure is transformed into action within, and not just between, national political traditions.

VI. THE PERSPECTIVES OF THE VOLUME

We thus arrive at the essays collected in this volume. Convinced that the American and European approaches summarized in parts one and two of this introduction have much to offer both to one another and to an understanding of collective action, we have "connected" them in one volume. Persuaded that they could be fruitfully combined, we propose a tentative synthesis around a three-phase process model: from mobilization potential through recruitment networks and consensus mobilization to the motivation to participate in social movements.

Because we think there are general similarities between recent social movement activity in Europe and America but are nonetheless struck by the differences among specific movements, we believe that these specific movements should be seen comparatively. For such a comparison, it seemed best to use a small number of movements in only four countries as our empirical base. We have outlined the characteristics of the four "core" movements that to us seemed central to both the new social movement and resource mobilization approaches, illustrating some of the ways in which they seemed similar, and then turning to how national differences could affect their strategies, their structures, and their outcomes.

Throughout this introduction, we have emphasized, not the empirical findings of our authors, but the themes that guided the choice of topics elaborated in the rest of the volume. (For an attempt at synthesis, see Hanspeter Kriesi's final chapter.) Four such themes have emerged from this introductory chapter:

First, an emphasis on the intermediate phases between the structural potential for movements and collective action suggests the importance of the *process* by which mobilization potentials are tapped and consensus mobilized into action. All three sections of the book follow this processual logic.

Second, rather than finding an absolute division between new and old movements, we have discovered that the old and new interpenetrate each other, the old influencing the new social movements of the last two decades, the new working changes upon existing organizations. These interfaces are distinguished and described in many of the contributions to the volume.

A third theme concerns the tremendous number of national variations and permutations of movements in the same sectors in different countries. We think this variation testifies not only to the differentiating role of political institutions but also to the importance of consensus mobilization on the part of movement strategists trying to build on existing ideological packages while fashioning new interpretive frames.

Fourth, we maintain that only systematic comparative analysis can succeed in isolating the effects particular national traditions have on particular movements and on their strategy, structure, and success.

The contributions to this volume are not explicitly comparative, for the raw materials for such comparisons are not yet available. But they make a start in this direction by their concentration on parallel themes and similar movements and phases of the mobilization process in different countries. Through the juxtaposition of differences and commonalities among the movements and countries we have studied, we hope to indicate a comparative and a theoretical direction for future research.

Focusing first on recruitment networks, then consensus mobilization, and finally the construction and careers of social movements, the chapters draw amply on national research traditions and, in our view, contribute richly to the reformulation of social movement theory and research in both Western Europe and the United States. At least, that is our hope.

Part I centers on the networks, support structures, and subcultures that form the bases of the mobilizational potentials we have discussed above. Hanspeter Kriesi, Karl-Dieter Opp, and Mario Diani and Giovanni Lodi discuss each of these aspects of mobilization potentials. Both Kriesi and Opp demonstrate the importance of subcultures in the mobilization of movement participants. The former reveals the role of countercultures in the mobilization of the Dutch peace movement, while the latter focuses on the role of neighborhood integration in the West Germans' willingness to participate in the antinuclear power movement. In their chapter, Diani and Lodi show how different currents within the Milanese ecological movement—some more "movement-like" than others—rely on different though overlapping networks for the recruitment of participants.

Micromobilization is the subject of both Doug McAdam's and Donatella della Porta's contributions. McAdam describes the importance of immediate social networks in decisions to participate in the "Freedom Summer" of the American civil rights movement; della Porta analyzes the roles both of friendship networks and of previous political involvements in the recruitment of members of Italian terrorist organizations. These two essays demonstrate the significance of networks, support structures, and subcultures for participation not only in low-risk and conventional movements but even in very high-risk and clandestine activities.

In Part II, our attention shifts to several aspects of consensus mobilization and of the construction of meaning in social movements. Bert Klandermans elaborates the notions of consensus formation (i.e., the unplanned convergence of meaning in social networks and subcultures) and consensus mobilization (i.e., deliberate attempts by an actor to create consensus) and provides suggestions for their further application. David Snow and Robert Benford develop their concept of "interpretive frames" to show how these constrain and conduct movements into taking particular directions, and how, when strategically deployed, they affect the success of participant mobilization. William Gamson, in analyzing the discourse of the American antinuclear movement, examines how the changing strength of different ideological "packages" affects the ability of that movement to achieve its aims.

Part III turns from individual decisions to participate to the creation and careers of collective actors in several of the four countries we are studying. Ben Schennink describes the sequential phases of consensus and action mobilization in a major peace movement organization in the Netherlands, observing the salience of different protest cultures within each phase. Sidney

Tarrow shows how the strategies and themes of the new collective actors in a protest cycle can be found even among the oldest kind of movements, religious movements.

Dieter Rucht argues that the career of movements is determined by, among other factors, the underlying "logics" to which social movement actors adhere. Rucht finds different logics in the women's and ecological movements, and holds them responsible for the differences in the organizational make-up of the two kinds of movements. Finally, Alberto Melucci links individual and group identity formation in his representation of the process of consensus building in a variety of Italian movements.

Our conclusions, presented by Hanspeter Kriesi, both summarize the main results of our current research and try to draw together some comparative and theoretical dimensions that we hope will contribute to the next phase of research on social movements in Western Europe and the United States. Kriesi distinguishes and differentiates six different types of movements, showing that, while "new" movements represent significant innovations in western democracies, not all recent movements are in fact "new." In new movements as in old, Kriesi argues, the mobilization process introduces significant change into political life in western democracies, producing the strategies, the forms of organization, and the interactions that transform structure into action.

NOTES

1. The two authors bear equal responsibility for this chapter, but—for the record—the introduction was written by Tarrow, parts one and two mainly by Klandermans, part three by Tarrow, part four by Klandermans, part five by both authors, and the conclusion by Tarrow. And although our collaborators have heard the views we advance all too often, we alone bear responsibility for the synthesis we propose.

2. An earlier, more fully elaborated version of this section can be found in Klandermans (1986).

3. Hirschman (1982, p. 78) observes that "Olson proclaimed the impossibility of collective action for large groups . . . at the precise moment when the Western world was about to be all but engulfed by an unprecedented wave of public movements, marches, protests, strikes and ideologies."

4. There are many versions and definitions of new social movements. The literature we have surveyed includes: Brand (1982), Brand et al. (1983), Melucci (1980, 1981), Offe (1985), Van der Loo et al. (1984). No single author will agree with all the elements of the composite picture we have drawn in this section.

5. These criticisms can be found in summary form in Tarrow (1986).

6. Tilly, for example (1978, p. 69), following Etzioni (1968, pp. 388-89), defines mobilization as "the process by which a unit gains significantly in the control of assets it previously did not control."

7. This section draws on a more elaborate statement in Tarrow (1986).

8. The indexes of seven popular texts were scanned for the following entries: "anomic groups," "civil strife," "collective action," "dissent," "movements," "terrorism," and "violence." The treatment of all of these terms was remarkably scant. The term "social movement" appeared least often,

turning up in none of the seven indexes, while the most frequent term, "revolution," was found in six out of seven texts.

9. Such "accidents of birth" were evident in the large number of studies of communism carried out in the United States. An observer from Mars might be forgiven for thinking that the CP-USA was a major force in American society during this period. Yet the only truly comparative study of American communism—that of Almond and his collaborators (1954)—showed how truly marginal the party was to American society, compared to its British, French, and Italian counterparts.

10. Strictly speaking, Milan is a typical "advanced industrial" city, in which the problems discussed by northern European theorists are well in evidence. But the same is true of many Italian cities, where some of the same movements have developed. See Tarrow (1988, chap. 12).

11. This section is based on the following publications: for the Netherlands: Briet, Klandermans, and Kroon (1987), Janssen and Voestermans (1978), Klandermans and Oegema (1987 a and b), Van der Loo, Snel, and Van Steenbergen (1984); for West Germany: Brand, Busser, and Rucht (1983), Ferree (1987), Mushaben (1983a and b), Rucht (1984a and b), Rutig (1983); for the U.S.: Barkin (1979), Benford (1984), Ferree (1987), Gitlin (1980), Heirich (1971), Lo (1982), Mitchell (1979, 1984), Obserchall (1978), Perrow (1979), Rucht (1984b), Rudig (1983), Wasmuht (1984); for Italy: Ergas (1982, 1986), Hellman (1987), Lodi (1984), Lumley (1983), Melucci (1982), Melucci et al. (1985), Tarrow (1983)

12. But note the brief revival of the Italian student movement in 1977 and again in 1985. Further, continued activism in America suggests that the women's movement is far from moribund; see Katzenstein (1987).

13. The next section owes much to the contributions in Katzenstein and Mueller, eds. (1987), to whom we are grateful for allowing us to consult their long-gestating manuscript prior to its publication.

14. But not all the empirical evidence supports this widely held claim. See Bürklin (1985) for an excellent empirical analysis of Green supporters which cuts through much recent speculation on the party.

15. We are grateful to Ida Regalia, whose 1986 paper is the general source of the summary presented in this section. See in addition Regalia, Regini, and Reyneri (1978), which provides a general view of the interaction between the labor cycle, and Tarrow (1988, chaps. 6-8), for evidence on the diffusion of protest repertoires from one sector to another in Italy.

16. Our discussion in this section is indebted to Huberts and van Noort (1986).

REFERENCES

Almond, Gabriel, Herbert E. Krugman, Elsbeth Lewin, and Howard Wriggens. 1954. *The Appeals of Communism*. Princeton: Princeton University Press.

Barkin, Steven. 1979. "Strategic, tactical and organizational dilemmas of the protest movement against nuclear power." *Social Problems* 27:19-37.

Barnes, Samuel H., Max Kaase, and Klause R. Allerbeck. 1979. *Political Action: Mass Participation in Five Western Democracies*. London: Sage.

Beckwith, Karen. 1987. "Response to feminism in the Italian parliament: Divorce, abortion and sexual violence legislation." In Mary Katzenstein and Carol Mueller (eds.), *The Women's Movements of the United States and Western Europe: Consciousness, Political Opportunity, and Public Policy*. Philadelphia: Temple University Press.

Benford, Robert. 1984. "The interorganizational dynamics of the Austin peace movement." Unpublished Ph.D. dissertation, University of Texas at Austin.

Berger, Peter L., Brigitte Berger, and Hansfried Kellner. 1975. *Das Unbehagen in der Modernität*. Frankfurt: Campus.

Berger, Suzanne, 1979. "Politics and antipolitics in Western Europe in the seventies." *Daedalus* 108:27-50.

Boender, Kees. 1985. *Sociologische Analyse van Milieusolidariteit onder Elites en Publiek.* Rijswijk: Sythoff.

Brand, Karl-Werner. 1982. *Neue soziale Bewegungen, Entstehung, Funktion und Perspektive neuer Protestpotentiale, eine Zwischenbilanz.* Opladen: Westdeutscher Verlag.

Brand, Karl-Werner, Detlef Büsser, and Dieter Rucht. 1983. *Aufbruch in eine andere Gesellschaft. Neue soziale Bewegungen in der Bundesrepublik.* Frankfurt: Campus.

Briet, Martien, Bert Klandermans, and Frederike Kroon. 1987. "How women become involved in the women's movement." In Mary Katzenstein and Carol Mueller (eds.), *The Women's Movements of the United States and Western Europe: Consciousness, Political Opportunity, and Public Policy.* Philadelphia: Temple University Press.

Bürklin, Wilhelm. 1985. "The German Greens." *International Political Science Review* 6 (October):63-81.

Carden, Maren Lockwood. 1978. "The proliferation of a social movement: Ideology and individual incentives in the contemporary feminist movement." Pages 179-96 in Louis Kriesberg (ed.), *Research in Social Movements, Conflict and Change.* Vol. 1. Greenwich, Conn.: JAI.

Costain, Anne N. and W. Douglas Costain. 1987. "Strategy and tactics of the women's movement of the United States: The role of political parties." In Mary Katzenstein and Carol Mueller (eds.), *The Women's Movements of the United States and Western Europe: Consciousness, Political Opportunity, and Public Policy.* Philadelphia: Temple University Press.

Crozier, Michel, S. Huntington, and J. Watunaki (eds.). 1975. *The Crisis of Democracy* New York: New York University Press.

Dalton, Russell et al. 1987. "Environmental action in Western democracies." Project Report. Unpublished paper. Department of Political Science, Florida State University, Tallahasse, Fla., March.

della Porta, Donatella and Sidney Tarrow. 1986. "Unwanted Children: Political Violence and the Cycle of Protest in Italy." *European Journal of Political Research* 14: 607-632.

Dubois, Pierre. 1978. "New forms of industrial conflict, 1960-1974." Pages 1-34 in Colin Crouch and Alessandro Pizzorno (eds.), *The Resurgence of Class Conflict in Western Europe since 1968.* Vol. 2. London: Macmillan.

Eisinger, Peter K. 1973. "The Conditions of Protest Behavior in American Cities." *American Political Science Review* 67:11-28.

Ercole, Enrico, Peter Lange, and Sidney Tarrow. 1985. "I comunisti nei movimenti." *Politica ed Economia* 16: 33-45.

Ergas, Yasmine. 1982. "1968-1979. Feminism and the Italian Party System." *Comparative Politics* 14:253-79.

Ergas, Yasmine. 1986. *Nelle maglie della politica. Femminismo, istituzioni e politiche sociali nell' Italia degli anni '70.* Milan: F. Angeli.

Etzioni, Amitai. 1968. *The Active Society.* New York: Free Press.

Ferree, Myra Marx. 1987. "Equality and autonomy: Feminist politics in the United States and West Germany." In Mary Katzenstein and Carol Mueller (eds.), *The Women's Movements of the United States and Western Europe: Consciousness, Political Opportunity, and Public Policy.* Philadelphia: Temple University Press.

Ferree, Myra Marx, and Frederick D. Miller. 1985. "Mobilization and meaning: Toward an integration of social psychological and resource perspectives on social movements." *Sociological Inquiry* 55:38-61.

Fireman, Bruce and William A. Gamson. 1979. "Utilitarian logic in the resource mobilization perspective." Pages 8-45 in Mayer N. Zald and John D. McCarthy (eds.), *The Dynamics of Social Movements.* Cambridge, Mass.: Winthrop.

Gamson, William A. 1975. *The Strategy of Social Protest.* Homewood, Ill.: Dorsey Press.

Garner, Roberta and Mayer N. Zald. 1985. "The political economy of social movement sectors." In Gerald D. Suttles and Mayer N. Zald (eds.), *The Challenge of Social Control: Citizenship and Institution Building in Modern Society*. Norwood, N.J.: Ablex.

Geest, de A. 1984. "Nieuwe Sociale Bewegingen en de Verzorgingsstaat." *Tijdschrift voor Sociologie* 5: 39-67.

Gitlin, Todd. 1980. *The Whole World Is Watching: The Media in the Making and Unmaking of the New Left*. Berkeley: University of California Press.

Goldstone, Jack A. 1979. "The weakness of organization: A new look at Gamson's *The Strategy of Social Protest*." *American Journal of Sociology* 85:1017-42.

Habermas, Jürgen. 1973. *Legitimationsprobleme im Spätkapitalismus*. Frankfurt: Suhrkamp.

Heirich, Max. 1971. *The Spiral of Conflict: Berkeley, 1964*. New York: Columbia University Press.

Hellman, Judy. 1987. "Women's struggle in a workers' city: Feminist movements in Turin." In Mary Katzenstein and Carol Mueller (eds.), *The Women's Movements of the United States and Western Europe: Consciousness, Political Opportunity, and Public Policy*. Philadelphia: Temple University Press.

Hirsch, F. 1980. *Die soziale Grenzen des Wachstums. Ein ökonomische Analyse der Wachstumskrise*. Hamburg: Reinbek.

Hirsch, J. 1980. *Der Sicherheitsstaat*. Frankfurt: EVA.

Hirschman, Albert O. 1982. *Shifting Involvements*. Princeton: Princeton University Press.

Horn, Klaus (ed.). 1973. *Gruppendynamik und der "subjektive Faktor." Repressive Entsublimierung oder politische Praxis*. Frankfurt: Suhrkamp.

Huberts, Leo W. and Wim J. Van Noort. 1986. "Participation in radical social movements in the Netherlands: A description and a possible explanation." Paper presented at the International Symposium on New Social Movements. Amsterdam, Free University. June, 12-14.

Inglehart, Ronald. 1971. "The silent revolution in Europe: Intergenerational change in post-industrial societies." *American Political Science Review* 65:991-1017.

Inglehart, Ronald. 1977. *The Silent Revolution: Changing Values and Political Styles among Western Publics*. Princeton: Princeton University Press.

Janssen, J. and P. Voestermans. 1978. "De Verguisde Universiteit. Een Cultuurpsychologisch Onderzoek naar voorbije en actuele Ontwikkelingen in de Nijmeegse Studentenwereld." Unpublished dissertation, Catholic University, Nijmegen.

Jenkins, J. Craig. 1983. "Resource mobilization theory and the study of social movements." *Annual Review of Sociology* 9:527-53.

Jenkins, J. Craig. 1985. *The Politics of Insurgency*. New York: Columbia University Press.

Jenkins, J. Craig and Charles Perrow. 1977. "Insurgency of the Powerless: Farm Worker Movements (1946-1972)." *American Sociological Review* 42:249-68.

Katzenstein, Mary F. 1987. "Comparing the feminist movements of the United States and Western Europe: An overview." In Mary Katzenstein and Carol Mueller (eds.), *The Women's Movements of the United States and Western Europe: Consciousness, Political Opportunity, and Public Policy*. Philadelphia: Temple University Press.

Katzenstein, Mary Fainsod and Carol McClurg Mueller (eds.). 1987. *The Women's Movement of the United States and Western Europe: Consciousness, Political Opportunity, and Public Policy*. Philadelphia: Temple University Press.

Killian, Lewis M. 1984. "Organization, rationality and spontaneity in the civil rights movement." *American Sociological Review* 49:770-83.

Kitschelt, Herbert. 1986. "Political opportunity structures and political protest: Anti-nuclear movements in four democracies." *British Journal of Political Science* 16: 57-85.

Klages, H. 1980. *Verdrossene Bürger-überlastete Staat*. Frankfurt: Suhrkamp.

Klandermans, Bert. 1984. "Mobilization and Participation: Social-Psychological Expansions of Resource Mobilization Theory." *American Sociological Review* 49:583-600.

Klandermans, Bert. 1986. "New Social Movements and Resource Mobilization: The European and the American Approach." *International Journal of Mass Emergencies and Disasters.* Special issue, *Comparative Perspectives and Research on Collective Behavior and Social Movements* 4:13-37.

Klandermans, Bert and Dirk Oegema. 1987a. "Campaigning for a nuclear freeze: Grassroots strategies and local government in the Netherlands." In Richard G. Braungart (ed.), *Research in Political Sociology.* Vol. 3. Greenwich, Conn.: JAI.

Klandermans, Bert and Dirk Oegema. 1987b. "Potentials, networks, motivations and barriers: Steps toward participation in social movements." *American Sociological Review* 52:519-531.

Kornhauser, William. 1985. *The Politics of Mass Society.* New York: The Free Press.

Kriesi, Hanspeter. 1985. *Bewegung in der Schweizer Politik, Fallstudien zu politischen Mobilierungsprozessen in der Schweiz.* Frankfurt: Campus.

Lipsky, Michael. 1968. "Protest as a political resource." *American Political Science Review* 62:1144-58.

Lo, Clarence Y. H. 1982. "Countermovements and conservative movements in the contemporary U.S." *Annual Review of Sociology.* 8:107-34.

Lodi, Giovanni. 1984. *Uniti e diversi: Le mobilitazioni per la pace nell' Italia degli anni '80.* Milan: Unicopli.

Loo, Hans van der, Erik Snel, and Bart van Steenbergen. 1984. *Een Wenkend Perspectief. Nieuwe Sociale Bewegingen en Culturele Veranderingen.* Amersfoort: De Horsink.

Löwenthal, R. 1979. *Gesellschaftswandel und Kulturkrise. Zukunftproblemeder westlichen Demokratien.* Frankfurt: Fischer Taschenbuch.

Lumley, Robert. 1983. "Social movements in Italy, 1968-1978." Ph.D. dissertation, Centre for Contemporary Cultural Studies, University of Birmingham, England.

McAdam, Doug. 1982. *Political Process and the Development of Black Insurgency.* Chicago: University of Chicago Press.

McAdam, Doug, 1983. "Tactical innovation and the pace of insurgency." *American Sociological Review* 48:735-54.

McAdam, Doug. 1984. "Structural vs. attitudinal factors in social movement recruitment." Paper presented at the Annual Meeting of the American Sociological Association, San Antonio, Texas, August, 27-31.

McAdam, Doug. 1986. "Recruitment to high-risk activism: The case of Freedom Summer." *American Journal of Sociology* 92:64-90.

McCarthy, John D. 1983. "Social infrastructure deficits and new technologies: Mobilizing unstructured sentiment pools." Unpublished paper, Catholic University, Washington, D.C.

McCarthy, John D. and Mayer N. Zald. 1973. *The Trend of Social Movements in America.* Morristown, N.J.: General Learning Press.

McCarthy, John D. and Mayer N. Zald. 1977. "Resource mobilization and social movements: A partial theory." *American Journal of Sociology* 82:1212-41.

Melucci, Alberto. 1980. "The new social movements: A theoretical approach." *Social Science Information* 19:199-226.

Melucci, Alberto. 1981. "Ten hypotheses for the analysis of new movements." Pages 173-94 in Diana Pinto (ed.), *Contemporary Italian Sociology.* Cambridge: Cambridge University Press.

Melucci, Alberto. 1982. *L'invenzione del presente.* Bologna: Il Mulino.

Melucci, Alberto (ed.). 1984. *Altri codici. Aree di movimento nella metropoli.* Bologna: Il Mulino.

Mitchell, Robert C. 1984a. "National environmental lobbies and the apparent illogic of collective action." In Clifford S. Russell (ed.), *Collective Decision-Making: Applications from Public Choice Theory.* Baltimore: Johns Hopkins University Press.

Mitchell, Robert C. 1984b. "Moving Forward vs. Moving Backwards: Motivation for Collective Action." Paper presented at the Annual Meeting of the American Sociological Association, San Antonio, Texas, August, 27-31.

Morris, Aldon. 1981. "Black Southern Students' Sit-in Movements: An Analysis of International Organization." *American Sociological Review* 46:744-67.

Muller, Edward N. and Karl-Dieter Opp. 1986. "Rational choice and rebellious action." *American Political Science Review* 80:471-88.

Mushaben, Joyce Marie. 1983a. "Cycles of peace protest in West Germany: Experiences from three decades." Paper presented at the Annual Meeting of the American Sociological Association, Detroit, August 31-September 4.

Mushaben, Joyce Marie. 1983b. "Innocence last: Environmental images and political experiences among West German 'Greens'." Paper presented at the Annual Meeting of the International Society for Political Psychology, Oxford, July 19-22.

Narr, N. D. 1979. "Hin zu einer gesellschaftbedingter Reflexe." In Jürgen Habermas (ed.), *Stichworte zur geistigen Situation der Zeit.* Frankfurt: Suhrkamp.

Nelkin, Dorothy and Michael Pollak. 1981. *The Atom Beseiged: Extraparliamentary Dissent in France and Germany.* Cambridge, Mass.: MIT Press.

Oberschall, Anthony. 1973. *Social Conflict and Social Movements.* Englewood Cliffs, N.J.: Prentice-Hall.

Oberschall, Anthony. 1978. "The Decline of the 1960s Social Movements." In Louis Kriesberg (ed.), *Research in Social Movements, Conflict, and Change.* Vol. 1. Greenwich, Conn.: JAI.

Oberschall, Anthony. 1980. "Loosely Structured Collective Conflict: A Theory and an Application." Pages 45-68 in Louis Kriesberg (ed.), *Research in Social Movements, Conflict and Change.* Vol. 3. Greenwich, Conn.: JAI.

Offe, Claus. 1985. "New Social Movements: Challenging the Boundaries of Institutional Politics." *Social Research* 52:817-68.

Oliver, Pamela. 1984. "If You Don't Do It, Nobody Else Will": Active and Token Contributors to Local Collective Action." *American Sociological Review* 49:601-10.

Oliver, Pamela, Gerald Marwell, and Ruy Teixeira. 1985. "A Theory of the Critical Mass. I. Group Heterogeneity, Interdependence and the Production of Collective Goods." *American Journal of Sociology* 91:522-56.

Olson, Mancur, Jr. 1968. *The Logic of Collective Action: Public Goods and the Theory of Groups.* Cambridge: Harvard University Press.

Oudijk, Corrine. 1983. *Sociale Atlas van de Vrouw.* The Hague: Staatsuitgeverij.

Perrow, Charles. 1979. "The Sixties Observed." In Mayer N. Zald and John D. McCarthy (eds.), *Dynamics of Social Movements.* Cambridge, Mass: Winthrop.

Pinard, Maurice. 1971. *The Rise of a Third Party: A Study in Crisis Politics.* Englewood Cliffs, N.J.: Prentice-Hall.

Pinard, Maurice. 1983. "From deprivation to mobilization." Paper presented at the Annual Meeting of the American Sociological Association, Detroit, August 31-September 4.

Piven, Frances Fox and Richard A. Cloward. 1979. *Poor People's Movements: Why They Succeed, How They Fail.* New York: Vintage.

Pizzorno, Alessandro. 1978. "Political exchange and collective identity in industrial conflict." Pages 277-98 in Colin Crouch and Alessandro Pizzorno (eds.), *The Resurgence of Class Conflict in Western Europe since 1968.* Vol. 2. London: Macmillan.

Raschke, Joachim. 1980. "Politik und Wertwandel in den westlichen Demokratien." *Aus Politik und Zeitgeschichte.* 36:23-46.

Regalia, Ida. 1986. "Evolving patterns of participation in the trade union movement: Membership, strikes, and militancy in Italy." Paper presented at the International Symposium on New Social Movements. Amsterdam, Free University, June, 12-14.

Regalia, Ida, Marino Regini, and Emilio Reyneri. 1978. "Labour conflicts and industrial relations in Italy." Pages 101-58 in Colin Crouch and Alessandro Pizzorno (eds.), *The Resurgence of Class Conflict in Western Europe since 1968.* Vol. 1. London: Macmillan.

Reich, Michael. 1984. "Mobilizing for environmental policy in Italy and Japan." *Comparative Politics* 16:379-402.

Rucht, Dieter. 1984a. "Comparative new social movements, organizations, and strategies in a cross-sectional and a cross-national view." Paper presented at the Conference of the European Group of Organizational Sociologists on New Social Movements, Aarhus, Denmark, August 27-29.

Rucht, Dieter. 1984b. "Zur Organisation der neuen Sozialen Bewegungen." In Jürgen W. Falter, C. Fenner, and M.Th. Greven (eds.), *Politische Willensbildung und Interessenvermittlung.* Opladen: Westdeutscher Verlag.

Rudig, Wolfgang. 1983. "Clustered nuclear siting, anti-nuclear opposition." Paper presented at the Sixth Annual Meeting of the International Society of Political Psychology, Oxford, July 19-22.

Sherif, C.W., M. Sherif, and R.E. Nebergall. 1965. *Attitude and Attitude Change: The Social Judgment-Involvement Approach.* Philadelphia: W. B. Saunders.

Snyder, David and Charles Tilly. 1972. "Hardship and collective violence in France, 1830-1960." *American Sociological Review* 37:520-32.

Tarrow, Sidney. 1983. *Struggling to Reform: Social Movements and Policy Change during Cycles of Protest.* Western Societies Paper No. 15. Ithaca, N.Y.: Cornell University.

Tarrow, Sidney. 1986. "Comparing Social Movement Participation in Western Europe and the United States: Problems, Uses, Examples, and a Proposal for Synthesis." *International Journal of Mass Emergencies and Disasters.* Special issue, *Comparative Perspectives and Research on Collective Behavior and Social Movements* 4:145-70.

Tarrow, Sidney. 1988. *Democracy and Disorder: Society and Politics in Italy, 1965-1975.* Oxford: Oxford University Press (forthcoming).

Teulings, Ad and Frans Leynse. 1975. *Nieuwe Vormen van Industriele Actie.* Nijmegen: SUN.

Tilly, Charles. 1978. *From Mobilization to Revolution.* Reading, Mass.: Addison-Wesley.

Tilly, Charles. 1979. "Repertoires of contention in America and Britain, 1750-1830." Pages 126-56 in Mayer N. Zald and John D. McCarthy (eds.), *The Dynamics of Social Movements.* Cambridge, Mass.: Winthrop.

Tilly, Charles. 1984. "Social movements and national politics." In Charles Bright and Susan Harding (eds.), *Statemaking and Social Movements.* Ann Arbor: University of Michigan Press.

Touraine, Alain. 1971. *The Postindustrial Society.* New York: Random.

Touraine, Alain, 1978. *La voix et le regard.* Paris: Seuil.

Van Noort, Wim. 1984. *De Effecten van de Kraakbeweging op de Besluitvorming van Gemeentelijke Overheden.* Leiden: COMT.

Visser, J. 1985. "Vakbondsgroei en Vakbondsmacht in West Europa." *Tijdschrift voor Arbeidsvraagstukken* 1:18-39.

Wilson, James Q. 1973. *Political Organization.* New York: Basic Books.

Wilson, Kenneth L. and Anthony M. Orum. 1976. "Mobilizing people for collective political action." *Journal of Political and Military Sociology* 4:187-202.

Zald, Mayer N. and Michael Berger. 1978. "Social movements in organizations: Coup d'état, insurgency, and mass movements." *American Journal of Sociology* 83:823-61.

PART I

NETWORKS, SUPPORT STRUCTURES, AND SUBCULTURES

LOCAL MOBILIZATION FOR THE PEOPLE'S SOCIAL PETITION OF THE DUTCH PEACE MOVEMENT

Hanspeter Kriesi

I. INTRODUCTION: THE STRUCTURE OF NEW SOCIAL MOVEMENTS

In the fall of 1985, the Dutch peace movement organized a large-scale event, the people's petition. About 3.8 million Dutch were mobilized to sign this petition against the deployment of cruise missiles in the Netherlands. This mobilization process can serve as an example of how contemporary social movements in Western Europe mobilize. To study this example I start out from the assumption underlying the resource mobilization approach: that understanding organizational structure is of crucial importance for understanding mobilization processes. In doing so, however, I do not restrict my attention to formal organizational structures (SMOs); in the notion of organizational structure I include informal networks at the level of the supporters (adherents) of social movements as well. As Oberschall (1973) has shown, traditional communities can serve as functional equivalents of formal

International Social Movement Research, Vol. 1, pages 41-81.
Supplement to Research in Social Movements, Conflicts and Change
Copyright © 1988 by JAI Press Inc.
All rights of reproduction in any form reserved.
ISBN: 0-89232-955-6

SMOs in mobilization processes; Tilly's (1978) CATNET is not only a necessary structural precondition for a mobilization process to take place, in some instances it may also supply sufficient organizational capacity to mobilize the shared grievances of those linked by more or less informal network ties. In this chapter I want to show that informal network structures are not only important for the mobilization of traditional communities, but that they also play a crucial role in the mobilization of those contemporary movements which have come to be called "new social movements" (NSMs).

Together with a number of other contemporary movements (the antinuclear movement, the women's movement, the ecology movement, and the squatters' movement), the peace movement can be counted among these NSMs. Although these movements apparently pursue quite different goals, they tend to be run by the same kind of people: Studies on NSMs in several Western European countries have shown that these movements are rooted especially strongly in a specific part of the new middle class, the professionals employed in social and cultural services (Alber 1985; Cotgrove and Duff 1980, 1981; Gundelach 1984; Kriesi 1985; Parkin 1968). The supporters of NSMs also tend to subscribe to value patterns different from the dominant ones. In his early work on the British CND, Parkin (1968, pp. 21-31) noted the "alienation" of its activists from dominant values. Later studies confirmed his results: Cotgrove and Duff (1980, 1981), for example, pointed out how supporters of the environmental movement opposed the dominant value of "economic individualism." Moreover, the pronounced postmaterialism of those engaged in or closely associated with NSMs has often been noted (Bürklin 1982, 1984; Fietkau et al. 1982; Inglehart 1981; Müller-Rommel 1982, 1985; Reuband 1985). The social and cultural background of the activitists in the Dutch peace movement also corresponds to this general pattern (Kriesi and van Praag, Jr. 1987). The different NSMs tend to articulate different aspects of a *new general cultural design*. This new general design can be termed *"countercultural"* because to some extent it represents an "inversion of," is "in sharp opposition to," the historically created designs, as is typical of the designs of the counterculture (Yinger 1982, pp. 39f.). Indeed, the fact that this new design is a very elusive phenomenon may be one of the reasons why the "newness" of these movements turns out to be so difficult to grasp.

The individual actors who form these movements not only come from comparable structural and cultural backgrounds, they also are closely interlinked. For one thing, activists from a specific NSM tend to be or to have been active in other NSMs as well. Even if they do not participate in other NSMs, they at least tend to share their goals and to be related to their activists via friendship ties. This interconnection is true of the Dutch peace movement in particular (Kriesi and van Praag, Jr. 1987). Moreover, these activists' networks are generally tied into broader and more diffuse network structures interconnecting people who sympathize with the goals of the various NSMs and who support them in different ways. These broader networks in turn are also based on common structural background characteristics and common cultural orientations. They have developed in the course of the cycle of protest (Tarrow 1983) that took off in the late 1960s and came to an end in the late 1970s. They have been built around groups, communes, projects, and media and communication centers begun by the protest generation of the late sixties (the New Left), and they are made up of people living, working, communicating, and making politics together in pursuit of a countercultural design for an alternative way of life. I shall call these broader networks *countercultural networks.*

If integration into these networks is based on structural and cultural preconditions, interaction within these networks entails structural and cultural consequences for those involved. If one is drawn into these networks on the basis of one's specific location in the social structure and one's value orientations, one's interactions with others within these network structures are likely to further develop one's original orientations and to change one's structural position accordingly. Interaction leads not only to sympathy with those one interacts with (Homans 1971, pp. 153ff.), but supposedly to an elaboration of ideas, value-conceptions, and identities, too. Most important, the interactions involved in the mobilization of NSMs in particular are most likely to contribute to the elaboration of countercultural designs and identities.

Countercultural networks make up the core of the *mobilization potentials* of NSMs, but they do not exhaust them. Depending on the issue articulated and the means employed, NSMs can reach beyond the boundaries of these rather circumscribed networks. These boundaries typically are highly diffuse: Individuals are involved in these networks to varying degrees, and the extent to which they break with the dominant culture varies considerably. The development of countercultural identities most often remains a partial one, given that most people are usually integrated into multiple networks and have quite contradictory experiences in their everyday life. Because there are different degrees of integration into countercultural networks, the counterculture is not isolated from the dominant culture; the two interpenetrate, and one shades off into the other.[1]

Just as it is difficult to draw the boundaries of the countercultural networks, it is hard to delimit the *activists' networks.* As McAdam (1986) points out, movements are ephemeral phenomena that resist boundary demarcation. In the case of the NSMs, this problem of demarcation is especially pronounced, because these movements are—consciously or unconsciously—trying to initiate societal de-differentiation processes (Rucht 1982, p. 285) to link personal and institutional change. That is, these movements tend to be scarcely differentiated from everyday activity within the countercultural networks, as Melucci (1984, p. 829) observes:

The normal situation of today's "movement" is to be a network of small groups submerged into everyday life which require a personal involvement in experiencing and practising cultural innovation.

These movements do not form organizational structures that are highly differentiated from the grass-roots level of everyday activity within the countercultural networks.[2] The local organizational structure of these movements tends to be of a highly *informal* character; typically they do not have any formal statutes, institutionalized role-differentiation, or regular dues. They even lack clear-cut membership criteria. Participation in the activities of the local/regional cores of these movements is highly irregular, dependent on political attention cycles (Downs 1972), mobilization attempts, and personal circumstances determining individual availability. Corresponding to the highly individualistic goals of these movements (defense and extension of individual autonomy in the face of ever increasing systems' imperatives), the participation pattern is also highly *individualistic* (Nelles 1984, p. 434; Kriesi 1982). The potential NSMs draw upon is, therefore, rather volatile, posing a serious problem for the stabilization of a minimal infrastructure over time. On the other hand, the fact that they are rooted in countercultural networks makes NSMs very flexible. Figure 1 summarizes the relationships between activists' networks of different NSMs, countercultural networks, and mobilization potential in a highly schematic way.

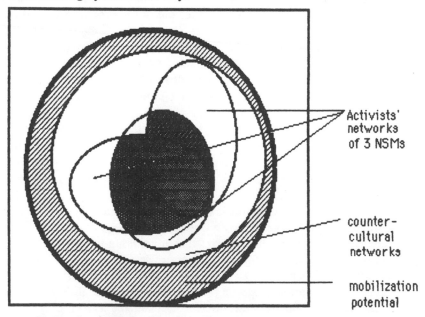

Activists'
networks
of 3 NSMs

counter-
cultural
networks

mobilization
potential

Figure 1.   Mobilization potential, countercultural networks,
and activists' networks of NSMs.

The emergent picture needs further elaboration along at least three lines. First, we need to distinguish between the *national* and the *local/regional level* of structuration. Given their general structural roots in countercultural networks, NSMs typically have a highly decentralized structure with local/ regional cores enjoying a large measure of autonomy. At the national level, the organizational capability is characteristically limited, and most often the national core-group has little more than a coordinating function. It is the local/ regional cores (activists' networks) which are the crucial organizational level of the NSMs, because they typically bear the brunt of mobilization efforts and they connect the grass-roots level of the countercultural networks with the national, coordinating level. The relative importance the national structures assume in a NSM seems to depend on at least two factors: the structure of the political system and the kind of issue involved. If the movement is operating in a centralized political system and if it deals with an issue that touches matters of national or even international politics, organization on the national level will be of greater relevance. For both of these reasons, we may expect the Dutch peace movement to be relatively more centralized than other NSMs.

Second, countercultural networks are not distributed evenly throughout a country, they are primarily *an urban phenomenon.* As Fisher (1982, p. 196) observed, urbanization stimulates the formation of countercultural networks in at least three different ways:[3]

By *selective migration:* Cities attract all kinds of cultural, ethnic, and ideological minorities. A wide range of outsiders and of specific population groups settle in cities,

By reaching a "*critical mass*": In cities, these different groups reach a critical mass facilitating the establishment and intensification of countercultural networks.

By *conflict between groups:* Contact between different cultures generally causes friction and conflict which in turn strengthen individual identification and involvement in the countercultural networks.

Although these networks are found mainly in cities, they are not confined to cities. As is observed, for example, by Craven and Wellman (1974, p. 80), communities in the urban world have become increasingly nonlocal and specialized in character, which is to say that someone living in a rural area may well be connected to countercultural networks by ties to people living in the cities. Moreover, countercultural groups may also develop in smaller towns, groups supported by their links to more firmly rooted countercultural cores in cities. Some of these groups may be local/regional activist networks of NSMs. The interconnected network of local/regional activist networks of NSMs forms what Melucci (1984, p. 828) has called *"movement networks."* This concept is, as he notes, similar to that of McCarthy and Zald's (1977) "social movement industry"; it includes not only "formal" organizations but also the network of "informal" relationships connecting activists among themselves as well as to a broader area of (countercultural) participants.

Finally, the activists' network within one and the same movement may be less coherent than one may expect. Movements are made up of different *tendencies* that form specific sub-networks within the more encompassing structure of a movement's overall activists' network. These sub-networks may not all be interconnected to the same degree, and they may be differentially linked to the countercultural networks in particular and to other elements of their environment in general. Militant currents typically are more isolated from their environment, as well as from the other parts of a movement's activists' network, than moderate ones. Very moderate tendencies may reach far beyond countercultural networks and may be able to enlarge the mobilization potential of a movement to a considerable degree. The Dutch peace movement in particular is made up of different currents. It is to the specific structure of this movement and to its campaign for the people's petition that I now turn.

II.   THE STRUCTURE OF THE DUTCH PEACE MOVEMENT AND THE CAMPAIGN FOR THE PEOPLE'S PETITION

Peace movements, pacifism, and antimilitarism have a long tradition in the Netherlands. Since the end of the nineteenth century, groups representing various intellectual and political currents have been active. We can roughly distinguish *four such currents:* an antimilitaristic tradition inspired by an anarchistic vision of the state, a socialist tradition whose primary goal is disarmament, a Christian tradition that condemns war and violence on ethical and moral grounds, and a women's peace movement. Between the two World Wars, when Holland was pursuing a neutral policy, the activities of these different currents peaked for the first time. In the new peace movement, reactivated in the seventies, the same four tendencies can again be discerned.

Before we examine the different currents, it is important to note that, although there are ideological similarities between the old and the new peace movements, there is *little organization continuity* between the two. In the past, large-scale activities were more heavily influenced by party politics, and the radical and (Christian)-pacifist traditions had more influence than they do today. The "grass-roots" approach over the last ten years is a sign of the impact other NSMs have had on it, an impact due, among other things, to the influx of former activists from the ecology movement and the antinuclear movement. The peace movement has adopted various forms of action from other NSMs, and it has become increasingly concerned with the security of one's own life world (van der Loo et al. 1984; Everts and Walraven 1984).

The *Christian tradition* is represented by the Catholic Pax Christi and above all by the ecumenical IKV (Inter-kerkelijk Vredesberaad). The IKV was founded in 1967 by seven churches (the Catholic church, the Calvinists, the Dutch Reformed Church, and several smaller churches). Originally, the IKV consisted of only a national core group made up of a general secretary and a few staff members, financed by the member churches. Its central task was to stimulate contemplation in the churches on the problems of war and peace and to advise the churches in these matters (IKV 1984, p. 13). Consciousness-raising was an important part of its strategy. Its activities—such as, at first, the distribution of information and discussion papers—were mainly concentrated on a yearly "peace week" held nationally in September. In 1977 the IKV started with a more distinctly political campaign against nuclear weapons in general and against the nuclear task-force of the Dutch army in particular. At the same time, the IKV also set out to stimulate activities at the grass-roots level by encouraging the foundation of local IKV cores. In 1985 some 450 local cores were active all over the country. The organization, however, was still characterized by a top-down model. Only recently, has the IKV been trying to restructure its internal relations to give the local cores some measure of influence on the policy made at the national top. At the national level, the IKV does not have individual members; individuals can only join a local core or subscribe to the monthly of the IKV (3,000 subscribers).

The second important current in the new peace movement, the *socialist current*, is represented by the action group Stop-de-Neutronenbom/Stop-de-Kernwapenwedloop (SNB), a loosely structured cluster of autonomous local groups under the umbrella of a national coordinating committee. The number of local cores varies considerably according to the political attention cycle. There are around 75-100 stable groups and about 200 groups inactive in quiet times but ready to be called upon if needed during a mobilization campaign. The people who founded this action group in 1977 came from a communist background (Maessen 1979). Although the communist element in this group is still very strong today, it should be considered an independent organization that recruits its activists from all three small Dutch leftist parties and from the nonorganized on the left. In contrast to the IKV, the SNB is not primarily engaged in consciousness-raising and discussing problems of peace but in mobilizing as many people as possible for direct actions with clearly identifiable goals concerning questions of war and peace. The first campaign the SNB organized was directed against President Carter's plan to introduce the neutron bomb. In 1977-78 this group organized the first massive postwar peace actions—a petition with 1.2 million signatures and a demonstration of 50,000 people. Later, this group also concentrated on preventing the deployment of cruise missiles in the Netherlands.

Women for Peace (Vrouwen voor Vrede; VVV) was founded in 1979, and a few years later could count on 6,000 subscribers to its periodical. VVV defines itself as part of an international movement for peace without a central policy. Like the SNB, it is made up of autonomous local cores. The scope of their activities, however, is more encompassing than that of the SNB cores. The VVV groups are active not only in issues regarding peace and disarmament but also on such issues as relations with the Third World and problems of nuclear energy. Their activities consist of both demonstrative actions and the organization of discussions and information-evenings.

The *radical peace tendency* is composed of many small groups. In general, their policy is to express their opposition to the arms race and the military-industrial complex. They do not have any confidence in the political system and in traditional political organizations. The different groups are loosely structured and have connections to the squatters' movement and to the antinuclear movement. The number of adherents is limited, but their actions—sometimes ludicrous, sometimes provocative—get a great deal of publicity. The antimilitarist and anarchist group "Onkruit" (Weed) has for several years been the most important element in this current.

The local cores of all the different currents share the overall structural characteristics described for the general model above. They are highly informal and have no clear-cut membership criteria. The number of activists regularly participating in their activities is small, typically varying from five to ten persons. Their financial resources are limited, too, and typically depend upon the sale of propaganda material supplied by the national coordinating institution of the appropriate current. These cores do develop actions of their own, but our study of local cores has left me with the impression that their level of activity is highly dependent on impulses from the national level. They are indeed responsible for mobilization at the grass-roots level, but most likely within the framework of a campaign launched at the national level. This is a strong indication of the importance of the national coordination for this particular NSM.

If we are to get a more complete picture of the organizational structure of the Dutch peace movement, however, we must look at more than these different currents. In fact, the peace movement has a two-tiered structure in which more *encompassing coordinating committees* exist alongside the different currents. At the national level, this more encompassing structure first was of an ad hoc and temporary nature: It was set up specifically for organizing large-scale national events. The first large demonstration of the new peace movement, the one that took place in Amsterdam in 1981 with about 400,000 people participating, was organized by an ad hoc committee (the "21-november Komitee"). This committee consisted not only of all the large peace organizations but also of political parties ranging from the small leftist parties—CPN (communists), PSP (pacifist socialists), PPR (radicals)—via the Social Democrats to the progressive liberals of D'66, some smaller peace organizations, and the union of conscripts. After the demonstration, this committee ceased to function as a national coordinating body. Significantly, however, it was not dissolved but continued as a coordinating committee for the City of Amsterdam. Moreover, elsewhere in the country similar committees were set up to coordinate the activities of the different currents and to establish links between the peace movement and political parties on the local/regional level.

In 1983 a second national committee was established to organize another large-scale demonstration, this time in The Hague, in which over half a million people participated. This committee (Komitee Kruisraketten Nee, KKN) was even more encompassing than the first one, representing as well the FNV, the largest peak organization of the Dutch trade unions. This time, the national committee continued to carry out national coordinating functions after the demonstration and became a more or less permanent structure for organizing large-scale national events. First it organized the "action-week," a campaign to influence the government's decision on the deployment of 48 cruise missiles in the Netherlands to be taken on June 1, 1984. After that decision had been deferred to November 1, 1985, it set up the campaign for the people's petition to be held just before that final decision of the government.

The emergence of a second tier of organizations within the Dutch peace movement has served to integrate the different currents and to strengthen its ties with established political organizations (see Kriesi and van Praag, Jr. 1987). This development, however, has not been unproblematic for the movement. The organization of encompassing national campaigns has siphoned off resources from the organizations in the different currents and it has to some extent undermined their identity and visibility for their supporters.[4] Moreover, since all the organizations participating in the encompassing structure have to agree to a common national campaign, such a campaign has to take into account the more limited action-repertory of established political organizations, which is to say that such a campaign can only be a moderate one. This enforced moderation brought the KKN much criticism from more radical groups which think that the KKN has sold out the peace movement to the political parties and the unions.

The links between the KKN and the local coordinating committees are even looser than the links between the organizations within the different currents and their local branches. The KKN has roughly 700 contacts all over the country, but not all these contacts are local committees. Some are local cores of an organization of one of the currents, some are individual activists or people interested in the activities of the KKN. The KKN itself does not know how many local committees exist. The KKN also has a top-down structure: Although the ideas and opinions of the local committees are taken into account, the decisions on the kind of campaigns to be held are made at the top by the representatives of the different organizations that compose the committee. The implementation of national campaigns, however, is determined mainly by the peace movement itself. Thus the organization and national coordination of the campaign for the people's petition was carried out by a group of five people who had already organized the first demonstration in Amsterdam and who had strong ties to the peace movement: two of the five came from Stop-de-N-Bom, one from the IKV, and two from political parties (one from the Social Democrats and one from the PSP). The mobilization at the local/regional level was carried out almost entirely by local cores of the peace movement.

The *campaign for the people's petition* was set up as follows. Every one of the 5.5 million households in the Netherlands was to receive by official mail a card with the text of the petition against the deployment of cruise missiles in the Netherlands.[5] This card could be signed by as many as five persons and sent back at the signers' expense to the national headquarters of the campaign. No age limit was set for signers of the petition. The card also contained a section that could be filled in by those who wanted to support the campaign financially. Since the KKN did not have the money to pay for the return mail, it expected that many people would not participate for this reason. It therefore called upon its local contacts to organize local collection campaigns. The idea was that the local groups would mobilize their grass-roots supporters to stage a door-to-door collection drive covering all addresses in every locality in the Netherlands. Such a campaign would have the additional advantage of allowing people who had not received cards or had lost them the opportunity to sign. One million additional cards were supplied to the local groups for this purpose. The cards collected by the local groups were to be sent to national headquarters, where the signatures were checked and counted.

The campaign was launched with a widely publicized national demonstration, and it continued to attract much publicity throughout the eight weeks of collection. At the time of the campaign, the issue of the cruise missiles was a very visible one and, according to a survey held immediately after the presentation of the petition at the end of October, virtually all the Dutch (95%) were to some extent informed about the issue. For about two-fifths of them, the issue was very important and another two-fifths considered it of at least some importance. The petition was signed by 3.8 million people, which is roughly one-fourth of the Dutch population[6]. No other petition in the Netherlands has ever been signed by so many people.

III.   DATA AND INDICATORS FOR INTEGRATION IN COUNTERCULTURAL NETWORKS

The setup of the campaign for the people's petition allows us to analyze the impact of local countercultural networks on both the mobilization of activists for the local collection campaigns and the mobilization of the broader potential of supporters to sign the petition. To study the differential impact of these networks structures *six specific localities* in the Netherlands were selected: two districts in Amsterdam and two in Utrecht—the largest and the third largest Dutch city, a locality in the north and one in the south of the country. With respect to the city districts, we chose an inner-city district and a peripheral one in both cities. The reason why we did not choose entire cities but districts within cities has to do with the way the peace movement is organized. The local cores of the different currents, and to some extent the encompassing committees too, are formed at the district level within cities, and city cores and city committees coordinate all the activities of all the cores/committees within one city.

Both Amsterdam and Utrecht are university towns with a rather young population and an intensive countercultural life in the center of the city. In each of the two cities we chose inner-city districts—the "Kinkerbuurt" in Amsterdam and the "Vogelenbuurt" in Utrecht—that have large areas of rather run-down housing with many young, single, and highly educated inhabitants and a relatively large percentage of foreigners (15% in Amsterdam and 13% in Utrecht). The two peripheral districts chosen were both built in the 1960s and 1970s to relieve the serious Dutch housing shortage. Designed under the impact of the booming postwar economy, they first consisted mainly of enormous apartment buildings. Because of the social problems that arose in these areas, later stages of the large-scale projects were then constructed in a different style—mainly family homes. In the district chosen in Amsterdam, the social problems have not, however, disappeared. In spite of a housing shortage in the inner city, a large number of flats in this peripheral district (the "Bijlmer") are empty, and the turnover among the local population of now approximately 65,000 is very high and still increasing. The population on the whole resembles that of the inner-city districts but there are more families with children. If there is an example of a highly "alienating" environment in Holland, then it is the Bijlmer. The situation in the peripheral district in Utrecht ("Overvecht"), where about 30,000 people live, is less extreme. Here, in contrast to the Bijlmer, the population more closely resembles the national average: the level of education is much lower than in the inner cities and in the Bijlmer, and the proportion of working-class and lower-middle-class inhabitants is larger, there are many families with children and, because of the large number of homes built for the elderly, many old persons. The two rural localities, finally, were chosen to represent the average Dutch community as closely as possible. Their population is not very different from that of Overvecht, except in the extent to which the people practice their religion. Since religion still plays a major role in rural Dutch communities and in Dutch politics in general, we chose a typical Protestant community in the north of the country ("Joure") and a typical Catholic one in the south ("Waalwijk").

In each of these 6 localities we gathered information on the organizational structure of the movement by interviewing key representatives of the local cores. In addition, we conducted written *surveys among the activists* who took part in the organization and the collection of the signatures of the people's petition. These surveys were organized in collaboration with the local groups, which we found to be very cooperative.[7] Eighty percent of the roughly 600 activists who received a questionnaire immediately after the close of the campaign for the petition responded to the survey. In each of the 6 localities we also took a sample of 250 people of the *local population* 18 or older, to whom we administered a written questionnaire at the same time.[8] Only 52% of the people in these samples responded, a considerably smaller proportion than that of the activists. Several checks with statistical information available through other sources have shown that certain groups are overrepresented among the respondents, in particular men and Dutch citizens (as compared to the foreign inhabitants), but also the highly educated, those sympathetic to the Social Democrats and D'66, and those who were in favor of the petition.

Three different indicators *define the strength of a local counterculture.* A first indicator pertains to how the people in the respondent's personal environment reacted to the petition.[9] In a given locality, the larger the number of people who live in an environment supportive of the petition, the stronger, presumably, the local counterculture. A second indicator is based on a question that asked, for five different NSMs, whether one had a friend or several friends who had already participated or were still participating in the movement.[10] In a given locality, the larger the number of individuals having several ties to activists in at least one NSM, the stronger we may again assume the local counterculture to be. Both these indicators are somewhat deficient, however, because the questions they are based upon do not have any territorial reference. The friends or family members who approve of the petition and the friends active in NSMs may not live in the same community as the respondent. If this is the predominant pattern in a certain locality, the local counterculture may be relatively weak, even if there are many people tied to countercultural networks living there. It is only when these people are interlinked among themselves that we can speak of a strong local counterculture.

In order to overcome the deficiencies of the first two indicators, I devised an indirect measure for the likelihood that someone has friendship ties to individuals in the local counterculture. This indirect measure corresponds to the number of contacts one has with people living in one's community in general, weighted by the proportion of the local population integrated into countercultural networks.[11] The larger the share of the local population who is integrated into countercultural networks (as measured by the second indicator above), the greater the chance that contacts with persons living in the same community will be with people integrated into countercultural networks. This third indicator has deficiencies of its own, since it measures only the probability of integration into local countercultures and not actual integration. Where an individual says he or she has no contact at all with the local population, we can be sure that he or she is not integrated into the local counterculture. But when someone claims to have some or many ties to the local population, the indicator assumes that these ties are evenly distributed among those integrated into countercultural networks and those not integrated into these networks, which may be contrary to what in fact obtains.

Table 1 shows how peace movement activists and the local population in the six localities selected differ with respect to countercultural integration according to the three indicators described. Examining these results, we see that the two inner-city districts and the peripheral district from Amsterdam clearly differ from the other three localities, the first three not unexpectedly being characterized by much stronger local countercultures. This fact becomes readily apparent if we look at the three columns in this table pertaining to local population. The proportion of those living in an environment supportive of the peace movement is considerably greater in all three of the former localities; the proportion of those who have several friends in NSMs is on the average twice as high in the first group as in the second, and the discrepancies between the scale values for the indirect indicator are even more pronounced. For the activists, differences between the two groups of localities are negligible regarding the first two indicators. With respect to the indirect measure, however, activists in the inner-city districts and in the periphery of Amsterdam turn out to be more integrated into the counterculture than activists in the other localities. This result is quite plausible in the light of the specific deficiencies of the three indicators. Everywhere, activists seem to be highly integrated into countercultural networks in general, but in localities with a strong counterculture, this integration apparently is much more locally based than in localities where local countercultural networks are weak. As it turns out, activists in the three localities with a relatively strong counterculture have more contact with people in the community than does the population at large, while the reverse is true of the southern town of Waalwijk and of the northern town of Joure.[12]

If we compare the results for the activists with the ones for the population at large on the third indicator, the pattern becomes even clearer. Overall, the activists are more strongly integrated in the local countercultural networks than is the population at large. But in the localities where these networks are strong, the population at large is more strongly integrated into the counterculture than are the activists in places with a weak counterculture. The countercultural activist in a city like Amsterdam can count upon many potential supporters of his cause, while his or her colleague in a town like Waalwijk or Joure is faced with a more or less indifferent or even hostile environment. How this general difference affects the local mobilization processes is the subject of the following empirical analysis. First, I will report the results with respect to the mobilization of the activists, then I shall turn to the mobilization of the supporters.

Table 1. Three Indicators for Countercultural Integration for Activists and Population at Large in the Six Chosen Localities

Locality	Supportive environm.[1]		Friends in NSMs[2]		Int into local c.-c.[3]		Sample size[4]	
	Activists	Population	Activists	Population	Activists	Population	Activists	Population
inner-city Amsterdam	93%	64%	94%	61%	.77	.55	69	105
periphery Amsterdam	94%	60%	80%	51%	.74	.38	84	126
inner-city Utrecht	97%	63%	79%	50%	.63	.35	34	113
strong counterculture	94%	62%	85%	54%	.73	.42	187	344
periphery Utrecht	97%	45%	84%	31%	.36	.15	78	116
Joure (North)	91%	43%	85%	29%	.36	.18	91	127
Waalwijk (South)	84%	44%	75%	22%	.20	.09	97	115
weak counterculture	91%	44%	81%	27%	.31	.14	263	358

Notes:

[1] Integration into an environment supportive of the peace movement: percentage of those whose personal environment approved of the petition.

[2] Percentage of those who have several friendship ties to activists in at least one NSM.

[3] Average scale values (see text).

[4] Sample sizes for "supportive environment." The size varies somewhat between the three indicators due to missing values.

IV. THE FIRST STEP IN LOCAL MOBILIZATION: RECRUITING ACTIVISTS

Except in the inner-city district of Utrecht, in all the localities selected, the movement could fall back on preexisting local SMOs to initiate the first step. The local organizational patterns in these places did not deviate very much from the pattern outlined above for NSMs in general. As is shown in Table 2, the *specific configurations of local cores,* however, were quite distinct in each of the localities studied.

In the inner-city district of Amsterdam we find small local cores of the IKB and SNB as well as a local committee encompassing representatives of the three main branches of the peace movement, local branches of different parties, and the local churches. Also represented is the neighborhood center ("buurthuis") of the city. The committee, which was established upon the initiative of the SNB, is activated only if national events are to be organized, and it is the IKV or the SNB that take the initiative in reactivating it. The "Bijlmer," the peripheral district of Amsterdam, has an active IKV-core and a committee encompassing the IKV, VVV, local parties, and a Third World group (the "Wereldwinkel"). In this case, the committee was established at the initiative of the citywide committee (the "21-november-komitee"). The SNB had been very active in the "Bijlmer" in the past, but because several activists had moved away, the group had disappeared by the time the petition took place. The fact that VVV is represented on the local committees, although it does not have an established group in either of these districts, is due to the way VVV is represented on the local committees, although it does not have an established group in either of these districts, is due to the way VVV is organized in Amsterdam. VVV has only a citywide group, but some of the individual members living in the different parts of the city join their local committees to represent the organization at that level.

Table 2. Configuration of Local Cores in the Six Localities at the Time of the Petition[1]

| | strong counterculture | | weak counterculture | | | |
Local core	inner c. Amst.	periph. Amst.	inner c. Utrecht	periph. Utrecht	Prot. North	Cath. South
IKV	x	x	—	x	x	x
SNB	x	—	—	(x)	—	x
VVV	—	—	—	—	—	x
local committee	x	x	—	x	x	x

Note:

[1] x: local core exists; —: local core does not exist anymore; (x): local core integrated into local committee

In the third locality with a strong countercultural network—the inner-city district in Utrecht—no local cores existed at the time the campaign for the petition took place. There had initially been an unusually large (about 20 members) and very active SNB-group in this district, which organized a yearly local peace festival. By the time of the second national peace demonstration in The Hague, however, this group had lost faith in the moderate strategies of SNB and joined the radical branch of the movement, only to disappear completely in 1985. In the peripheral district of Utrecht, another large and very active SNB-group had existed for some time. This group, however, developed quite differently. It sought to enlarge its base and tried to become a more · encompassing local committee, embracing the small local IKV-core as well. This strategy was not entirely successful because of the distrust of some local IKV-members who tried to preserve the autonomy of their local core. Like Amsterdam, Utrecht also has a citywide committee that tries to coordinate the activities of all the local cores and to keep in contact with the political parties.

In the two rural localities selected, the organizational situation is different again. In Joure, the predominantly Protestant town in the north, the movement has a strong IKV-core and a local committee including representatives of the local peace groups, parties, unions, and the previously mentioned Third World organization. Between the IKV-core and the committee a kind of division of labor has been established with the committee organizing the local actions of the movement and the IKV-core concentrating on study activities. An SNB-core that had existed in Joure for some time had disappeared by the time of the petition. Because of the prevailing Christian orientation in rural areas, one might expect the IKV to be generally strong there. This is not the case, however, as the example of the predominantly Catholic town of Waalwijk in the south illustrates. Here, all three currents of the peace movement are represented, but the local IKV-core turns out to be rather weak, while the local SNB-group has been quite active for several years. In the local committee, we find all three currents, but, significantly, no other organizations. The activists from the local branch of Amnesty International and of the Third World organization mentioned above sympathize with the peace movement but do not dare to associate with it publicly. They are afraid they will lose their support in the local population if they do so! Tensions between the three local currents further weaken the local committee in this, for the peace movement, rather inhospitable town.

A *common element* in these local organizational patterns is that traces of the two-tiered overall structure of the movement can be found everywhere. The way the two tiers relate to each other, however, differs from locality to locality, as does the configuration of currents represented and their relative strength. Another common characteristic is the high degree of instability exhibited by the groups at the local level. Both these elements reflect the generally low level of institutionalization of this movement, as does the fact that in all the places studied only a small number of the activists subsequently engaged in the mobilization for the people's petition regularly contributed more than a few hours a week to peace movement activities in the months preceding this campaign. In all the 6 localities together, only 17 activists had devoted 1 day per week or more to the movement earlier that year.

The configurations of local cores in the six places selected do not reveal systematic differences between localities with strong countercultural networks and localities with weak ones. But it is possible to find differences in *the way they relate to the local countercultural networks*—differences that are very significant when it comes to the recruiting of activists. Local cores of the peace movement generally form focal points in these networks, but in localities where the counterculture is weak, we can expect them to be *the only focal points* or the most important ones. Here they become the rallying points for people who share the preferences of the entire countercultural design. The local networks tend to be centered around the local peace groups and to be relatively isolated from other local networks. Conversely, strong integration into countercultural networks in such places tends to imply active membership in the local peace group. In localities where the counterculture is strong, on the other hand, it is very likely that the local cores form *one focal point among many*. Local projects (newspapers, alternative shops, etc.), local cores of other NSMs, and local branches of the small activist parties of the left tend to coexist with local cores of the peace movement. The latter not only have to compete for resources with the other cores but, given the great overlap between these different organizational structures, which in turn is due to the general makeup of the countercultural networks, the other structures also provide additional recruitment channels. Using Granovetter's (1973) distinction between *strong* and *weak ties,* we can expect that in localities with weak countercultural networks the recruitment process has to rely on "strong" ties linking potential constituents directly to activists in the local cores. In localities where the countercultural networks are strong, on the other hand, recruitment can also take place via "weak" ties bridging different parts of these more elaborate network structures. The "strength of weak ties" in this case consists in their connecting a large number of potential constituents to a mobilizing local core group. Where such a local core group does not exist—in the inner-city district of Utrecht, for example—other focal groups may even fill the gap, serving as functionally equivalent recruitment channels.

The figures presented in Table 3 generally support these expectations.[13] These figures show how the activists who participated in the collection of signatures were recruited in the two types of localities; in both types of places the activists are also distinguished according to degree of integration into the local countercultural networks. As is immediately apparent from these figures, the local cores of the peace movement have been much more central to the

Table 3. Recruitment Patterns of Peace Movement Activists, by Type of Locality and Degree of Countercultural Integration: in Percentages[1]

Localities with strong countercultural networks

recruited via	countercultural integration				Total
	none	weak	moderate	strong	
local core	3	22	39	45	34
party	21	44	25	27	27
friends	21	17	18	15	17
self-application	46	22	25	22	27
Sum	91%	105%	107%	109%	105%
N	(33)	(18)	(71)	(85)	(207)

Localities with weak countercultural networks

recruited via	countercultural integration				Total
	none	weak	moderate	strong	
local core	68	75	75	100	74
party	11	12	5	0	10
friends	16	9	12	0	11
self-application	11	12	12	0	11
Sum	106%	108%	104%	100%	106%
N	(56)	(147)	(57)	(7)	(267)

Note:
[1] more than one answer possible

mobilization process in localities with weak countercultural networks than in areas with strong networks. In the former localities, those who participated in the collection of signatures were, typically, either part of a local core already or they had been recruited via a local core. In localities with strong countercultural networks, recruitment much more often took place through other channels. This observation is true independent of the level of activists's countercultural integration. Level of integration, however, does make some difference if we consider each type of locality separately. The more integrated into local countercultural networks an individual is, the more likely it is that he or she was recruited via the local peace movement cores. This fact holds for both types of localities. In localities with a weak counterculture, strong integration means that one is recruited via the local core *only*. This result supports the idea that the local core forms *the* focal point of the countercultural networks in such places, but, since we have looked only at peace movement activists, it does not rule out the existence of other such local cores. In localities with a strong counterculture, strong integration means only that one is *more likely* to be recruited via the local core. This result is consistent with the idea of several focal points existing in such places. Strong integration into local countercultural networks does not necessarily imply that one is also part of the local cores of the peace movement, but those who are highly active in such cores—and therefore recruited directly via those cores—are very likely to be strongly integrated into the local countercultural networks as well, because these local cores form one of the focal points of the local counter-culture.

In localities with a strong counterculture, political parties and friendship networks are important alternative recruitment channels, and the chances that an individual will initiate contact with the local group are also significant. With respect to *those recruited via parties,* it is very interesting to note an additional difference between the two types of localities. While virtually all the activists are party-members, those who are recruited via parties in localities with weak countercultural networks come predominantly (64% of them) from the Social Democratic Party (PvdA), whereas the corresponding group in localities with a strong counterculture comes predominantly (71% of this group) from the small radical parties on the left (PPR, PSP, and CPN). Here we note the importance of these small parties as alternative recruitment channels for the peace movement. But because these parties are very much part of the countercultural networks, they can fulfill this function only in localities where these networks are strong.[14]

Table 3 contains one more piece of outstanding information. Almost half the activists who did not have any ties to the local countercultural networks in places where these networks are strong themselves took the initiative to contact the local cores. The corresponding proportion in the other localities amounts to only one-ninth. This difference could be interpreted in terms of differential thresholds for joining NSMs. In localities where the counterculture is already strong, it is probably easier for potential constituents to approach an SMO than in localities where these SMOs are rather isolated. To put this result into perspective, we have to note, however, that, even among those activists who—according to the indicator used here—do not have any ties to the local counterculture, we find few people who had not already participated in activities of the peace movement before participating in the petition. Of all the activists who participated in the organization of the petition, only nine percent were involved as peace movement activists for the first time, and in this respect the differences between the two types of localities are negligible.[15]

The connectedness of elaborate countercultural networks explains why even in the inner-city district of Utrecht, where an active local core no longer existed, it was possible to get together a group of people for the collection of the cards. Here the initiative was taken by the ad hoc local committee that was established by the permanent encompassing committee on the city level to coordinate the activities concerning the petition in the city of Utrecht. This ad hoc committee had divided the city into 13 districts, one of them being the "Vogelenbuurt," the inner-city district in question. The idea was to rely on existing local cores or to set up ad hoc committees for the organization of the activities in each of these districts. Since there was no longer any group active in the "Vogelenbuurt," the city committee contacted the people who had organized the peace festival before. These people, for their part, got in touch with their own friends, and these contacts led to the formation of an ad hoc committee of six people who, in turn, contacted their friends and acquaintances in the groups and small leftist parties to which they belonged.

This *snowball system* of recruiting is found in all the places with strong countercultures. In Amsterdam, too, it was the encompassing committee at the city level which took the initiative. The city was divided into 28 districts and, here, as in the Vogelenbuurt, it turned out that the local committees in most of these districts no longer existed. Here, too, old contacts were reactivated and new ones created. On the one hand, the city committee reached back to existing lists of earlier participants, such as the lists that had been compiled at the time of the great demonstrations, when many local committees had organized a number of buses or trains to get local supporters of the movement to the site of those demonstrations in The Hague and Amsterdam. Lists of the addresses of the people who had taken those buses or trains had been made, and they could still be used to some extent at the time of the petition campaign. Quite a few of the earlier activists could be reached through these lists. At the same time, new lists of potential supporters were compiled. During the yearly peace festival organized by the committee in the Vondelpark on Liberation Day (5th of May), for example, more than a hundred people from Amsterdam signed up to participate in organizing the petition. Moreover, people who had peace movement posters in their windows were personally called upon, and local hospitals and workers councils ("ondernemingsraden") were approached as well. The contacts established along these lines in turn mobilized their own local acquaintances. In the "Bijlmer," the activists from the local committee first placed articles in the local newspaper and contacted people within their own circles of acquaintances. In this way, 125 participants were found; that number, however, was still short of what the local committee thought it needed. In order to get a sufficient number of participants, all those who had already been successfully contacted were asked to mobilize one more person, which they did. The local cores in the localities with a weak counterculture in principle followed the same strategy, but because of the structure of their local networks they could not as easily reach people outside their immediate circles of acquaintances.

The number of activists in the entire country who were mobilized to participate in the collection of signature-cards is quite impressive. In the city of Amsterdam their number reached several thousands, in a city such as Utrecht about one thousand people were involved, and in smaller towns such as Waalwijk no less than a hundred people participated in this activity. I will now take a closer look at how successful they were in their mobilization attempt and what their relative success or failure depended upon at the local level.

V.   THE SECOND STEP IN LOCAL MOBILIZATION: MOBILIZING THE LOCAL POTENTIAL CONSTITUENTS

A.   Local Campaign Setups

As already indicated, according to the general framework of the campaign the local activists were supposed to go from door to door to collect the cards with signatures. With one exception this general plan was followed in the six localities selected. Typically, the districts or towns were subdivided into smaller units that were then assigned to teams of two or more people. In some places, first a car with a loudspeaker went into a neighborhood to announce the action, and then a large group of collectors followed. In other places, teams of two persons worked their way along the assigned streets. The number of attempts to visit a specific address differed from place to place. In Overvecht, for example, only one attempt was made, because there were not enough activists to make return visits to all those not reached initially. In the Vogelenbuurt, on the other hand, up to three attempts were supported by committees of local notables who declared their approval of the petition by placing advertisements in the local newspapers. Activists wrote articles for local newspapers, they opened stands on the local market and organized "circles of silence" to call attention to the petition. Finally, in the Bijlmer, for example, a number of voting boxes were set up in crucial public locations (such as senior citizens' homes, hospitals, libraries, neighborhood centers, or churches), where the cards could be returned by those not contacted at home.

The only one among our six localities where the chosen strategy deviated from this general plan was *Joure,* the predominantly Protestant town in the north. Here the local core did not want to collect the cards by making personal visits from door to door. The reason was that the group had gotten the impression from earlier experience with similar campaigns that people reacted much more to social pressure than to the issue in question if confronted at their front door with activists whom they knew. In order to avoid any kind of social pressure, the local core decided not to go from door to door to collect the cards. At the beginning of the campaign, however, the activists did distribute to all the local households leaflets underscoring the importance of the petition. Later, they went once more from door to door to personally hand out a reminder to all the households. This was done once. The purpose of this undertaking was not to collect signatures, but to persuade people of the significance of the action against the deployment of cruise missiles. Incidentally, a considerable number of cards was nevertheless collected in the course of this reminder campaign.

Joure is a special case in one other respect: it was the only locality in our selection where some measure of *counter-mobilization* took place. The ICTO— a counterpeace movement organized by believers of different churches who do not accept the position taken by the IKV with respect to cruise missiles and who strongly emphasize the need for *bilateral* disarmament—tried to mobilize against the petition by placing advertisements in the local newspaper with an appeal not to sign the petition and by distributing leaflets with this same message to all the local households. Because Joure represents a special case, I shall treat it separately in most of the following presentation of the results concerning the outcome of the mobilization campaign. I will compare the outcome of the campaign in localities that have a strong countercultural network with, on the one hand, the outcome in Joure and, on the other hand, the outcome in the remaining two localities (those with weak countercultural networks). In some instances, it is also possible to compare these figures with those taken from a national sample interviewed at the same time as our local samples.

B. Success of the Campaign

Let us look first at the *degree* to which the mobilization attempts of the peace movement *reached* the local population. In doing so, we can distinguish: those who received a card and were visited by an activist member of the peace movement, those who received a card but were not visited by an activist, and those who did not even receive a card.[16] As is shown in Table 4, roughly one-tenth of the population maintained they did not receive a card at all. The post office had some problems in distributing the cards, and some households may actually have never received a card. In some cases, the cards may not have been recognized and so were thrown away, perhaps because they were put into the mailbox together with advertising material, or perhaps for some other reason. In some cases, however, people probably simply denied having received a card, although they had gotten one. An indication that this may, indeed, be the case is the fact that there are somewhat more opponents of the peace movement among those who said they did not receive a card than among those in the other two categories (30% vs. 21%). Because this "silent" opposition to the campaign is inherently difficult to measure, the answers of the respondents will be taken at face value in the subsequent analysis.

In general, roughly one-third of the population was visited by an activist of the movement. Only in Joure is the latter figure somewhat lower, because of the specific arrangements described above. The other localities chosen seem to be fairly representative of the country as a whole in this respect. The largest

Table 4.   Degree to which Local Population was Reached by Mobilization
in Different Localities (Percentages)

Degree reached	strong counter-c	weak counter-c	Joure	national sample
visited by activists	51	58	37	55
received cards, not visited	36	29	55	33
received no cards	13	13	9	13
Total[1]	100%	100%	101%	101%
N	(349)	(238)	(128)	(585)

Note:
[1]The columns do not always sum to 100% because of rounding errors.

percentage of people contacted by an activist (66%) was in the town in the
south. This result is not necessarily a consequence of particularly intensive
campaigning but is probably primarily due to the fact that people in rural areas
are more likely to be contacted at home than people living in urban areas.

How many *signatures were collected,* and how many people eventually
signed the petition in the different localities? These two measures of success
are not identical, because there were two different ways to return the cards:
they could either be handed over to an activist at the door or they could be
mailed directly to the national headquarters of the campaign. Table 5 presents
the relevant figures for the two measures.[17] Because of the bias in the sample,
the figures for the number of people who signed are almost certainly too high;
it can be assumed, however, that the kind of bias is the same in all the localities
and that, therefore, these figures are at least comparable among themselves.
It is difficult to assess to what extent the first column in Table 5 reflects
differences in local campaigning efforts. Joure indeed stands out as the place
where the fewest signatures were collected, but as we have seen, this outcome
was not intended at all. In the case of the peripheral district in Utrecht, one
could assume that a greater number of signatures could have been collected
if more than one attempt had been made to meet people personally. The case
of the inner city of Amsterdam, on the other hand, probably testifies more
to the difficulty of meeting people at the door in a neighborhood with a large
number of singles' households than to a lack of campaigning effort.

If we compare the two columns of Table 5, the question arises whether the
local campaigning efforts did in fact contribute very much to the final outcome
of the petition. Irrespective of the number of signatures collected by the local
groups, the proportion of people who said they signed the petition is
considerably higher in all the localities with a strong counterculture than in
the localities with a weak one. Moreover, this proportion is of about equal

Table 5.   Success of the Campaign in the Six Localities, in Percentages
of the Local Population 18 or Older

Locality	Percentage collected	Percentage who signed
inner-city Amsterdam	23	66
periphery Amsterdam	32	65
inner-city Utrecht[1]	29	60
periphery Utrecht[1]	22	53
South (Waalwijk)	33	48
North (Joure)[1]	10	36

Note:
[1]In these locations, percentages had to be taken of the population 15 or older.

size in all three instances of strong countercultural networks, and the same
distribution applies to two of the three localities with weak networks. Only
the special case, Joure, deviates markedly, having a much lower proportion
of signatures than the other two places with weak countercultural ties.

The impression of *a rather limited impact of the local campaign* is
strengthened if we now look at the proportion of those who signed, controlling
for type of locality as well as for degree to which people were reached. Table
6 gives the relevant figures, including the corresponding figures for the national
sample.[18] Looking at these figures, we see immediately that the most crucial
factor for determining the campaign's success was whether or not a respondent
had received a card. In all localities, those who did not receive a card were
very unlikely to have signed the petition. Among those who received a card,
a visit by a movement activist only marginally increased the overall likelihood
that one would sign the petition. This fact applies to localities with a strong
counterculture (increase from 67% to 72%) as well as to localities with a weak
one (increase form 51% to 59%). In Joure, the visits designed to persuade people
to sign seem to have had no impact at all.

Table 6.   Percentage of Supporters of Petition, by Degree Reached and
Type of Locality of Residence

Degree reached	strong counter-c	weak counter-c	Joure	all 6 places	National sample
visited	72	59	38	63	56
received card	67	51	41	56	44
no card	16	13	0	13	11
Total	64	50	37	54	45

The relatively limited impact of the local campaigns in the six localities must be interpreted first in terms of the *low threshold* involved in participating in the petition. The only steps an isolated conscience adherent who was against the deployment of cruise missiles in the Netherlands had to take was to sign the card, pay for a 70-cent stamp, and mail it. The rather limited impact of the local campaigns can be attributed, secondly, to the fact that these campaigns took place within the *framework of a highly publicized national campaign.* Almost everyone everywhere in the Netherlands read about it in the newspaper and heard about it on the radio and on television. Finally, we must take into account that this campaign came as a more or less *final event in a long series of campaigns* against the cruise missiles. The different branches of the peace movement were all very well known all over the country because of their earlier campaigns both local and national. Thus 70% of our sample said they knew VVV, 78% said they knew SNB, 80% the IKV, and 87% indicated that they knew the KKN. Moreover, these organizations were not only well known, they also received a great deal of sympathy.

The results of Table 6 show further that, for those who received a card, the chances that they would sign the petition were considerably greater in localities with strong countercultural networks than in localities with weak ones. For those not visited, the respective figures are 67% and 51%. This differential success of the campaign in the two types of localities can hardly be attributed to differences in campaigning. It is much more likely to be related to the implications of the differential strength of the local countercultures. Strong preexisting countercultural networks tie the movement to a particularly *large and receptive mobilization potential* and provide it with *latent mobilization channels* that are indirectly activated by a specific campaign.

C.   The Size of the Local Mobilization Potentials

To measure the size of the local mobilization potentials, two different indicators were constructed. The first indicates *attitude toward cruise missiles.* It distinguishes the proponents of deployment from three categories of opponents: (1) those who do not regard the petition as a suitable means to oppose deployment, (2) those who do regard the petition as an effective means and are moderately against deployment, and (3) those who favor the petition and are strongly opposed to deployment.[19] The second indicator measures *sympathy for the peace movement,* with categories ranging from opponents to passive supporters to potential activists and actual activists. Opponents have little or no sympathy for the movement. Passive supporters have some or a great deal of sympathy but are not prepared to participate in the movement's further activities. Potential activists, in contrast, say they are ready to participate and activists have already done so.[20] Tables 7 and 8 show that there are actually sizable differences among the different types of localities with

Table 7. Size of Mobilization Potential in Different Types of Localities: Distribution of Attitudes with Respect to Deployment (Percentages)

attitude with respect to deployment	strong counter-c	weak counter-c	Joure	all 6 places
proponent of deployment	23	31	40	29
opponent, against petition	9	11	8	9
moderate opponent, for petition	27	32	23	28
strong opponent, for petition	42	26	29	34
Total[1]	101%	100%	100%	100%
N	(341)	(233)	(125)	(699)

Note:
[1]The columns do not always sum to 100% because of rounding errors.

Table 8. Size of Mobilization Potential in Different Types of Localities: Distribution of Sympathy with Peace Movement (Percentages)

sympathy with peace movement	strong counter-c	weak counter-c	Joure	all 6 places
opponent	17	26	33	23
passive supporter	32	45	41	38
potential activist	14	20	18	17
activist	37	8	8	22
Total[1]	100%	99%	100%	100%
N	(348)	(235)	(126)	(709)

Note:
[1]The columns do not always sum to 100% because of rounding errors.

respect to the local mobilization potential for the petition campaign. Opponents of deployment, and in particular strong opponents favoring the petition, are considerably more numerous in localities with strong countercultures. Moreover, many more people in these localities have already participated in peace movement activities before than in localities with weak counterculutres. The town of Joure in the north has again been treated separately in these two tables. There are somewhat more proponents of deployment and opponents of the peace movement in Joure, but on the whole this town does not deviate significantly from the other two localities with weak countercultures.

It must now be shown that these attitudes and sympathies supportive of the peace movement are in part *a consequence of one's integration into the local counterculture*. Following the general line of reasoning set out in the introduction, which argues that interaction leads to change of values and new sympathies, we can expect integration into local countercultural networks to imply stronger attitudes against deployment and greater sympathy for the movement. More specifically, independent of one's social structural background and one's general value-position, it can be expected that:

- the stronger the local counterculture in general, the stronger one's integration into the local counterculture;
- the more integrated one is into the local counterculture in general, the stronger one's integration into an environment supportive of the peace movement;
- the more integrated one is into the local counterculture in general and into an environment supportive of the peace movement in particular, the stronger one's opposition to deployment;
- the more integrated one is into the local counterculture and into a supportive environment and the more one is opposed to deployment, the stronger one's sympathy with the peace movement.

To test these hypotheses, a series of regressions were conducted, one for each hypothesis. Age, education, and church attendance were the indicators for general social structural background; position on the left-right spectrum and postmaterialism were the indicators for general value-position. *Age* and *level of education* play an important role in the context of unconventional political activities (see Barnes, Kaase et al. 1979; Kriesi and Castenmiller 1986). The younger and more educated one is, the more generally prepared one is to participate in unconventional political activities. Concerning *church attendance*, we have shown elsewhere (Kriesi and van Praag, Jr. 1987) that active members of the churches are unlikely to have great sympathy with the peace movement in Holland, despite the fact that one of the currents of the movement has close ties to the churches. With reference to general values, it is to be supposed that those who support the peace movement generally tend to have *postmaterialist* rather than materialist values. With reference to general political position, it can be assumed, again in view of our earlier results (Kriesi and van Praag, Jr. 1987), that peace movement supporters are for the most part *on the left* of the general political spectrum.

Two additional indicators characterizing the local context of the respondents were introduced into the regressions: a dummy variable for those living in *Joure* and accounting for the very special circumstances in that locality, and an indicator for the *strength of the local counterculture,* measured by the proportion of the local population having several friends in at least one NSM (see col. 4 in Table 1). The dependent variables were already introduced.[21] Table A-1 in the Appendix gives an overview of the operational definitions of all

Table 9. Determinants of Integration into Countercultural Networks and Mobilization Potential for Petition: Standardized Regression Coefficients[1]

independent variable	integration into local counter-c.	integration into supp. environm.	against deploy- ment	sympathy with peace-m.
age			-.11**	
education	.16***		-.13***	
church attendance	.09*			
left-right	-.19***	-.34***	-.32***	-.13***
postmaterialism	.23***	.16***	.14***	.20***
Joure				
strength of local c.c.	.24***			
int. into local c.c.	—	.27***		.11***
int. into supp. environm.	—	—	.34***	.20***
against deployment	—	—	—	.31***
R²adj.	.26	.38	.39	.59

Note:
[1]levels of significance .05 (*), .01 (**), .001 (***)

the variables involved, and Table A-2 presents the correlation matrix the analysis is based upon. The results of the regression analyses are shown in Table 9.

All four hypotheses specified above are supported by these results, with one minor exception. Integration into the local counterculture does not have a direct effect on one's attitude with respect to deployment; it strengthens the opposition to deployment only indirectly, through integration into an environment supportive of the peace movement. The dummy for Joure does not have any effect at all, that is the mobilization potential in Joure does not seem to be determined by any specific local conditions other than those specified by the independent variables of the analyses. In addition, the results indicate that one's general value-position is highly significant for the integration into countercultural networks as well as for one's potential for mobilization by the peace movement. The direction of this impact is as expected. Social structural background variables, on the other hand, are shown to have rather limited direct effects on the dependent variables, effects that in two instances— church attendance on integration into local counterculture and education on opposition to deployment—are somewhat unexpected. I will not go any further into the details of these results, however, because that would lead us away from the major theme.

D.   Latent Mobilization Channels

Where countercultural networks are elaborate, chances are relatively high for *informal contacts with people* attempting to mobilize others for a campaign

Table 10.   Percentage of People Approached Personally
in Different Ways, by Locality

way approached	strong counter-c	weak counter-c	Joure
on the street	15	8	8
in another way	12	8	8
in the family etc.	11	6	5
at work	4	2	0
in at least one way[1]	36	21	16
N	(351)	(239)	(128)

Note:
[1]Because one could have been approached in more than one way, these figures are not column totals.

Table 11.   Percentage of Local Population that Noticed local
Peace Groups in the Six Localities

| Local core | strong counterculture | | | weak counterculture | | | |
	inner c. Amst.	periph. Amst.	inner c. Utrecht	periph. Utrecht	Joure North	Waalw. South
KKN, local comm.	58	39	33	24	18	18
IKV	37	31	23	16	38	5
SNB	40	26	25	17	7	12
VVV	21	16	13	9	2	5

such as the people's petition. Table 10 shows that this has, indeed, been the case. The number of people who were personally approached on the street, in their immediate surroundings, at work or in some other way, and asked to sign the petition was greater in localities with a strong counterculture than in localities with a weak counterculture.[22] In such localities, moreover, chances are relatively high that one will come into *contact with general activities of the peace movement.* Because in these contexts the movement is integrated into everyday activities, it is possible to come into contact with it even if the local groups are not well organized and even if at first glance they seem to be rather inactive. Table 11 supports this point.[23] With one exception—the IKV in Joure in the north of the country—the proportion of the local population that has taken notice of local activities of the different peace groups is greater in places with a strong countercultural network and, for all the important groups considered, it is greatest in the inner-city district of Amsterdam, where, as we have seen, the counterculture is strongest.[24] This is not to say that the relative strength of the different local groups which we noted in the discussion of Table 2 is irrelevant; again, Table 11 makes that point clear, too. Most notable are the prominence of the strong IKV-core in Joure and the general weakness of the different groups in Waalwijk in the Catholic south. Some minor differences, such as the relative importance of SNB here and in the peripheral district of Utrecht, come out as well. What is also striking is the fact that everywhere, again except in Joure, the local branch of the KKN is the group most often noticed. This may be a spill-over effect of the activities surrounding the petition, but it incidentally shows to what extent the encompassing structure has encroached on the structure of the four currents within the movement.

E.   The Determinants of Signing the Petition

It remains to be shown whether the specific campaign activities—distributing cards and visiting people at the front door—were indeed of minor or no importance if we control for degree of elaboration of local countercultural networks, size of local mobilization potentials, and indirect mobilization attempts based on preexisting ties. In order to do so, a logit regression was performed using the signing of the petition as dependent variable. Among the independent variables introduced into the regression were all those discussed so far plus a variable indicating one's attitude with respect to the effectiveness of the petition as a means of influencing the government. Several authors have shown that the expected success of a mobilization process is an important determinant of one's participation in it (see, for example, Klandermans 1984). People who do not regard the petition as an effective means or who consider the petition to be a danger to democracy will have an additional reason for not signing it. Dummies were used to indicate those who did not receive a card and those who were visited. For the indirect mobilization attempts, the number of ways one could be approached was added and a dummy variable was introduced to indicate whether the respondent took any notice of local movement activities. A definition of all the variables used can be found in Table A-1 in the Appendix. Results are presented in Table 12.

The most important result is the fact that being visited by an activist did not have any direct impact whatsoever on one's support of the petition, while not receiving a card was one of the decisive reasons for not signing it. Second, the results show that one's support of the peace movement, and especially one's opposition to deployment, were important determinants of signing. Aspects of integration into countercultural networks, on the other hand, were of limited or no direct relevance to support for the petition. From the previous analysis, however, we know that integration into these networks has a considerable effect on one's attitudes and sympathies with regard to the movement and therefore that it, too, indirectly affected the signing of the petition. Third, we note some effects of indirect mobilization attempts, which, we have seen, are stronger in

Table 12. Logit Regression on Effect of Independent Variables
on Signing the Petition (n = 566)

Independent Variable	Dependent Variable: Signing the Petition	
	b	SE(b)[1]
received card	-1.979***	.322
was visited	-.060	.175
was approached otherwise	.473**	.193
took notice of local movement	.068	.175
regards petition as effective	.361*	.206
age	.004	.006
education	-.034	.053
church attendance	-.173**	.063
left-right	.018	.044
postmaterialism	.067*	.029
Joure	-.742***	.222
Strength of local c.c.	-.931	.690
int. into local c.c.	.225	.278
int. into supportive environm.	.159*	.072
against deployment	.341***	.044
support of peace-movement	.324**	.116

Note:
[1]signed petition = 1, otherwise = 0
significance levels: .05 (*), .01 (**), .001 (***)

localities with elaborate countercultural networks than in localities with weak networks. Whether one has taken note of the local movement before, on the other hand, is of no significance. Fourth, it is clear that residents of Joure have a significantly smaller chance of having signed the petition than people from other localities. This condition holds independent of their lower mobilization potential, independent of the weak ties they generally have to countercultural networks, and independent of whether they were visited by movement representatives. Which specific aspects of this locality are responsible for this outcome is difficult to determine: the strong presence of a countermovement indicates a political climate in this community that may have helped to raise the threshold for signing among those inclined to do so.

Fifth, one's evaluation of the petition does make a small, but significant difference in the expected direction. Sixth, one's general value-position is shown to have no (position on left-right spectrum) or only a minor (postmaterialism) direct impact on one's chance of signing. But this is not to say that one's value-position is unimportant in the present context, for, as we have seen, it has a highly significant influence on one's relevant attitudes and sympathies. Finally, with respect to social structural background indicators, a quite surprising result emerges. While age and education do not have any direct effect on the support of the petition independent of all the other variables involved, church attendance does. The more integrated into a church one is, the less likely one is to have signed the petition, regardless of one's mobilization potential, general value-position as measured here, and integration into countercultural networks. This may suggest that churches have actively mobilized opposition to the petition among their members. As far as I can tell, however, this has not been the case; churches have more or less remained neutral vis-à-vis the campaign. Why active churchgoers have been particularly resistant to the drive for the petition remains an open question.

There is no statistic for logit models that would assess the degree to which the dependent variable is explained by the independent ones. But Aldrich and Nelson (1984, p. 57) suggest an alternative measure that is quite useful for the present case: the probability of signing the petition can be predicted on the basis of the estimated coefficients, and the predicted value can then be compared to the actual one. If the predicted probability for a given person is greater than .5, we predict that he or she has signed the petition; if it is smaller than .5, we predict that this was not the case. Following this procedure, we can, in 90% of the cases, predict correctly whether an individual has signed the petition. This degree of accuracy lends a considerable amount of plausibility to the model used and to the conclusion drawn from it: that the local door-to-door campaign had no appreciable direct impact on the success of the petition at all.

Even if the campaign did not have any direct impact, it may still be that it had some indirect effect by influencing people's evaluation of the petition as a means of action or by influencing their attitudes with respect to deployment. But we find very little evidence of this effect in our data. Concerning the evaluation of the petition, 77% of those visited, but also 73% of those who received a card but were not visited, regarded the petition as at least somewhat effective at the time of the interview. The distributions over the different attitudes with respect to deployment and with respect to sympathy with the movement turn out to be virtually identical for these two groups. If there is little to suggest a change of mind as a consequence of the visits at the front door, the visits may nevertheless have led some particularly hesitant people to sign in spite of serious doubts about the movement, the petition or both. There is some indication that, to a limited extent, this was the case. Among those who were against deployment, but did not regard the petition as an appropriate means to fight it, 63% of those visited, as compared to only 53% of those who received a card but were not visited, signed. Similarly, 59% of the passive supporters who were visited, but only 52% of the passive supporters who were not visited, signed. It may be that in localities where the movement met with more of such skeptics than were found in the localities chosen for this analysis the impact of the explicit local mobilization attempts was somewhat more pronounced than is evident here.[25] If, however, we try to take account of the specific situation of the skeptics who were visited in our sample by introducing into the logit regression special interaction terms for them—in addition to all the other independent variables already in the regression—these terms, it turns out, do not contribute significantly to the explanation of who signed and who did not. For this sample, the general conclusions drawn are not modified.

VI. SUMMARY AND CONCLUSION

In this chapter I have tried to show the effects of preexisting local countercultural network structures on the mobilization of a NSM. I have tried to show first, how these network structures provide elaborate channels for ad hoc mobilizations of sizeable numbers of activists by linking, via weak ties, a large number of potential recruits to a mobilizing core group. Second, I have tried to show how these networks are tied to larger mobilization potentials that provide the movement with a large reservoir to draw upon, and how they serve as latent mobilization channels that increase the movement's drive in an indirect way. Elaborate countercultural networks seem to have a kind of auto-mobilizing capacity that makes direct mobilization attempts almost superfluous—at least for widely publicized national campaigns with a low threshold, such as the campaign for the people's petition. Given a national framework for a campaign that draws much attention from the media, the potential constituents embedded in these networks become active in large numbers, whether or not they are directly approached by movement organizations.

The other side of the coin is that direct mobilization attempts of local movement organizations can, to only a limited extent, compensate for the lack of such networks. Where people are not embedded in larger countercultural networks, they are less likely to live in an environment supportive of NSMs and are therefore less likely to develop corresponding attitudes and sympathies, at least in the short run, as in a campaign such as the one studied here. In this analysis, I have treated the presence or absence of countercultural networks as a permanent feature of a local context, an assumption which, in the longer run, does not hold and so puts the rather pessimistic conclusion concerning the impact of local mobilization attempts in a somewhat different perspective. As observed above, local cores of NSMs form focal points in the local countercultural networks. Where these networks do not exist, the establishment of a local group of a moderate current of a rather broadly accepted movement, such as the peace movement, may serve as the starting point for the development of such a local network. Where the networks are weak, local cores of this kind of movement may contribute to their elaboration and stabilization.

The success of a campaign such as that for the people's petition must be measured not only against its short-run impact (as I have done here). The impact of the campaign on the local cores themselves may be even more important. It may have served to strengthen them by giving them a sense of purpose and tying them more closely into the national framework of the movement. By strengthening them, it may have contributed to the elaboration of the local countercultural networks, thereby contributing to future campaigns of its own or of other NSMs. On the other hand, the campaign may have weakened the local cores, since the entire effort may have seemed futile—I refer not only to the results presented here but also to the fact that the Dutch government chose to completely ignore the petition and decided for deployment on November 1, 1985.

These considerations remain tied to an instrumental view of collective action. As is stressed by students of NSMs, these movements seek to do more than influence government policy—indeed, such an effect may not be their most important goal at all. Most important, they strive to construct new collective identities (Cohen 1985). Viewed from the point of view of identity-formation, the campaign for the petition may have had its greatest impact by contributing to the formation of new identities of those most intensely involved in it, especially in the localities where the countercultural networks are still weak and where reinforcement through participation in national events is most needed.

APPENDIX

Table A-1.   Description of the Variables Used in the Causal Model

Variable	Description
1. signed petition	(0) did not sign (1) signed
2. sympathy for peace movement	as described in the text: (1) opponent, (2) passive supporter, (3) potential activist, (4) activist
3. attitude concerning deployment	a combination direction (for or against) and intensity (very important, important, less important, unimportant) of attitude; ranging from (-4) very important/for deployment to (+4) very important/against deployment
4. Integration in environment supportive of peace movement	(1) approving environment and friends in peace movement, (2) approving environment and one friend in movement, (3) approving environment and no friend in movement, (4) neutral environment, (5) disapproving environment
5. integration in local counterculture	constructed as described in section 3 of the text

Table A-1 (continued)

6.	Joure	(1) lives in Joure (0) others
7.	strength of local counterculture	variable characterizing the locality where one lives: percentage of local population that has several friendship ties to at least one NSM (see Table 1 above)
8.	evaluation of petition	(0) petition is not regarded as an effective means and/or is regarded as dangerous to democracy (1) petition not regarded as dangerous to democracy and as at least somewhat effective
9.	visited	(0) not visited (1) visited
10.	no cards received	(0) card received (1) no card received
11.	approached by others	number of ways one was approached (on the street, in the family, at work, in another way) see Table 10
12.	taken notice of local movement	"Have you ever noticed activities of peace groups in your place of residence?" (1) no, (2) yes
13.	age	number of years
14.	education	highest level attained, ranging from (1) lower education (LO) to (7) university
15.	church attendance	frequency of church attendance, ranging from (1) never to (5) once a week or more
16.	materialism/post-mat.	scale constructed on the basis of 6 of the items used by Inglehart, 3 post-materialist and 3 materialist ones with values ranging from 1 to 7 per item. Values for post-materialist items were added, values for materialist ones subtracted to form the scale
17.	left-right	self-evaluation on a scale ranging from 1 (left) to 10 (right)

Table A-2.	Correlation Matrix for the Variables of the Causal Model

Variables	1	2	3	4	5	6	7	8	9	10	11	12	13	14	15	16	17
1. signed petition	—																
2. sympathy for peace mov.	.59	—															
3. against deployment	.69	.61	—														
4. supportive environment	.52	.63	.50	—													
5. int. in counterculture	.27	.41	.24	.43	—												
6. Joure	-.16	-.16	-.12	-.13	-.11	—											
7. strength local c.-c.	.18	.28	.14	.24	.34	-.38	—										
8. evaluation of petition	.38	.39	.43	.38	.14	-.06	.11	—									
9. Visited	.17	.04	.06	.10	.06	-.13	.00	.04	—								
10. no card received	-.30	-.08	-.05	-.13	-.03	-.05	.01	.01	-.38	—							
11. approached by others	.18	.19	.09	.20	.16	-.12	.18	.09	.10	-.10	—						
12. taken notice of local mov.	.18	.28	.12	.25	.29	.04	.19	.08	.09	-.12	.16	—					
13. age	-.09	-.20	-.15	-.17	-.02	-.04	-.03	-.08	-.02	.06	-.06	-.18	—				
14. education	.11	.25	.07	.27	.24	-.12	.19	.04	.05	-.11	.07	.29	-.44	—			
15. church attendance	-.23	-.26	-.22	-.19	-.07	.22	-.33	-.15	-.03	-.04	-.07	-.06	.13	-.07	—		
16. postmaterialism	.38	.48	.36	.37	.31	-.10	.19	.27	.07	-.13	.10	.25	-.18	.31	-.16	—	
17. left-right	-.47	-.56	-.54	-.30	-.32	.14	-.31	-.35	-.02	.05	-.09	-.19	.07	-.10	.37	-.41	—

Abbreviations used

CPN   Dutch Communist Party
D'66   Dutch Progressive Liberal Party
FNV   National Federation of Dutch Unions (social-democratic)
ICTO   Dutch counter-peace movement
IKV   Dutch Inter-Church Peace Council
KKN   Dutch Committee against Cruise Missiles
NSM   New social movement
PPR   Dutch Radical Party
PSP   Dutch Pacifist Party
SMO   Social Movement Organization
SNB   Stop-de-Neutronenbom-Bomb (leftist tendency in Dutch peace movement)
VVV   Women for Peace (Vrouwen voor Vrede)

ACKNOWLEDGMENTS

I would like to thank my colleague Philip van Praag, Jr., and all the participants in the student research group on the Dutch peace movement: Chris van de Borgh, Ellen Couvret, Leonieke Daalder, Nanda Hagemeijer, Ronald de Klein, Ruud Koopmans, Richard Matenko, Ben Mertens, Klaske van der Meulen, Michael The, and Roel Wessels. They have not only helped with the collection of the data, they have also written special reports about the peace movement in the six localities selected, reports that have been valuable sources for this paper. In addition, their perceptive comments on an earlier version of this paper have helped to improve the arguments presented here.

NOTES

1. Huber (1983) uses the term "intermediary culture" to characterize the field of interpenetration. This intermediary culture is made up of people participating in both of these cultures.

2. The line between political and nonpolitical groups becomes blurred and, following Nelles (1984, p. 429), one could talk about an emergent "informal political sector."

3. Fisher speaks not of "counter" but of "subcultures." Quite clearly, subculture cannot be subsumed under counterculture, but the reverse might be true. Whether one wants to do this, Yinger (1982, p. 41) argues, rests largely on whether it seems wiser to emphasize the similarities or the differences between the two terms: "Both refer to normative systems that are less comprehensive than and to some degree separate from the total culture. One is defined primarily by its reversal of the dominant norms, however, whereas this characteristic is incidental or lacking in the other." While Yinger prefers to keep the two terms analytically separate, I would rather emphasize their similarities. For a recent empirical study supporting Fisher's theses, see Wilson (1986).

4. The conflict that erupted within the IKV after the campaign for the people's petition can be viewed in terms of the strain introduced into the different currents by the emergence of the second tier (see NRC, 22-2-96; 24-2-86; 24-3-86).

5. Whether the cards should be spread by official mail or by a private distributor was a matter of considerable discussion within the KKN, because financial considerations (in favor of a private

distributor) clashed with matters of principle (in favor of a public solution). It was finally decided to stick to principles and use the services of the Dutch post office.

6. Children, too, could sign and they made use of this opportunity to a considerable extent, although the percentage of children who signed is smaller than the percentage of adults belonging to the electorate. On the basis of survey information, one can estimate that between one-seventh and one-sixth of the signers were younger than 18 years old.

7. It is remarkable, however, that none of the groups let us have their address material. All the groups preferred that we come to their quarters and do the administrative task of addressing and packing the material under their surveillance. It was always the groups themselves who did the mailing. The reminders were also sent out by the groups themselves.

8. The sample was drawn from the phonebook. Since it was concentrated in six localities, we distributed the questionnaires ourselves and we also collected them ourselves as far as possible, following the strategy of the peace movement's petition-campaign. We received the impression that our collection of the questionnaires did much to raise the response.

9. The question for this indicator was worded as follows: "How did people who are important to you, such as friends or members of the family, in general react to the people's petition?" The available categories were "approvingly," "neutrally," and "disapprovingly."

10. The question was: "Do you have friends who have already participated or still participate in the activities of these groups?" The "groups" mentioned were: ecology movement, women's movement, antinuclear movement, and squatters' movement. For the peace movement, an analogous but separate question was posed: "Do you have friends who have participated in peace movement activities before the people's petition took place?"

11. The number of contacts one has with people living in the same community was measured by a straightforward question: "How many contacts do you have with people from your neighborhood ('buurt')?" The response categories were: "very many," "many," "few," and "none." The proportion of the local population integrated into countercultural networks corresponds to the local aggregate of people who had several friends among the activists of at least one NSM, as measured by the second indicator. To arrive at the third indicator, the response to the "contact" question was multiplied with the percentage of the local population integrated into countercultural networks.

12. The peripheral district of Utrecht (Overvecht) is an exception to this general pattern, because there the activists also have more contact with people in the community than does the population at large, although the locality is considered to be one with a weak counterculture. The differences are most striking for the periphery of Amsterdam, where 62% of the activists but only 25% of the local population have many or very many contacts with the people in the neighborhood, and for Waalwijk in the south, where only 20% of the activists but 43% of the population at large say they have many/very many such contacts.

13. These figures are based on the following question we put to all the activists: "How did you get involved in the people's petition?" The categories given were: "was already involved in a peace group"; "have myself applied"; "was approached by a union;" "approached by party;" "approached by peace group;" "approached by acquaintances, friends;" and "approached in another way." More than one answer was possible, which is why the columns in Table 4 do not sum to 100%. The number of people who had been recruited via unions or in another way was negligible and these categories have therefore been omitted from Table 3.

14. This is not to say that there are no members of these parties among the activists from localities with weak countercultural networks. It is noteworthy, however, that the proportion of these party members is much smaller in places with weak networks (11%) than in places where these networks are strong (32%).

15. The peripheral district in Amsterdam and the town in the Catholic south deviate from the general pattern in this respect: 12% of the activists in the former and 19% in the latter were mobilized for the first time, as compared to an average of 5% in all the other places.

16. Those who did not receive a card originally but were visited by someone in the movement we count among those who were visited, because the activists who collected the cards were also provided with additional copies to hand over to those who had not received a card or did not have one anymore.

17. The first measure was calculated by dividing the number of signatures collected by the local peace movement by the number of those in the local population who were 18 or older. In three cases (Joure and the two districts from Utrecht) the available statistics were categorized somewhat differently; thus the figures in Table 5 to some extent underestimate this type of success for these three localities. The second measure was calculated from the response to our survey question of whether or not one had signed the petition.

18. Incidentally, by comparing the total proportion of those who signed in all six places with the total of the national sample one notes that our sample is not representative in this respect, partly because of the bias noted above and partly because of the type of selection of the six localities. This lack of representativity does not affect the general argument of the paper, however. As it turns out, the national sample itself is not representative on this point, for it also tends to overestimate the proportion of people who signed. Although the national survey of people 18 years and older was conducted by interviewers in personal interviews, the national sample is to some extent subject to the same bias we found in our local samples.

19. This categorization is based on two direct attitudinal questions concerning deployment—the first asking whether one was an opponent or a proponent of deployment, the second asking for the importance one attached to the issue—and on two questions concerning the petition as instrument—one asking for an evaluation of its effectiveness, the other, whether one regarded the petition as dangerous for democracy. Those who said the petition was an ineffective instrument or a danger to democracy were coded as being "against the petition."

20. This categorization is based on two questions, one asking how much sympathy one feels for the movement and the other asking about one's readiness to participate in further activities of the movement.

21. Two of the variables previously introduced were modified for the regression analyses in order to make them more "continuous." With respect to the indicator for "integration into an environment supportive of the peace movement," those who said that their environment was approving of the petition were further differentiated according to whether or not they had friends among the activists in the peace movement. The indicator for the attitude with respect to deployment now indicates a combination of direction and intensity of attitude.

22. The question was: "Have you personally been approached for a signature for the petition?" Several answers were possible, using the following categories: "by member of family, friend or acquaintance," "on the street," "at my work," "in another way," or "no, not at all."

23. This table is based on an open question that asked the respondents to name all the groups that they had already noticed to be active in their own community. Up to four groups could be named.

24. In this district, the peace movement, for example, is literally very visibly present because of a huge mural that cannot be overlooked by those who pass by.

25. This circumstance may, incidentally, explain why the corresponding figures for the national sample in Table 6 show a somewhat greater impact of the visits than do the figures for our six localities.

REFERENCES

Alber, Jens. 1985. "Modernisierung, neue Spannungslinien und die politischen Chancen der Grünen." *Politische Vierteljahresschrift* 26:211-26.

Aldrich, John H. and Forrest D. Nelson. 1984. *Linear Probability, Logit, and Probit Models.* London: Sage.

Barnes, Samuel H., Max Kaase, and Klause R. Allerbeck. 1979. *Political Action: Mass Participation in Five Western Democracies.* London: Sage.

Brand, Karl-Werner (ed.). 1985. *Neue soziale Bewegungen in Westeuropa und den USA. Ein internationaler Vergleich.* Frankfurt: Campus.

Bürklin, Wilhelm. 1984. *Grüne Politik.* Opladen: Westdeutscher Verlag.

Cohen, Jean L. 1985. "Strategy or identity: New theoretical paradigms and contemporary social movements." *Social Research* 52:663-716.

Cotgrove, Stephen and Andrew Duff. 1980. "Environmentalism, middle class radicalism and politics." *Sociological Review* 28:333-51.

Cotgrove, Stephen and Andrew Duff. 1981. "Environmentalism, values and social change." *British Journal of Sociology* 32:00-00.

Craven, Paul and Barry Wellmann. 1974. "The network city." Pages 57-88 in M. Pelly Effrat (ed.), *The Community: Approaches and Applications.* New York: Free Press.

Downs, Anthony. 1972. "Up and down with ecology—The issue attention cycle." *Public Interest* 28 (Summer):38-50.

Everts, Philip P. and G.Walraven. 1984. *Vredesbeweging.* Utrecht: Het Spectrum.

Fietkau, Hans-Joachim et al. 1982. *Umwelt im Spiegel der öffentlichen Meinung.* Frankfurt: Campus.

Fisher, Claude S. 1982. *To Dwell among Friends: Personal Networks in Town and City.* Chicago: University of Chicago Press.

Granovetter, Mark S. 1973. "The strength of weak ties." *American Journal of Sociology* 78:1360-80.

Gundelach, Peter. 1984. "Social transformation and new forms of voluntary associations." *Social Science Information* 23:1049-81.

Homans, George C. 1972. *Elementarformen sozialen Verhaltens.* 2d edition. Opladen: Westdeutscher Verlag.

Huber, Joseph. 1983. "Help yourself—the German way." Pages 48-61 in A. Sicinski and M. Wemegah (eds.), *Alternative Ways of Life in Contemporary Europe.* Tokyo: The United Nations.

IKV. 1984. *Wat wil het IKV nu eigenlijk? Achenveertig vragen aan de vredesbeweging.* Amersfoort: De Horstink.

Inglehart, Ronald. 1981. "Post-materialism in an environment of insecurity." *American Political Science Review* 75:880-900.

Inglehart, Ronald. 1983. "Traditionelle politische Trennungslinien und die Entwicklung der neuen Politik in westlichen Gesellschaften." *Politische Vierteljahresschrift* 24:139-65.

Klandermans, Bert. 1984. "Mobilization and participation: Social-psychological expansions of resource mobilization theory." *American Sociological Review* 49:583-600.

Kriesi, Hanspeter. 1982. *AKW-Gegner in der Schweiz.* Diessenhofen: Rüegger.

Kriesi, Hanspeter. 1984. *Die Zürcher Bewegung. Bilder, Interaktionen, Zusammenhänge.* Frankfurt: Campus.

Kriesi, Hanspeter and Peter Castenmiller. 1987. "De ontwikkeling van politiek protest in Nederland sinds de jaren zeventig." *Acta Politica* 22:61-84.

Kriesi, Hanspeter and Philip van Praag, Jr. 1987. "Old and new politics: The Dutch peace movement and the traditional political organizations." *European Journal of Political Science* 15:319-46.

Loo, Hans van der, Erik Snel, and Bart van Steenbergen. 1984. *Een wenkend perspectief? Nieuwe sociale bewegingen en culturele veranderingen.* Amersfoort: De Horsink.

McAdam, Doug. 1986. "Recruitment to high-risk activism: The case of freedom summer." *American Journal of Sociology* 92:64-90.

McCarthy, John D. and Mayer N. Zald. 1977. "Resource mobilization and social movements: A partial theory." *American Journal of Sociology* 82:1212-41.

Maessen, Pieter J.J. 1979. "Wie stopt de neutronenbom?"—de geschiedenis van een aktie." *Transaktie* 4:423-57.

Melucci, Alberto. 1984. "An end to social movements?" *Social Science Information* 23:819-35.

Melucci, Alberto. 1985. "The symbolic challenge of contemporary movements." *Social Research* 2:789-816.

Müller-Rommel, Ferdinand. 1982. "'Parteien neuen Typs' in Westeuropa: Eine vergleichende Analyse." *Zeitschrift für Parlamentsfragen* 13:369-90.

Müller-Rommel, Ferdinand. 1985. "New social movements and smaller parties: A comparative perspective." *West European Politics* 8:41-54.

Nelles, Wilfried. 1984. "Kollektive Identität und politisches Handeln in Neuen sozialen Bewegungen." *Politische Vierteljahresschrift* 25:425-40.

Oberschall, Anthony. 1973. *Social Conflict and Social Movements*. Englewood Cliffs, N.J.: Prentice-Hall.

Parkin, Frank. 1968. *Middle Class Radicalism: The Social Bases of the British Campaign for Nuclear Disarmament*. Manchester: Manchester University Press.

Reuband, Karl-Heinz. 1985. "Politisches Selbstverständnis und Wertorientierungen von Anhängern und Gegnern der Friedensbewegung." *Zeitschrift für Parlamentsfragen* 16:25-45.

Rucht, Dieter. 1982. "Neue soziale Bewegungen oder: Die Grenzen bürokra-tischer Modernisierung." *Politische Vierteljahresschrift,* Sonderheft 13:272-92.

Snow, David A., E. Burke Rochford, Jr., Steven K. Worden, and Robert D. Benford. 1986. "Frame alignment processes, micromobilization, and movement participation." *American Sociological Review* 51:464-81.

Tarrow, Sidney. 1983. *Struggling to Reform: Social Movements and Policy Change during Cycles of Protest*. Western Societies Paper No. 15. Ithaca, N.Y.: Cornell University.

Tilly, Charles. 1978. *From Mobilization to Revolution*. Reading, Mass.: Addison-Wesley.

Wilson, Thomas C. 1986. "Community population size and social heterogeneity: An empirical test." *American Journal of Sociology* 91:1154-69.

Yinger, J. Milton. 1982. *Countercultures: The Promise and the Peril of a World Turned Upside Down*. New York: Free Press.

COMMUNITY INTEGRATION AND INCENTIVES FOR POLITICAL PROTEST

Karl-Dieter Opp

I. INTRODUCTION

The relationship between integration into social groups and political participation has long been a concern of social scientists. Integration or, equivalently, social solidarity is defined here as "the extent to which people participate in organized groups and are objectively and subjectively attached to their community" (Useem 1980, p. 361). This paper focuses on the latter type of integration.

Mass society theory and resource mobilization theory, two intensively discussed theoretical perspectives in the social movement literature, entail different predictions about the relationship between integration and participation.

Kornhauser (1959), the main advocate of the *theory of mass society,* claimed that social groups are, so to speak, a "safety for the elites." Social groups protect the elite from widespread participation by the general population. The uprooted, marginal citizens are those participating in mass movements. If this

International Social Movement Research, Vol. 1, pages 83-101.
Supplement to Research in Social Movements, Conflicts and Change
Copyright © 1988 by JAI Press Inc.
All rights of reproduction in any form reserved.
ISBN: 0-89232-955-6

reasoning is correct, high integration should be associated with low participation.

Proponents of the *resource mobilization perspective* argue that integration into groups "furnishes individuals with a communication network, a set of common values and symbols around which members can be mobilized, a tradition of participation in group activity, and an authority structure" (Useem 1980, p. 357). As for community integration, it is argued that integration within a neighborhood "is an important element in a neighborhood's ability to act collectively in response to some threat" (Oliver 1984, p. 604). In general, groups provide resources that make participation easier for their members. Contrary to mass society theory, the resource mobilization perspective holds that a positive correlation between integration and participation is thus to be expected (see McAdam 1982, 1983; Morrison 1971; Oberschall 1973; Pinard 1971; Pollock III 1982; Snow et al. 1980).

The results of empirical research are inconclusive. Snow et al. (1980) showed that interpersonal ties, including extra-movement networks, play a major role in recruitment. This study and others indicate that, in contradiction of the theory of mass society, integration does promote political participation.

Other studies, however, found no relationship or even a negative relationship between integration and participation. Useem (1980), for example, reported negative or zero correlations between primary group participation and participation in or support for the Boston anti-busing movement. Orbell and Uno (1970) found that remedial action to solve neighborhood problems decreased rapidly with length of residence, a factor which is one of the indicators of community integration frequently employed in empirical research. According to Isaac et al. (1980, p. 203) "integration with friends and into the neighborhood all show moderately large, significant negative effects" on protest orientation.

In summary, then, (1) the effects of integration differ, depending on the kind of group and thus on the kind of community individuals are integrated into, and (2) the theoretical approaches mentioned above make assumptions referring to the kinds of incentives for participation being related to integration into groups. The resource mobilization perspective, for example, posits that, in general, integrated people are exposed to positive incentives for participation. If, then, differential integration does in fact have different effects on participation, the incentives for participation will be different in different groups.

In this chapter we will examine the effects of community integration on political protest using data of a survey of opponents of nuclear power in West Germany. We will attempt to explain our findings about the relationships between community integration and participation in political protest as the outcome of various incentives provided by the community individuals are integrated into.

II. EXPLAINING THE EFFECTS OF INTEGRATION

What are the incentives for participation which may be connected with integration into social groups? We want to distinguish three possible effects of integration which are more or less clearly specified in the literature on political participation: (1) A high degree of integration may provide opportunities for participation and thus may raise perceived political efficacy; (2) the group may exert social control in the sense that it provides positive or negative incentives for participation; and (3) groups may have a socializing effect in the sense that they change values and attitudes of their members.

In this section we discuss these three types of effects, and then propose a general model based on these hypotheses which links integration, incentives for protest, and protest behavior more explicitly.

A. Political Efficacy, Social Control, Preference Change, and Social Integration

Integration and Political Efficacy

One of the main propositions of solidarity theorists, in contrast to adherents of mass society theory, is that integration facilitates mobilization and thus political participation (see McAdam 1982, 1983; Morrison 1971; Oberschall 1973; Oliver 1984; Pinard 1971; Pollock III 1982; Snow et al. 1980; Useem 1980). If this claim holds true, we can expect that integration will correlate positively with perceived political efficacy: if groups do in fact provide opportunities for protest, then the member of a group disposes of a greater amount of resources than a nonmember and is thus more influential than a nonmember. If we assume that the increased influence is also perceived, we can expect a positive relationship to obtain between integration and perceived political efficacy.

Social Control and Integration

If integration affects political participation, one would expect people who are integrated into social networks to be exposed to political stimuli encouraging participation (see, for example, Finifter 1974; Oberschall 1973; Putnam 1966; Wilson and Orum 1976). Reference persons are to a great extent members of the network to which an individual belongs. Integrated persons will thus have greater exposure to normative expectations of reference persons than will less integrated persons. We can expect, moreover, that integrated persons will be confronted more often with positive sanctions and less often with negative sanctions for participation than weakly integrated persons would be.

The Socializing Effects of Social Networks

According to mass society theory, intermediate groups socialize members to accept the 'rules of the game' (Pinard 1971, p. 183). A rule most groups will subscribe to is to avoid using violence to achieve political goals. Integrated people therefore should be inclined not to accept violence. Legal participation, however, is part of the "game." We can thus expect to find a negative correlation between norms of violence and integration and a positive correlation between norms of protest and integration.

Group members should, furthermore, strengthen preferences for the public goods the group is concerned with. If a member enters a group he will be faced with new arguments and justifications in favor of the goals of the group and against the aims of the group's opponents. This should lead to stronger preferences for the group's goals.

The data set that we used to test our hypotheses consists of a sample of opponents of nuclear power whose primary aim is to reduce the utilization of nuclear energy. As casual observations suggest, many nuclear power opponents (hereafter referred to as "antinuclears") also seem to reject the present economic and political order, that is, they are alienated from the political system. We surmised that integration affects or strengthens the preference for non-provision of both these public bads. Therefore we could expect that integration would correlate positively with discontent with nuclear energy as well as with political alienation.

If political actions are rewarded for a long time, these actions will become intrinsically rewarding. We supposed that for individuals who are members of groups in which participation is rewarded, political actions become rewarding per se: they acquire an entertainment value, and they are performed in order to displace or eliminate aggression on the part of the group members, thus acquiring a catharsis value.

Our data include various indicators of the incentive variables. The sources of the incentives were not identified. We assumed, however, that if people are integrated into a group, at least some rewards and costs for participation will come from the respective group, provided that integration correlates with participation.

B.   Linking Incentives, Integration, and Political Protest

We have argued that if integration is associated with political protest (or with political participation in general), it is because integration is associated with incentives for protest that affect protest behavior.

This is exactly the argument by rational choice theory. It posits that the choice to be politically active depends on the costs and benefits associated with political action. If, accordingly, groups (or, to be more precise, members of groups) provide relatively strong positive (or negative) incentives for political participation to their members, integration into groups can be expected to correlate positively (or negatively) with political participation. Further, there may be groups that provide neither positive nor negative incentives for participation. In such a case we can expect to find no relationship at all between integration and participation.

To explain the relationship between integration and participation it is not enough to look at the incentives provided by the respective groups. An individual may obtain rewards and costs from outside specific membership groups. A student, for example, may share the expectations of the protest group to which he belongs—expectations of investing enough time to initiate various actions. Yet he may have to restrict his activities in the protest group because he wants to pass an examination in the near future. Thus, his opportunity costs for participation are high. Accordingly, if we want to explain effects of integration on participation, we need to take into account not only the incentives provided by members of specific groups, we have to control for other incentives as well.

Figure 1 displays the *general model* outlined thus far. The arrows symbolize causal relationships, whereas the line denotes a noncausal relationship. The relationship between integration and political participation thus may obtain because integration is connected with various costs and benefits of participation, and because these costs and benefits, together with other costs and benefits coming from outside the specific groups, determine participation. If, furthermore, integration and participation are not related, we can expect that the respective groups will not provide any incentives for participation.

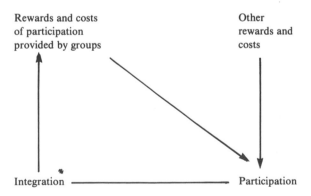

Figure 1. The General Model for Explaining the Relationship between Integration and Political Participation

In sum, then, we contend that the relationship between integration and participation is spurious and can be explained by the presence or absence of incentives for protest by the groups.

Given the variety of social groups, we expect that membership in different groups will have different effects on participation. This view converges with a differential socialization hypothesis (see particularly Portes 1971; Isaac et al. 1980) that in this context may be called the *differential integration hypothesis* (a term suggested by Bert Klandermans): groups differ with respect to the ideologies, information, and other stimuli to which members are exposed.

In order to test the rational choice explanation of the relationship between integration and participation it is reasonable to proceed in *four steps*.

The starting point and first step is to ascertain the relationship between integration and participation itself. As we want to explain why this relationship does or does not exist, we first need to determine whether there is a positive, negative, or zero correlation between integration and participation.

Since we claim that integration correlates with protest only if it is connected with incentives to protest, we must examine whether the rewards and costs outlined above correlate with integration. This is the second step of our analysis.

Explaining the correlation between integration and participation by means of costs and benefits implies that these costs and benefits actually are determinants of participation. Consequently, in a third step it must be tested whether costs and benefits have significant effects on participation.

The final question to be answered is to what extent the rational choice model can explain the relationship at issue. This explanation can be achieved in a fourth step by computing partial correlations between integration and participation, controlling for the incentive variables.

III.   METHODS

A.   The Sample

One of the objectives of our study of opponents of nuclear power was to explain why only a few of those who oppose the use of nuclear energy engage in protest behavior. Our sample consisted of 398 opponents of nuclear power from two different locations: a district of Hamburg (West Germany), where many counterculture people—and thus supposed opponents of nuclear power—live (229 people were interviewed there), and a small town near Hamburg close to an atomic power station (169 interviews were conducted there).

One hundred eighty-seven respondents were from a random sample of the population of the two locations. Two hundred eleven respondents represented a snowball sample, people whom we were led to by the interviewees of the random sample.

Demographic differences between the samples were not large enough to require a separate analysis of both samples.

B.   Dependent Variables

Participation in Legal and Illegal Protest

Respondents were first presented with a list of legal and illegal behaviors described as actions people may take to protest against the construction of nuclear power plants. The referents of the legal and illegal protest items were: participation in a petition-signing campaign; participation in a permitted political demonstration; participation in a citizen's initiative; seizing factories, offices or other buildings; damaging other people's property; using violence against persons.

Respondents were also asked about their intention of performing the respective action in the future. They were given five response categories ranging from "in no case" to "quite certain."

Each behavior response (scored "1" for "have not done," "2" for "have done") was multiplied by the respective intention response (scored 1 to 5, where a high score means that there is a high probability the behavior will be performed in the future).

The resulting six product terms were subject to a principal component analysis. Two factors were extracted, one exhibiting high loadings of the legal, the other showing high loadings of the illegal protest product terms. Due to this pattern a legal and an illegal protest scale were constructed by adding the product terms of the legal and illegal items respectively.

The possible and observed range of the legal protest scale is from 3 to 30 with a mean of 17.00 and a standard deviation of 6.17. The possible range of the illegal protest scale is from 3 to 30 and the observed range is from 3 to 22.83 with a mean of 6.07 and a standard deviation of 3.67.

C.   Independent Variables

Community Integration

This variable was measured by five items similar to those used by Useem (1980, p. 361): "length of residence in the town where the respondent now lives" and "tenant/lives in own house or apartment" are indirect indicators of community integration. It was assumed that living for a relatively long time at the same place or owning one's own home or apartment leads to close ties to people in the immediate environment.

In order to measure neighborhood integration more directly we used two other indicators: strength of the respondent's ties to people of the neighborhood (two categories, not strong = 0, strong = 1) and how much the respondent feels he has in common with people of the neighborhood (not much = 0, much = 1).

Incentive Variables

Our questionnaire included, first, items measuring perceived influence and the two public good variables, "discontent with nuclear energy" and "system alienation." The rational choice model requires that the public good variables be weighted by perceived influence. We thus had to construct two multiplicative terms: "discontent with nuclear energy * influence" and "system alienation * influence." As the correlation between both interaction terms is .71, which is due to the common variable "influence," we constructed additive scales of the two public good variables. We first regressed legal protest on the two public good variables, weighted each variable by its unstandardized regression coefficient, and added the products and the constant. We then regressed illegal protest on both public good variables and constructed a similar scale. The scales were called "public good constructs." Each construct was weighted by the perceived influence scale.

Other items measure expectations of reference persons to protest, positive sanctions, negative sanctions, norms of protest, norms of violence, catharsis value of protest, and entertainment value of protest.

We will not go into the details of the measurement. They are described elsewhere (Mueller and Opp 1986; Opp 1985, 1986).

IV. RESULTS

A. Community Integration and Political Protest

Since this chapter focuses on explaining the relationship between community integration and protest, it is first necessary to examine how our integration items and protest are correlated.

As Table 1 indicates, the three indirect integration items correlate negatively with legal as well as with illegal protest. Two of the six correlation coefficients are not statistically significant. The correlations of the two direct measures of integration with legal as well as with illegal protest are close to zero. Our data thus contradict the hypotheses advanced by advocates of the resource mobilization perspective: community integration either is not related to protest at all or, if it correlates with protest, the correlation is negative, that is, integration does not foster but inhibits protest.

Table 1. Neighborhood Integration, Legal and Illegal Protest:
Bivariate Correlations

Items measuring neighborhood integration	Legal Protest	Illegal Protest
Length of residence in present apartment	-.21**	-.12**
Length of residence in town	-.12**	-.03
Owns home/apartment	-.02	-.14**
Feels strong ties to people in neighborhood	.01	.04
Feels a great deal in common with people in neighborhood	.07	.04

*p < .05   **p < .01

B. The Community as a Social Context:
Testing and Implication of Rational Choice Theory

We presume that positive rewards for protest are exchanged in neighborhoods where many people reject the utilization of nuclear energy. In such a community context close relationships with neighbors should thus enhance protest. We assume, furthermore, that opponents of nuclear power in particular reward protest that is directed against the construction of nuclear power plants. These rewards, however, can only reach those individuals who interact with the antinuclears. A friendship group can exert control over its members because "it can deprive them of much, if they do not conform" (Homans 1974, p. 150). We thus predict *that in neighborhoods with a high percentage of opponents of nuclear power, integrated individuals will be faced with rewards for protest and, accordingly, will protest relatively frequently.*

In statistical terms, we expected to find an *interaction effect* between the strength of personal relationships to neighbors and the proportion of opponents of nuclear power in the neighborhood on the one hand and protest on the other. If individuals are weakly integrated into the community, the percentage of antinuclears in the neighborhood will have no or only a small effect on protest. If, however, individuals are strongly integrated, the relationship between the percentage of antinuclears and participation will be particularly strong.

We predicted, in addition, that the interaction effect would be particularly strong for our two direct measures of community integration (ties to neighbors and perceived similarity with neighbors) because they are more valid measures of close relationships with neighbors than the three indirect items.

As an indicator for the percentage of opponents of nuclear power in the community we used an estimate of the respondents. The interview question was: "Can you tell me approximately what percentage of the people in your neighborhood are opponents of nuclear power?" Although it would be of interest to know the objective percentage of antinuclears in the neighborhood of the respondents, a subjective measure is superior to an objective one for explaining protest behavior, because the estimate of the respondent better reflects his actual contacts with opponents of nuclear power and thus his expectations about rewards and punishments in his neighborhood.

In order to examine whether the predicted interaction effect was present, we computed, first, bivariate correlations between legal/illegal protest and the percentage of antinuclears in the neighborhood for those respondents reporting low similarity and for those respondents reporting high similarity with their neighbors. Interaction effects would lead to relatively low correlations of the perceived percentage of antinuclears in the neighborhood with legal/illegal protest among those reporting low similarity with their neighbors.

The same correlations were computed for respondents reporting weak and strong ties to their neighbors: for each group the variable "percentage of antinuclears in the neighborhood" was correlated with legal as well as with illegal protest.

The correlations in Table 2 clearly confirm the predicted interaction effect: if respondents say they have not much in common with people in the neighborhood, the perceived percentage of opponents of nuclear power in the neighborhood has no effect on either legal or illegal protest. If, however, respondents report having much in common with their neighbors, "percentage of antinuclears" correlates significantly with legal as well as illegal protest.

The same results are obtained if we compute correlations for respondents reporting weak and strong ties to their neighbors.

We want to examine in yet another manner whether there are additive effects of the integration items and the context variable on protest. For "legal protest" two regression analyses were performed, one for each integration item. As independent variables of the first regression analysis we employed the

Table 2.   Bivariate Correlations between Percentage of Opponents of Nuclear Power in the Neighborhood and Protest for Respondents with Strong and Weak Neighborhood Integration (Hamburg Data)

Groups of respondents	Correlations of "percentage of antinuclears in the neighborhood" with:		
	Legal protest	Illegal protest	No. of respondents
Similarity with neighbors *low*	-.01	-.07	322
Similarity with neighbors *high*	.35**	.39**	64
Ties with neighbors *weak*	-.01	-.06*	311
Ties to neighbors *strong*	.35**	.22*	81

*p < .05   **p < .01

integration items "similarity with neighbors" and "percentage of antinuclears" as additive variables as well as interaction term consisting of the product of those two variables. In the second regression analysis we employed the second integration item, "ties with neighbors," and again "percentage of antinuclears in the neighborhood" as additive terms, as well as a product term constructed from these two variables.

In the two other regression analyses "illegal protest" was regressed on the same terms as in the two regression analyses carried out for "legal protest."

The results presented below confirm, first, the interaction effects found in our previous analyses: for each of the four regression analyses the coefficients of the interaction terms are significant (twice at the .01 level and twice at the .05 level). The additive effect of the context variable "percentage of antinuclears" was in each case insignificant and the coefficients were close to zero. Each additive integration item, however, has a negative effect, which is significant at the .05 level in two of four instances.

$$LP = -.01 \ \%Ant. - .12 \ \ SimN \ + .24* \ \ (\%Pct \ x \ SimN)$$
$$LP = -.01 \ \%Ant. - .19* \ Ties \ \ + .26** \ (\%Pct \ x \ Ties)$$
$$IP \ = -.09 \ \%Ant. - .23* \ SimN \ + .37** \ (\%Pct \ x \ SimN)$$
$$IP \ = -.06 \ \%Ant. - .11 \ \ Ties \ \ + .23* \ \ (\%Pct \ x \ Ties)$$

with

LP	=	Legal protest
IP	=	Illegal protest
%Pct	=	Percentage of antinuclears in neighborhood
SimN	=	Similarity with neighbors
Ties	=	Close relationships with neighbors

Multicollinearity was not a serious problem in these analyses. In the regression analyses with the similarity item the highest intercorrelation between two independent variables was .65 (the two others were .59 and .37) so that the results have substantive value.

The negative additive effect of community integration on participation means that *if the percentage of opponents of nuclear power in the community is estimated as zero, an increase in integration leads to a decrease—not to an increase—in participation.* If our assumption is correct that a relatively high percentage of opponents of nuclear power is indicative of ample rewards for protesting the use of nuclear energy, a negative additive effect of integration on participation means that, in the absence of social incentives for participation, greater integration leads to less participation and probably greater involvement in other social activities.

In sum, then, integration into the neighborhood, as measured by our two direct indicators, has either no effect on protest, if we proceed from the results of the bivariate correlation analyses, or it has a negative effect, if we accept the results of the regression analyses. If we take the three indirect indicators of community integration into account (see Table 1), and if we take the results of the regression analyses more seriously than the bivariate correlation coefficients because we are interested in the *joint effects* of the additive variables and the interaction terms, we may conclude that in general the additive effect of integration into the community on protest is negative.

Our previous analyses of the interaction effects of community integration were based on the two direct indicators of community integration because they are the more valid measures. The same analyses that we have reported before have been performed with the three indirect indicators (length of residence in apartment/town, ownership of home/apartment). There were, however, no interaction effects.

C.   Community Integration and Incentives for Protest

The next step of our analysis uses our data to examine to what extent community integration is associated with incentives for protest. Let us first consider the integration effect of community integration and percentage of opponents of nuclear power in the neighborhood. The reason for this effect is, we hypothesized, that individuals who are highly integrated into neighborhoods with a large percentage of antinuclears are to a large extent exposed to incentives for protest.

In testing this assumption we employed only our similarity item because it revealed the strongest interaction effects and thus provided a better opportunity to test the extent to which the incentive variables can explain the relationship between the interaction term and protest.

The relationships between the incentive variables and our interaction term are displayed in Table 3. The first column shows the incentive variables. Lines 1 to 4 refer to the public good variables and perceived influence. Lines 5 to 11 include the selective incentive variables referred to above.

In columns 2 and 3 the effects of the (perceived) percentage of antinuclears in the neighborhood on protest are exhibited for those respondents who are weakly integrated into the neighborhood and for these who are strongly integrated. We saw above that the percentage of antinuclears in the neighborhood had a particularly strong effect on protest (legal as well as illegal), if the respondents were strongly integrated. We explained this by claiming that strongly integrated individuals are faced with more incentives for protest than those who are weakly integrated, if there are many opponents of nuclear power in the neighborhood.

Table 3. Community Integration and Incentives for Protest
(Bivariate Correlations)[1]

		% Antinuclears		Length of residence in apartm.	Length of res. in town	Owner of home/ap.
Incentive variables		simil. low	simil. high			
	1	2	3	4	5	6
(1)	Discontent with nuclear energy	.05	.29*	-.08	-.02	-.01
(2)	System alienation	.01	.31*	-.14**	-.05	-.18**
(3)	Influence	-.05	.24*	-.11*	-.11*	-.06
(4)	Public good construct	.01	.36**	-.15**	-.10*	-.11*
	* general influence[2]	.00	.36**	-.16**	-.10*	-.15**
(5)	Expectations of reference	-.04	.18	-.14**	-.04	-.03
	persons[3]	-.07	.22*	-.16**	-.03	-.08
(6)	Positive sanctions	.01	.35**	.00	-.04	-.08*
(7)	Negative sanctions	-.01	-.09	.11*	.03	.06
(8)	Norms of protest	.07	.25*	-.06	-.03	-.03
(9)	Norms of violence	.01	.32**	-.23**	-.11*	-.19**
(10)	Catharsis value	-.01	.11	.11*	-.02	.03
(11)	Entertainment value	.05	.35**	-.08*	.00	-.15**

[1] The N for column 2 is 322, for column 3 it is 64. For all other columns N = 398.
[2] The first row of coefficients refers to the composite public good variable, which was constructed on the basis of a regression analysis for legal protest, whereas the second row displays the coefficients constructed on the basis of a regression analysis for illegal protest.
[3] The first coefficient describes the correlations for the expectation variable being constructed for legal protest, the second coefficients refer to the construct for illegal protest.
$*p < .05;$ $**p < .01$

If our reasoning is correct we can expect that the correlations between "percentage of antinuclears in the neighborhood" and the incentive variables will be low for weakly integrated individuals, whereas the correlation between "percentage of antinuclears" and the incentive variables should be high for individuals who say they have much in common with their neighbors. If we compare the coefficients of column 2 with those of column 3, we find that our hypothesis is clearly substantiated: with one exception, which is the variable "negative sanctions," all correlation coefficients in column 3 are higher than those in column 2. In other words, those respondents who are highly integrated into a neighborhood with a relatively large number of antinuclears are faced with much stronger incentives for participation than those who are weakly integrated.

Let us look more closely at the effects of the single incentive variables. We find clear differences between the public good variables and percentage of antinuclears: those respondents who are strongly integrated into a neighborhood with many antinuclears are more dissatisfied with nuclear energy and more alienated from the social order than weakly integrated respondents.

The former respondents also perceive that participation in the antinuclear movement has a greater influence on achieving the respective goods. The differences in the correlations are even stronger for the public good construct, weighted by perceived influence.

The other incentive variables also clearly differ according to whether an individual is strongly or weakly integrated into the neighborhood, if the neighborhood has a high percentage of antinuclears. Highly integrated persons encounter high expectations of participation from reference persons, if there are many antinuclears in the neighborhood; they experience particularly strong positive sanctions for participating; they have internalized norms of protest; and they accept norms of violence to a high degree.

The variable "positive sanctions" is a factor scale consisting of the utility and subjective probability of occurrence of seven reactions within the social environment in regard to participation. For five of these sanctions the differences between the correlations for weakly and strongly integrated persons were particularly great (the correlations are given in parentheses):

> I get social approval from opponents of nuclear power (.12, .20); I am encouraged to continue my activity (.05, .27); I have a feeling of solidarity with other opponents (.02, .25); I meet interesting people (.01, .22); I get information about atomic power stations and political problems (.02, .20).

It thus seems that positive rewards for participation are common in a social environment with strong social ties and with many people who have antinuclear views.

The difference in the correlations of *negative sanctions* for strongly and weakly integrated antinuclears is not great (-.01 vs. -.09, which are statistically not significant), so it does not require further discussion.

The correlations of the variables referring to the *intrinsic reward value of protest* (see lines 10 and 11 of Table 3) do differ: strongly integrated people in particular experience an intrinsic reward value of protesting if they live in neighborhoods with many antinuclears.

Let us deal with our three *indirect indicators of community integration*. For each of these items the sign of the correlation coefficient with protest is negative, although two of the six correlations are not significant (see Table 1). These results suggest two predictions: (1) since low horizontal mobility and ownership inhibit protest, most of the incentive variables should in general show negative correlations with our indirect indicators; (2) "length of residence in the apartment where the respondent lives at present" exhibits higher negative correlations with legal *and* illegal protest, whereas for the other two items there is a significant correlation with either legal or illegal protest (see Table 1). We can thus predict that "length of residence in present apartment" will show stronger negative correlations with most of our incentive variables than will the other two items.

Both predictions are clearly substantiated by our data. The correlation coefficients between the three integration items at issue and our incentive variables are with a few exceptions negative (see columns 4 to 6 in Table 3). Furthermore, the correlations of "length of residence in present apartment" are in general stronger (i.e., more negative) than the coefficients for the other two items.

In general, then, low mobility and ownership have negative additive effects on protest. They are, in addition, connected with disincentives for protest. Thus they inhibit rather than instigate protest.

D. Explaining the Relationship between Community Integration and Protest

The relationship between community integration and protest can only be explained by our incentive variables if these variables exhibit statistically significant relationships with legal and illegal protest. Regressions of legal and illegal protest on the public good construct, weighted by "perceived influence," and the other incentive variables showed that each variable—with the exception of the "entertainment value of protest"—significantly affects at least one of the two dependent variables (with explained adjusted R^2's of .47 for legal and .32 for illegal protest).

The fourth step of our analysis can be accomplished by computing partial correlations, controlling for those incentive variables which have a statistically significant correlation with the respective integration item as well as a statistically significant regression coefficient in the respective equation for legal/illegal protest. Comparing the partial correlation coefficient with the respective bivariate correlation coefficient, we can expect that the partial coefficient will be lower than the bivariate one. The greater the difference, the better we have succeeded in explaining the relationship between the integration item and protest.

The results of our analysis are exhibited in Table 4. Since we found an interaction effect between similarity with neighbors and percentage of antinuclears in the neighborhood with legal as well as illegal protest, we constructed the respective interaction terms and computed bivariate correlations with legal as well as illegal protests. As Table 4 shows, the bivariate correlations of these interaction terms with legal as well as illegal protest are .13. The respective partial correlation coefficients (controlling for the variables indicated in the last column of Table 4) are, as expected, lower than the bivariate correlation coefficients.

We will investigate in yet another manner the extent to which the interaction effect can be explained by our incentive variables. For those respondents who say that they have much in common with their neighbors, the correlation

Table 4.   Community Integration and Political Protest:
Bivariate and Partial Correlations

Integration items	Bivariate r's with legal or illegal protest	Partial r's	Variables controlled for (see Table 3)
Similarity with neighb. * % antinuclears			
Legal protest	.13**	.07	4, 6, 8
Illegal protest	.13**	.11*	4, 8
% antinuclears in neighb. reporting high similarity			
Legal protest	.35**	.09	4, 6, 8
Illegal protest	.39**	.20	4, 5, 8, 9
Length of residence in apartment			
Legal protest	-.21**	-.12**	4, 5, 7
Illegal protest	-.12**	.00	4, 5, 7, 9, 10
Length of residence in town			
Legal protest	-.12**	-.08	4
Owner of apartment/house			
Illegal protest	-.14**	-.03	4, 9

*p < .05   **p < .01

between "percentage of antinuclears" and legal protest is .35, while the respective correlation with illegal protest is .39 (see Table 4). If we control for the incentive variables that satisfy the two requirements mentioned above, we see that the partial correlation coefficients are reduced to .09 and .20 respectively. Thus the interaction effect of similarity with neighbors and percentage of antinuclears in the neighborhood can be clearly explained by our incentive variables.

Let us now turn to our three indirect indicators of community integration. If we compute the partial correlation coefficients for the significant bivariate correlations with legal or illegal protest, controlling for the variables fulfilling the two criteria previously described, we find, as expected, that the partial correlations are, without exception, lower than the bivariate correlation, as Table 4 indicates.

The question arises as to why the two groups of indicators of community integration are related differently to political protest and to the incentive variables. People who say they are similar to their neighbors or have close relationships with them seem to be distinct from people who are immobile and own an apartment or a house. This distinction is clear if we perform a principal component analysis using the five integration items. Two factors with eigenvalues greater than 1 were extracted, which explain 34.5 and 30.9% of the variance. On the first factor only the similarity and relationship items exhibit a high loading, whereas the three other items load highly on the second factor. There are thus *two dimensions of community integration*. The first seems to refer to relationships with neighbors, whereas the second seems to capture length of stay in a neighborhood. The important point is that community integration, as measured by the five items, does not have a homogenous effect on protest.

SUMMARY AND CONCLUSIONS

The proposition that integration into social life may be an important determinant of political participation will not be challenged by any political scientist or sociologist. Major theoretical traditions, however, differ with respect to the kind of effect that social integration is assumed to have. Mass society theory, in particular, implies that integration into groups deters individuals from extensive participation, whereas the resource mobilization perspective implies the contrary. Results of empirical studies are contradictory. Some studies yield a positive relationship between integration and participation, some studies a negative relationship, and others no relationship at all. These findings raise the question: under which conditions does integration affect political participation?

The present paper aims at contributing an answer to this question. Applying rational choice theory, it argues that the effects of integration depend on the costs and benefits of participation associated with social integration. If integration is, thus, (positively or negatively) related to political participation, this relationship should be attributable to the fact that integration is associated with various incentives enhancing or inhibiting political participation.

A study of opponents of nuclear power in West Germany showed that *there is no consistent effect of integration into the community on either legal or illegal protest*. Theoretical perspectives such as the resource mobilization perspective or mass society theory postulating such effects are not confirmed by our data.

If integration is positively or negatively related to protest, then, according to the rational choice model, integration also should be related to incentives or disincentives for protest. We tested various predictions specifying expected relationships between particular integration variables and perceived costs and benefits. Further, we tested to what extent incentives were able to explain relationships between integration and protest.

The results clearly confirm our hypothesis that the relationship between integration on the one hand and legal and illegal protest on the other can be explained by incentives for participation.

This chapter was concerned with one type of integration, namely community integration. In a related paper the same argument was tested for integration into voluntary associations (Opp forthcoming). The results of this analysis support the arguments presented in this chapter.

To conclude, one of our major findings can be formulated as a more general hypothesis to be tested in future research:

> The higher the perceived percentage of individuals living in a community who share preferences for collective goods and the more cohesive a group these individuals form, the more these individuals will participate in political actions to reduce discontent.

In many sociological and economic studies in which the social context is taken into account, objective measures of context variables are used on the assumption that most of the time people perceive the situation as it really is. Our own study casts some doubts on this procedure and on the related assumption. Our respondents show great differences in their perception of the percentage of antinuclears in their neighborhood: the standard deviation is 28.36% (with a mean of 28.47, where the range is from a minimum of 0 to a maximum of 100%). It is hardly plausible that these estimates reflect reality. But if these estimates are correct, the social contexts of our respondents are so different that objective data of extremely small units would be required. Such data, however, will not usually be available.

This implies that in studies taking the social context into account it is not enough to look at the social environment as it is objectively given, that is, as it exists from the viewpoint of an observer. Rather, for explanatory purposes it is important to ascertain how the environment is perceived by the subjects of the investigation in order to determine the extent to which objective conditions are perceived correctly.

The theoretical argument and the empirical results presented in this paper suggest a new research strategy for exploring the relationship between integration and participation. The emphasis should lie on ascertaining the incentives for participation provided by groups and the effects of these incentives on participation.

ACKNOWLEDGMENTS

Financial support of this research by the *Volkswagenwerk-Foundation* (Stiftung Volkswagenwerk) is gratefully acknowledged. I would also like to thank Peter Hartmann for his assistance in analyzing the data and for valuable suggestions.

The present paper is a continuation of an earlier paper (Opp, forthcoming) which focuses on integration into *voluntary associations*. In both papers the same theoretical approach and the same hypotheses are used. For ease of reference the sections of both papers referring to the common theoretical bases are largely identical.

REFERENCES

Finifter, Ada W. 1974. "The friendship group as a protective environment for political deviants." *American Political Science Review* 68:607-25.

Homans, George C. 1961. (rev. 1974). *Social Behavior: Its Elementary Forms.* New York: Harcourt.

Isaac, Larry, Elizabeth Mutran, and Sheldon Stryker. 1980. "Political protest organizations among black and white adults." *American Sociological Review* 45:191-213.

Kornhauser, William. 1959. *The Politics of Mass Society.* New York: Free Press.

McAdam, Doug. 1982. *Political Process and the Development of Black Insurgency, 1930-1970.* Chicago: University of Chicago Press.

McAdam Doug. 1983. "Tactical innovation and the pace of insurgency." *American Sociological Review* 48:735-54.

Morrison, Denton E. 1971. "Some notes toward a theory on relative deprivation, social movements and social change." *American Behavioral Scientist* 14:675-90.

Muller, Edward N. and Karl-Dieter Opp. 1986. "Rational choice and rebellious collective action." *American Political Science Review* 80:471-87.

Oberschall, Anthony. 1973. *Social Conflict and Social Movements.* Englewood Cliffs, N.J.: Prentice-Hall.

Oliver, Pamela. 1984. " 'If you don't do it, nobody else will': Active and token contributors to local collective action." *American Sociological Review* 49:601-10.

Opp, Karl-Dieter. 1985. "Konventionelle und unkonventionelle politische Partizipation." *Zeitschrift für Soziologie* 14:282-96.

Opp, Karl-Dieter. 1986. "Soft incentives and collective action: Participation in the anti-nuclear movement." *British Journal of Political Science* 16:87-112.

Opp, Karl-Dieter, Forthcoming. "Social Integration into Voluntary Groups and Incentives for Legal and Illegal Protest." In Bert Klandermans (ed.), *Organizing for Change: Social Movement Organizations across Cultures.* Greenwich, Conn.: JAI.

Orbell, John M. and Toru Uno. 1972. "A theory of neighborhood problem solving: Political action vs. residential mobility." *American Political Science Review* 66:471-89.

Pinard, Maurice. 1971. *The Rise of a Third Party: A Study in Crisis Politics.* Englewood Cliffs, N.J.: Prentice-Hall.

Pollock, III, Philip H. 1982. "Organizations as agents of mobilization: How does group activity affect political participation?" *American Journal of Political Science* 26:485-503.

Portes, Alejandro. 1971. "Political primitivism, differential socialization, and lower-class leftist radicalism." *American Sociological Review* 36:820-35.

Putnam, Robert D. 1966. "Political attitudes and the local community." *American Political Science Review* 60:640-54.

Snow, David A., Louis A. Zurcher, Jr., and Sheldon Ekland-Olson. 1980. "Social networks and social movements: A microstructural approach to differential recruitment." *American Sociological Review* 45:787-801.

Useem, Bert. 1980. "Solidarity model, breakdown model, and the Boston anti-busing movement." *American Sociological Review* 45:357-69.

Wilson, Kenneth L. and Anthony M. Orum. 1976. "Mobilizing people for collective action." *Journal of Political and Military Sociology* 4:187-202.

THREE IN ONE:

CURRENTS IN THE MILAN

ECOLOGY MOVEMENT

Mario Diani and Giovanni Lodi

I. INTRODUCTION

Many students of collective action have questioned the long-accepted belief that social movements consist of homogeneous collective actors (Touraine 1978; Melucci 1982; Tarrow 1983). Though starting from quite different theoretical viewpoints, these authors have stressed that each protest event involves many different actors, who attribute differing and frequently contradictory meanings to the same processes of mobilization.

The ecology movements that have arisen in Western societies in the last decade provide us with ample empirical evidence of such heterogeneity (see for instance Nelkin and Pollack 1981; Lowe and Goyder 1983; Papadakis 1984; Rudig 1986, 1987; Rucht 1987). Milan's ecology movement, the subject of this paper, is no exception. In our examination of this movement, we first analyze its composition, focusing on the most committed activists. We then draw a

International Social Movement Research, Vol. 1, pages 103-124.
Supplement to Research in Social Movements, Conflicts and Change
Copyright © 1988 by JAI Press Inc.
All rights of reproduction in any form reserved.
ISBN: 0-89232-955-6

picture of the main political and cultural currents within the movement. Next (in Section III) we show how such currents differ according to the characteristics of their respective constituencies and (Section IV) also ask whether the persisting differences in approaches to ecology action have any effect on the processes of recruitment and patterns of participation. In the final section the paper's mainly descriptive perspective gives way to a more interpretive one, aimed at providing some suggestions for further analysis.

The empirical evidence for the analysis performed in Sections III and IV was gathered through semistructured questionnaires. Although we tried to interview all full members of the 55 groups and associations active in the Milan metropolitan area, we actually succeeded in contacting only 204 out of an estimated total of 400.

II.   CURRENTS IN THE ECOLOGY MOVEMENT

Cooperation between the organizations concerned with the defense of the natural and urban environment in Italy has increased sharply in recent years, particularly among the most important groups, such as Italia Nostra, WWF (World Wildlife Fund), and Lega per l'Ambiente.[1] Indeed, one could even say that these three organizations today represent a permanent coordinating body for environmentalist action. Their influence was confirmed by the recent campaigns (Spring 1986) to promote two popular referendums against nuclear energy and hunting, conducted jointly with other ecology organizations and political groups such as the Radical Party or the Worker's Democracy Party (Democrazia Proletaria). Furthermore, a wider research project on the structure of the ecology movement in Milan, some of the results of which are presented in this paper, stresses the relevance of interorganizational links even at the local level (Diani 1987).

These interconnections should not however be taken as a sign of increasing social and cultural integration of the basic components within the ecology movement. On the contrary, the differences between them are still very deep. More specifically, we can identify at least three distinct cultural and political approaches to the ecology issues. The first, which we will describe as *conservationist,* represented until the 1960s the only active form of ecology action in Italy. Groups such as Italia Nostra, Pro Natura, and various animal rights leagues fall into this category. The main aim of the conservationist group is, as the term suggests, the defense of the environment understood largely in terms of natural heritage (parks, fauna, coasts, etc.). The conservationists' objectives often include protection of the nation's artistic and architectural heritage as well. In their view, the primary cause of environmental decay is the irrationality of human behavior in its broadest sense, our inability to free ourselves from short-sighted utilitarianism. What is necessary above all, they argue, is to stimulate awareness of the environment through education of the public and by action to inform and put pressure on institutions.

Toward the mid-1970s, and especially after the accident at Seveso (1976), Italy also saw the development of *political ecology,* whose base largely coincided with that of the other social movements of the day. Unlike the conservationists, those in the political ecology movement blamed environmental degradation on the capitalist pattern of development and called for closer links between ecology action and other expressions of social protest. During this first phase political ecology mobilizations tended to coincide (not by chance) with actions against nuclear power plants, whose target was not so much the source of energy in itself as the social model it presupposed — the "nuclear society" (Nelkin and Pollack 1981). With respect to conservationism, attention tended to shift from the natural to the urban or social environment; and the orientation changed from one of integration in the political system to one of confrontation with the system.

We might summarize the differences between conservationism and political ecology in terms of the distinction between a basically "reactive" approach, adopted by the former, and a "proactive" approach, stressed by the latter (see Tilly 1978). In fact, the groups of the conservationist current are primarily concerned with the preservation of the natural and urban habitat. We can therefore consider their mobilizations as actions oriented toward defending "already established" rights, for example, the right to live in a nonpolluted environment. Such rights, which were never questioned in the past, have, with the increasing development of an industrial society, now become threatened.

Political ecology organizations, in contrast, desire wider social change. Thus they mobilize to impose new rights and claims, not only to defend already legitimate ones, and they stress the quest for grass-roots democracy and for direct control by the citizens over industrial production and over energy and economic policies.

A third component of the ecology movement, possibly less conspicuous in numerical terms but of considerable importance on the political level, again since the 1970s, is what we will call *environmentalism.* This approach differs from the other two principally in the eclecticism of its theoretical background and its willingness to draw from several and often very different traditions of ecologist thought and collective action. Borrowing widely from the strategies and tactics introduced for the first time in Italy by the Radical Party, organizations such as Friends of the Earth or LIPU (Italian League for the Protection of Birds) have on different occasions mobilized in defense of the natural environment or expressed strong criticism of industrial society through support of the antinuclear movement. Their mobilizations are therefore a mix of reactive (the defense of what still survives) and proactive action (the quest for a new pattern of social and economic development), and differ from those of the other currents in their essentially pragmatic nature. Currently the Italian

CONSERVATIONISM

Italia Nostra (Let's Save Our Italy)

Animal rights groups:
ENPA (Ente Nazionale Protezione Animali/National Association for the Protection of Animals); LeAL (Lega Antivivisezionista Lombarda/Lombardy Anti-vivisection Legaue); Lega Nazionale per la Difesa del Cane (National League for the Protection of Dogs); MondoGatto (Cats' World); LAN (Lega Antivisezionista Nazionale/National Anti-Vivisection League)

Moderate Citizens' Action Groups:
Trezzano, Opera, Fiera (Milan), San Siro (Milan), Sempione (Milan)

Other organizations:
Istituto Ecologico Internazionale (International Ecology Institute); Gruppo Naturalistico Brianza (Brianza Association for the Preservation of Nature)

ENVIRONMENTALISM

Local branches of the WWF (World Wildlife Fund):
Regional Office, Milan, Cinisello, San Donato, Rho

Animal Rights Leagues:
LIPU (Lega Italiana per la Protezione degli Uccelli/Italian League for the Protection of Birds); LAC (Lega per l'Abolizione della Caccia/League for the Abolition of Hunting); LAV (Lega Anti Vivisezione/Anti-vivisection League)

Associazione per il Parco Sud (Association for the Southern Milan Area Park)

Libertarian ecology grass-roots groups:
Associazione Citta' Verde (Green City Association); Liberta' Futura (Future Freedom); Studenti Verdi (Green Students)

POLITICAL ECOLOGY

Local branches of Lega per l'Ambiente (League for the Environment):
Milan, Novate, Bollate, Cinisello, Cologno

Local green parties:
Regional Party, Milan, Cologno, Rho, Sesto S. Giovanni

Autonomous grass-roots groups:
Sesto S. Giovanni, Ecology 15 (Milan), Ecology 10 (Milan), Cologno

Action on health organizations:
Medicina Democratica (Democratic Medicine); Gruppo Locale di Figino (Figino Health Action Group)

Technical/scientific action groups:
Geologia Democratica (Democratic Geology); Istituto Uomo/Ambiente (Man and Environment Institute)

Countercultural organizations:
Agrisalus (Alternative Food and Agriculture); AAM Terra Nuova (AAM New Land/Alternative Agriculture); Associazione Culturale Roccabrivio (Roccabrivio Cultural Association)

Figure 1.   Currents in the ecology movement in Milan

section of the WWF would also seem to fall into this environmentalist category. Though the WWF was founded on strictly conservationist principles, its long history of single-issue mobilization and its willingness to commit itself to specific and not necessarily coherent objectives have brought together within the organization a variety of different approaches to the ecological problem. For instance, it is quite common in the WWF to find collaboration between rigidly conservationist, apolitical activists and militants critical of the dominant model of social relations.

In terms of its capacity for action and organization, if not of the size of its membership, the most important conservationist group in Milan is undoubtedly Italia Nostra. The majority of animal rights groups also share a conservationist approach, and so represent a significant and consolidated presence. A more recent phenomenon, however, is the emergence of rather conservative local committees and neighborhood organizations, usually active on specific issues. Altogether we placed sixteen groups in this category for a total of 51 activists—about 25% of the sample.

Under the environmentalist heading fall various local WWF groups; a few single-issue committees; some animal rights groups, such as LIPU, LAC, and LAV, originally close to the Radical Party; and libertarian ecology groups— 11 groups in all, with 53 activists, thus making up 26% of the total.

The principal political ecology groups are, on the one hand, the different sections of the League for the Environment and, on the other, the various green lists formed at the time of the 1985 local administrative elections. Also represented in this current are autonomous leftist groups, health-action organizations, and technical/scientific action committees—altogether twenty-eight groups, 99 militants, for 49% of the total (see Figure 1).

III. THREE CONSTITUENCIES OF ECOLOGY ACTION

Socio-demographic Traits

Most studies of the ecology movement show that interest in environmental issues is highest among young people of medium-high education; the data thus support Inglehart's hypothesis (1977) about the spread of postmaterialist values (see among others, Papadakis 1984; Müller-Rommel 1985a). But other researchers find that concern for the environment cuts right across social distinctions, however these are defined (age, gender, occupation, education) (see Lowe and Rudig 1986 for an overview of this debate). There seems to be some agreement about the fact that active participation in ecology movements is essentially a middle-class phenomenon (Cotgrove and Duff 1981, 1982; Lowe and Goyder 1983). Our research does not contradict these findings: Table 1 shows that ecology activists in Milan tend to be young, with a higher than average education, and are involved primarily in intellectual activities

Table 1.   Sociodemographic Profiles of Ecology Activists
and General Population in the Province of Milan (in percentages)

	Ecology Activists	Milan Population*
Gender:		
Men	73	48
Women	27	52
Age:		
Under 36	58	40
Over 36	42	60
Education Level:		
Compulsory	16	82
High School	48	14
Graduate	36	4
Occupation:		
Nonemployed	8	36
Students	18	9
Blue-collar	11	25
Shopkeepers	6	7
White-collar	27	18
Teachers	10	3
Professionals	20	2
Total	100%	100%
N	(204)	(2,976,000)

* These percentages are computed on the basis of the population in the Milan province falling into the same age range (18-78) as the ecology activists.
Source: ISTAT (National Institute for Statistics), *Dati del censimento nazionale 1981* (National Census, 1981). Rome, 1983.

(they are professionals, teachers, students, and office workers). Although the activists are for the most part male, the incidence of women is far from insignificant, given the traditionally low levels of women's political participation in Italy.[2]

Nonetheless, one common shortcoming of studies of ecology militancy is that they tend to underestimate the heterogeneity of the actors involved, neglecting the sometimes very significant differences in the social composition of the various currents. A more detailed analysis of the socio-demographic data will allow us to pinpoint such differences more accurately.

The first point to emphasize is that the more traditional approach to ecology action proves by far the most effective in mobilizing female activists. In fact, half the militants in the conservationist current are women, who are

Table 2.   Gender by Ecological Current (in percentages)

	Conserva-tionism	Environ-mentalism	Political Ecology	All
Men	49	79	82	73
Women	51	21	18	27
Total	100%	100%	100%	100%
N	(51)	(53)	(99)	(203)

concentrated in particular in the various animal rights organizations. The proportion of women activists is much smaller in environmentalist and political ecology groups, in neither case exceeding one-fifth of the total number of members (Table 2).

Ages among members range from 18 to 78, with an overall average of 36; the analysis was conducted on five age groups: 18-25, 26-35, 36-45, 46-60, and 61-78. In determining these ranges we took into account the probable life experience of each age group, in particular its relation to collective movements of the 1960s and 1970s. By "relation" we mean not direct participation in those movements but contact with specific cultural attitudes and worldviews. We can assume that the age groups most directly influenced by that cycle of mobilization are the middle ones (26-35 and 36-45 years); contact tends to decrease among younger members and falls off dramatically among the older activists. Further, our data clearly show that the conservationist current is much more successful among older activists, while younger activists are more attracted to the environmentalism and political ecology currents (Table 3).

We isolated seven groups by occupation: nonemployed (housewives and retired people), students, blue-collar workers, white-collar workers, teachers, shopkeepers and craftsmen, and professionals (Table 4). The relative weight of these categories is consistent with the picture of ecology activism (and participation in the "new" social movements in general) as an intellectual middle-class phenomenon. On the other hand, the various currents of ecology action do not appear to differ significantly in terms of their members' occupation. There is certainly an overwhelming presence of retired people and housewives within the conservationist groups; students are slightly over-represented in the environmentalist current; a political ecology approach is more likely than a traditional conservationist approach to attract activists from the working class. Yet the analysis of occupation reveals a far less heterogeneous movement than one might expect, given our initial assumptions in this chapter.

Table 3.   Age by Ecological Current (in percentages)

	Conserva-tionism	Environ-mentalism	Political Ecology	All
18-25	6	28	27	22
26-35	22	42	41	36
36-45	20	13	21	19
46-60	42	13	8	18
61-78	10	4	3	5
Total	100%	100%	100%	100%
N	(50)	(53)	(97)	(200)

Table 4.   Occupation by Ecological Current (in percentages)

	Conserva-tionism	Environ-mentalism	Political Ecology	All
Nonemployed	26	6	0	8
Students	8	28	18	18
Blue-collar	4	8	17	11
Shopkeepers	10	2	5	6
White-collar	18	26	32	27
Teachers	8	9	11	10
Professionals	26	21	17	20
Total	100%	100%	100%	100%
N	(50)	(53)	(99)	(202)

Finally a word about both the level of general education and the specialized technical enterprise among the activists, an aspect of particular relevance to environmental protection, where the scientific and cultural elements are especially important. We have already emphasized the overwhelming presence of well educated activists in the movement (Table 1). Furthermore, our research data show that 26% of the militants have some specific ecology-related expertise, either as a result of past studies (e.g., a university degree in scientific disciplines) or through their present occupation. On the other hand, our sample of activists reveals no differentiation among the various sectors in terms of education or these more specific skills.

Political Background

The three currents of the ecology movement differ much more clearly with respect to the past experience of their activists. Many studies have pointed out that past militancy provides individuals with political and organizational skills

Table 5. Political Participation in the Past by
Ecological Current (in percentages)

	Conserva-tionism	Environ-mentalism	Political Ecology	All
No Participation	78	66	24	49
Political Parties	10	15	24	18
Other Political Organizations	6	11	43	25
Clubs, Circles	6	8	9	8
Total	100%	100%	100%	100%
N	(51)	(53)	(96)	(200)

they can call upon afterward in new and different circumstances (McCarthy and Zald 1973, 1977). At the same time, personal contacts and solidarity networks set up for one cause can always be reactivated later to produce new episodes of mobilization.[3] We would therefore have expected a high incidence of past commitment among our sample, ecological and otherwise. More particularly, we would have expected to find: first, a marked presence of political commitment among the political ecology militants; second, among the conservationists and environmentalists, a substantial number of people with experience of membership in other organizations such as cultural circles or voluntary groups.

The findings only partially confirmed our expectations. About half the sample proved to have been active in nonecology-oriented organizations. If we examine the different currents individually, however, we find that the incidence of former activists is especially high in the political ecology current, much lower among the environmentalists, and still lower among the conservationists. This conclusion remains valid irrespective of the type of past commitment involved, be it membership in political parties, other sociopolitical organizations (trade unions, SMOs, etc.), or clubs and circles (see Table 5).

It is worth noting that the low figure for conservationists and, to a lesser extent, for the environmentalists, cannot be attributed to their being involved in the ecology movement over a longer period. In effect, while the vast majority of conservationists and a significant proportion of the environmentalists were already active before 1982, only a quarter of the political ecology militants were active before that date (Table 6). Furthermore, figures for the period of active involvement in ecology militancy (not necessarily in the present group but also in previous ones) show a median value of six years for conservationists, against four for environmentalists and two for political ecology, the relation being wholly unaffected by the activists' age. Nevertheless, even introducing the length of ecology militancy as a control variable does not modify the original

Table 6. Adhesion Before/After 1982 by Ecological Current (in percentages)

	Conserva- tionism	Environ- mentalism	Political Ecology	All
Before 1982	69	42	27	42
After 1982	31	58	73	58
Total	100%	100%	100%	100%
N	(48)	(50)	(95)	(193)

relation: the conservationists are still characterized by little experience with political activity; the political ecologists are the most experienced; and the environmentalists fall somewhere in between.

We can therefore conclude that the different interpretations of ecology action embodied in the various currents are capable of mobilizing constituencies that are quite distinct in terms of political background. The stronger an organization's effort to relate environmental issues to goals of radical social change, the greater its attraction for people with a past experience of political participation. The reverse follows for reactive patterns of action. This conclusion is largely consistent with findings of other authors (Walsh 1981, 1986; Walsh and Warland 1983). These authors have shown, in analyses of the campaigns following the Three Mile Island incident, how previous political experience is no longer a strictly necessary precondition for mobilization when individuals are faced with exceptionally serious events, when certain fundamental rights such as the right to life itself are placed in peril. We might suggest that any event *perceived* as threatening, even though of minor importance (e.g., a proposal to build a motorway, the use of public parkland for construction, etc.), affects people's willingness to participate in much the same way that previous activist experience does.

Frames

The final dimension in which we want to analyze the differences between the various constituencies is that of cultural orientation. In conducting this analysis we assumed from the outset that the choice of one current rather than another does not occur on the basis of a perfect congruence between the opinions of individuals and the group's official ideology. Various studies have in fact shown how choice many often precede a full socialization to the values upheld by the organization (Snow et al. 1980; Ferree and Miller 1983). However, the individual's own attitudes must be minimally congruent with certain central ideas or cores of the group and the individual's own attitudes (Snow et al. 1986). More specifically, we identified two such cores over which the various currents of the ecology movement have been divided in recent years. The first is the

Table 7. Preferred Solutions to Ecological Problems by
Ecological Current (in percentages)

	Conserva-tionism	Environ-mentalism	Political Ecology	All
Radical Social Change	15	41	60	44
Conservation	70	42	20	38
Both Important	13	17	20	17
Both Unimportant	2	0	0	1
Total	100%	100%	100%	100%
N	(47)	(53)	(98)	(198)

previously mentioned distinction between a conception of ecology as the mere preservation of the environment and as action to change the social causes underlying environmental degradation. The second criterion concerns the weight given to political as opposed to direct action (direct action intended here not in the sense of violence, but as personal responsibility for change, thus involving voluntary action, altering individual behavior, etc.). We assumed the conservationists would favor defense of the existing situation and direct action, and so would express characteristics typical of a movement of moderate orientation: priority given to reactive action and hostility toward the political system in general. Conversely, from the political ecologists we anticipated a clear preference for transformation of social relations and for political action. The pragmatic nature of environmentalists should, we assumed, result once again in greater eclecticism, not only in the choice of ends (defense vs. transformation) but in the choice of means as well (in fact, their collective action repertoire has included from the outset both direct action and political pressure).

Our findings fully bear out our assumptions as far as attitudes to transformation are concerned: even taking into account the opinions of those who consider both criteria of equal importance, the percentage of those who give priority to the transformation of social relations drops off rapidly when we pass from the political ecologists to environmentalists to the conservationists, while consensus in favor of defending the existing natural heritage decreases if we consider the currents in the opposite order (Table 7).

As regards the most suitable form of action there appears to be a general preference for direct action. Here again, however, the overall distribution of opinion relative to the various options bears out our expectations: support for political action decreases from political ecologists to environmentalists and to conservationists, even if there appears to be little difference between the last two. On the other hand, support for direct action decreases inversely (Table 8). Once again, from the point of view of attitudes and orientations, we have two relatively polarized sectors with a third less well-defined group in between.

Table 8.   Patterns of Action by Ecological Current (in percentages)

	Conserva-tionism	Environ-mentalism	Political Ecology	All
Political Action	10	21	29	22
Direct Action	70	68	36	53
Both Important	18	9	33	23
Both Unimportant	2	2	2	2
Total	100%	100%	100%	100%
N	(49)	(53)	(97)	(199)

IV.   PATTERNS OF RECRUITMENT AND PARTICIPATION

Ever since Gerlach and Hine's classic work (1970) introduced the concept of social network, this idea has been widely used to analyze social movement structure and mobilization processes. In this chapter we deal first with patterns of recruitment and then go on to analyze forms of participation and the contribution of overlapping membership to the circulation of resources within the movement and without.

Recruitment Networks

It has often been held that an individual's involvement in existing relational networks facilitates his decision to commit himself to collective action. There is some disagreement, however, about what kind of involvement to emphasize. "Solidarity" theorists (see Jenkins 1983 for an overview) have stressed the importance of participation in other generically communal activities, thus supporting the hypothesis that someone who is well integrated into a community is more likely to commit himself than is someone who is isolated. But this theory has been partly disputed by some scholars (Crenson 1978; Oliver 1984; Walsh 1986) who maintain that integration itself does not necessarily encourage mobilization. What counts in reality is membership in specific networks, that is to say direct contact with people who are already active, or who at least sympathize with the movement (see the essays of Opp and Kriesi, pp. 83-101 and 41-81 in this volume). In our analysis of recruitment patterns we have concentrated on the role of specific networks in an attempt to determine whether—and, if so why—the networks have greater influence in certain currents rather than in others, and if different types of networks prevail in different currents.

In general our findings (Table 9) confirm the importance of personal contacts with militants in encouraging the move to activism: the vast majority of

Table 9. Patterns of Recruitment by Ecological Current (in percentages)

	Conserva-tionism	Environ-mentalism	Political Ecology	All
Associative Networks	12	25	39	28
Private Networks	51	36	29	37
Unspecified Networks	16	4	16	13
Other Channels	21	35	16	22
Total	100%	100%	100%	100%
N	(51)	(52)	(99)	(202)

interviewees (78%) had in fact joined their group through these channels, while only a few (22%) joined via other routes (after participating in a specific initiative, after hearing of the group through the media, etc.). The role of networks does appear to have a different weight from one current to another, however. While there is little appreciable difference between the role of networks among conservationists and among political ecologists (79% in the first case, 84% in the second), the influence of networks among environmentalists is smaller, although still significant (65%).

To explain this imbalance we might relate the influence of networks to the presumed costs of mobilization. By "costs" we mean that the greater the resocialization the potential participant has to go through when he joins a specific group, the more costly his decision to participate will be. A number of studies that take a similar line (see among them McAdam's and della Porta's contributions to this volume) demonstrate the link between networks and costs by reference to certain high-risk kinds of mobilization, such as racial equality militancy in the USA in the 1950s and 1960s or Italian terrorism in the 1970s. In these cases the decision to join a group implies a fairly radical transformation of one's frames of reference, requiring specific relational contexts (in McAdam's terminology, micromobilization contexts). Obviously, in the case of ecology action the distinction between high-cost and low-cost action has to be redefined. Let us assume then that the decision to join is easier, and the role of networks less important, when the group in question (a) tries to contact potential participants through specific recruitment campaigns; (b) promotes activities open to nonmembers which make it easier for them to come into contact with the organization; (c) does not espouse particularly coherent cultural frames that the potential member must to some extent accept before joining. These three conditions are most frequently found in the environmentalist current. The WWF is certainly the only large-scale ecology organization in Italy to pay special attention to the question of recruitment, resorting, in a fashion similar to that of the American ecology lobbies, to advertising and the media. Mobilization of "atomized" individuals is also made easier by the presence of short-term initiatives (week-long voluntary work programs or environmental education courses in schools) which sympathizers can participate in without feeling committed to a project whose costs and duration are difficult to calculate. Initiatives of this type are of course not exclusive to environmentalism (Italia Nostra has been running similar schemes for some time), but they do seem to play a special role in organizations such as the WWF or LIPU. A final factor is the greater ideological incoherence of the environmentalist current. Its more limited set of shared beliefs compared to the other currents suggest that its members have less need for a process of socialization by means of specific social networks.

A further distinction among the various currents concerns the different roles played by private and associative networks. By "associative networks" we mean relationships with other people formed on the occasion of mutual participation in other associative activities (which in the case of our sample tend, as we have seen, to involve political/social militancy). "Private networks," on the other hand, are contacts made through personal acquaintance in the activist's ordinary daily life: friends (besides those who are at the same time companions in militancy), colleagues at work, even in some cases, relatives. Overall, private networks have a slightly higher profile than associative ones. Their relative influence, however, varies sharply from current to current. The influence of associative networks declines as we move from political ecology to environmentalism and conservationism, while that of private networks tends to increase (see Table 9). Once again a connection emerges between the type of network (private or associative) and the type of collective action (reactive or proactive). In other words, the more an action concentrates on asserting new rights and values rather than merely defending what is currently threatened, the greater the role of associative networks in giving rise to that action.

Participation Networks

Although networks linking the organizations that are active within the movement to potential constituents are essential for recruitment, a network of interorganizational contacts (both within the movement itself and with the outside world) is important for encouraging the circulation of available resources and thus making the process of mobilization more effective (Gerlach and Hine 1970; Tilly 1978). Because of the often informal structure of the SMOs, such contacts are frequently made by individuals (Aveni 1978; Rosenthal et al. 1985). The analysis of overlapping membership thus assumes a special importance. In addition to examining overlapping membership in the strict sense, we also considered other less formalized ties in order to investigate the extent of persisting differences between the sectors in their forms of participation. In all we used six indicators.

Table 10. Patterns of Participation in the Ecology
Movement by Ecological Current (in percentages)

	Conserva- tionism	Environ- mentalism	Political Ecology	All
(A) Attendance at Other Groups' Activities, Meetings, etc.				
Yes	59	77	68	68
No	41	23	32	32
(B) Membership in Other Ecology Organizations				
No Membership	64	42	63	58
Passive Membership	24	16	8	14
Active Membership	12	42	29	28
(C) "Consistent" vs. "Eclectic" Membership				
"Consistent"	32	27	27	28
"Eclectic"	4	31	10	14
No Membership	64	42	63	58
(D) Friendship Ties with Activists in Other Groups				
No	89	58	77	75
Yes	11	42	23	25
Total	100%	100%	100%	100%
N	(50)	(52)	(97)	(199)

The first indicator concerns the activist's level of information about the existence of other ecology groups. A list of 40 organizations active in Milan was submitted to the respondents. Members of the environmentalist sector scored highest, with a median value of recognition of 15 groups. Political ecology members had heard of 13 groups (the same as the overall population), while conservationists recognized 9.

The second indicator refers to individual participation in the activities of other ecology groups, for example meetings, lectures, and demonstrations. Among the total population, a large majority of activists take part, even occasionally, in such activities. This kind of participation increases when we move from the conservationist current to the political ecologists to the environmentalists (Table 10A).

The third variable relates to simultaneous support given to other ecology organizations, either by paying a membership fee or by active participation. Thirty-six percent of the conservationists and 37% of the political ecologists choose this type of support, compared to 58% of the environmentalists. These statistics suggest a similarity between the first 2 currents, both of which show a more exclusive pattern of participation, while environmentalists show a stronger interest in multiple commitments. Nevertheless, a difference does exist between conservationists and political ecologists, as the former prefer the simple payment of a membership fee. This finding is hardly a surprise, for this form of commitment is typical of formally structured organizations acting largely as institutionalized pressure groups. Political ecologists, on the other hand, are more active in other groups than are conservationists, though multiple participation is most popular with environmentalists (Table 10B).

Another indicator concerns the distinction we drew between "consistent" and "eclectic" choices to support other organizations. By consistent choice we mean simultaneous support of different groups in the same current. Eclectic choice, on the other hand, is the choice to support groups in more than one current. If we apply these two categories, we see that the environmentalists are more "eclectic" than the other currents (Table 10C).

The fifth indicator is the existence of friendships between members of different organizations. This indicator reveals a trend similar to that shown by the other indicators, with a higher incidence of these relations among environmentalists (Table 10D).

It still remains for us to analyze active participation in nonecology groups, which involve 27% of the respondents.[4] Here again conservationism appears to be the least disposed toward overlapping membership, a phenomenon concerning only 12% of its activists. It is worth noting, however, how the gap between political ecologists and environmentalists, so marked when we analyzed previous experience, has now more or less closed: 33% of the former and 31% of the latter participate in other forms of action. If we now combine this figure with that for participation in other ecology groups, we see that the environmentalists have the highest proportion of activists involved in at least one other organization, whereas the conservationists have the lowest (73% vs. 42%: see Table 11).

Table 11.   Present Participation by Ecological Current (in percentages)

	Conserva-tionism	Environ-mentalism	Political Ecology	All
No participation	58	27	44	43
Sociopolitical Organizations	6	15	20	15
Other Ecology Organizations	30	42	23	30
Both	6	16	13	12
Total	100%	100%	100%	100%
N	(50)	(52)	(96)	(198)

If we exclude the figures for participation by nominal membership, in any case involving very few individuals, all the evidence so far points to widely differing patterns of participation among the various currents. The environmentalists appear to be characterized by a strongly inclusive approach, in sharp contrast with the typical exclusiveness of the conservationists. In this respect, the political ecologists fall somewhere in between the two other currents.

It is interesting to ask whether these differences might be due to the personal characteristics of the individual activists or, rather, to implicit differences among the currents themselves. One possible hypothesis is that the propensity for multiple participation is related to the greater availability of free time: certain activists simply have more time than others. If, however, we analyze the principal data on participation together with that on age and occupation, the only correlation that emerges is one between age and friendships, friendship ties being more common among younger activists. There appears to be no real connection between age and participation in more than one organization. Nor does the fact that certain occupations afford a greater freedom to manage one's time seem to have any bearing on patterns of participation.

The differences between the various currents, then, appear to be attributable to their own specific characteristics. The reactive, and frequently parochial, nature of the conservationist current might perhaps explain the preference for single-group participation. A large number of its members mobilize because they are concerned about one specific problem, often circumscribed by the metropolitan quarter or the district in which they live. The aversion to politics and the absence of past commitment would provide a further explanation for the lack of interest in forms of collective action which go beyond the boundaries of the single group. But these characteristics are also reflected to some extent in the environmentalist current, which stands poles apart from the conservationists in terms of patterns of participation. Thus to us it seems more useful to return to the notion of mobilization costs, introduced above in our explanation of the role of networks in the processes of recruitment. Applying this notion, we found that environmentalist organizations seem to be somewhat easier to join than conservationist or political ecology organizations. There are various reasons for this phenomenon, but we would pinpoint the weaker ideological coherence within the environmental sector and the greater opportunity for short-term commitment. These factors also seem to us to explain the prevalence among environmentalists of an inclusive pattern of participation. In the first place, greater ideological incoherence may favor simultaneous membership in organizations expressing at least partly diverging positions. Second, because single-issue and short-term forms of participation are more frequent in the environmental sector than in the other sectors, its members have a greater flexibility of commitment. In other words, activists can commit themselves fully for a given period, then reduce their activity in order to devote themselves to other organizations, and eventually return to full commitment should a new campaign arise.

V. CONCLUSIONS

In this chapter we began by asking whether the three distinct approaches to ecology action might vary in their appeal to different constituencies. Broadly speaking, we can say that this variation does indeed seem to occur, but our conclusion requires certain important qualifications.

The conservationist current is marked by the higher average age of its membership and by a sizable proportion of female activists. For the majority of its constituents, this involvement is their first and only experience of collective action; they share a preference for an approach aimed at defense of the threatened natural heritage and the transformation of individual behavior. At the other extreme, male and younger militants are over-represented in the political ecology current. Strongly rooted in a tradition of sociopolitical commitment, these activists favor a more proactive interpretation. The environmentalist current proves the most representative of the movement as a whole: in fact, the distribution of data for this current reflects the values of the population more precisely than do the data for the other currents. Although similar to conservationism in terms of the activists' political background, the environmentalist sector stands out for the extreme heterogeneity of its members' orientations and for its larger proportion of young people and male participants.

The three currents do not seem to differ so much in terms of sociodemographic variables, with the partial exception of gender and age, as they do in terms of their activists' political background and cultural orientations.

It may prove worthwhile to ask whether, and how far, our findings are consistent with those analyses which stress the postmaterialism of contemporary social movements. Such approaches postulate that the mobilization potential of New Social Movements, and of the ecology movements as well, is constituted primarily of young and well-educated people, employed for the most part in the tertiary and professional sectors, and with some background of political activism. But, no one has yet tried—as far as we know—to discover how such characteristics are distributed among the different sectors of any social movement. This is hardly a secondary point, since it is difficult to see how all the various currents can be described as "postmaterialist." If we look at the ecology movement in Milan, for instance, political ecology and environmentalism (in part) are probably fairly close to a "postmaterialist" pattern of collective action; but we would hesitate to apply the term "postmaterialism" to the conservationists, who identify much more with traditional patterns of nonpolitical participation.

On the other hand, it is significant that the sociodemographic indicators of postmaterialism tend to be evenly distributed throughout all sectors. At least from this point of view then, the activists of the more traditional groups appear just as "postmaterialistic" as the members of the more recent groups.

To conclude: the use of social and demographic characteristics as the key to differentiating emerging patterns of collective action from those which are more traditional, and better established, is thrown increasingly into question. In fact, all these movements are largely heterogeneous phenomena, whose membership cannot reliably be analyzed in terms of "class (or social) constituency." On the contrary, greater emphasis must be placed on the concept of "conscience constituency," an element that cuts across traditional class boundaries.

Meanwhile we consider it essential to concentrate on the process by which such conscience constituencies are activated. Our analysis of recruitment patterns provided some useful, if only preliminary, insights. We described above how preexisting social networks play a crucial role in encouraging potential members to participate. Their somewhat diminished importance in the environmentalist current was accounted for in terms of this current's more eclectic and pragmatic nature, which makes it easier for potential activists to join some form of collective action without having to undergo a relatively thorough socialization process.

We also highlighted the different roles played in the various currents by private and associative networks. The latter became more important as we go from conservationism to political ecology; the reverse holds true for the former.

How can this difference be explained? In effect, the more proactive the collective action, the more radical the criticism of dominant values, and the greater the activists' need for socialization to alternative frames. Socialization is made easier if the potential participants have personal links with current activists who share the same beliefs and political background. In this case, therefore, bonds forged through common participation in specific activities are more likely than merely private ties to provide the preconditions for individual mobilization.

The role of networks changes somewhat when the action is reactive. In this case, the appeal to radical and antagonistic beliefs is quite weak, as the action is essentially designed to preserve widely established and accepted values and rights. Consequently, the role played by personal ties must also be viewed differently. These ties no longer serve to socialize potential members to alternative worldviews but to provide them with an opportunity to begin an activity (collective action) of which the majority have no previous experience. Whereas most members of proactive groups know quite well "how" to mobilize (they have already done so in the past) and basically need only some strong cultural frame to identify with, reactive-oriented militants are in the opposite position. Above all they lack specific expertise and skills in the field of mobilization: for example, frequently they do not know who is already active on the same issues, how to call a meeting or a demonstration, or they doubt whether collective action may prove effective. Contact with other activists may help them overcome their lack of past experience, but it is relatively unimportant whether such contacts are made through previous political action or via private networks. Thus it is not difficult to see why bonds of personal acquaintance and friendship are more influential in promoting adhesion to reactive groups than to proactive groups.

ACKNOWLEDGMENTS

The data employed in this article were gathered by the authors during the period June 1985-February 1986 within the scope of research activities of LAMS (Collective Action and Social Movement Research Workshop), under the direction of Alberto Melucci at the Department of Sociology of the University of Milan. Data processing was performed by PENELOPE, a statistical package for social sciences created by Franco Rositi (University of Turin). A modified version of this paper was published under the title "Militanti ecologisti in un'area metropolitana" in Biorcio and Lodi, 1987.

NOTES

1.   Italia Nostra was formed in 1955 for the express purpose of protecting the artistic and architectural patrimony and limiting the damaging effects of unchecked urban development, which at that time was rapidly beginning to take off in Italy. It has gradually extended its area of concern to cover the countryside and natural heritage. It presently has around 15,000 members. The Italian branch of the WWF was set up in 1966 and has devoted most of its energies to the preservation of the natural environment. Since the 1970s it has also voiced a vigorous protest against the construction of nuclear power plants. Its membership topped 115,000 in 1987. The League for the Environment is a coordinating body linking hundreds of locally based ecological groups of leftist orientation. Founded in 1979, it initially relied on the organizational structure of ARCI, a cultural association run jointly by the Italian Communist and Socialist Parties, but it maintains a certain independence from these two, which has increased of late. The latest figures speak of around 40,000 members.

2.   Recent findings confirm the persistent low levels of political participation among Italian women, though they also suggest changing trends for the younger generations (Barbagli and Maccelli 1985).

3.   There is by now a wealth of literature on this subject. For a summary and further data see the essays by della Porta and McAdam in this volume.

4.   The figures presented in this paragraph have been computed by adding the percentage of ecology militants who are also active in sociopolitical organizations, but not in other ecology groups (see Table 11, row 2) to the one of those who are active in both (Table 11, row 4).

REFERENCES

Aveni, Adrian F. 1978. "Organizational linkages and resource mobilization: The significance of linkage strength and breadth." *Sociological Quarterly* 19:185-202.

Barbagli, Marzio and Alessandro Maccelli. 1985. *La partecipazione politica a Bologna*. Bologna Il Mulino.

Biorcio, Roberto and Giovanni Lodi (eds.) 1987. *La sfida verde. Il movimento ecologista in Italia*. Padua: Liviana.

Cotgrove, Stephen and Andrew Duff. 1980. "Environmentalism, middle class radicalism and politics." *Sociological Review* 28:333-51.

Cotgrove, Stephen and Andrew Duff. 1981. "Environmentalism, values, and social change." *British Journal of Sociology* 32:92-110.

Crenson, M.A. 1978. "Social networks and political processes in urban neighborhoods." *American Journal of Political Science* 22:578-94.

Diani, Mario. 1987. "Le mobilitazioni ecologiste tra lobby e movimento sociale. Un'analisi strutturale." Ph.D. dissertation, University of Turin.

Ferree, Myra Marx and Frederick D. Miller. 1985. "Mobilization and meaning: Toward an integration of social psychological and resource perspectives on social movements." *Sociological Inquiry* 55:38-61.

Gerlach, Luther P. and Virginia H. Hine. *People, Power, and Change: Movements of Social Transformation*. Indianapolis: Bobbs-Merrill.

Inglehart, Ronald. 1977. *The Silent Revolution: Changing Values and Political Styles among Western Publics*. Princeton: Princeton University Press.

Jenkins, J. Craig. 1983. "Resource mobilization theory and the study of social movements." *Annual Review of Sociology* 9:527-53.

Klandermans, Bert. 1986. "New social movements and resource mobilization: The European and the American approach." *International Journal of Mass Emergencies and Disasters*. Special issue, *Comparative Perspectives and Research on Collective Behavior and Social Movements* 4:13-37.

Lowe, Philip D. and Jane M. Goyder. 1983. *Environmental Groups in Politics*. London: Allen & Unwin.

Lowe, Philip D. and Wolfgang Rudig. 1986. "Political ecology and the social sciences. The state of the art." *British Journal of Political Science* 16:513-50.

McCarthy, John D. and Mayer N. Zald. 1973. *The Trend of Social Movements in America: Professionalization and Resource Mobilization*. Morristown, N.J.: General Learning Press.

McCarthy, John D. and Mayer N. Zald. 1977. "Resource mobilization and social movements: A partial theory." *American Journal of Sociology* 82:1212-41.

Melucci, Alberto. 1982. *L'invenzione del presente*. Bologna: Il Mulino.

Melucci, Alberto. 1984. (ed.) *Altri codici. Aree di movimento nella metropoli*. Bologna: Il Mulino.

Müller-Rommel, Ferdinand. 1985a. "The Greens in Western Europe. Similar but different." *International Political Science Review* 6:483-99.

Müller-Rommel, Ferdinand. 1985b. "Social movements and the Greens: New internal politics in Germany." *European Journal of PoliticalResearch* 13:53-67.

Nelkin, Dorothy and Michael Pollack. 1981. *The Atom Besieged: Extraparliamentary Dissent in France and Germany*. Cambridge, Mass.: MIT Press.

Oberschall, Anthony. 1973. *Social Conflicts and Social Movements*. Englewood Cliffs, N.J.: Prentice-Hall.

Oberschall, Anthony. 1978. "Theories of social conflict." *Annual Review of Sociology* 4:291-315.

Oliver, Pamela. 1984. "If you don't do it, nobody else will": Active and token contributors to local collective action." *American Sociological Review* 49:601-10.

Papadakis, Elmer. 1984. *The Green Movement in West Germany*. London: Croom Helm.

Piven, Frances Fox and Richard A. Cloward. 1979. *Poor People's Movements: Why They Succeed, How They Fail*. New York: Vintage.

Rosenthal, Naomi, Meryl Fingrutd, Michele Ethier, Roberta Karant, and David McDonald. 1985. "Social movements and network analysis: A case study of nineteenth-century women's reform in New York State." *American Journal of Sociology* 90:1022-54.

Rucht, Dieter. 1987. "Environmental movement organizations in West Germany and France. Structure and interorganizational relations." In Bert Klandermans (ed.), *Organizing for Change: Social Movement Organizations across Cultures.* Greenwich, Conn.: JAI.

Rudig, Wolfgang. 1986. "Energy, Public Protest, and Green Parties. A Comparative Analysis." Ph.D. dissertation, University of Manchester.

Rudig, Wolfgang. Forthcoming. *Antinuclear Movements: A World Survey.* London: Longman.

Simcock, Bradford L. 1979. "Developmental aspects of anti-pollution protest in Japan." In Louis Kriesberg (ed.), *Research in Social Movements, Conflict and Change.* Vol. 2. Greenwich, Conn.: JAI.

Snow, David A., Louis A. Zurcher, Jr., and Sheldon Ekland-Olson. 1980. "Social networks and social movements: A microstructural approach to differential recruitment." *American Sociological Review* 51:464-81.

Tarrow, Sidney. 1983. *Struggling to Reform: Social Movements and Policy Change during Cycles of Protest.* Western Societies Paper No. 15. Ithaca, N.Y.: Cornell University.

Tarrow, Sidney. 1986. "Comparing Social Movement Participation in Western Europe and the United States: Problems, Uses, Examples, and a Proposal for Synthesis." *International Journal of Mass Emergencies and Disasters.* Special issue, *Comparative Perspectives and Research on Collective Behavior and Social Movements* 4:145-70.

Tilly, Charles. 1978. *From Mobilization to Revolution.* Reading, Mass.: Addison-Wesley.

Touraine, Alain. 1978. *La voix et le regard.* Paris: Seuil.

Useem, Bert. 1980. "Solidarity model, breakdown model, and the Boston anti-busing movement." *American Sociological Review* 45:357-69.

Walsh, Edward J. 1981. "Resource mobilization and citizen protest in communities around Three Mile Island." *Social Problems* 29:1-21.

Walsh, Edward J. 1986. "Discontent, networks, and social movement participation: Reflections occasioned by the TMI mobilization processes." Paper presented at the International Symposium on New Social Movements, Amsterdam, Free University, June 12-14.

Walsh, Edward J. and Rex H. Warland. 1983. "Social movement involvement in the wake of a nuclear accident: Activists and free riders in the TMI area." *American Sociological Review* 48:764-80.

MICROMOBILIZATION CONTEXTS AND RECRUITMENT TO ACTIVISM

Doug McAdam

Up until the mid-1970s, the study of social movements was dominated by theory and research focused at the micro-level of analysis. This characteristic focus betrayed the underlying view that social movements were less a variety of rational political action than a form of "collective behavior" that operates primarily at a social psychological level. Thus answers to both the macro question of movement emergence as well as the micro question of individual participation tended to be sought in the characteristic psychological profile— however described—of the activist and the presumed psychological functions attendant to participation. Among the variants of this traditional social psychological approach to the study of social movement are the mass society (Kornhauser 1959; Selznick 1970), collective behavior (Lang and Lang 1961; Smelser 1962; Turner and Killian 1972), and relative deprivation (Crawford and Naditch 1970; Davies 1962, 1969; Feierabend et al. 1969; Geschwender 1964; Gurr 1970; Searles and Williams 1962) models.

In the 1960s and 1970s social movement activity reached levels not seen since the 1930s, not only in the United States but in many European countries as well. The political turbulence of the era caught the sociological community

International Social Movement Research, Vol. 1, pages 125-154.
Supplement to Research in Social Movements, Conflicts and Change
Copyright © 1988 by JAI Press Inc.
All rights of reproduction in any form reserved.
ISBN: 0-89232-955-6

off guard and demonstrated some glaring deficiencies in the traditional social psychological conceptions of social movements. These developments sparked something of a renaissance in the sociological study of social movements, triggered initially by a critical rethinking of the dominant theories in the field.

The theories were criticized on both theoretical and empirical grounds by many movement analysts (Aya 1979; Gamson 1975; Jenkins and Perrow 1977; McAdam 1982; McCarthy and Zald 1973, 1977; Oberschall 1973; Rule and Tilly 1975; Schwartz 1976; Shorter and Tilly 1974; Tarrow 1983; Tilly 1978). The effect of these critiques was to shift the focus of movement analysis from social psychological to more macro political and structural accounts of movement dynamics.

In the United States, the principal new theoretical perspectives to emerge in the field are the resource mobilization and political process models. In Europe, the "new social movements" approach has come to dominate research and writing on social movements. In contrast to earlier classical formulations, all of these perspectives attribute rationality to movement participants and posit a fundamental continuity between institutionalized and movement politics. The differences between the two models, then, are ones of emphasis rather than kind. Resource mobilization theorists tend to emphasize the constancy of discontent and the variability of resources in accounting for the emergence and development of insurgency (cf. McCarthy and Zald 1973, 1977; Oberschall 1973). Accordingly, a principal focus of attention in their work is on how burgeoning movement organizations seek to mobilize and routinize—frequently by tapping lucrative elite sources of support—the flow of resources to ensure movement survival.

Though compatible with the resource mobilization approach, the political process model represents a slightly different perspective on social movements. As formulated by its chief proponents (McAdam 1982; Tilly 1978), the political process model emphasizes two sets of macro structural factors believed to facilitate the generation of social insurgency. The first is the level of organization within the aggrieved population; the second, the political realities confronting members and challengers at any given time. The first can be conceived of as the degree of structural "readiness" within the minority community and the latter, following Eisinger, as the "structure of political opportunities" available to insurgent groups (Eisinger 1973).

Though marked by considerable diversity, the new social movements perspective attributes the rise of social movements in Europe over the past 15 years to new political, economic, and social strains that have accompanied modernization processes in postwar Europe (Brand 1982; Klandermans 1986; Melucci 1980). These processes are variously described as having undermined traditional ways of life, reduced the political and social importance of various social groups, and decreased the ability of society and its political institutions to respond to social problems.

As valuable as the recent theoretical shift toward more macro determinants of movement dynamics has been, we now run the risk of merely substituting one conceptual orthodoxy for another. Just as the earlier social psychological conceptions of social movements oversimplified the complexity of collective action, so too do those models that attribute exclusive importance to macro structural factors. Reflecting a desire to redress the new macro bias in movement theory, several authors (Jenkins 1983, p. 527; Klandermans 1984, pp. 583-84; Snow et al. 1985, pp. 2-3) have recently voiced calls for the development of a new and viable social psychology of collective action. While I agree with their assessment of the current macro bias in the field, I am not persuaded that a reassertion of the social psychological is the best way to redress this imbalance. Such an assertion reifies the micro/macro distinction and reinforces the notion that the two constitute distinct levels of analysis. What is missing is not so much a viable social psychology of collective action—the broad contours of which already exist in the literature—but intermediate theoretical "bridges" that would allow us to join empirical work at both levels of analysis. In the absence of such "bridges" we are doomed to perpetuate two important but ultimately incomplete accounts of collective action. Movements may occur in a broad macro context, but their actual development clearly depends on a series of more specific dynamics operating at the micro level. Just as clearly, these micro dynamics must be seen against the backdrop of the larger political-economic context in which they occur if we are to fully understand the timing and specific form they take. This chapter, then, has two aims. In the first or theoretical section of the chapter, I intend to sketch the relationship between macro political factors and the individual decision to participate as mediated through the crucial conceptual "bridge" of the "micromobilization context." In the second or empirical section of the chapter, I will present data that document the crucial importance of these "micromobilization contexts" in the recruitment of volunteers to a specific campaign in the American Civil Rights Movement. The campaign in question took place in 1964 and was termed the Mississippi Freedom Summer project. As a preface to the empirical section of the chapter, I will provide a fuller account of this project. Before I do so, however, it will be necessary to lay a conceptual foundation for the analysis that will follow later in the chapter.

I. POLITICAL FACTORS IN MOVEMENT EMERGENCE

One of the major contributions of the recent paradigm shift in the field of social movements has been the reassertion of the political. Both the resource mobilization and political process perspectives locate social movements squarely within the realm of rational political action. In contrast to institutionalized politics, social movements are simply "politics by other means," often the *only* means open to relatively powerless challenging groups. As such, social movements should be as responsive to the broad political trends and characteristics of the regions and countries in which they occur as are institutionalized political processes. Recent research in the field suggests as much. Among the macro political factors that have been linked to the development of collective action are expanding political opportunities, regime crisis and contested political arenas, the absence of political repression and the imposition of "suddenly imposed grievances," and the unchecked expansion of the welfare state. Each of these factors will be discussed in turn.

Structure of Political Opportunities

Considerable evidence now exists suggesting the crucial importance of changes in the "structure of political opportunities" (Eisinger 1973) for the ebb and flow of movement activity. By "structure of political opportunities" we mean the distribution of member support and opposition to the political aims of a given challenging group. Characteristically, challengers are excluded from any real participation in institutionalized politics because of strong opposition on the part of most polity members. This unfavorable structure of political opportunities is hardly immutable, however. In so saying our:

> attention is directed away from systems characterizations presumably true for all times and places, which are basically of little value in understanding the social and political process. We are accustomed to describing communist political systems as "experiencing a thaw" or "going through a process of retrenchment." Should it not at least be an open question as to whether the American political system experiences such stages as fluctuations? Similarly, is it not sensible to assume that the system will be more or less open to specific groups at different times and at different places? (Lipsky 1970, p. 14).

The answer to both of Lipsky's questions is yes. Challenging groups *can* count on facing very different levels of support and opposition over time. It is these variations in support and opposition that constitute the shifting structure of political opportunities confronting challengers and members which have been shown to be related to the ebb and flow of movement activity.

For example, Jenkins and Perrow (1977) attribute the success of the farm workers movement in the 1960s to "the altered political environment within which the challenge operated" (263). The change, they contend, originated "in economic trends and political realignments that took place quite independent of any 'push' from insurgents" (266). In similar fashion, McAdam (1982) has attributed the emergence of widespread black protest activity in the 1950s and 1960s, in part, to several broad political trends—expansion of the black vote, its shift to the Democratic party, postwar competition for influence among emerging Third World nations—that served to enhance the bargaining position of civil rights forces. In his analysis of the emergence of the contemporary environmental movement, Gale (1982) has also noted the importance of a "political system which included agencies already sympathetic to the movement" (p. 6). Indeed, with increased historical perspective has come the realization that the ascendant liberal-left coalition of the 1960s created a broad political context facilitating the emergence of a wide variety of leftist movements. Similarly, the conservative backlash of the 1970s and the contemporary dominance of the political right has encouraged the mobilization of the Moral Majority and pro-life forces while dimming the prospects for successful leftist movements. More generally, Tarrow (1983) has proposed a similar pattern of thaw and contraction in political opportunities as a standard feature of most liberal democratic regimes.

Regime Crises and Contested Political Arenas

Related to, yet distinct from, the previous category are regime crises and general contests for political dominance within a particular region or country. Both situations translate into a net gain in political opportunity for all organized challengers. In this sense the result is the same as in the cases discussed in the previous section. The difference stems from the conditions that give rise to the improved bargaining situation confronting the challenger. In the previous section we cited instances in which broad macro processes—demographic, political, etc.—had increased the leverage of a *particular* challenger without affecting the system-wide distribution of political power. By contrast, regime crises or periods of generalized political instability improve the relative position of *all* challenges by undermining the hegemonic position of previously dominant groups or coalitions.

Despite this difference, both situations are expected to stimulate a rise in social movement activity. Certainly the literatures on regime crises and major contests for political dominance support this assumption. Shorter and Tilly, for example, marshall data to show that peaks in French strike activity correspond to periods in which organized contention for national political power is unusually intense. They note that "factory and white-collar workers undertook in 1968 the longest, largest general strike in history as student unrest reopened the question of who were to be the constituent political groups of the Fifth Republic" (Shorter and Tilly 1974, p. 344). Similarly, Schwartz (1976) argues that a period of political instability preceded the rise of the Southern Farmers Alliance in the post-Civil War South. With the southern planter aristocracy and emerging industrial interests deadlocked in a struggle for political control of the region, a unique opportunity for political advancement was created for any group able to break the stalemate. In like fashion, Skocpol (1979) has located the source of revolution in major regime crises, typically precipitated by military losses and fiscal overextension. To this list of well-researched examples one might also add the generalized political instability in Germany following World War I as the facilitative context in which the Nazis came to power.

Absence of Repression

A third macro political factor often associated with the rise of a social movement is the absence or relatively restrained use of repressive social control by movement opponents. Although analytically distinct from the other two conditions, the absence of repression frequently occurs in conjunction with both of these factors. In a situation in which expanding political opportunities have significantly improved the bargaining position of a particular group, movement opponents are likely to exercise more restraint in dealing with the challenger.

Now, the movement's improved position increases the risk of political reprisals against any who would seek to repress it, whereas before, the powerless status of the challenger made it a relatively "safe" target. Thus repression is less likely to be attempted even in the face of an increased threat to the interests of other groups. For, as Gamson notes in summarizing the evidence from his survey of challenging groups, insurgents "are attacked not merely because they are regarded as threatening—all challenging groups are threatening to some vested interest. They are threatening *and* vulnerable" (1975, p. 82). To the extent, then, that shifting political conditions increase the power of a particular challenger, they also render them less vulnerable to attack by raising the cost of repression. This argument figures prominently in McAdam's (1982) account of the rise of widespread black protest activity in the 1950s and 1960s. Using the annual number of lynchings as a crude measure of repression, he has documented a significant decline in lynching during the period when black political fortunes were on the rise nationally (87-90). The implication is that the enhanced political significance of blacks at the national level increased the South's fear of federal intervention and thus restrained the use of extreme control measures. This restraint in turn created a more favorable context in which blacks could mobilize.

Recourse to repressive measures is also likely to decline during regime crises as the coercive capacity of the state deteriorates. Skocpol (1979) places great stress on this dynamic in her analysis of revolution, arguing persuasively that it is the collapse of the state as a repressive agent that sets in motion peasant mobilization. One need look no further than Iran under the Shah for a recent example of the same dynamic. As the crisis in Iran deepened, the Shah's ability to utilize the repressive measures he had once used so successfully declined rapidly. When, at last, large segments of the armed forces abandoned the regime, the last restraints on mobilization were removed, a development that precipitated the Shah's ouster.

One could also argue that the rise of the Solidarity Movement in Poland was aided by the unusual restraint showed by the Soviet leadership in failing to repress the burgeoning movement. This failure in turn can be linked to the unique political opportunity created by the Soviet Union's earlier invasion of Afghanistan. Having mounted the invasion only months before the strikes by Polish workers, the Soviet leadership was already smarting from the criticism the invasion had triggered in international political circles. No doubt their desire to avoid another major foreign policy setback, the likes of which would surely have followed an invasion of Poland, greatly restricted their resources to the type of repressive action that they had earlier used so successfully in Hungary and Czechoslovakia.

Suddenly Imposed Grievances

One final macro political factor that has been linked to the outbreak of collective action is the imposition of what Walsh (1981) has termed "suddenly imposed grievances" (p. 1). Rejecting the claim of some resource mobilization theorists that grievances are relatively constant, Walsh argues that the sudden imposition—whether through accident or conscious decision—of onerous conditions on a population is likely to stimulate widespread collective action. In support of his claim, Walsh provides convincing evidence of a sharp rise in protest activity in the area around Three Mile Island immediately following the accident there.

Nor is Walsh's the only example of this phenomenon. Useem's (1980) analysis of the antibusing movement in Boston leaves little doubt that the imposition of court-ordered busing precipitated widespread mobilization efforts among the residents of South Boston. Molotch (1970) documents a similar rise in protest activity among residents of Santa Barbara, California, in the wake of a major oil spill there. Even rising national opposition to the Vietnam War in the late 1960s can be interpreted within this framework. The war itself can be seen, as it was at the time, as a series of suddenly imposed grievances—higher draft quotas, the "secret" bombing of Cambodia, the elimination of student deferments—each of which, in turn, fueled growing protest against the war.

Welfare State Expansion and the Politicization of Private Life

One final political factor that has been linked to the generation of social movements is the penetration of the state into previously private areas of life. This factor has been stressed primarily by proponents of the new social movements approach (cf. Hirsch 1980; Klandermans 1986; Melucci 1980, 1981), and often is couched in terms of a broader Marxist view of the state. The argument is straightforward. The contradictions inherent in postindustrial capitalist economies have forced the state to intervene in previously private areas of life. The state is required to do so both to underwrite the process of capital accumulation (O'Connor 1973) as well as to satisfy needs no longer satisfactorily addressed by an ailing market economy. New social movements have then emerged in response to this unprecedented state penetration into various private spheres of life. In this view, movements as diverse as the women's movement, the environmental movement, and the gay rights campaign can be seen as efforts to regain control over decisions and areas of life increasingly subject to state control.

II. MICRO PROCESSES AND THE INDIVIDUAL DECISION TO PARTICIPATE

Although important, these macro political conditions do not, in any simple sense, produce a social movement. They only offer insurgents a certain objective "structural potential" for collective political action. Mediating between opportunity and action are people and the subjective meanings they attach to their situations. This crucial attribution process has been ignored by proponents of both the collective behavior and resource mobilization processes. As Edelman has pointed out, "our explanations of mass political response have radically undervalued the ability of the human mind . . . to take a complex set of . . . cures into account [and] evolve a mutually acceptable form of response" (1971, p. 133). As one form of response, social protest depends upon two related yet analytically distinct social psychological processes.

Cognitive Liberation

For all the recent emphasis on macro political or other structural "determinants" of social movements, the immediate impetus to collective action remains a cognitive one. As William Gamson's recent book (1982) makes abundantly clear, successful collective action proceeds from a significant transformation in the collective consciousness of the actors involved. This process of "cognitive liberation" depends upon the generation and widespread adoption of the following three cognitions described by Piven and Cloward:

> The emergence of a protest movement entails a transformation both of consciousness and of behavior. The change in consciousness has at least three distinct aspects. First, "the system"—or those aspects of the system that people experience and perceive—loses legitimacy. Large numbers of men and women who ordinarily accept the authority of their rulers and the legitimacy of institutional arrangements come to believe in some measure that these rulers and these arrangements are unjust and wrong. Second, people who are ordinarily fatalistic, who believe that existing arrangements are inevitable, begin to assert "rights" that imply demands for change. Third, there is a new sense of efficacy; people who ordinarily consider themselves helpless come to believe that they have some capacity to alter their lot (Piven and Cloward 1979, pp. 3-4).

The absence of any of these cognitions is likely to deprive insurgents of either the motive or will to engage in collective action.

One of the central problematics of insurgency, then, is whether favorable political conditions will be defined as such by a large enough group of people to facilitate collective protest. This process, however, is not independent of the macro political conditions discussed above. Indeed, one effect of improved political conditions is to render this process of "cognitive liberation" more likely.

As noted earlier, favorable shifts in political opportunities decrease the power disparity between insurgents and their opponents and, in doing so, increase the cost of repressing the movement. These are objective structural changes. Such shifts, however, have a subjective referent as well. That is, challengers experience shifting political conditions on a day-to-day basis as a set of "meaningful" events communicating much about their prospects for successful collective action.

Sometimes the political significance of events is apparent on their face, as when mass migration significantly alters the electoral composition of a region. Thus, as early as the mid-1930s black leaders began to use the fact of rapidly swelling black populations in key northern industrial states as bargaining leverage in their dealings with presidential candidates (Sitkoff 1978, p. 282). Even when evolving political realities are of a less dramatic nature, however, they will invariably be made "available" to insurgents through subtle cues communicated by other groups. The expectation is that, as conditions shift in favor of a particular challenger, members will display a certain increased symbolic responsiveness to insurgents. Thus in a tight labor market we might expect management to be more responsive to workers than they had previously been. Or, as regards the earlier example, should internal migration significantly increase the proportion of a certain population residing in a region, we could expect area politicians to be more symbolically attentive to that group than before.

As subtle and substantively meaningless as these altered responses may be, their significance for the generation of insurgency would be hard to overstate. As Edelman notes, "political actions chiefly arouse or satisfy people not by granting or withholding their stable substantive demands, but rather by changing the demands and the expectations" (1971, p. 7). In effect, the altered responses of members to a particular challenger serve to transform evolving political conditions into a set of "cognitive cues" signifying to insurgents that the political system is becoming increasingly vulnerable to challenge. Thus, by forcing a change in the symbolic content of member/challenger relations, shifting political conditions supply a crucial impetus to the process of cognitive liberation.

Value Expectancy

Should the three cognitions discussed above come to be widely shared within a particular population, the chances that collective action will occur are quite good. This likelihood still tells us nothing about whether a given number of that population will take part in any resulting action. To better understand that process we need a model of individual decision making. Through his application of value expectancy theory to the phenomenon of individual activism, Klandermans (1984) has offered us such a model. At the heart of his model is a view of the individual as a rational, calculating actor weighing the costs and benefits of activism. The key point though is that these anticipated costs and benefits are not independent of the individual's assessment of the likely actions of others. Instead, the perceived efficacy of participation for the individual will depend upon the following three sets of expectations he or she brings to the decision-making process:

a.   expectations about the number of participants;
b.   expectations about one's own contribution to the probability of success;
c.   expectations about the probability of success if many people participate (Klandermans 1984, p. 585).

As regards participation, individual activism is most likely to occur in a situation where the individual has high expectations on all three of these counts.

It should be obvious, however, that the formulation of these expectations does not occur in a social vacuum. Rather, the prevailing assessment of the chances for successful collective action within the individual's immediate social circle is likely to exert a powerful influence on his or her own thinking. In this sense, the process of cognitive liberation is not independent of the individual decision-making process described by Klandermans. Rather it is the context within which these individual choice processes occur. The individual's own expectations regarding the prospect for collective action cannot then be separated from the collective attribution processes discussed earlier. For an individual actor to formulate expectations regarding the behavior of others, he or she must be (a) attuned to, and (b) *in contact with* other prospective activists. This point brings us to the all-important structural bridge mediating the relationship between macro political conditions and the individual decision to act on those conditions.

III.   THE MICROMOBILIZATION CONTEXT

The key intermediate concept linking macro and micro processes is that of the micromobilization context. A micromobilization context can be defined as that small group setting in which processes of collective attribution are combined with rudimentary forms of organization to produce mobilization for collective action. Several examples of such settings will help to clarify the concept. Perhaps the most obvious example is that of the preexistent political group. Unions, for instance, provide a previously organized context in which political attributions are generated and translated into concrete forms of action. But the concept is not synonymous with the union as a formally constituted, bureaucratic entity. Subgroups within the union, organized informally on the basis of seniority or along task, racial, or even friendship lines may provide a basis for mobilization independent of the broader union context. This is precisely the situation in the case of a wildcat strike, or in instances where small, informally organized groups of workers become active in other movements. An example of the latter would be the "hardhat marches" organized in the early 1970s by construction workers supporting the war in Vietnam.

This example of "extracurricular" mobilization can apply to nonpolitical groups as well. That is, groups organized for ostensibly *nonpolitical* purposes can serve as the setting within which attribution and organization come together to produce collective *political* action. Several authors have, for example, noted the importance of black churches as collective settings in which early civil rights organizing took place (cf. McAdam 1982; Morris 1984; Oberschall 1973, pp. 126-27). Curtis and Zurcher (1973) assign similar importance to a variety of "nonpolitical" organizations—but especially "fraternal/service" groups—in their analysis of the emergence of a local anti-pornography movement in Texas (56).

Finally, micromobilization may also take place in smaller, informal groups of people. For instance, friendship networks have been known to furnish the crucial context for micromobilization. Perhaps the best known example is the case of the four Greensboro A & T students who initiated the 1960 sit-in movement with a demonstration that originated in informal "bull sessions" in one another's dorm rooms. Similarly, Sarah Evans (1980) locates the roots of the women's liberation movement in informal networks of women who had come to know one another in the context of civil rights and New Left organizing. Finally, Wilson and Orum (1976), see such networks as providing an important collective basis for riot participation. They write: "Many analysts have found themselves baffled by the riots of the 1960s; explanations presumed to work, such as those based on conventional psychological theories, do not. On the basis of our limited experience with and observations of these events, it appears to us that social bonds alike, i.e., friendship networks, drew many people to become active participants" (198).

Despite these differences in the size and degree of formal organization of these various collective settings, all serve to encourage mobilization in at least three ways. First, they provide the context in which the all-important social-psychological processes discussed above can occur. I will discuss this factor in greater detail later in the chapter. For now I will only note its significance in the generation of social insurgency.

Secondly, these settings provide the rudiments of organization—leaders, whether formally designated or not, communication technologies, etc.—needed to translate attributions into concrete action. It is not enough that people define situations in new and potentially revolutionary ways; to create a movement they must also act on these definitions. As preexisting groups, these contexts provide the established roles and lines of interaction necessary for action to unfold.

Finally, these collective settings supply the established structures of solidary incentives on which most social behavior depends. By "structures of solidary incentives" I refer to the myriad interpersonal rewards that attend ongoing participation in any established group or informal association. It is expected that these incentive structures will solve or at least mitigate the effects of the "free rider" program.

First discussed by Mancur Olson (1965), the "free rider problem" refers to the difficulties insurgents encounter in trying to convince participants to pursue goals whose benefits they would reap even if they did not participate in the movement. The fact is, when viewed in the light of a narrow economic calculus, movement participation would indeed seem to be irrational. Even if we correct for Olson's overly rationalistic model of the individual, the "free rider" mentality would still seem to pose a formidable barrier to movement recruitment. The solution to this problem is held to stem from the provision of selective incentives to induce the participation that individual calculation would alone seem to preclude (Gamson 1975, pp. 66-71; Olson 1965).

In the context of these settings, however, the provision of selective incentives would seem unnecessary. These organizations already rest on a solid structure of solidary incentives that insurgents can appropriate by defining movement participation as synonymous with group membership. Accordingly, the myriad of incentives that have heretofore served as the motive force for participation in the group is now simply transferred to the movement. Thus insurgents have been spared the difficult task of inducing participation through the provision of new incentives of either a solidary or material nature.

For all these reasons, then, established groups or associational networks such as those discussed earlier are expected to serve as the basic building blocks of social movements. In effect, they constitute the "cellular structure" of collective action. However, this discussion still leaves the issue of micro-macro bridges unexamined. How *do* these mobilization contexts serve to link the macro conditions and micro dynamics discussed earlier? Quite simply, their significance lies in the important interpersonal context they create within which the two social-psychological processes outlined above can occur.

Cognitive Liberation and the Process of Collective Attribution

As regards the process of cognitive liberation, I earlier emphasized the importance of three cognitions that result from the process. It is important to realize, however, that these cognitions "are overwhelmingly not based upon observation or empirical evidence available to participants, but rather upon cuings among groups of people who jointly create the meanings they will read into current and anticipated events" (Edelman 1971, p. 32). The key phrase here is "groups of people." That is, the chances that cognitive liberation (McAdam 1982) will occur are assumed to be greatest in precisely the kind of collective settings I have called mobilization contexts.

This assumption would seem to be intuitively reasonable. Even in the unlikely event that a single person were to generate these necessary cognitions, his or her isolation would almost surely prevent their spread to the minimum number of people required to afford a reasonable basis for successful collective action. More to the point, perhaps, is the suspicion that under such conditions these cognitions would never arise in the first place. The consistent finding that links feelings of political efficacy to social integration supports this judgment (Neal and Seeman 1964; Pinard 1971; Sayre 1980). In the absence of strong interpersonal links to others, people are likely to feel powerless to change conditions even if they perceive present conditions as favorable to such efforts.

To this finding one might add the educated supposition that what Ross (1977) calls the "fundamental attribution error"—the tendency of people to explain their situation as a function of individual rather than situational factors—is more likely to occur under conditions of personal isolation than under those of integration. Lacking the information and perspective that others afford, isolated individuals would seem especially prone to explain their troubles on the basis of personal rather than "system attributions" (Ferree and Miller 1977).

The practical significance of this distinction comes from the fact that only system attributions afford the necessary rationale for movement activity. For movement analysts, then, the key question becomes, What social circumstances are productive of "system attributions?" If we follow Ferree and Miller, the likely answer is that the chances "of a system attribution would appear to be greatest among extremely homogeneous people who are in intense regular contact with each other" (1977, p. 34). In our terms, the chances that "cognitive liberation" will occur would seem greatest in the type of mobilization context described earlier. These settings also provide a favorable context for a second important interpersonal process.

Value Expectancy and the Aggregation of Choice

Finally, the generation of favorable expectations regarding the prospects for successful collective action would also seem most likely to occur in the kind of collective settings under discussion here. As useful as Klandermans' application of value expectancy theory is, it nonetheless tends, as most choice theories do, to divorce the individual actor and the subjective utilities that shape his or her choices from the collective settings in which these utilities are derived.

This is not to deny that the individual remains the ultimate focus of choice processes. At the same time the generation of expectancies on which choice depends remains a profoundly social process requiring attention to and information about other relevant actors. The significance of these micromobilization contexts, then, stems, in part, from the ready access to information they afforded members. Imagine two students trying to decide whether to attend an antinuke rally to be held on campus. Imagine further that one of the students lives in a dorm and is a member of several political groups on campus, while the other commutes to school and is not a member of any campus groups. Irrespective of their attitudes concerning nuclear power, which of the two students is more likely to attend the rally? Probably the student who is more integrated into campus life. Why? There are several reasons but among the most significant is the fact that our erstwhile activist is involved in several collective settings—the dorm and political group—that favor the generation of high expectations concerning the prospects for successful group action. To the extent that others in either setting are indicating that they might attend the rally, the likelihood that our potential recruit will go are increased as well.

But it isn't just that these collective settings encourage choices favoring participation. They also serve as contexts within which these individual choices can be aggregated into a collective plan of action. It isn't enough that individual actors choose to participate in activism. Their choices must then be combined with those of others in such a way as to make group action possible. Micromobilization contexts provide the setting within which this aggregation process can occur.

We are now in a position to assess the role of these micromobilization contexts in the recruitment of volunteers to a specific instance of activism: the 1964 Mississippi Freedom Summer project. That campaign brought nearly one thousand primarily white college students from the northern United States to Mississippi—a state in the American South—for all, or part of, the summer of 1964. While there, the volunteers taught black children, attempted to register black voters, and, by their mere presence, dramatized the continued denial of civil rights throughout the American South. As instances of activism go it would be hard to imagine many more costly or potentially risky than the Freedom Summer campaign. Volunteers were asked to commit an average of two months of their summer to a project that was to prove physically and emotionally harrowing for nearly everyone. Moreover, in this effort they were expected to be financially independent. Thus they were asked not only to give up their chance of summer employment elsewhere but to support themselves as well.

The project itself began in early June with the first contingent of volunteers arriving in Mississippi fresh from a week of training at Oxford, Ohio. Within 10 days 3 project members, Mickey Schwerner, James Chaney, and Andrew Goodman, had been kidnapped and beaten to death by a group of segregationists led by Mississippi law enforcement officers. That event set the tone for the summer as the remaining volunteers endured beatings, bombings, and arrest. Moreover most did so while sharing the grinding poverty and unrelieved fear that was the daily lot of the black families that housed them.

A. The Study

Preliminary to their participation in the campaign all prospective volunteers were required to fill out detailed applications providing information on, among other topics, their organizational affiliations, college activities, reasons for volunteering, and record of previous arrest. On the basis of these applications (and, on occasion, subsequent interviews), the prospective volunteer was either accepted or rejected. Acceptance did not necessarily mean participation in the campaign, however. In advance of the summer many of the accepted applicants informed campaign staffers that they would not be taking part in the summer effort after all. Completed applications for all three groups—rejects, participants, and withdrawals—were copied and coded from the originals, which now repose in the archives of the Martin Luther King, Jr., Center for the Study of Nonviolence in Atlanta, Georgia and the New Mississippi Foundation in Jackson, Mississippi.[1] A total of 1,068 applications were coded in connection with this study. The breakdown of these applications by group is as follows: 720 participants, 239 withdrawals, 55 rejections, 54 whose status regarding the summer project is unclear. Together these applications provide a unique source of archival data for assessing the relative importance of various factors in recruitment to activism.

B. Results

Attitudinal Affinity

Attitudinal accounts of activism are based on the assumption that people participate in social movements because of some underlying ideological affinity with the movement. At one level this claim is unobjectionable. Certainly the Freedom Summer volunteers were supportive of the general goals and ideals of the American civil rights movement. The real question is, were the prior attitudes of the volunteers sufficient in themselves to account for their participation. The answer I would offer here is a qualified no. While there were small, suggestive differences between participants and withdrawals in the ideological motivations they brought to the project, these differences would not appear to be enough to account for their very different courses of action that summer.

Not surprisingly, *all* of the applicants—participants and withdrawals alike—emerge as highly committed, articulate supporters of the goals and values of

Table 1.   Percentage of Participants and Withdrawals Reporting Various Motivations for Participation in the Freedom Summer Project

	Participants		Withdrawals	
Self-oriented Motives	%	(N = 300)	%	(N = 300)
As a vehicle for personal witness	39	(116)	32	(44)
As a vehicle for personal education (regarding the "plight of the Negro," regarding the "southern way of life," etc.)	21	(64)	24	(32)
As a vehicle for expiating guilt	3	(8)	6	(8)
As a vehicle for personal growth ("to test myself," etc.)	4	(12)	6	(8)
To formally affiliate with SNCC or the civil rights movement	24	(72)	26	(36)
As a vehicle for formal academic study	1	(4)	3	(4)
To experience the excitement of the project ("to be where the action is," etc.)	4	(12)	6	(8)
To gain teaching or other career related experience	11	(32)	3	(4)
Other self-oriented motives	4	(12)	4	(16)
Total self-oriented motives*	—	(332)	—	(150)
Other-oriented Motives				
To aid in the full realization of democracy in the United States	12	(36)	18	(24)
To help improve the lot of blacks generally	82	(246)	65	(89)
To aid in the equalization of black educational opportunities	15	(44)	21	(28)
To aid in the equalization of black political opportunities	13	(40)	6	(8)
To demonstrate white concern for black civil rights	3	(8)	9	(12)
To dramatize the depths of racism in the United States	3	(8)	6	(8)
To act as an example to others	7	(20)	0	(10)
To demonstrate the power of nonviolence as a vehicle for social change	5	(16)	3	(4)
Total other-related motives +	—	(418)	—	(172)

*Average number of self-oriented motives per: participants = 1.11
                                                                    withdrawals = 1.10
+Average number of other-oriented motives per: participants = 1.37
                                                                    withdrawals = 1.21

the summer campaign. The logic of the application process virtually assured this outcome. To apply, interested parties had to seek out and obtain a five page application from a campus representative of the project. The applicant then had to fill out the form and in many cases submit to a formal "screening interview" by the campus coordinator of the summer project. In short, applying to the project required considerable effort on the applicant's part, no doubt ensuring a kind of natural selection in the application process. Presumably, only those with considerable attitudinal affinity for the project would have been willing to expend the time and energy required of an applicant.

One question from the application provides a kind of crude confirmation of this presumption. Applicants were asked simply to explain why they "would like to work in Mississippi."[1] As noted earlier, *all* the answers to this item reflected an overwhelmingly positive stance toward the goals of Freedom Summer as well as the movement in general. More relevant for our purposes, there were only slight differences between participants and withdrawals in the thematic content of their answers.

An open-ended list of 17 motivational "themes" was used to capture the applicant's reason(s) for applying to the project. In addition, a single dichotomous code was used to distinguish between answers that reflected either a "self" or "other" motivation for participating. Statements that stressed the *personal* challenge of the campaign or the *individual* benefits of the experience (e.g., teaching experience), were coded as "self-interested" motives. Those that reflected more general, "selfless" concerns were categorized as "other-oriented" motives. However, neither of the above code dimensions captured any significant distinctions between participants and withdrawals. The average number of motives ascribed to both groups that were categorized as "self" or "other interested" was not statistically different.[2] Nor did the 17 thematic code categories produce a characteristic motivational "profile" for participants distinct from that of the no-shows. Both groups tended to rely on the same mix of themes in explaining their reasons for participating.

Admittedly, the single open-ended question described above hardly tells us all we would want to know about the underlying attitudes and values of the applicants. What is clear is that the participants' ideological identification with the project was not irrelevant to their later participation. Rather the participants' consistently strong attitudinal support for the project would seem to have been a necessary prerequisite for their later involvement. What is equally clear, however, is that it was not sufficient to ensure that involvement. On both attitudinal dimensions participants and withdrawals are virtually indistinguishable.

If the motivations underlying participation do not differ significantly for withdrawals and participants, what does? One possible answer to this question is that participants were integrated into a variety of micromobilization contexts to a greater degree than were withdrawals. By micromobilization contexts I mean any formal organizations, informal networks, or social relationships that serve to "pull" the potential recruit into activism. At least three different micromobilization contexts have been identified in the literature as midwives to the recruitment process. The first of these agents, formal organizations, can facilitate recruitment in two ways. First, individuals can be drawn into a movement by virtue of their involvement in organizations that serve as the associational network out of which a new movement emerges. This was true, as Melder (1964) notes, in the case of the nineteenth-century women's rights movement in the United States, with a disproportionate number of the movement's recruits coming from existing abolitionist groups. Curtis and Zurcher (1973) have observed a similar pattern in connection with the rise of two antipornography groups. In their study, the authors provide convincing data to support their contention that recruits were overwhelmingly drawn from the broad "multiorganizational fields" in which both groups were embedded.

Second, established organizations can serve as the primary source of movement participants through what Oberschall (1973, p. 125) has termed "bloc recruitment." In this pattern, movements do not so much emerge out of established organizations as they represent a merger of such groups. Hicks, for instance, has described how the Populist party was created through a coalition of established farmers' organizations (1961). The rapid rise of the free-speech movement at Berkeley has been attributed to a similar merger of existing campus organizations (Lipset and Wolin 1965). Both of these patterns, then, highlight the organizational basis of much movement recruitment and support Oberschall's general conclusion: "mobilization does not occur through recruitment of large numbers of isolated and solitary individuals. It occurs as a result of recruiting blocs of people who are already highly organized and participants" (1973, p. 125).

Individual activists have also been identified as an important agent in the recruitment process. Here it matters little whether the potential recruit is involved in formal organizations or not. Instead, the emphasis is on the necessity for prior *personal* contact with a *single* activist who introduces the recruit to the movement. Empirical support for the importance of a prior relationship with a single activist can be found in the work of Gerlach and Hine (1970), and Snow, Zurcher, and Ekland-Olson (1980).

With respect to these relationships it is useful to ask two empirical questions. First, are they more important than formal organizations in encouraging activism? Second, what *type* of relationship is more effective in recruiting other activists? Here Granovetter's (1973) distinction between "strong" and "weak" ties is of special interest. Granovetter and others have found that weak ties, more so than strong, are crucial to diffusion processes. We will want to see whether, in fact, this pattern holds true in the case of the Freedom Summer project. Did participants know more volunteers prior to the summer than did withdrawals? And, if so, did these prior contacts represent primarily weak or strong ties?

Finally, to these two agents—organizations and individual activists—we can add a third. I am referring to the movement in which the high risk episode is embedded. Here the micromobilization context is not a specific organization or person but the subcultural "world" of the movement. In such cases, prior involvement in the movement is expected to have embedded the individual in a network of organizational and interpersonal ties that are likely to draw him or her into subsequent actions.

In assessing the importance of these three micromobilization contexts, each will be looked at separately in terms of how well they differentiate Freedom Summer participants from withdrawals. Then the effects of all three will be measured simultaneously by means of a logit regression equation predicting participation in the summer project.

1. *Organizational affiliations.* One of the most significant of these contexts is the total number of organizational affiliations listed by the two groups on their applications. Table 2 clearly shows that participants tend to belong to more organizations than do withdrawals. To highlight this contrast we can compare the percentage within each group that belongs to less than or more than two organizations. Forty-eight percent of the withdrawals fall into the former category, as compared to only 35% of the participants. On the other hand, 66% of the participants, but only 52% of the withdrawals, belong to two or more organizations.

But as Table 3 indicates, it is not simply that participants and withdrawals differ in the number of organizations they belong to; the *type* of organizations

Table 2. Number of Organizational Affiliations by the Summer Status of the Freedom Summer Applicants* (in percentages)

Number of Organizations	Summer Status			
	Participants		Withdrawals	
	%	N	%	N
0	14	(99)	18	(43)
1	21	(143)	30	(71)
2	23	(157)	20	(48)
3	19	(131)	15	(36)
4	13	(87)	10	(23)
5 or more	11	(74)	7	(17)
Totals	101	(691)	100	(238)

Note:
    * Average number of organizations by project status:
        Participants = 2.4
        Withdrawals = 1.9
    difference significant at the .01 level using a two-tailed t-test.

Table 3. Percentage of Participants and Withdrawals Who Belong
to Various Types of Organizations

Type of Organization	Summer Status			
	Participants		Withdrawals	
	%	N	%	N
Civil rights organization	50	(347)	40	(96)
Peace or disarmament group	12	(84)	7	(18)
Socialist organization	3	(23)	2	(6)
Democratic or Republican party organizations	13	(91)	11	(26)
Other political organizations	16	(108)	12	(29)
Church or religious groups	22	(150)	18	(43)
Student club or social organization	20	(140)	24	(56)
Student government	8	(57)	9	(21)
Student newspaper	6	(43)	7	(17)
Academic club or organization	12	(81)	16	(37)

differs as well. Participants tend to be members of more explicitly political organizations than withdrawals. Especially significant, given the focus of the summer project, is the difference in the percentage of each group that included civil rights organizations among their affiliations. Fifty percent of the participants did so against 40% of the withdrawals. Similar percentage differences are evident in regard to all other major categories of political organizations. Conversely, withdrawals came disproportionately from the ranks of social or academic organizations. Thus not only do participants belong to more organizations but the political nature of these organizations means that participants were likely exposed to more pressure or encouragement to honor their applications than were withdrawals.

2. *Prior ties to other applicants.* The data also allow us to measure the strength and the type of interpersonal ties that existed between the applicants prior to the summer project. One question on the application asked the subject to list at least ten persons they wished to be kept informed of their summer activities. Reflecting the public relations goals of the project, these names were gathered in an effort to mobilize a well-heeled northern liberal constituency who might put pressure on the federal government to alter civil rights policy. Judging from the names they listed, most of the applicants seem to have been very aware of this goal. The names most often provided by the applicants were those of parents, parents' friends, professors, ministers, or any other noteworthy or influential *adults* they had contact with. Quite often, however, the applicant would include another applicant or well-known activist in their list of names.

Table 4. Percentage of Participants and Withdrawals
Reporting Strong and Weak Ties to Other Participants,
Known Activists, and Withdrawals

	Participants				Withdrawals			
	Yes		No		Yes		No	
	%	(N)	%	(N)	%	(N)	%	(N)
Strong tie to participant	25	(177)	75	(540)	12	(28)	88	(213)
Weak tie to participant	21	(150)	79	(567)	14	(33)	86	(208)
Strong tie to known activist	11	(81)	89	(636)	4	(10)	96	(231)
Weak tie to known activist	5	(35)	95	(682)	3	(7)	97	(234)
Strong tie to withdrawal	3	(25)	97	(692)	5	(12)	95	(229)
Weak tie to withdrawal	7	(52)	93	(665)	8	(19)	92	(222)

This enabled me to construct a measure of the interpersonal ties connecting participants and withdrawals to (a) other Freedom Summer volunteers, (b) known activists, and (c) withdrawals from the project. In doing so, I was careful to distinguish between "strong" and "weak ties" (Granovetter 1973). Persons listed directly on the subject's application were designated as strong ties. Weak ties were defined as persons who were listed on the application of one of the subject's strong ties.

The interesting finding for our purposes is that participants supplied many more names of other volunteers and well-known activists than did the withdrawals. The differences were especially pronounced in the case of strong ties, with participants listing better than twice the number of volunteers and nearly three times the number of activists as did those subjects who withdrew from the project. This finding makes a great deal of intuitive sense. While weak ties may be more effective as diffusion channels (Granovetter 1973), strong ties would seem to embody a greater potential for influencing behavior. Having a close friend engage in some behavior is certainly going to have more of an impact on a person than if a friend of a friend does so.

It is also interesting to note that participants listed a smaller percentage of withdrawals in both strong and weak ties categories than did the withdrawals. However, the relevant comparison here is not these percentage differences but the distribution of participants and withdrawals among all ties to other applicants listed by the two subject groups. In this case, the contrast is especially striking. Of the 202 strong ties to other applicants listed by participants, only 25 were to persons who later withdrew from the project. This is a withdrawal rate of 12%, as compared to the 25% rate for all applicants. By contrast, 30% (12 of 40) of the withdrawals' strong ties to other applicants were to persons who later withdrew from the project. Just as having a close friend participate in the project increased the subject's chances of participation, so too did the withdrawal of a close friend decrease those chances. Withdrawals, then, were not only less likely to list another applicant as a friend, but those they did list were two and one-half times more likely to withdraw from the project than those identified by participants.

Finally, we can assess the combined effect of each applicant's interpersonal ties by assigning a numeric value to each of the six classes of contacts shown in Table 4. Shown below, the value assigned to each category of tie is intended to capture its hypothesized effect on the subject's likelihood of participation:

Category of Tie	Numeric Value
strong tie to participant	+3
weak tie to participant	+2
strong tie to activist	+2
weak tie to activist	+1
no tie	0
weak tie to withdrawal	−1
strong tie to withdrawal	−2

Using these point values, an "interpersonal contact score" was computed for each applicant. The distribution of these scores for both groups of applicants is shown in Table 5.

Table 5. Percentage Distribution of Interpersonal Contact Scores by Applicant Status*

Scores	Participants		Withdrawals	
	%	N	%	N
-1 to -4	2	(11)	5	(11)
0	64	(459)	76	(184)
1-3	13	(96)	8	(19)
4-6	7	(49)	6	(14)
7-9	7	(47)	3	(7)
10+	8	(55)	2	(6)
	101	(717)	100	(241)

Note:
  * Average score by applicant status:
      Participant = 2.36
      Withdrawal = .97
  Difference significant at the .001 level using a two-tailed t-test.

Clearly there is a strong positive relationship between participation and the weighted sum of an applicant's interpersonal ties. The average score for participants was nearly two and one-half times greater than that for withdrawals. Even more dramatic, of those applicants who listed at least one interpersonal tie, 19% of the withdrawals, but only 4% of the participants, had scores below zero. Taken together, these findings suggest a simple conclusion. Both the nature and greater number of interpersonal ties enjoyed by participants would appear to have had a significant effect on their decision to go to Mississippi.

3. *Extent of prior civil rights activism.* The final comparative measure of integration into micromobilization contexts concerns the extent of prior civil rights activism by both participants and withdrawals. Both participants and withdrawals were asked to list on their applications any previous civil rights activities they had been involved in. In coding these activities, a numeric value was assigned to each activity based on its intensity relative to all other forms of civil rights activism. Each subject then received a final activity score computed as the sum of the points total for the activities reported on their applications. Table 6 affords a comparison of the distribution of these scores for both participants and withdrawals.

Table 6.   Percentage of Participants and Withdrawals
by Level of Prior Civil Rights Activity*

Level of Prior Activity+	Participants		Withdrawals	
	%	N	%	N
None	24	(174)	34	(81)
Low	31	(224)	37	(88)
Moderate	25	(177)	19	(46)
High	20	(145)	10	(24)
TOTAL	100	(720)	100	(239)

Note:
   * Average score by applicant status:
      Participant = 5.4
      Withdrawal = 3.9
   Difference significant at the .001 level using a two-tailed t-test.

+ For the purpose of this table, the four activity categories correspond to the following range of scores on
  the activity scale:
     none = 0
     low = 1-4
     moderate = 5-10
     high = 11 +

Table 7.   Logit Regression on the Effect of Various Independent Variables
            on Participation in the Freedom Summer Project

Independent Variable	Dependent Variables b	Summer Status+ SE(b)
Integration measures		
number of organizational affiliations	.182**	.058
interpersonal contact score	.005**	.002
level of prior activism	.044	.023
Major		
Social Science	-.236	.156
Other Majors	-.123	.156
Home Region		
West North Central	.265	.297
New England	.014	.256
Mid-Atlantic	.096	.216
East North Central	.045	.224
West	.401	.309
South	-.009	.262
College Region		
West North Central	-.348	.276
New England	-.222	.182
Mid-Atlantic	-.304	.173
East North Central	-.378	.265
West	-.440*	.193
South	-.012	.246
Race-White	.070	.107
Gender-Female	-.209*	.088
Age	.277*	.141
Highest Grade Completed	.026	.075
Distance from home to Mississippi	-.00003	.0003
Constant	-.159	1.06

N = 794
** = p < .01
* = p < .05
+ = summer status: 0 = withdrawals
                  1 = participants

Goodness of fit chi-square = 860.486 with 771 d.f. (p-value = .013)

As expected, participants had significantly higher levels of prior involvement than did withdrawals. Moreover, a closer look at the data shows that the differences are more pronounced at the upper end of the distribution, so that the proportion of participants ajudged to have "high" activity scores was twice as great as the comparable figure for withdrawals. At the other extreme, better than a third of the withdrawals, but fewer than a quarter of the participants, reported no previous civil rights activity.

Finally, we can assess the combined effect of these and a number of other factors on the applicant's chances of participation. By treating the individual's summer status—either participant or withdrawal—as a dichotomous dependent variable, we can attempt to explain participation by means of a logit regression equation comprising the following independent variables: age, gender, race, highest grade level completed, home region, college region, distance from home to Mississippi, major in school, number of organizational affiliations, interpersonal contact score, and level of prior activism. The results of this analysis are reported in Table 7.

The data presented in Table 7 attest to the importance of integration into micromobilization contexts as a predictor of activism. Of all the independent variables it is the three "integration measures" that bear the strongest relationship to variation in participation. Here several specific findings are worth highlighting. First, it is interesting to note that "level of prior activism" does *not* make a significant contribution to variation in the dependent variable. While participants clearly displayed higher levels of prior civil rights activity— see Table 6—than withdrawals, these involvements did not significantly affect the likelihood that they would participate in the summer project. Apparently, their involvement in Freedom Summer did not, in any amorphous way, grow out of their prior civil rights activities. Rather, even these veteran activists required tangible contact with a recruiting agent—either organizational or interpersonal—to encourage their involvement. Thus researchers who stress the facilitative effects of recruitment through either existing organizations or by means of prior interpersonal ties will find support in these data.

Perhaps the most interesting finding concerns the differential impact of various types of interpersonal contacts on likelihood of participation. Table 7 shows that of all the independent variables it is the sum of a person's ties to other applicants or known activists (interpersonal contact score) that bears the strongest relationship to participation. However, when this variable is broken down into the three dichotomous variables that are its principal components—presence or absence of (a) strong ties to participants or known activists, (b) weak ties to participants or activists, (c) strong ties to withdrawals—the explanatory significance of the measure emerges in Table 8 as exclusively a function of strong rather than weak ties. When the analysis is rerun substituting the three dichotomous contact variables for the single contact score, only the two strong tie variables remain significant. Having a close friend participate or withdraw from the project did, in fact, affect a subject's chances of participation, while the presence or absence of weak ties to other volunteers seems to have had little impact in most cases.

Table 8. Logit Regression on the Effect of Various Independent Variables on Participation in the Freedom Summer Project

Independent Variable	Dependent Variable b	Summer Status+ SE(b)
Integration measures		
number of organizational affiliations	.194**	.059
level of prior activism	.032	.018
categories of interpersonal contact		
strong tie to participant or		
known activist	.604**	.144
weak tie to participant or		
known activist	.259	.149
strong tie to withdrawal	-.395*	.201
Major		
Social Sciences	-.258	.158
Other Majors	-.140	.158
Home Region		
West North Central	.236	.298
New England	.065	.257
Mid-Atlantic	.063	.218
East North Central	.011	.226
West	.444	.311
South	.008	.263
College Region		
West North Central	-.340	.288
New England	-.245	.203
Mid-Atlantic	-.364	.193
East North Central	-.469*	.200
West	-.395	.216
South	-.029	.257
Race-White	.063	.108
Gender-Female	-.206*	.089
Age	.315*	.142
Highest Grade Completed	.030	.076
Distance from home to Mississippi	-.0001	.0003
Constant	-.348	1.12

N = 794
** = p < .01
* = p < .05
+ = summer status: 0 = withdrawals
　　　　　　　　　1 = participants

Goodness of fit chi-square = 843.761 with 769 d.f. (p-value = .028)

Summary

The evidence reviewed above clearly suggests the crucial importance of micromobilization contexts in shaping participation in the Freedom Summer campaign. Participants consistently scored higher than withdrawals on both organizational and interpersonal items measuring integration into activist networks. Although the differences between the two groups on these items were not always large, the direction of those differences remained consistent, suggesting but a single conclusion: regardless of their level of ideological commitment to the project, it was the extent and nature of the applicant's structural location vis-à-vis the project that best accounts for his or her participation in the Freedom Summer campaign.

Does this mean that the applicants' attitudes or values had no influence on their chances of participating? Absolutely not. Both their willingness to go through the application process and their answers to the open-ended item attest to the participants' high levels of attitudinal support for the project. It is simply that, according to these measures, participants and withdrawals exhibit similar levels of support. Thus attitudinal affinity must be thought of as a necessary, but not sufficient, cause of participation in activism. The suggestion, then, is that neither a strict structural nor individual motivational model can account for participation in this or any other instance of activism. An intense ideological identification with the values of the campaign acts to "push" the individual in the direction of participation, while a prior history of activism and integration into supportive networks acts as the structural "pull" encouraging the individual to make good on his or her strongly held beliefs.

What do these findings have to say about the broader macro political perspectives—resource mobilization, political process, new social movements—that have recently come to dominate theorizing about social movements? In one sense, not a whole lot. That is, these perspectives are concerned with those broad political factors that give rise to widespread *collective* action, while the findings presented here concern the dynamics of *individual* recruitment to activism. On the other hand, these findings serve to remind us that whatever macro factors underlie collective action, it is the microdynamics of mobilization and recruitment that produce and sustain a movement. In their basic dynamics, then, "new" movements are not likely to differ from "old" movements. The macro political roots of movements may vary, but the micro structural dynamics of collective action are likely to look very similar from movement to movement.

ACKNOWLEDGMENTS

My deep appreciation goes to Louise Cook, Head Librarian and Archivist at the King Center, and to Jan Hillegas—herself a summer volunteer—of the New Mississippi

Foundation for all their help in locating and copying the application materials used in this project. Without their help, this research would have been impossible.

NOTES

1.   In actuality, not all applicants were asked this open-ended question. At least 6 different application forms were used in this project, and only two included this item. In all, 300 of the participants and 136 of the withdrawals answered the question. A comparison of those who answered and those who did not answer this question turned up no significant differences between the two groups.

2.   While not statistically significant, the greater number of other-oriented motives invoked by participants in their narratives is certainly suggestive. It is also interesting, in light of the singular importance attributed to selective incentives by many theorists (cf. Olson 1965), to note that participants listed no more self-oriented motives—or selective incentives—than withdrawals. Following Olson and the rational choice theorists (Hechter, Friedman, and Applebaum 1982), we would have expected withdrawals to have listed significantly fewer such motives than participants.

REFERENCES

Aya, Rod. 1979. "Theories of revolution reconsidered: Contrasting models of collective violence." *Theory and Society* 8:39-99.

Brand, Karl Werner. 1982. *Neue soziale Bewegungen, Entstehung, Funktion und Perspektive neuer Protestpotentiale, eine Zwischenbilanz.* Opladen: Westdeutscher Verlag.

Crawford, Thomas and Murray Naditch. 1970. "Relative deprivation, powerlessness and militancy: The psychology of social protest." *Psychiatry* 33:208-23.

Curtis, Russell L. and Louis A. Zurcher, Jr. 1973. "Stable resources of project movement: The multi-organizational field." *Social Forces* 52:53-60.

Davies, James C. 1969. "The J-curve of Rising and Declining Satisfactions as a Cause of Some Great Revolutions and a Contained Rebellion." In Hugh Davis Graham and Ted Robert Gurr (eds.), *Violence in America: Historical and Comparative Perspectives.* Washington, D.C.: U.S. Government Printing Office.

Donati, Paolo R. 1984. "Organization between movement and institution." *Social Science Information* 23:837-59.

Edelman, Murray. 1971. *Politics as Symbolic Action.* New Haven: Yale University Press.

Eisinger, Peter K. 1973. "The conditions of protest behavior in American cities." *American Political Science Review* 67:11-28.

Evans, Sarah. 1980. *Personal Politics.* New York: Vintage.

Feierabend, Ivo, Rosalind Feierbend, and Betty Nesvold. 1969. "Social Change and Political Violence: Cross National Patterns." Pages 497-545 in Hugh Davis Graham and Ted Robert Gurr (eds.), *Violence in America: Historical and Comparative Perspectives.* Washington, D.C.: U.S. Government Printing Office.

Ferree, Myra Marx and Frederick D. Miller. 1977. "Winning Hearts and Minds: Some Social Psychological Contributions to the Resource Mobilization Perspective of Social Movements." Unpublished paper.

Gale, Richard P. 1982. "Social Movements and the State: The Environmental Movement, Countermovement, and the Transformation of Natural Resource Agencies." Unpublished paper.

Gamson, William A. 1975. *The Strategy of Social Protest.* Homewood, Ill.: Dorsey Press.

Gamson, William A., Bruce Fireman, and Steve Rytina. 1982. *Encounters with Unjust Authority*. Homewood, Ill.: Dorsey Press.

Gerlach, Luther P. and Virginia H. Hine. 1970. *People, Power, Change: Movements of Social Transformation*. Indianapolis: Bobbs-Merrill.

Geschwender, James. 1964. "Social structure and the Negro revolt: An examination of some hypotheses." *Social Forces* 43:250-56.

Granovetter, Mark. 1973. "The Strength of Weak Ties." *American Journal of Sociology* 18: 1360-80.

Gurr, Ted. 1970. *Why Men Rebel*. Princeton: Princeton University Press.

Hicks, John D. 1961. *The Populist Revolt*. Lincoln: University of Nebraska Press.

Hirsch, J. 1980. *Der Sicherheitsstaat*. Frankfurt: EVA.

Jenkins, J. Craig. 1983. "Resource Mobilization Theory and the Study of Social Movements." *Annual Review of Sociology* 9:527-53.

Jenkins, J. Craig and Charles Perrow. 1977. "Insurgency of the Powerless: Farm Workers Movements (1946-1972)." *American Sociological Review* 42:249-68.

Klandermans, Bert. 1984. "Mobilization and participation: Social-psychological expansions of resource mobilization theory." *American Sociological Review* 49:583-600.

Klandermans, Bert. 1986. "New social movements and resource mobilization: The European and the American approach." *International Journal of Mass Emergencies and Disasters*. Special issue, *Comparative Perspectives and Research on Collective Behavior and Social Movements* 4:13-37.

Kornhauser, William. 1959. *The Politics of Mass Society*. Glencoe, Ill.: Free Press.

Lang, Kurt and Gladys Lang. 1961. *Collective Dynamics*. New York: Crowell.

Lipset, Seymour Martin and Sheldon Wolin. 1965. *The Berkeley Student Revolt*. New York: Doubleday Anchor.

Lipsky, Michael. 1970. *Protest in City Politics*. Chicago: Rand-McNally.

McAdam, Doug. 1982. *Political Process and the Development of Black Insurgency, 1930-1970*. Chicago: University of Chicago Press.

McCarthy, John D. and Mayer N. Zald. 1973. *The Trend of Social Movements in America: Professionalization and Resource Mobilization*. Morristown, N.J.: General Learning Press.

McCarthy, John D. and Mayer N. Zald. 1977. "Resource mobilization and social movements: A partial theory." *American Journal of Sociology* 82:1212-41.

Melder, Keith Eugene. 1964. "The Beginnings of the Women's Rights Movement in the United States." Ph.D. dissertation, Yale University.

Melucci, Alberto. 1980. "The new social movements: A theoretical approach." *Social Science Information* 19:199-226.

Melucci, Alberto. 1981. "Ten Hypothesis for the Analysis of New Movements." Pages 173-94 in Diana Pinto (ed.), *Contemporary Italian Sociology*. Cambridge: Cambridge University Press.

Molotch, Harvey. 1970. "Oil in Santa Barbara and power in America." *Sociological Inquiry* 40:131-44.

Morris, Aldon D. 1984. *The Origins of the Civil Rights Movement*. New York: Free Press.

Neal, Arthur G. and Melvin Seeman. 1964. "Organizations and powerlessness: A test of the mediation hypothesis." *American Sociological Review* 29:216-26.

O'Connor, James. 1973. *The Fiscal Crisis of the State*. St. Martin's Press: New York.

Olson, Mancur, Jr. 1965. *The Logic of Collective Action: Public Goods and the Theory of Groups*. Cambridge: Harvard University Press.

Opp, Karl-Dieter. 1985. "Soft incentives and collective action: Participation in the anti-nuclear movement," *British Journal of Political Science* 16:87-112.

Pinard, Maurice. 1971. *The Rise of a Third Party: A Study in Crisis Politics*. Englewood Cliffs, N.J.: Prentice-Hall.

Piven, Frances Fox and Richard A. Cloward. 1979. *Poor People's Movements: Why They Succeed, How They Fail.* New York: Vintage.

Rule, James and Charles Tilly. 1975. "Political Process in Revolutionary France, 1830-1832." Pages 41-85 in John M. Merriman (ed.), *1830 in France.* New York: New Viewpoints.

Sayre, Cynthia Woolever. 1980. "The Impact of Voluntary Association Involvement on Social-Psychological Attitudes." Paper presented at the Annual Meeting of the American Sociological Association, New York City, August 27-31.

Schwartz, Michael. 1976. *Radical Protest and Social Structure.* New York: Academic Press.

Searles, Ruth and J. Allen Williams, Jr. 1962. "Negro college students' participation in sit-ins." *Social Forces* 40:215-20.

Selznick, Phillip. 1960. *The Organizational Weapon.* New York: Free Press.

Shorter, Edward and Charles Tilly. 1974. *Strikes in France, 1830-1968.* London: Cambridge University Press.

Sitkoff, Harvard. 1978. *A New Deal for Blacks.* New York: Oxford University Press.

Skocpol, Theda. 1979. *States and Social Revolutions.* New York: Cambridge University Press.

Smelser, Neil J. 1962. *Theory of Collective Behavior.* New York: Free Press.

Snow, David A., E. Burke Rochford, Jr., Steven K. Worden, and Robert D. Benford. 1984. "Frame alignment processes, micromobilization, and movement participation." *American Sociological Review* 51:464-81.

Tarrow, Sidney. 1983. *Struggling to Reform: Social Movements and Policy Change during Cycles of Protest.* Western Societies Paper No. 15. Ithaca, N.Y.: Cornell University.

Tilly, Charles. 1978. *From Mobilization to Revolution.* Reading, Mass: Addison-Wesley.

Turner, Ralph H. and Lewis M. Killian. 1972. *Collective Behavior.* 2d ed. Englewood Cliffs, N.J.: Prentice-Hall.

Useem, Bert. 1980. "solidarity model, breakdown model, and the Boston anti-busing movement." *American Sociological Review* 45:357-69.

Walsh, Edward J. 1981. "Resource mobilization and citizen protest in communities around Three Mile Island." *Social Problems* 29:1-21.

Wilson, Kenneth L. and Anthony M. Orum. 1976. "Mobilizing people for collective political action." *Journal of Political and Military Sociology* 4:187-202.

RECRUITMENT PROCESSES IN CLANDESTINE POLITICAL ORGANIZATIONS:
ITALIAN LEFT-WING TERRORISM

Donatella della Porta

I. RECRUITMENT IN TERRORIST ORGANIZATIONS: AN INTRODUCTION

Of all the phenomena that characterized the history of Italy in the 1970s, terrorism has had the most dramatic impact on the collective memory. At that time many questions arose about the causes of such a widespread and lasting wave of political violence. The peculiarity of the political culture and the gravity of some social problems were singled out as the environmental preconditions for its emergence. Some legal organizations were accused of offering structures and legitimation to terrorist groups. The fact that a large number of people were believed to be involved increased the need to understand the motivations that led to the violent behavior of individuals who had been politically socialized in a consolidated democratic regime.

International Social Movement Research, Vol. 1, pages 155-169.
Supplement to Research in Social Movements, Conflicts and Change
Copyright © 1988 by JAI Press Inc.
All rights of reproduction in any form reserved.
ISBN: 0-89232-955-6

Many of these questions remained unanswered at the time. It is only recently, with the change in the political climate and the availability of new sources of information, that it has become possible to analyze this phenomenon with a greater degree of historical precision. As part of a wider research project on Italian left-wing terrorism (della Porta in preparation), this essay deals with one aspect of individual motivations for engaging in noninstitutional forms of political behavior: recruitment into clandestine organizations.

In the sociological literature the most radical forms of protest have often been explained by the assumed pathology of the militants. In the case of clandestine political groups, participation has been related to personality dependence, low intelligence, egocentrism (Livingstone 1982), and frustrated attempts to build positive identities (Billing 1984; Ivianski 1983; Russell and Miller 1983; Knutson 1981; Steinoff 1976). These interpretations, however, have never been proven true by empirical research. In the few cases in which former terrorists were given personality tests, the tests were administered after their arrest, that is after the individuals involved had passed through at least two total institutions, the clandestine organization and the prison system.

Considering terrorist groups as forms of political organizations, albeit with particular characteristics, may suggest alternative hypotheses about individual participation. As I have attempted to show elsewhere (della Porta 1985 and 1986), left-wing underground groups originated inside a wider social movement sector (Garner et al. 1983) whose dynamics should be taken into account in explaining terrorism and its development. What I assume, therefore, is that the motivation to join terrorist groups can be understood within the framework of categories used for other types of political organizations, especially those which are less well-equipped with institutional resources.

The main suggestion in the sociological literature on protest movements is that one should look at recruitment as an interactive process. The decision to join an organization has been explained as a result of a calculation of costs and benefits within the framework of *exchanges* (Homans 1958) conducted between the individual and the organization. Following Olson's well-known analysis of the logic of collective action (1968), many studies have taken the risks and rewards of participation into account (Wilson 1973). It has already been suggested that the different actors in conflict try to influence the determinants of the "participation function." Political activists try to increase the value of the collective good by using propaganda; to foster loyalty by strengthening moral cohesion; and to reduce costs by finding new allies (Oberschall 1973). Moreover, the value of costs and benefits cannot be objectively defined. On the contrary, it is largely dependent on the perceptions of the actors (Pizzorno 1978a; Hirschman 1982). Thus it is necessary to analyze the characteristics of the people who participated in the activities of terrorist groups in order to understand their specific evaluation of the advantages and disadvantages of their militancy.

In this context the main question is why some persons are mobilized, why some show greater sensitivity than do others to the incentives political organizations offer. It would be possible to answer this question by saying that this inclination derives from the structural characteristics of some groups of individuals. From this perspective, the militants of the less institutionalized forms of political participation would be marginal—or alienated— and looking for alternative rewards (Kornhauser 1959). But they could just as well be individuals who are very strongly rooted in the social system. A high social status could be considered conducive to collective action since it implies that an individual has more specific skills as well as a greater probability of success (see for instance, Walsh et al. 1973; Wood et al. 1984). More free time and a smaller risk of social sanction have been mentioned to account for the higher propensity for mobilization among young people.

All these hypotheses about the structural preconditions that could facilitate individual mobilizations are plausible. But none is able to explain why a person—however marginal or influential she or he may be—decides to join a political organization rather than a voluntary association, nor how she or he chooses from among different political groups. This problem can be dealt with by relating political participation to the characteristics of the primary groups to which individuals belong (Pinard 1971; Rogers et al. 1975; Aveni 1977 and 1978; Rochford 1982) and, especially, to their positive affective ties with valued others (Gerlach et al. 1970).

This hypothesis will be discussed in greater detail in the first part of this chapter. Individual participation in tight-knit social networks will be singled out as a very important precondition for joining clandestine organizations. Consequently it will be necessary to specify which kind of interpersonal network has positive effects on the kind of political militancy we are trying to explain, and this effort will lead us to look at recruitment as an interactive and cumulative process (Lofland et al. 1965; Gerlach 1970; Snow 1980; Snow et al. 1983) that brings about deep personal transformations. Individual recruitment into a clandestine political organization will therefore be examined as a stage in the collective identity building process (Pizzorno 1978a; Melucci 1985).

I will analyze the recruitment process by presenting original data on the social origins and political background of terrorists. Information has been collected on members of most of the left-wing clandestine groups active in the Italian political system during the seventies. The data refer to the four most important organizations; the Red Brigades (*Brigate Rosse*), the Proletarian Armed Groups (*Nuclei Armati Proletari*), the Front Line (*Prima Linea*), and the Communist Fighting Formations (*Formazioni Comuniste Combattenti*)—and to "minor" groups such as the Armed Fighting Formations (*Formazioni Armate Combattenti*), the Communist Fighting Units (*Unità Comuniste Combattenti*), the Communist Attack Division (*Reparti Comunisti d'Attacco*), the armed Proletarians for Communism (*Proletari Armati per il Comunismo*), the Red Guerrilla (*Guerriglia Rossa*), later called the 28th of March Brigade (*Brigata 28 Marzo*), the Lo Muscio Brigade (*Brigata Lo Muscio*), the Revolutionary Communist Movement (*Movimento Comunista Rivoluziona-rio*), the For Communism (*Per il comunismo*), and the "Nuclei". The trial records referring to judicial proceedings for crimes of political subversive association and membership in paramilitary groups were my main sources for this research. Additional reflections are the product of interviews with former terrorists which I conducted in the framework of the research on political violence in Italy carried out at the Carlo Cattaneo Institute.

II. TERRORIST MILITANCY AND SOCIAL NETWORKS

The available biographical information on terrorists shows that recruitment took place within homogeneous groups aggregated on the basis of multiple ties. Table 1 presents some quantitative data on the number of personal ties between new recruits and the members of the underground groups that they eventually joined. Some caution is needed in analyzing this table. The existing ties are, in fact, more numerous than those which can be deduced from judicial sources. Indeed the category "no ties" has been dropped, since it is very likely that personal ties existed even when they were not revealed by my source. Nevertheless, the data yields at least two important results. The first is that, in at least 843 cases out of 1,214, the decision to join an underground organization was taken by people who had at least one friend already involved in that organization. Second, in 74% of these cases, the recruit had more than one friend and in 42% he or she had even more than seven.

My data reveal some qualitative characteristics of these ties. They show, for example, that they were both multiple and strong. Decisions to join underground organizations were taken by clusters (Barnes 1969) or cliques (Burt 1980) of people connected to each other by joint involvements in more than one activity. For example, quite frequently new recruits were next-door neighbors who worked in the same department of a big factory; school friends who used to spend their vacation together; cousins who belonged to the same voluntary association. Moreover, the intensity of the relations is also shown by the high frequency of kinship ties: in 298 cases of my quantitative sample, militants in underground organizations had at least one relative—usually a husband/wife or brother/sister—who shared their commitment. These statistics thus confirm the hypothesis, which has already been suggested for the analysis of other kinds of high-cost commitment (Erickson 1981), that participation in clandestine groups is more likely when it is strengthened by previous affective ties.

Examinations and interviews allow us to understand the role of solidarity with peer groups in the decision to become a terrorist. First, they indicate how this decision is influenced by the peculiar dynamics of face-to-face relations

Table 1.   Number of Personal Ties inside the Terrorist Organizations
for the New Recruits

No. of personal Ties	N	Percent of responses	Percent of cases
One	220	26.1	28.6
Two	123	14.6	16.0
Three	40	4.7	5.2
Four	64	7.6	8.3
Between 5 and 7	45	5.3	5.9
8 and more	351	41.6	45.6
Total Responses*	843	100.0	109.6
Missing values: 371			
Valid cases: 769			

*Some people were active in more than one clandestine organization.

(Verba 1961; Coombs 1979), governed by the desire to conform and to avoid disagreements that would create cognitive dissonance. All the interviewees stressed a sense of harmony as one of the more positive aspects of the phases of their life which preceded or coincided with their recruitment into clandestine groups. A temporary lack of agreement, on the other hand, is a reason for doubts and changes of mind. The subjective perceptions of the importance of friendship network support are confirmed by the evidence of a series of choices made together with the same small groups of people. The decision to enter terrorist organizations seems to have been motivated, at least to a certain extent, by the desire to obtain the approval of friends who had made or were going to make the same decision.

The interviews yielded some data that could be used to support previous analyses of cognitive dissonance when applied to political groups. Not only solidarity with friends was in general valued very highly, but there is also a second kind of explanation: the social network in which the individual was embedded was the main source of political information. Indeed, the life histories of former terrorists show the development of a kind of oral culture of which the peer group served as the main means of diffusion. The hypothesis that interpersonal relations are a powerful communication channel through which information is passed and acquires meaning and relevance (Smith et al. 1946; McPhail et al. 1973) is therefore confirmed also in the case of Italian terrorists I interviewed, whose responsiveness to external stimuli was particularly low.

A third explanation of the role of personal ties is related to activities that involve high personal risks. For terrorist groups, and secret societies more generally, recruitment is less risky when the recruiter can trust the recruit, and vice versa. In such cases networks help to ensure a general base of loyalty.

Table 2.   Relationships Between Terrorist Recruits and their Recruiters

Relationship with recruiter	N	Percent of responses	Percent of cases
Unknown	42	11.6	12.3
Wife/husband	51	14.0	15.0
Other kin	22	6.1	6.4
Friend	159	43.8	46.6
Work mate	34	9.4	10.0
Political comrade	55	15.2	16.1
Total Responses*	363	100.0	106.4
Missing cases: 799			
Valid cases: 341			

*Some people were active in more than one clandestine organization.

The relevance of personal contacts in recruitment into the Italian terrorist organization is confirmed by the data on the relations between recruiters and recruits. As Table 2 reveals, in as many as 88% of the cases in which the nature of the tie with the recruit is known, she or he is not a stranger to the recruiter, in 44% of the cases she or he is a personal friend, and in 20% she or he is a relative.

These results are confirmed by a militant of Front Line. Speaking of the recruitment process during an interrogation, he said, "[it] happened . . . through personal ties. In this way the comrades of the *Squadre* contacted people whom they had known for a long time, who would have entertained the idea of joining the *Squadre* or at least would not have been shocked by the proposal or have not created problems for the security of the comrade who made the contact" (quoted in the Court of Turin 1980, pp. 66-69). The presence of reciprocal affective ties is therefore essential for the reducing of the risks a clandestine organization takes in contacting a potential militant.

III.   TERRORIST MILITANCY AND POLITICAL CAREERS

The presence of strong affective ties is thus a powerful explanation of individual motivations. But, quite obviously, not all the cliques of friends or the friends of terrorists joined clandestine groups. It is therefore necessary to specify which kinds of personal relations are more likely to incentivate some forms of political participation. The research on social movements has singled out the importance of such variables as ideological affinity (Wallis et al. 1982; Stark et al. 1980), common structural positions (Tilly 1978; Snow et al. 1983), or previous membership in voluntary associations (Parkin 1968; Walsh et al. 1973; Stark

Table 3.   Legal Political Organizations to which Terrorists Belonged
before Joining Underground Groups.

Legal organization	N		Percent responses		Percent cases
Italian Communist Party	17		2.1		2.8
Trade Unions	40		4.9		6.5
New Left	232		28.5		37.7
of which:					
Lotta Continua		75	9.2		12.2
Potere Operaio		52	6.4		8.5
"Autonomous" Collectives	518		63.6		84.2
of which:					
Comitati Comunisti		56	6.9		9.2
Senza Tregua		32	3.9		5.2
Rosso		42	5.2		6.8
Others	7		0.8		1.2
Total of Responses*	814		100.0		132.4
Missing cases: 525					
Valid cases: 615					

*Some people were active in more than one clandestine organization.

et al. 1980; Oberschall 1973 and 1980) in determining the capacity of a social
network for influencing the political behavior of its members. My research on
the members of terrorist groups stresses the particular importance of
participation in other political organizations. A widespread motive for joining
was the desire to show solidarity with a network of friends who all participated
in small legal political groups.

The quantitative data on the political origins of clandestine militants allow
us to make some initial observations. Table 3 provides information on the legal
organizations to which militants belonged, before joining terrorist groups. With
regard to this table it is important to remember that the data refer only to
those cases in which information about a terrorist's previous legal militancy
was gathered. Nevertheless, it is still striking in how many cases terrorists had
been committed to legal political activity before joining the underground
groups. The data indicate that recruitment to terrorism involved "political"
people, that is people who already had a political identity.

Other considerations must be taken into account in analyzing the internal
distribution of legal political involvement. First, the percentage of people
coming from the traditional left is very low: only 3% for the Communist Party
and a slightly higher 6.5% for the trade unions. Simplistic hypotheses that refer
to the disillusion felt by "hard" communist militants when faced with the
softening of their party would not fit reality. By contrast, 38% of the terrorists

had been involved in the New Left. In this group the percentage of people who had participated in *Potere Operaio* (Worker Power) and *Lotta Continua* (Continuous Struggle) is quite high. These organizations have often been accused of having provided the structures for the emerging terrorist groups, in particular by forming semi-legal bodies that have been defined as "strategic articulations of an organic terrorist project" (Ventura 1984). My data show that the breakdown of *Potere Operaio,* as well as the almost contemporaneous crisis of *Lotta Continua,* had important effects on the fortunes of the Italian radical left. But the careers of individual militants show that very few people shifted to terrorism directly from these two groups. Rather, the breakdown of these groups gave rise to a process of "autonomization" of *Comitati di Base* (Rank and File Committees) and *Collettivi Operai* (Workers Collectives) from under the guardianship of the more structured groups of the New Left (Palombarini 1982). It was in these small political nuclei, characterized by radical ideologies and violent repertoires, that many future terrorists continued their political involvement.

But the number of late 1960s militants who chose a radicalization of the conflict was quite small. The sharp increase in recruitment came about only when the entrepreneurial efforts of these people found a large potential base in another group of violence-prone political militants. While the breakdown of *Lotta Continua* and *Potere Operaio* occurred in 1973, only after 1976 did a large number of people, as many as 78% of all the recruits, join terrorist groups. Too young to have been involved in the first phases of the late 1960s protest cycle, the members of the "second generation" of terrorists began their political socialization in those groups which had their origins in the crisis of the New Left. As many as 84% of the terrorists had been active in the nuclei that formed around 2 magazines called *Rosso* (Red) or *Senza Tregua* (Without Truce), in the *Circoli del Proletariato Giovanile* (Circles of Youth Proletariat), or in the small *Comitati di Quartiere* active in the working-class neighborhoods of the largest cities.

One characteristic of these groups was their very small size. In Table 3, the category "Autonomous Collectives" combines 93 sub-categories. In at least 89 of these sub-categories, the size of the organization was small enough to suggest that strong personal bonds developed among all the members. In 65 of these sub-categories the frequency is more than 1; in other words, within these groups, at least 2 future terrorists were sharing the same legal political experience. Very often the decision to join a clandestine organization involved an even larger network of "political" companions: 47 of these groups produced at least three future terrorists; 35 at least 4; and 112 more than 5. Decisions to join the "armed struggle" were, in all these cases, collective ones.

In-depth interviews and examinations allow for a better interpretation of these quantitative data. As the testimony of former members reveals, membership in the small legal political group was of great importance in their daily lives. Even where friendship ties external to the political milieu did exist, their importance tended to diminish as political socialization developed. In a spiraling series of interrelationships, as the amount of time a member spent in political activities increased, so did his contacts with political companions. At the same time, the strengthening of friendship ties inside the political environment increased the value attached to political involvement and encouraged people to dedicate more and more time to political activities. In this way, other ties lost their power to exert countervailing effects on the formation of the personality. As Keniston (1968) has suggested is typical of other kinds of political socialization, commitment among the militants involved a process of isolation from the outside world, and this isolation reinforced loyalty to the new group. Political friends became the most important peer group, capable of influencing any individual choice.

IV. TERRORIST MILITANCY AND POLITICAL IDENTITIES

To summarize what has been said so far, Italian clandestine organizations recruited their militants from tight-knit networks of social relations in which political ties were strengthened by primary solidarity based on friendship and kinship relations. These networks offered loyalty channels of communication to the underground groups. Individual motivations can be traced, to a large extent, to solidarity with groups of people with whom an individual shared a political identity. But the understanding of personal motivation requires a deeper analysis of the process of political socialization that helps to build a collective identity.

Examinations and interviews with former terrorists support the hypothesis that the formation of collective political identities is influenced by the political climate in which sectors of the population have their first political experiences. Specific political sub-cultures influence both the degree of importance political identity has in a person's life and the specific meaning that political activities have for an individual.

Life stories of Italian terrorists confirm that a characteristic of people recruited to clandestine organizations is previous experience of using violence as a political means. Many of the members of armed groups had previously belonged to the semimilitary structures of nonclandestine organizations. They had been involved, for example, in the *servizio d'ordine* (marshall body) of *Lotta Continua,* in the semilegal structures of *Potere Operaio* and of the groups organized around the review *Linea di Condotta* (Line of Conduct), and in the military body of *Rosso,* the so-called *Brigate Comuniste* (Communist Brigades), appointed for the armed defense of public demonstrations and illegal activities. Some of the militants of *Nuclei Armati Proletari* and of *Proletari*

Armati per il Comunismo were experienced in illegal activities, though, in the case of ordinary delinquents who became involved in politics during their stay in prison, for nonpolitical aims. Many of the small clandestine groups that arose after 1979 were founded by terrorists from the major armed organizations. And, conversely, many people recruited into the larger terrorist organizations had previously been involved with illegal groups active in some working class neighborhoods.

The relevance of the previous use of violent repertoires in the political socialization of Italian terrorists is indicated by other data as well. Previous legal convictions for violent crime were traced in 67 cases. Moreover, many of the younger terrorists of the late seventies had been charged with the "proletarian expropriations" and "armed demonstrations" carried out by semilegal groups. A number of others had been prosecuted as members of the most violent groups of *Autonomia Operaia* (Workers Autonomy), the *Collettivo di Via dei Volsci* in Rome, for instance.

The importance of previous experiences with violence is often stated in former militants' accounts of their lives. The political episodes most frequently mentioned are squattings, confrontations with police, fascist assaults, and use of "Molotov cocktails" to "defend" marches and arrests. The use of violence by right-wing activists and police is cited as a justification for personal involvement in illegal and violent activities. The militants' emphasis on their participation in violent events is, therefore, often a device to justify choices that were seen as a necessary response.

To conclude, previous experience in violent political activities predisposes individuals to involvement in terrorist groups. My analysis suggests that participation in violent practices produces a kind of militant for whom political commitment is identified with physical violence rather than with negotiation. The lack of possibilities for concrete gains through bargaining activities increases the need for symbolic substitutes, which are often found in radical ideologies that maintain that social changes can be obtained only through a long war against the enemy.

The spread of terrorist organizations in Italy was, therefore, connected to the presence of political militants whose political socialization took place in the long protest cycle of the late sixties-early seventies. In this period, political activities were characterized by strategies aimed at the formation of new collective identities, rather than at the use of already existing solidarity bonds for bargaining (Pizzorno 1978b). When the protest cycle was over, networks of militants—more accustomed to physical violence than to mediation— constituted a potential base for violent political groups. This group of people interacted, then, with other militants who were politically socialized during periods of identity building and high violence rates. This interaction produced the base from which the second generation of terrorists would emerge. For these people, the use of physical violence preceded rather than followed the joining of terrorist organizations. The threshold of clandestinity was often passed involuntarily and sometimes even unconsciously.

A fair conclusion would be, therefore, that an individual has a greater propensity to become involved in terrorist activities when she or he belongs to tight-knit political networks and has been socialized to accept violent forms of action.

V. THE RECRUITMENT TO CLANDESTINE ORGANIZATIONS AS A CASE OF POLITICAL PARTICIPATION: A CONCLUSION

Analyzing recruitment is not sufficient to give a full account of individual motivations in joining underground groups. We must examine other processes in order to understand the way in which the militants were integrated in the organizations and the evolution of their activities in them. In concluding, I will simply summarize my main findings, arranging them around three foci of attention: mobilization potential, consensus mobilization, and action mobilization (Klandermans 1984 and 1985; Tarrow 1985).

Consensus mobilization, that is, "the creation of network arenas and mentalities in which predispositions favorable to action mobilization are formed" (Tarrow 1985, p. 15) has been the main focus of my analysis. Our findings show that terrorist groups are able to recruit in homogeneous political networks. The reservoir for terrorist organizations is composed of people who share (1) strong political identities, that is, people whose personality-building process relies heavily upon a political commitment; and (2) a political socialization to violence, that is, people whose political ideology and, in particular, whose practice, admits the use of physical violence.

The high risks involved in terrorist recruitment may require a greater emphasis on personal networks in terrorist organizations than in other political groups. Moreover, the total commitment that a terrorist organization requires may dramatically increase the degree of personality investment in political participation.

Even allowing for important peculiarities, some general statements can be made here. First, the categories of social network and political ideology are only partially useful in defining consensus mobilization. Neither participation in a social network nor adoption of a certain ideological framework is indeed sufficient to foster political loyalties. They can, in fact, be important constraints on the formation of collective political identities. Second, solidarities that develop during the formation of these collective identities tend to persist and often to direct the groups of people they bind together toward political problem solving attitudes. Faced with crises in social movements, groups of friends keep their solidarity with each other by looking together for other political involvements. Third, collective identities are formed during periods of regular contact, a fact that in turn helps explain why some individuals consider their political role so important to the structure of their personality.

Although this research concentrated on consensus mobilization, it also offers insights into the other two levels of analysis of political participation. As far as the mobilization of people into action is concerned, the main findings refer to the importance of symbolic incentives. Such incentives are somewhat specific to terrorist organizations, because the high risks involved in participation, diminish the importance of economic incentives. Actually, this situation seems to hold true for other kinds of social movement organizations as well. Indeed, social movements in general are rarely able to offer more than very low-paying and temporary jobs and rely heavily upon volunteer work.

The third subject for analysis, the structural factors that produce groups and individuals with a predisposition to left-wing clandestine organization has not been systematically reviewed. Nevertheless, my data suggest that left-wing groups emerged in Italy as the unforeseen consequences of harsh social conflicts (on this point, see Caselli et al. 1984; della Porta et al. 1986). The lack of a timely policy response to the late 1960s protest cycle, together with the relatively high level of police intervention, favored a gradual deterioration of the repertoires. In the second half of the seventies a very intense outburst of youth protest quickly gave rise to violence. One of the reasons for this outburst may be found in the repressive way through which the new demands were dealt with. In both cases, the environmental conditions encouraging the emergence of terrorism were characterized by the spread of violent patterns of political behavior. The presence of violent repertoires, indeed, creates the preconditions for political entrepreneurs to orient their efforts to a specific constituency formed by those who use radical forms of action.

While these structural preconditions may seem very specific to terrorist groups, nonetheless some general conclusions can be drawn on this point. First, political variables have to be taken into account in analyzing mobilization potential. This potential is defined not only by class position or economic variables but also by the structure of political opportunities (Tarrow 1983). Second, political variables are particularly necessary when the research addresses the potential constituency, not of a social movement in general, but of a specific social movement organization. The two problems have to be differentiated analytically. Third, the mobilization potential is not a naturally existing reservoir; rather, it is in some way shaped by the political organization. The organization's strategic choices define the boundaries of a certain constituency and in this way contribute, if not to the creation, at least to the exploitation of some structural preconditions.

ACKNOWLEDGMENTS

The information used in this paper has been gathered by the author as part of a wider research program on "Political Violence and Terrorism" coordinated by the Carlo Cattaneo Institute of Bologna, Italy.

REFERENCES

Aveni, Adrian F. 1977. "The not-so-lonely crowd: Friendship groups in collective behavior." *Sociometry* 40:96-99.

Aveni, Adrian F. 1978. "Organizational linkages and resource mobilization: The significance of linkage strength and breath." *Sociological Quarterly* 19:185-202.

Barnes, J.A. 1969. "Network and political process." Pages 51-76 in J. Mitchell (ed.), *Social Networks in Urban Situations*. Manchester: Manchester University Press.

Billing, Otto. 1984. "The case history of a German terrorist." *Terrorism: An International Journal* 7:1-10.

Burt, Ronald S. 1980. "Models of network structure." *Annual Review of Sociology* 6:79-141.

Caselli, Giancarlo and Donatella della Porta. 1984. "La storia delle Brigate Rosse: Strutture organizzative e strategie d'azione." In Donatella della Porta (ed.), *Terrorismi in Italia*. Bologna: Il Mulino.

Coombs, G. 1979. "Network and exchange: The role of social relations in a small voluntary association." *Journal of Anthropological Research* 29:96-112.

Court of Turin. 1980. "Left-wing terrorism in Italy during the seventies: The formation of terrorist organizations." Paper presented at the 13th International Conference of the IPSA, Paris, July.

della Porta, Donatella and Sidney Tarrow. 1986. "Unwanted children: Political violence and the cycle of protest in Italy, 1966-1973." *European Journal of Political Research* 14: 607-32.

della Porta, Donatella. In preparation. *Il Terrorismo di Sinistra in Italia*.

Elder, Glen. 1981. "History and the life course." In D. Bertaux (ed.), *Biography and Society*. Beverly Hills: Sage.

Erickson, Bert H. 1981. "Secret societies and social structures." *Social Forces* 60:188-210.

Garner, Roberta and Mayer N. Zald. 1983. "Social movement sectors and systemic constraints: Towards a structural analysis of social movements." University of Michigan, CRSO Working Paper No. 238.

Gerlach, Luther P. 1970. "Corporate groups and movement networks in America." *Anthropological Quarterly* 43:123-45.

Gerlach, Luther P. and Virginia H. Hine. 1970. *People, Power, Change: Movements of Social Transformation*. New York: Bobbs-Merrill.

Hirschman, Albert O. 1982. *Shifting Involvements: Private Interest and Public Action*. Princeton: Princeton University Press.

Homans, George C. 1958. "Social behavior as exchange." *American Journal of Sociology* 63: 596-606.

Ivianski, Zeev. 1983. "A chapter in the story of individual terror: Andrey Zhelyabol." In L. Z. Freedman and Y. Alexander (eds.), *Perspectives on Terrorism*. Wilmington, Del.: Scholarly Resource.

Keniston, Kenneth. 1968. *Young Radicals: Notes on Committed Youth*. New York: Harcourt, Brace and World.

Klandermans, Bert C. 1984. "Mobilization and participation: Social-psychological expansions of resource mobilization theory." *American Sociological Review* 49:583-600.

Klandermans, Bert. 1986. "New social movements and resource mobilization: The European and the American approach." *International Journal of Mass Emergencies and Disasters.* Special issue, *Comparative Perspectives and Research on Collective Behavior and Social Movements* 4:13-37.

Knutson, Jeanne N. 1981. "Social and psychological pressures toward a negative identity: The case of an American revolutionary terrorist." In Y. Alexander and J. M. Gleamson (eds.), *Behavioral and Quantitative Perspectives on Terrorism.* New York: Pergamon.

Kornhauser, William. 1959. *The Politics of Mass Society.* Glencoe, Ill.: Free Press.

Livingstone, Neil C. 1982. *The War against Terrorism.* Lexington, Mass.: Lexington Books.

Lofland, John and Robert Stark. 1965. "Becoming a world-saver: A theory of conversion to a deviant perspective." *American Sociological Review* 30:362-74.

McPhail, C. 1971. "Civil disorder participation: A critical examination of recent research." *American Sociological Review* 34:1058-73.

McPhail, C. and D. Miller. 1973. "The assembling process: A theoretical and empirical examination." *American Sociological Review* 38:721-35.

Melucci, Alberto. 1984. "Alla ricerca dell'azione." In A. Melucci (ed.), *Altri codici. Aree di movimento nella metropoli.* Bologna: Il Mulino.

Melucci, Alberto. 1985. "Multipolar action system. Systemic environment and individual involvements in contemporary movements." Paper presented at the Planning Meeting on New Social Movements, Ithaca, N.Y., August 16-18.

Oberschall, Anthony. 1973. *Social Conflict and Social Movements.* Englewood Cliffs, N.J.: Prentice-Hall.

Oberschall, Anthony. 1980. "Loosely structured collective conflict: A theory and an application." Pages 45-68 in Louis Kriesberg (ed.), *Research in Social Movements, Conflicts, and Change.* Vol. 3. Greenwich, Conn.: JAI.

Olson, Mancur, Jr. 1968. *The Logic of Collective Action: Public Goods and the Theory of Groups.* Cambridge: Harvard University Press.

Palombarini, Giovanni. 1982. *Il 7 aprile. Il processo e la sua storia.* Venice: Arsenale.

Parkin, Frank. 1968. *Middle Class Radicalism: The Social Bases of the British Campaign for Nuclear Disarmament.* Manchester: Manchester University Press.

Pinard, Maurice. 1971. "A reformulation of the mass society model." In Maurice Pinard, *The Rise of a Third Party. A Study in Crisis Politics.* Englewood Cliffs, N.J.: Prentice-Hall.

Pizzorno, Alessandro. 1978a. "Political exchange and collective identity in industrial conflict." Pages 277-98 in Colin Crouch and Alessandro Pizzorno (eds.), *The Resurgence of Class Conflict in Western Europe since 1968.* Vol. 2. London: Macmillan.

Pizzorno, Alessandro. 1978b. "Intervento su terrorismo e quadro politico." *Mondo operaio,* no. 4, pp.5-18.

Rochford, E. Burke. 1982. "Recruitment strategies, ideology, and organization in the Hare Krishna movement." *Social Problems* 29:400-10.

Rogers, David L. and Gordon L. Bultena. 1975. "Voluntary association and political equality: An extension of mobilization theory." *Journal of Voluntary Action Research* 4:172-83.

Rogers, David L., Gordon L. Bultena, and Ken H. Barb. 1975. "Voluntary association membership and political participation: An exploration of the mobilization hypothesis." *Sociological Quarterly* 16:305-18.

Russell, Charles and Bowman H. Miller. 1983. "Profile of a terrorist." In L. Z. Freedman and Y. Alexander (eds.), *Perspective on Terrorism.* Wilmington, Del.: Scholarly Resource.

Smith, Bruce L., Harold D. Lasswell, and Ralph D. Casey. 1946. *Propaganda, Communication and Public Opinion: A Comprehensive Reference Guide.* Chicago: University of Chicago Press.

Snow, David A. and Robert Machalek. 1983. "The convert as a social type." In R. Collins (ed.), *Sociological Theory.* San Francisco: Jossey-Bass.

Snow, David A. and Cynthia Phillips. 1980. "The Lofland-Stark conversion model: A critical reassessment." *Social Problems* 27:430-47.

Snow, David A., Louis A. Zurcher, Jr., and Sheldon Ekland-Olson. 1980. "Social networks and social movements: A microstructural approach to differential recruitment." *American Sociological Review* 45:787-801.

Stark, Rodney and William S. Bainbridge. 1980. "Networks of faith: Interpersonal bonds and recruitment to cults and sects." *American Journal of Sociology* 85:1376-95.

Steinhoff, Patricia. 1976. "Portrait of a terrorist: An interview with Kozo Okamoto." *Asian Journey:* 830-45.

Tarrow, Sidney. 1983. *Struggling to Reform: Social Movements and Policy Change during Cycles of Protest.* Western Societies Paper No. 15. Ithaca, N.Y.: Cornell University.

Tarrow, Sidney. 1986. "Comparing social movement participation in Western Europe and the United State: Problems, uses, examples, and a proposal for synthesis." *International Journal of Mass Emergencies and Disasters.* Special issue, *Comparative Perspectives and Research on Collective Behavior and Social Movements* 4:145-70.

Tilly, Charles. 1978. *From Mobilization to Revolution.* Reading, Mass.: Addison-Wesley.

Ventura, Angelo. 1984. "Il problema delle origini del terrorismo di sinistra." In Donatella della Porta (ed.), *Terrorismi in Italia.* Bologna: Il Mulino.

Verba, Sidney. 1961. "The primary groups and politics." In Sidney Verba (ed.), *Small Groups and Political Behavior: A Study of Leadership.* Princeton: Princeton University Press.

Wallis, Roy and Steve Bruce. 1982. "Network and clockwork." *Sociology* 16:102-7.

Walsh, Edward J. and Rex H. Warland. "Social movement involvement in the wake of a nuclear accident: Activists and free riders in the TMI area." *American Sociological Review* 4:764-80.

Wilson, James Q. 1973. *Political Organizations.* New York: Basic Books.

Wood, Michael and Michael Hughes. 1984. "The moral basis of moral reform: Status discontent vs. culture and socialization as explanations of the anti-pornography social movement adherence." *American Sociological Review* 49:86-99.

PART II

CONSENSUS MOBILIZATION OR THE
CONSTRUCTION OF MEANING

THE FORMATION AND MOBILIZATION OF CONSENSUS

Bert Klandermans

INTRODUCTION

In recent years several authors have described how collective actors are generated. The pictures they have drawn show striking resemblances, whether they apply to the civil rights movement (McAdam 1982; Morris 1984), the United Farm Workers (Jenkins 1985), the environmental movement (Boender 1985; Mazur 1981), the women's movment (Ferree and Hess 1985), the antibusing movement (Taylor 1985), the neighborhood movement (Henig 1982), or protest cycles in general (Kriesi 1985; Tarrow 1983). ~

The process all these authors describe can adequately be labeled a spiral of mobilization. Broad sociocultural changes in society, such as the transition into postindustrial society; changes in the position of social categories, as of blacks and women; and the emergence of a new middle class give rise to general concerns in the public. One result of these general trends is the development of societal niches of individuals who oppose the direction of society or challenge

International Social Movement Research, Vol. 1, pages 173-196.
Supplement to Research in Social Movements, Conflicts and Change
Copyright © 1988 by JAI Press Inc.
ISBN: 0-89232-955-6

the status quo. When changes occur in the political opportunity structure, changes that provide challengers with leverage in the realm of policy, the general climate becomes more conducive to insurgency. In such a climate, an open controversy among elites (Boender 1985; Mazur 1981) or a suddenly imposed grievance (Henig 1982; Morris 1984; Outshoorn 1986; Walsh 1981) can trigger a spiral of mobilization. Activists, political entrepreneurs, or indigenous leaders set out to mobilize popular support for insurgent action.

The strength of indigenous networks and organizations in a subculture is the crucial factor determining the level of mobilization that is reached initially. Successful mobilization draws mass-media attention, especially if innovative action strategies are used. Media coverage rapidly increases the number of individuals who are aware of the problem and strengthens the mobilization that is underway. As a consequence, tangential and nontangential resources available to the collective actor increase. The influx of resources makes it possible to strengthen organizations and to enlarge networks. And growing popular support makes it easier to co-opt existing networks and organizations (cf. Tierney 1982 for an example of this process). The result is a stronger collective actor capable of reaching higher levels of mobilization in the next confrontation with its opponent. Repression and counterattacks often fuel the movement because they reinforce support, especially among those who sympathize with the movement.

A complex interplay of strains, resources, and opportunities determines the structure of collective action. As Part I of this volume demonstrates, current social movement literature highlights the importance of indigenous social structures and subcultures in the mobilization for collective action. Long before actual mobilization campaigns take place, indigenous structures and subcultural networks develop and generate more or less elaborated collective identities that are the seedbeds in which future collective action can come to flower. Kriesi (1986) even argues that contemporary social movements such as the environmental movement, the peace movement, and the women's movement can afford to maintain loose structures because they are rooted in dense subcultural networks that serve as communication and mobilization channels in case of need.

This chapter emphasizes the deliberate attempts of social movement organizations to mobilize consensus among (a subset of) the population. First, consensus *mobilization* will be distinguished from consensus *formation*. Next I discuss consensus mobilization in the context of movement participation, and distinguish between consensus mobilization as the formation of mobilization potential and consensus mobilization in the context of action mobilization. The second part of the chapter addresses the questions of how consensus is mobilized and of what strategies and tactics are used. I will show how the characteristics of movement organizations, messages, channels, and audiences influence the success of consensus mobilization.

I. CONSENSUS FORMATION AND CONSENSUS MOBILIZATION

Much of what goes on within social networks concerns the formation of consensus. People tend to validate information by comparing and discussing their interpretations with significant others (Festinger 1954), especially when complex social information is involved. People prefer to compare their opinions with those of like-minded individuals. As a rule, the set of individuals interacting in one's social networks—especially one's friendship networks—is relatively homogeneous and composed of people not too different from oneself. Processes of social comparison produce collective definitions of a situation. Consequently, within these networks, consensus is formed and maintained. Consensus mobilization (e.g., attempts by an actor to spread its views and beliefs) has to take this social reality into account. Messages issued by an actor are not only filtered through the cognitive frames of individual receivers but also processed by reality-testing intercourse in the social networks and subcultures to which the receivers belong. So, consensus mobilization must target not only the beliefs and attitudes of individuals, but the collective definitions sustained in social networks.

Although individuals are part of networks and subcultures that often become engaged *en bloc* in collective action, it is still the individual who must make up his or her mind whether to join in collective action. Even in the case of *en bloc* engagement individuals have to consider whether they will conform to or defect from the collectivity.

Individuals behave within a perceived reality. They perceive the different actors in a social conflict; they have perceptions of actors' stands on relevant issues; and supporting these actors is perceived to be more or less rewarding. Since social reality is complex enough to allow for completely different interpretations of what is going on, a variety of definitions of the situation is available, sponsored by competing actors. In the case of social conflicts, actors try to persuade individuals to take their sides. In that way, governmental agencies, competing challengers, movement and countermovement organizations are struggling for the hearts and minds of the people (see, for example, Marshall and Orum 1987).

Attempts to spread the views of a social actor among parts of the population are what we call consensus mobilization (Klandermans 1984b). Consensus mobilization must be distinguished from consensus *formation:* it is a deliberate attempt by a social actor to create consensus among a subset of the population, whereas consensus formation concerns the unplanned convergence of meaning in social networks and subcultures. Although consensus mobilization can be practiced by any social actor, I will concentrate here on one single type of actor and its targets: social movement organizations sponsoring an ideological package and individuals faced with the question of whether to adopt the movement organization's definition of the situation.

Neither movement organizations nor individuals act in a vacuum. A movement organization operates in a field of competing sources of information, in which its views are continually challenged. Individuals are embedded in social structures and subcultures that reinforce indigenous beliefs and values. To conceptualize movement organizations as agents of consensus mobilization we must relate movement organizations to other agents attempting to influence public opinion. In an analogous way individuals must be viewed as taking part in networks of social relationships in which incoming information is validated.

Until now the social movement literature has paid scant attention to persuasion in the context of mobilization. In this context social psychological literature on persuasive communication has much to offer to students of social movements. This paper is an attempt to apply to social movement mobilization lessons learned from the study of persuasion in general. But before we turn to our discussion of consensus mobilization, it will be useful to reiterate what the introductory chapter of this volume stated about the meaning of consensus mobilization in the context of participation in social movement activities.

II.   CONSENSUS MOBILIZATION AND SOCIAL MOVEMENT PARTICIPATION

Participation in social movements—the Introduction argued—takes place in the context of the formation of mobilization potentials, the formation and activation of recruitment networks, the arousal of the motivation to participate, and the removal of barriers to participation. In the formation of mobilization potentials, movement organizations must win attitudinal and ideological support. In the formation and activation of recruitment networks, they must increase the probability that people who "belong" to their mobilization potential will be reached. In arousing motivation to participate, they must favorably influence the decisions of people who are reached by a mobilization attempt. And in removing barriers they must increase the probability that people who are motivated will eventually participate. These four kinds of actions together constitute the process of mobilization.

The efforts of a social movement organization to mobilize support have two different ends: consensus mobilization and action mobilization (Klandermans 1984b). The former has to do with the propagation of the views of the movement; the latter with the promotion of participation in activities organized by the movement. In Gamson's terms (1975), consensus and action mobilization distinguish the creation of commitment from the activation of commitment.

It will be clear from our previous distinctions that the formation of mobilization potentials occurs through consensus mobilization. This is not to say that the formation of mobilization potential is completely determined by an organization's attempts to mobilize consensus. On the contrary, much of the mobilization potential of a movement comes from the unplanned formation of consensus. Moreover, as indicated in the introductory chapter, agents other than the organization can contribute to the consensus, and, as we will see, this external stimulus is sometimes the *only* means to create consensus, especially in the initial phases of mobilization. However, the efforts of a movement organization to create a mobilization potential in society are, by definition, attempts to mobilize consensus. The three other aspects of mobilization are a mixture of consensus and action mobilization, as will be presented in the following section.

III. CONSENSUS MOBILIZATION

Consensus mobilization is necessary for every social movement organization. In Freeman's (1983) treatment of social movements, the desire to spread the message of the movement is even considered as one of the *defining* characteristics of social movements. Given its centrality to a social movement's concern, however, it is surprising how little empirical study it received. The available literature is primarily speculative. In general it is agreed that the message of a social movement implies a redefinition of the situation, a break with the discourse justifying the status quo (Skelly 1986). In this context Gamson et al. (1982) refer to "the process of replacing a dominant belief system that legitimizes the status quo with an alternative mobilizing belief system that supports collective action for change" (p.15). Like Turner (1969), these authors stress the importance, for mobilization, of defining a situation as unjust. Adopting an injustice framework is an important precondition for resistance (Gamson et al. 1982; Taylor 1986).

A social movement's message is framed by a more or less elaborated ideology. According to Wilson (1973), a movement's ideology contains a diagnosis (an indication of the causes of discontent and the agents responsible for it), a prognosis (an indication of what must be done), and a rationale (who must do the job, arguments to convince the individual that action must be taken, self-justification, and a description of the future of the movement). Individuals differ according to the degree of congruence between their belief systems and a movement ideology. Snow et al. (1986) were the first to design a theory of consensus mobilization that took this congruency factor into account. In their analyses, consensus mobilization can imply frame bridging, frame amplification, frame extension, or frame transformation, depending on the discrepancy between individual belief systems and movement ideologies.

In this literature the justification of the existence of a movement organization and the justification of its actions or activities are sometimes confused. From a consensus mobilization point of view, these are two rather different concerns. As will become clear in the following sections, movement organizations are faced with different problems and have to find different solutions depending on what form of consensus mobilization they seek to promote.

Consensus mobilization was described earlier as a social movement organization's search for support for its point of view. To win such support is easier said than done. In reality, it may be necessary to effect fundamental changes in peoples' views and attitudes, and mobilizing widespread consensus may take years to accomplish. For instance, the Dutch Interdenominational Peace Council (IKV) initially thought it would need ten years to gain some degree of acceptance for its motto "Stop nukes in the world, beginning with the Netherlands." It could not forsee when it was formed that, thanks to the cruise missiles affair, less than half this period would prove sufficient. This example illustrates as well that the results of consensus mobilization are not determined by the efforts of movement organizations alone. The rest of this paper elaborates further how social movement organizations mobilize consensus. The two questions I will examine are: "What is consensus mobilization?" and "How is it accomplished?"

IV.   WHAT IS CONSENSUS MOBILIZATION?

It is necessary to distinguish between consensus mobilization in the context of the formation of mobilization potential in a society and consensus mobilization in the context of action mobilization. The former refers to the generation of a set of individuals with a predisposition to participate in a social movement. The latter refers to the legitimation of concrete goals and means of action.

It can be inferred from this distinction that the two forms of consensus mobilization have different time frames: the formation of mobilization potential is a long term problem; action mobilization a short term matter. The target audiences differ as well: action mobilization means the activation of commitment; it restricts itself to people who already "belong" to the mobilization potential of a movement organization. The formation of mobilization potential means the creation of commitment; in this case, the audience is much broader, usually a social category of people who share some characteristic related to the movement's cause. It follows from these preliminary remarks that the two forms of consensus mobilization should be treated separately, as the next two sections make clear.

A.   The Formation of Mobilization Potentials

However successful a movement organization may be in interpreting grievances, it cannot create them. Scholars usually point to structural factors to explain the development of grievances in a society. In the literature expositions of the structural factors that contribute to the generation of grievances abound. One well-known explanation is Smelser's (1971) distinction between structural conduciveness (circumstances that allow protest behavior) and structural strain (ambiguities, conflicts, deprivations, and discrepancies in the social order). Recent European literature emphasizes marginalization of social groups and regions, decreasing legitimacy of regimes, groups that are hit the hardest by the negative consequences of modernization processes (cf. Brand 1982 for a review). Recent American contributions stress the importance of suddenly imposed grievances (McAdam 1982; Walsh 1981) and of the "transvaluation" of existing ones (Piven and Cloward 1977).

Although they are important in explaining where grievances come from, structural factors alone will never provide a sufficient explanation of the transformation of grievances into movement demands. Between the structural factors that make it more likely that certain social groups will become the breeding ground for social movements and the rise of social movements are people and the meanings they attribute to their situation. Consensus mobilization in the form of the interpretation of grievances is an essential stage in the formation of a mobilization potential.

Recently, various authors have formulated theories on grievance interpretation (Ferree and Miller 1985; McAdam 1982; Snow et al. 1986; Taylor 1986). With the exception of Taylor's study of public opinion and the antibusing movement, no empirical research appears to have been done on this topic. The causal attributions that people make are crucial in interpreting grievances. Particularly important is the distinction between personal and system attributions (Ferree and Miller 1985, Klandermans 1983b; Snow et al. 1986): the distinction between people who hold personal or individual factors responsible for what happens to them and those who hold situational factors responsible. It is generally argued that grievances that are attributed to situational factors predispose people to participate in social movements.

But interpreting grievances requires a more comprehensive perspective. Merely attributing grievances to situational factors is not enough. To use the words of Piven and Cloward (1979), it is also necessary that people who normally accept authority and are convinced of the legitimacy of institutions come to recognize that this authority and these institutions are unjust and wrong. In addition, people who are usually fatalistic and feel that the existing order cannot be changed must start to demand changes. Lastly, a sense of effectiveness must emerge; people who generally feel powerless must become convinced that they are capable of changing their condition. McAdam (1982) refers to such changes in people's belief systems as cognitive liberation. These are radical changes, and the formation of mobilization potentials often does not take place where one would expect it to.

For this reason Kriesi (1984) distinguishes between latent and manifest political potentials. The former is the set of people who—because of a similar social structural situation—share a specific set of interests. If people become aware of their shared interests and develop a collective identity, a manifest political potential is created. Consciousness-raising is the crucial link between the two potentials. Organizations and networks among individuals play an important role in the transition from latent to manifest political potential.

Discussing this transaction, McAdam (1985) has pointed to the importance of the micromobilization context. By micromobilization he means "that small group setting in which processes of collective attribution are combined with rudimentary forms of organization to produce mobilization for collective action" (p.15). Melucci (1985) had something similar in mind when he emphasized the importance of "intermediate relational systems" that produce "shared definitions of the field of opportunities and constraints offered to collective action" (p.3). The groups involved are not infrequently existing groups and networks based upon entirely dissimilar and nonpolitical goals, such as friendship circles, churches, or community organizations.

Thus interactions between individuals in friendship networks and existing organizations and alignments play an important role in the interpretation of grievances. Although movement organizations are not the only agents engaged in grievance interpretation, they take an active part (Tierney 1982). Like other social actors, movement organizations try to persuade people to accept their definition of a situation. Of course they do not always need to change people's perceptions in all respects. Consequently Snow et al. (1986) find it helpful to distinguish between frame bridging, frame extension, frame amplification, and frame transformation. Following Gamson et al. (1982), they adopted the frame concept from Goffman, who used it to indicate the frames of reference individuals employ to interpret events in the surrounding world. Consensus mobilization, or in Snow's terminology, frame alignment, links the frames of individuals and social movement organizations in such a way that "individual interests, values and beliefs and social movement organization activities, goals and ideology are congruent and complementary" (p.464).

Depending on the differences between frames, one of the four processes distinguished by Snow et al. takes place. Frame bridging occurs when the individual and social movement frames are congruent. In this case it is enough simply to point out the congruence to individuals. Frame amplification occurs when an interpretive frame is clarified and strengthened by linking it to values or beliefs held by the public. In the case of frame extension, a movement organization extends the boundaries of its primary frameworks: value and interests of potential adherents become aligned with participation in movement activities. Frame transformation occurs when individual frames need to be changed either in part or as a whole in order to make them congruent with the movement frame. It goes without saying that frame transformation demands a great deal more of a social movement than do the other forms of frame alignment.

The degree to which a social movement is successful in creating mobilization potential determines among other factors the size of the reservoir from which a movement can draw for action mobilization. The amount of time available for action mobilization is too short to allow for frame transformation. A social movement therefore must frequently turn to forms of consensus mobilization which do *not* require changing frames: frame bridging, frame extension, or frame amplification.

B. The Context of Action Mobilization

We have seen that dissatisfactions and aspirations and the conviction that a situation can be changed take hold among members of a society during the formation of mobilization potential. But the presence of such feelings does not in itself mean that people will actually take part in activities of a social movement, even if it tries to do something about their dissatisfactions and aspirations. For activities of a social movement have concrete goals, and it cannot be taken for granted that potential participants will feel these goals to be related to their dissatisfactions and aspirations. Nor can it be assumed that people will believe that participating in the movement's activities is effective. Action goals and means have to be legitimated and that is the challenge a movement organization faces in mobilizing consensus in the context of action mobilization.

Legitimating Action Goals

If they are to motivate people to participate, a movement's concrete goals must be considered instrumental for eliminating the dissatisfactions or fulfilling the aspirations that are at the root of a movement's mobilization potential. To be able to form an opinion about instrumentality, people must be familiar with the action goals and their most important implications. Thus dissemination of knowledge is an important aspect of consensus mobilization. Campaigns can easily run aground on this very first requirement.

Action goals are not constants. Influenced by circumstances, and interaction with opponents, among other factors, they can and do change. The danger to social movements here is that changes in the action goals will not become adequately known. Those who occupy more marginal positions in movement networks are especially likely to be left behind. The dissemination of knowledge has its limits. The great majority in the targeted group will never have more than a general idea of the action goals, and efforts to improve this knowledge will probably not be very effective.

However important the adequate dissemination of knowledge may be, it is of course never more than a condition for the actual objectives of consensus mobilization, which create a widespread positive attitude toward the action goals. The key concept here is the perceived instrumentality of the action goals for changes felt to be worth striving for, or for maintaining a preferred state of affairs. Campaigns for the mobilization of consensus attempt to convince people of this instrumentality, often in the face of counterarguments by opponents (cf. Marshall and Orum 1987). How successful a movement organization is in convincing people determines how successful it will be in creating a positive attitude toward action goals.

In discussing action goals, we must make another distinction, one that has important consequences for consensus mobilization. This is the distinction between reactive and proactive demands (Ferree and Miller 1985). Reactive demands involve changes that fit in with this dominant ideology in a society. They are based on claims that are legitimate for a group to make according to the dominant ideology. Proactive demands involve changes that do not fit in with the dominant ideology. They involve rights, privileges, or means to which a group is not entitled according to the dominant ideology. To legitimate proactive demands requires much more effort from a social movement organization than pursuing reactive demands, if only because proactive demands arouse greater resistance—as I can illustrate with an example drawn from our union research in the Netherlands.

In the Netherlands unions traditionally negotiate wages. The demands they usually make in bargaining are reactive ones. The particular wage increase demanded may itself be a matter of discussion, but the right of unions to demand higher wages is not. Because such demands fit into the familiar pattern, it is not difficult to mobilize consensus for them, first because they meet with little resistance, and second because they are easy to explain and to legitimate. But the reaction was very different when, a couple of years ago, the Dutch unions demanded manning agreements and shorter working hours. Resistance on the part of employers, the government, and even friendly economists was strong. In both cases, unions had great difficulty in legitimating demands to its own constituency (Klandermans 1984a).

In the case of proactive demands, frame transformation may be necessary in order to make them seem legitimate. Consequently, the time limits of an average action mobilization campaign will almost certainly be exceeded. Essentially, a movement is faced with the task of creating mobilization potential for the demands. A case in point is the demand for a shorter workweek, from our preceding example. With the help of skyrocketing unemployment, unions were eventually able to persuade their memberships and the government that shortening the workweek was an effective strategy to reduce unemployment. After ten years, the Dutch unions finally reached a first agreement on establishing a shorter workweek.

Legitimating Action Means

Several authors have stressed the important role expectation of success plays in motivating people to participate in social movement activities (Klandermans 1984b; Oberschall 1980; Pinard and Hamilton 1986). With the possible exception of very low risk activities (Klandermans and Oegema 1987; Pinard and Hamilton 1986), expectations of success seem to be a necessary condition for participation. The belief in the effectiveness of participation can be analyzed into three separate expectations, which vary independently: "(a) expectations about the number of participants, (b) expectations about one's own contribution to the probability of success, (c) expectations about the probability of success if many people participate" (Klandermans 1984b, p.585).

Legitimating a means of action implies convincing people that participation by others is above threshold level; that individual participation contributes significantly to success, or alternatively that nonparticipation threatens success; and by convincing people that the movement's action strategy will have an impact on the target institution. It is clear that persuasion is a delicate undertaking: too much optimism encourages people to take a free ride; too much pessimism creates concern as to whether participation makes sense at all. Thus intelligent organizers try hard to get people to believe that their contribution is critical. Sometimes it is an advantage to organizers if supporters of a movement organization tend to overestimate the number of participants (Granberg 1983; Granberg and Holmberg 1983; Taylor 1986). But overestimation can be a disadvantage as well, if, for example people decide to ride free because their participation does not seem necessary.

Collectively, expectation about the behavior of others can work as self-fulfilling prophecies. If a movement organization fails to convince people that others will participate, people are less motivated to join the movement and the prediction that few people will participate becomes reality.

Effectiveness is not the only criterion. Action means are also evaluated in terms of their efficiency, that is their cost/benefit ratios, both collectively (damage done to target institutions, society in general) and individually (risks and costs to be taken). Movement organizations have to convince their adherent that the costs of the means chosen stand in a reasonable proportion to the benefits to be gained. The higher the costs, the heavier the burden of legitimation, that is the more depends on the movement organization's ability to make people believe that participation will have some effect. This includes the guarantee that others will participate.

V.   HOW IS CONSENSUS MOBILIZED?

As the preceding section suggests consensus mobilization may involve a wide range of changes in views and attitudes. The type of procedures used will vary with the nature of the changes a movement organization wants to bring about. In the case of frame bridging, a written message may be enough, whereas frame transformation might require lengthy and intensive interpersonal contact. Movement organizations use a wide array of techniques to mobilize consensus. The following list is an incomplete sample from three compilations of methods of collective action (Mushaben 1986; Reckman 1971; Sharp 1973):

> Public speeches; letters of opposition or support; declarations by organizations and institutions; signed public statements, signed advertisements; declarations of indictment and intention; slogans; caricatures and symbols, banners, posters; displayed communications; expositions; leaflets, pamphlets, books, newspapers and journals; records, radio, television, audiovisual presentations; art; exhibits; films; information stands in shopping centers; organizing public events featuring well known intellectuals and political figures; organizing congresses, teach-ins, hearings; publicizing the results of public opinion surveys; symbolic public acts such as prayer and worship; painting; wearing of symbols; performances of plays; music; singing; street theater; concerts; organizing dramatic events such as marches, demonstrations, die-ins, pilgrimages; arranging sports events, door-to-door canvassing.

From this enumeration it is clear that techniques vary according to the nature of the intended audience: the general public, sympathizers, or target institutions. In many cases, however, techniques directed at target institutions are indirectly aiming at a much broader audience. This overlap is what makes discussions about the success and failure of movement strategies so complicated. For a movement organization, an instance of protest may have no other function than getting mass-media attention, raising public awareness, or winning public support for its cause. Even strategies that fail to have any impact on policy making, although they were intended to do so, can turn out to be a success in terms of consensus mobilization (Morris 1984).

Essentially, anything that can be used to communicate meaning is applicable in campaigns to mobilize consensus. I will not try to map out the variety of techniques used and their respective merits. The list suggests the variety of techniques and the creativity of movement organizations in continually inventing more. An analytical approach is preferable, one using a general framework borrowed from the literature on persuasive communication: characteristics of the source of information, the message, the channels employed, and the audience are discussed in terms of their contribution to a movement organization's effectiveness in mobilizing consensus. As indicated earlier, the audiences vary depending on the context of consensus mobilization. Characteristics of source, message, and channel vary with the context as well, as will become clear in the next sections.

Movement organizations as sources of information.   Credibility is the key characteristic of a source of information. Movement organizations are aware of this fact, and take serious trouble to build up credibility. They can use various strategies. Thorne (1983) compares two strategies employed by two different draft-resistance groups in the Boston area. The first group tried to profile itself by expertise and know-how, minimizing the differences between proselytizers and their targets. The second group sought to polarize rather than to promote identification, and used theatrical, dramatic events. Risk-taking, that is, making sacrifices for the cause, was meant to signify strong commitment, which in turn was supposed to promote credibility and to give the group a right to speak.

We can find the same diversity in strategies to promote credibility in other movements as well. In the environmental movement, for example, the conservation organizations take a different approach than does Greenpeace. The factors used in strategies to promote credibility, i.e., expertise, sacrifices, and identification with the audience has been proven to be effective. In the case of the draft-resistance groups, neither identification strategy nor the polarizing strategy succeeded in building up credibility among its principal target group, working-class youth, partially because the resistance stance itself was so unattractive. Working-class youth considered it foolish to volunteer for jail. For the civil rights movement, however, Terchek (1974) observed that the strategy of risk-taking was effective in improving credibility.

In addition to expertise, the sacrifices made for the cause of the movement organization, and the perceived similarities between source and target, other factors contribute to the credibility of a social movement organization. One tactic that movement organizations frequently use is to have attractive and prestigious persons speak on its behalf. Especially if the persuasive message is not in the communicator's best interest, this strategy can be very effective. Another factor: dramatic events that put a movement organization in the right can strongly increase its credibility. Ecological accidents, for example, have considerably increased the credibility of the environmental movement (Boender 1985).

The weight of a movement organization's credibility differs depending on the context of consensus mobilization. Because action mobilization restricts itself to people who already "belong" to the mobilization potential, in this context there is less pressure to gain credibility than in the case of the formation of mobilization potential. This is not to say that credibility in action mobilization does not matter. Credibility always counts—all the more so because the goals and means of a movement organization are by definition controversial. Opponents and competing organizations challenge the arguments of the organization and advance a great many counterarguments. Under such circumstances, differences in credibility do matter even among supporters of the movement organization. The case of the campaign by a Dutch labor union to mobilize consensus about a shorter workweek illustrates this point.

The union's campaign concentrated on the argument that reducing the workweek would reduce unemployment. Employers, government officials, economists, and specialists in industrial relations vehemently denied the truth of this claim. The union failed completely to mobilize consensus for its position:

at the beginning of the campaign, 60-70% of its members believed that a shorter workweek would reduce unemployment. Within a few months this percentage dropped to 40%, and eventually to 25%. The credibility of the union as a source of information in the context of contradictory publicity played a significant role in this decline. Among members who agreed with the union, those who found the union highly credible[1] never changed their minds, whereas a large proportion of the members who found the union less credible did change their minds and came to disagree with the union. Among those members who initially disagreed with the union, a large proportion of those who found the union highly credible changed their minds in the first two months of the campaign and came to agree with the union. Those who found the union less credible, however, did not change their minds. Later on in the campaign the union no longer succeeded in persuading opponents among its members, even among members who found the union a credible source of information.

On highly controversial issues, high credibility apparently is better in fostering consonant beliefs than in transforming discrepant beliefs. If this is true in the context of action mobilization—that is, even among adherents of a movement—then we have to assume that the formation of mobilization potential on highly controversial issues will be extremely difficult. Indeed, the credibility of a movement organization among nonadherents can be so low that only indirect ways—using other organizations or media not identified with the movement—can promise some success. Especially in the initial phases of a movement organization's development, recourse to indirect means can be the only alternative available.

Examples abound. Consider the role of the churches in the civil rights movement (Morris 1984) and the peace movement (Klandermans and Oegema 1987). Also traditional women's organizations (Brïet et al. 1987) and traditional environmental organizations (Kriesi 1985; Rucht 1988) have played an important role in reaching subsets of the population that more radical organizations would have failed to reach.

With these examples in mind we can speculate about what can be called the "diversion of credibility." What we often see happening is that the target group's indigenous sources of information (organizations, media, opinion leaders) adopt parts of the message of the movement organization. This move is nothing spectacular; it exemplifies the two-step or multi-step flow of communication so well known from communication literature. Because of their much greater credibility, these indigenous sources are able to diffuse beliefs the organization itself would have never been able to diffuse. As this target group, or subpopulation, comes to adopt parts of the message, the movement organization itself gains greater credibility (cf. Tierney 1982). Eventually, the movement can communicate directly with the members of the subpopulation.

The message of social movement organizations. A first requirement for a message is that it be understandable. If people do not comprehend a message, attitudes will change very little. The content of the message of course varies with the nature of the campaign. If frame bridging is involved, then the message will confine itself to an explanation of the frame and/or the action goals and means, along with the request to support the organization. In the case of frame extension or amplification, the organization will attempt to link its frame to the supposed interests and values of the intended audience and call on it for support. If frame transformation is involved, then the organization will argue that a certain situation is unjust, that situational factors are to blame, and that changes can be brought about (cf. Snow et al. 1986, for a further elaboration).

Several authors have asserted that the messages of movement organizations show striking similarities irrespective of the sources they stem from (Buss and Sleeking 1980; Godwin 1984; Mazur 1981). On the one hand, similarities are due to the unavoidable dynamics of "proponents vs. opponents" and "challengers vs. establishment." Proponents promote and opponents criticize; challengers blame a powerful establishment and elites discredit challengers. Much of a movement organization's message consists of arguments for its own stands and criticisms of opposite stands, praising its allies and discrediting its opponents (Buss and Sleeking 1980; Griffin et al. 1986; Mazur 1981). Apparently, too, in their efforts to mobilize consensus, actors behave according to the rules associated with the role they occupy in the conflict.

On the other hand, similarities are due to the persuasive character of a movement organization's message. In his analysis of direct-mail campaigns from both conservative and liberal origins, Godwin (1984) detected the same general features: immediacy, that is, the assertion that the addressee can do something immediately; personalization, that is, the use of personal appeals, calling addressees by name, appealing to values they are supposed to adhere to; and concentration, for example, using mailing lists of individuals with specific characteristics and lifestyles, or using different appeals for different subpopulations. In addition, it turned out that 60-70% of the content of campaigns involved information, 20-40% an appeal to one's citizenly duty, 35-45% concerned purposive incentives for participation, and 20% consisted of appeals to guilt or fear. These proportions were the same for conservative and liberal groups alike.

Literature on persuasive communication details the factors that influence the impact of persuasive messages. Some of these factors are directly relevant to the social movement field: newness versus familiarity, one-sidedness versus two-sidedness, messages with or without conclusion, the use of threat (cf. Rogers 1983; Gergen and Gergen 1986). The newness/familiarity factor is closely related to the distinction between proactive and reactive demands discussed above. The more familiar a message, the easier it is to get it accepted. In the context of action mobilization, familiarity can be advantageous as long as the message does not deviate from what adherents are used to. In the context of the formation of mobilization potential, however, familiarity can easily become a serious handicap, because the message of a movement organization is almost by definition new to the audience. Mitchell (1984) makes the interesting observation that the message of a movement can be better framed in terms of a collective evil (i.e., some collective good familiar to the audience is threatened) than in terms of a collective good (i.e., some good not familiar to the audience that is to be produced).

Whether it is preferable to present information as one-sided or two-sided, or with or without conclusions is immediately relevant to a movement organization's persuasive communications, which usually take a particular side in a controversy, and suggest a line of action. Research results seem to indicate that education is an important moderator: among the more educated, two-sided messages without conclusions are more effective. For the less educated, one-sided messages with conclusions are more effective. Although movement organizations often use fear appeals to make people aware of existing problems, fear appeals are not always effective. The most important factor determining the effects of fear appeals is the presence or absence of effective means of coping. If no effective remedies are mentioned in a fear-arousing communication, then people may easily engage in defensive avoidance.

The channels used by movement organizations.   Snow et al. (1980) classify the channels a movement organization can use for information dissemination, promotion, and recruitment according to the dimensions face-to-face vs. mediated, and public vs. private. There are thus four different categories of channels: (a) face-to-face, private (door-to-door leafleting or petitioning, social networks), (b) private, mediated (mail, telephone), (c) face-to-face, public (face-to-face leafleting or petitioning on sidewalks, participation in public events, staging events for public consumption), and (d) public, mediated (radio, television, newspapers). It is not easy to generalize about the differential effectiveness of these four approaches. Face-to-face channels are known to be more effective than mediated channels both in the diffusion of information (Rogers 1983) and in mobilization campaigns of movement organizations (Brïet et al. 1987; Gerlach and Hine 1970; Henig 1982; Mazur 1981; Snow et al. 1980). Yet direct mail (a private, mediated channel) turns out to be very effective in environmental campaigns (Godwin and Mitchell 1984), and mass media, when used by movement organizations in an intelligent way, can also be very efficacious (Gitlin 1980; Mazur 1981; Taylor 1986).

Much depends of course on the impact desired and the size of the target group. To oversimplify a little: the relationship of the impact, the range of a channel, and the size of the target group to the effectiveness of a channel can be summarized in the following formula:

$$\text{Effectiveness} \quad = \quad \frac{\text{Impact \& Range}}{\text{Size of target group}}$$

The effectiveness of a channel increases with its impact and range, and is inversely related to the size of the target group. If a campaign has a large target group, a channel with great impact but a narrow range is not effective. If a drastic change in thought is desired, a channel with great impact is needed. And if that message is to reach a sizable target group, the channel must have a wide range as well.

However attractive mass-media and direct-mail campaigns may be (because of their wide range), they have obvious disadvantages for a movement organization. It is never certain to what extent the target group is actually reached. Campaigns using mass media are costly if an organization has to pay for them, and hard to control if an organization makes use of free publicity (editorial space). The media may draw a biased picture of the movement and so reshape mobilization potential by attracting some people and discouraging others (Gitlin 1980). Besides, it is hazardous for a social movement organization to depend on free publicity, for the mood in the media can turn against it and the media can lose interest (Gitlin 1980; Oberschall 1979). A movement organization's failure to use mass media is primarily the result of inexperience. As soon as a movement organization develops expertise in dealing with mass media—often through the installation of specialized public relations officers—it becomes much more effective in exploiting public-mediated channels. One way it can achieve such effectiveness is by establishing relationships with people inside the media industry, such as sympathetic journalists, editors, or directors.

One strategy often employed to circumvent the mass media is the use of the organizations own media (newspapers, magazines). There is, however, one serious limitation to this strategy. Reading a movement's newspaper or magazine is already a degree of participation that many adherents, even if they are subscribers, never reach—much less people who are not adherents. This restricted impact was clearly shown in my research on the mobilization campaign of unions in the Netherlands. Only among shop stewards and union militants was the union newspaper the prime source of information on the negotiations. For the average member, radio, television, or newspapers were much more important (Klandermans 1983a). A movement organization's own media are very effective in communicating to the active core of the constituency, but much less effective outside this usually narrow circle. Provided they have a sufficient number of links to other people, however, activists can transmit information to other people in their environment and can thus expand the range of their movement's media considerably.

Often a movement organization will not be able to do without private face-to-face interaction, either because it lacks the means to use other channels or because the impact achieved through other channels is too weak. The range of a campaign based on interpersonal contact depends on how extensive a network the movement has. The network need not necessarily be within the movement. Co-optable networks outside the movement are often even more effective. For example, the peace movement in the Netherlands, which has a widespread network of local branches with ties to local organizations, was very successful in the mobilization of consensus in Dutch society. In the absence of any infrastructure, mediated channels are the best alternative (McCarthy 1983).

There are some indications that the four means of communication are differentially effective among different categories of the population. Social networks are apparently more effective channels among women, than among men (Rochford 1985). People recruited through direct mail are more committed to the goals of the movement organization, whereas people recruited through private face-to-face contact are more committed to the organization (Godwin and Mitchell 1984). Compared to other channels, direct mail seems to attract more alienated, apathetic figures (Godwin 1984).

The use of communication channels is not unrelated to the context within which consensus mobilization occurs. The two different processes—formation of mobilization potential and action mobilization—involve different requirements for communication channels. The formation of a mobilization potential requires channels with a relatively high impact but can usually employ long term strategies. Action mobilization on the other hand, is bound to short term strategies but can confine itself primarily to limited forms of frame alignment, especially in the case of low-risk participation. In both contexts the specific features of mass media and private channels lead to a mixture of the two, that operate in completely different ways. In the context of the formation of mobilization potential, the mass media publicize the message of the movement organization, while private channels—especially face-to-face contacts in social networks—take care of the necessary frame-alignment (Gamson and Modigliani 1981). In the context of action mobilization, private face-to-face channels are often the only ones that can compete in speed with the mass media. So in the heat of the collective action, we see mass media, together with private channels, taking care of the dissemination of information. In a peculiar division of labor, the media seems to concentrate on the *means* of action, and private channels deal with the *goals*. By their accounts of protest events mass media are often much more capable than are private channels of creating either belief or doubt that an effective collective action is in the making. Private channels, on the other hand, are more concerned with legitimating action goals in the face of counterargumentation. In times of collective action, a social movement's communication networks are the channels most frequently used by movement organizations and their adherents (Klandermans 1983). A special feature is the mass meeting, which can function as an extremely efficacious communication channel during episodes of collective action (Morris 1984).

The audience. Systematic empirical research on the interaction of characteristics of different audiences of movement organizations and campaign characteristics is completely lacking. Moreover, it is known from the literatures on attitude change and the diffusion of innovation, that the same characteristics have contradictory effects depending on the situation and the criterion. For example, education helps people to understand better complex messages, but makes it more difficult to persuade them (see Hall et al. 1986, for results along that line in the social movement area). It can be expected from the same literature however, that attitudes toward the movement organization and its goals and means clearly influence the effectiveness of attempts of movement organizations to persuade individuals in the audience. A negative attitude toward a source of information rapidly reduces that source's credibility (Jaspars 1978). The discrepancy between the individual's attitudes and a message together with the credibility of the source, determine whether a message has any impact. The higher the discrepancy and the lower the credibility, the lesser the impact. The work of Snow et al. (1986) on frame alignment can be seen as an elaboration of this assertion.

CONCLUSIONS

Consensus mobilization (the deliberate attempt by an actor to create consensus among sectors of the population) has been distinguished from consensus formation (the convergence of meaning within social networks) This is not to say that the two are not related. On the contrary, attempts by movement organizations to mobilize consensus give impetus to processes of consensus formation; and consensus formation prepares the soil for consensus mobilization. Despite this reciprocity, in this chapter I have chosen to concentrate on the mobilization of consensus. Much of the impact of the movement organizations is rooted in numbers; most of their resources stem from individual supporters. In short, movement organizations are largely dependent on their capability of generating mass support. Social movement literature has concentrated largely on actual participation. Surprisingly little attention has been paid to organizations' attempts to propagate their views.

Perhaps as a consequence of the neglect of consensus mobilization as a separate process, an important distinction in the study of convincing and activating people has escaped the attention of scholars of social movements: namely, the difference between consensus mobilization in the context of the formation of a mobilization potential and consensus mobilization in the context of action. Legitimating the existence of a movement organization is rather different from legitimating its strategy: different arguments are used, different time frames are pertinent, different audiences are targeted, and different communication networks are put into operation.

Focusing on consensus mobilization brings to the fore the problematic position of movement organizations in regard to their credible sources of information. We might expect the credibility of a movement organization to be minimal in those situations in which credibility is needed most, that is where the discrepancy between the views of the organization and its audience is greatest. In those situations, a movement organization might hope that indigenous organizations, networks, or leaders would be willing to transmit its message, and that is the way it sometimes works. The diversion of credibility—that is, the role that indigenous organizations, networks, or leaders play in making movement organization more credible—is rather neglected in the literature.

It may be assumed that attempts to create consensus among a population have a diminishing return. After some optimum point has been reached, it becomes more and more difficult to enlarge a mobilization potential and/or the pool of adherents who agree with the action strategy. Under these circumstances, in the context of the formation of mobilization potential, movement organizations would do better to spend their resources on the maintenance and activation of commitment instead of on enlarging their mobilization potential. In the context of action mobilization, the movement organization reaches a point where it no longer makes sense to use any more of its resources for the mobilization of consensus. Resources are better used in providing incentives to wavering adherents.

In the social movement literature little attention is paid to the different kinds of audiences to which movement organizations must address themselves. Although movement organizations are not unaware of the heterogeneity of their audience, they usually lack systematic information on audience characteristics. These characteristics range from rather simple ones, such as what media different members of the audience use and what organizations they belong to, to more complicated qualities, such as beliefs, attitudes, and values. But, relevant distinctions such as frame bridging, frame extension, frame amplification, and frame transformation are of no use if profiles of a movement organization's audience are not available. Research that could provide social movement organizations with information on audience characteristics is rarely done. Such research should compare the way a movement organization approaches different audiences, and figure out what differences and similarities appear in terms of credibility, message, and most frequently used channels.

Indigenous social networks appear to be of crucial importance in the mobilization of consensus. In an intriguing interplay, mass media, movement organization, and competing and opposing sources of information supply the information that is processed inside the social networks to which individuals belong. From this observation it is plausible to conclude that opinions alter collectively. Consensus is not created by convincing individual after individual; rather, groups of individuals linked by social networks learn to move together in the direction of the movement organization. Individuals must choose whether to go along or deviate from the groups they are involved in. Altogether, this element of collective change makes the task of social movement organizations and students of social movements in the performance and investigation of consensus mobilization rather complicated. With this chapter I hope to convince organizers and scholars alike of the relevance of this aspect of the mobilization process, and to urge them to generate the research necessary to arrive at a clearer understanding of how it works.

NOTE

1. The credibility of the union as a source of information was assessed in a separate measurement at a different point in time.

REFERENCES

Boender, Kees. 1985. *Sociologische Analyse van Milieusolidariteit onder Elites en Publiek.* Rijswijk: Sythoff.

Brand, Karl-Werner. 1982. *Neue Soziale Bewegungen, Entstehung, Funktion und Perspektive neuer Protestpotentiale, eine Zwischenbilanz.* Opladen: Westdeutscher Verlag.

Brïet, Martien, Bert Klandermans, and Frederike Kroon. 1987. "How women become involved in the women's movement." In Mary Katzenstein and Carol Mueller (eds.), *The Women's Movements of the United States and Western Europe: Consciousness, Political Opportunity, and Public Policy.* Philadelphia: Temple University Press.

Buss, Henk and Siem Sleeking. 1980. "Vakbondsacties en propaganda." Unpublished paper, Amsterdam, Free University.

Ferree, Myra Marx and Beth B. Hess. 1985. *Controversy and Coalition: The New Feminist Movement.* Boston: G. K. Hall.

Ferree, Myra Marx and Frederick D. Miller. 1985. "Mobilization and meaning: Toward an integration of social psychological and resource perspectives on social movements." *Sociological Inquiry* 55:38-61.

Festinger, Leon. 1954. "A theory of social comparison." *Human Relations* 7:117-40.

Freeman, Jo. (ed.), 1983. *Social Movements of the Sixties and Seventies.* New York: Longman.

Gamson, William A. 1975. *The Strategy of Social Protest.* Homewood, Ill.: Dorsey Press.

Gamson, William A., Bruce Fireman, and Steve Rytina. 1982. *Encounters with Unjust Authorities.* Homewood, Ill.: Dorsey Press.

Gamson, William A. and André Modigliani. 1983. "Political culture and cognition." Boston College/University of Michigan, National Science Foundation Research Proposal.

Gergen, Kenneth J. and Mary M. Gergen, *Social Psychology.* 2d ed. New York: Springer.

Gerlach, Luther P. and Virginia H. Hine. 1970. *People, Power, Change: Movements of Social Transformation.* Indianapolis: Bobbs-Merill.

Gitlin, Todd. 1980. *The Whole World Is Watching: The Media in the Making and Unmaking of the New Left.* Berkeley: University of California Press.

Godwin, R. Kenneth. 1984. "Direct mail appeals and the mass society." Paper presented at the Annual Meeting of the American Sociological Association, San Antonio, Texas, August, 27-31.

Godwin, R. Kenneth and Robert C. Mitchell. 1984. "The impact of direct mail on political institutions." *Social Science Quarterly* 66:829-39.

Granberg, Daniel. 1983. "Preferences, expectations and placement judgments: Some evidence from Sweden." *Social Psychology Quarterly* 46:363-68.

Granberg, Daniel and Sören Holmberg. 1983. "Modeling the relationship among preference, expectations and voting behavior," Unpublished Paper, University of Göteborg, Department of Political Science.

Griffin, Larry J., Michael E. Wallace, and Beth A. Rubin. 1986. "Capitalist resistance to the organization of labor before the new deal: Why? how? success?" *American Sociological Review* 51:147-67.

Hall, Robert L., Mark Rodeghier, and Bert Useem. 1986. "Effects of education on attitude to protest." *American Sociological Review* 51:564-73.

Henig, Jeffrey R. 1982. *Neighborhood Mobilization, Redevelopment and Response.* New Brunswick, N.J.: Rutgers University Press.

Jaspars, J.M.F. 1978. "Determinants of attitudes and attitude change." In H. Tajfel and C. Fraser, *Introducing Social Psychology.* Harmondsworth: Penguin.

Jenkins, J. Craig. 1985. *The Politics of Insurgency.* New York: Columbia University Press.

Jenkins J. Craig. 1987. "Interpreting the stormy sixties; Three theories in search of a political age." In Richard G. Braungart (ed.), *Research in Political Sociology.* Vol. 3. Greenwich, Conn.: JAI.

Judkins, Benneth M. 1983. "Mobilization of Membership: The Black and Brown Lung Movements." Pages 35-51 in Jo Freeman (ed.), *Social Movements of the Sixties and Seventies.* New York. Longman.

Klandermans, Bert. 1983a. *Participatie in een Sociale Beweging: een Mobilizatiecampagne onderzocht.* Amsterdam: Free University Press.

Klandermans, Bert. 1983b. "Rotter's I.E.-scale and socio-political action taking: The balance of 20 years of research." *European Journal of Social Psychology* 13:399-415.

Klandermans, Bert. 1984a. "Mobilization and participation in trade union action: A value expectancy approach." *Journal of Occupational Psychology* 57:107-20.

Klandermans, Bert. 1984b. "Mobilization and participation: Social-psychological expansions of resource mobilization theory." *American Sociological Review* 49:583-600.

Klandermans, Bert and Dirk Oegema. 1987. "Campaigning for a nuclear freeze: Grassroots strategies and local government in the Netherlands." In Richard G. Braungart (ed.), *Research in Political Sociology.* Vol. 2. Greenwich, Conn.: JAI.

Kriesi, Hanspeter. 1985. *Bewegung in der Schweizer Politik, Fallstudien zu politischen Mobilierungsprozessen in der Schweiz.* Frankfurt: Campus.

Kriesi, Hanspeter. 1986. "Nieuwe sociale bewegingen: Op zoek naar hun gemeenschappelijke noemer." Inaugural Address, University of Amsterdam, June 16.

Lawson, Ronald. 1983. "A decentralized but moving pyramid: The evolution and consequences of the structure of the tenant movement." Pages 119-32 in Jo Freeman (ed.), *Social Movements of the Sixties and Seventies.* New York: Longman.

McAdam, Doug. 1982. *Political Process and the Development of Black Insurgency.* Chicago: University of Chicago Press.

McCarthy, John, D. 1983. "Social infrastructure deficits and new technologies: Mobilizing unstructured sentiment pools." Unpublished paper, Catholic University, Washington, D.C.

McQuail, Denis. 1983. *Mass Communication Theory: An Introduction.* London: Sage.

Marshall, Susan E. and Anthony Orum. 1987. "Opposition then and now: Countering feminism in the twentieth century." In Gwen Moore and Glenna D. Spitze (eds.), *Research in Politics and Society*. Vol. 2. Greenwich, Conn.: JAI.

Mazur, Allan. 1981. *The Dynamics of Technical Controversy*. Washington, D.C.: Communication Press.

Melucci, Alberto. 1985. "Multipolar action systems: Systemic environment and individual involvement in contemporary movements." Paper presented at the Planning Meeting on New Social Movements, Ithaca, N.Y., August 16-18.

Mitchell, Robert C. 1984. "Moving forward vs. moving backwards: Motivation for collective action." Paper presented at the Annual Meeting of the American Sociological Association, San Antonio, Texas, August 27-31.

Morris, Aldon. 1984. *The Origins of the Civil Rights Movement: Black Communities Organizing for Change*. New York: Free Press.

Mushaben, Joyce Marie. 1986. "Grassroots and Gewaltfreie Aktionen: A study of mass mobilization strategies in the West German peace movement." *Journal of Peace Research* 23:141-54.

Oberschall, Anthony. 1979. "Protracted conflict." In Mayer N. Zald and John D. McCarthy (eds.), *The Dynamics of Social Movements, Resource Mobilization, Social Control and Tactics*. Cambridge, Mass.: Winthrop.

Oberschall, Anthony. 1980. "Loosely structured collective conflicts: A theory and an application." Pages 45-68 in Louis Kriesberg (ed.), *Research in Social Movements, Conflict, and Change*. Vol. 5. Greenwich, Conn.: JAI.

Oliver, Pamela. 1983. "The mobilization of paid and volunteer activists in the neighborhood movement." Pages 133-70 in Louis Kriesberg (ed.), *Research in Social Movements, Conflict, and Change*. Vol. 5. Greenwich, Conn. JAI.

Outshoorn, Joyce. 1986. *De Politieke Strijd rondom de Abortus Wedgeving in Nederland 1964-1984*. Amsterdam: Free University.

Pinard, Maurice and Richard Hamilton. 1986. "Motivational dimensions in the Quebec independence movement: A test of a new model." Pages 225-80 in Louis Kriesberg (ed.), *Research in Social Movements, Conflict, and Change*. Vol. 9. Greenwich, Conn.: JAI.

Piven, Frances Fox and Richard A. Cloward. 1979. *Poor People's Movements: Why They Succeed, How They Fail*. New York: Vintage.

Reckman, Piet. 1979. *Naar een Strategie en Methodiek voor Sociale Aktie*. Baarn: Bosch and Keuning.

Rochford, E. Burke, Jr. 1985. "Gender and differential recruitment to Hare Krishna." Paper presented at the Annual Meeting of the American Sociological Association, Washington, D.C., August.

Rogers, Everett M. 1983. *Diffusion of Innovation*. New York: Free Press.

Rucht, Dieter. Forthcoming. "Environmental movement organization in West-Germany and France: Structure and interorganizational relations." In Bert Klandermans (ed.), *Organizations for Change: Social Movement Organizations across Cultures*. Greenwich, Conn.: JAI.

Sharp, Gene. 1973. *The Politics of Non-Violent Action*. Boston: Porter Sargent.

Skelly, James M. 1986. "Power-knowledge: The problems of peace research and peace movement." Paper presented at the International Peace Research Biennial Meeting, Sussex, England, April 13-18.

Smelser, Neil J. 1971. *Theory of Collective Behavior*. New York: Free Press.

Snow, David A., E. Burke Rochford, Jr., Steven K. Worden, and Robert D. Benford. 1986. "Frame alignment processes, micromobilization, and movement participation." *American Sociological Review* 51:464-81.

Tarrow, Sidney. 1983. *Struggling to Reform: Social Movements and Policy Change during Cycles of Protest.* Western Societies Paper No. 15. Ithaca, N.Y.: Cornell University.

Taylor, D. Garth. 1986. *Public Opinion and Collective Action.* Chicago: University of Chicago Press.

Terchek, Ronald J. 1974. "Protest and bargaining." *Journal of Peace Research* 11:133-45.

Thorne, Barry. 1975. "Protest and the problem of credibility: Uses of knowledge and risk taking in the draft resistance movement." *Social Problems* 23:111-23.

Tierney, Kathleen J. 1982. "The battered women movement and the creation of the wife beating problem." *Social Problems* 29:207-20.

Tilly, Charles, Louise Tilly, and Richard Tilly. 1975. *The Rebellious Century: 1830-1930.* Cambridge: Harvard University Press.

Turner, Ralph H. 1969. "The theme of contemporary social movements." *British Journal of Sociology* 20:390-405.

Walsh, Edward J. 1981. "Resource mobilization and citizen protest in communities around Three Mile Island." *Social Problems* 29:1-21.

Wilson, John. 1973. *Introduction to Social Movements.* New York: Basic Books.

IDEOLOGY, FRAME RESONANCE, AND PARTICIPANT MOBILIZATION

David A. Snow and Robert D. Benford

The relationship between ideological factors—values, beliefs, meanings—and identification with social movements and participation in their activities has rarely been treated systematically or dialectically in either the theoretical or empirical literature. With the exception of a few general discussions of social movements (Turner and Killian 1987; Wilson 1973) and a scattering of critical essays (Ferree and Miller 1985; Zurcher and Snow 1981), ideational elements tend to be treated in primarily descriptive rather than analytical terms. What this treatment typically involves is a description of movement ideology or value orientation as prefatory to the analytic task of explaining the emergence and operation of social movements.

This tendency to sidestep or gloss ideological considerations in favor of other factors is particularly evident in the two current fashionable approaches to the analysis of social movements—the new social movements approach in Western Europe and the resource mobilization perspective in the United States. In the case of the former, movements are seen primarily as the carriers or transmitters of programs for action that arise from new structural dislocations. Collective action or social movement activity is seemingly contingent upon a kind of

International Social Movement Research, Vol. 1, pages 197-217.
Supplement to Research in Social Movements, Conflicts and Change
Copyright © 1988 by JAI Press Inc.
ISBN: 0-89232-955-6

immanent awakening that expresses the conditions of or divisions within a population's material situation. What is problematic from this vantage point are not ideas and cognitions but underlying structural precipitants and the emergent forms of action.[1] In the case of the resource mobilization perspective, even less attention is devoted to ideological considerations. Mobilizing beliefs and ideas are seen as ubiquitous and therefore relatively unimportant determinants of movement emergence, mobilization, and success. Analytic attention is focused, instead, on the resource acquisition and deployment activities of movement organizations and on the waxing and waning of political opportunity structures.[2]

Although these two perspectives differ in terms of focal considerations and levels of analyses, both tend to treat meanings or ideas as given, as if there is an isomorphic relationship between the nature of any particular set of conditions or events and the meanings attached to them. Since meanings are produced in the course of interaction with other individuals and objects of attention (Blumer 1969; Mead 1934), it strikes us as foolhardy to take meaning and other ideational elements for granted or to treat them purely descriptively in any equation attempting to account for movement participation. Movements function as carriers and transmitters of mobilizing beliefs and ideas, to be sure; but they are also actively engaged in the production of meaning for participants, antagonists, and observers. This productive work may involve the shaping and structuring of existing meanings. Movements can thus be construed as functioning in part as signifying agents and, as such, are deeply embroiled, along with the media and the state, in what Stuart Hall (1982) has referred to as the "politics of signification."

We use the verb *framing* to conceptualize this signifying work precisely because that is one of the things social movements do. They frame,[3] or assign meaning to and interpret, relevant events and conditions in ways that are intended to mobilize potential adherents and constituents, to garner bystander support, and to demobilize antagonists. In an earlier paper we argued that the mobilization and activation of participants are contingent upon "the linkage of individual and SMO interpretive orientations, such that some set of individual interests, values, and beliefs and SMO activities, goals, and ideology are congruent and complementary" (Snow et al. 1986, p. 464). We referred to this linkage as "frame alignment" and identified four alignment processes in which movements engage for the purpose of participant mobilization.[4] In that paper we proceeded, for heuristic purposes, as though all framing efforts are successful. But clearly that is not the case. In this chapter we turn to consideration of the conditions that affect or constrain framing efforts directed toward participant mobilization.[5] Why are potential constituents mobilized on some occasions while at other times framing efforts fall on deaf ears and may even be counterproductive? Under what conditions do framing efforts strike a responsive chord or resonate within the targets of mobilization? What are the key determinants of the differential success of movement framing efforts? What, in short, accounts for what might be termed *frame resonance?*

We attend to these questions by identifying and elaborating four sets of factors that affect the mobilizing potency of a movement's framing efforts and activities. The first set concerns the robustness, completeness, and thoroughness of the framing effort. Does it attend to both consensus and action mobilization, as conceptualized by Klandermans (1984), or is it partial and incomplete? A second set deals with the internal structure of the larger belief system with which the movement seeks to affect some kind of cognitive/ideational alignment. The third set concerns the relevance of the frame to the life world of the participants. Does it resonate phenomenologically? The fourth set concerns what Tarrow (1983a; 1983b) has referred to as "cycles of protest." In elaborating each of these considerations, we draw on our research on the peace movement for illustrative purposes.[6]

I. CORE FRAMING TASKS

Klandermans (1984) has argued that the success of any participant mobilization campaign is contingent upon its ability to affect both consensus and action mobilization. That is, movements must drum up support for their views and aims and activate individuals who already agree with those views and aims. While we find this distinction to be of considerable conceptual utility, we do not think it goes far enough in getting at the dynamic interactive relationship among ideational elements, movement activity, and participation. Additionally, the terms strike us as umbrella concepts of sorts in that they camouflage or gloss over the more specific tasks that need to be conducted in order to achieve consensus and to produce action.

We think the verb "framing" provides a conceptual handle for identifying and elaborating the more specific tasks. Following Wilson's (1973) decomposition of ideology into three component elements, we suggest that there are three core framing tasks: (1) a diagnosis of some event or aspect of social life as problematic and in need of alteration; (2) a proposed solution to the diagnosed problem that specifies what needs to be done; and (3) a call to arms or rationale for engaging in ameliorative or corrective action. The diagnostic and prognostic framing tasks are directed toward achieving consensus mobilization. The latter task, which concerns action mobilization, provides the motivational impetus for participation.

It is our thesis that variation in the success of participant mobilization, both within and across movements, depends upon the degree to which these three tasks are attended to. The more the three tasks are robust or richly developed and interconnected, the more successful the mobilization effort, *ceteris paribus*. The general proposition can be illustrated in part with reference to the peace movement.

A.   Diagnostic Framing

Diagnostic framing involves identification of a problem and the attribution of blame or causality. While consensus is often achieved within a movement with respect to problem identification, attributional consensus is less frequently realized or is more problematic. In the case of the peace movement, there is relatively little dispute regarding the nuclear threat. Indeed, the most richly developed imagery is represented by the mushroom cloud and the associated destructive capacity of nuclear weapons.[7] There is far less agreement, however, with respect to the factors underlying this threat (Benford 1987; Newman 1986; Yankelovich and Doble 1984). Disarmament proponents, as well as persons external to the movement, have identified a variety of factors as causes of the nuclear threat. While more than one factor is often blamed or combined in such causal attributions, the various wings or factions of a movement tend to elevate one factor above all other possible causes as the most salient or primary one. Our research indicates at least four distinctive sets of causal factors, each of which is claimed by different sections of the movement to be *the* most salient cause of the nuclear threat: (1) technological, (2) political, (3) economic, and (4) moral. Since our purpose is to illustrate our conceptual framework, we will attend to only the first two causal attributions.

Many view the nuclear threat as primarily a consequence of technological developments. Nuclear weapons are seen as representing the culmination of the Enlightenment and the industrial revolution and therefore as manifestations of our species' attempt to understand, harness, and overcome the forces of nature. Yet even among those who point to technology in general as the primary cause underlying the nuclear predicament there is disagreement regarding the more specific focus of blame. Some employ a Frankenstein analogy suggesting that our present lack of understanding of technology has led to the creation of a nuclear monster that could turn, out of control, on its creators. Others blame an overly optimistic faith in the capacity of science to solve global social and political problems. Still others stress the amoral commitment of technologists to their craft.

Within other sectors of the movement, political factors loom as most salient. There are those who argue that an anachronistic geopolitical structure is to blame, particularly one comprising sovereign states. Others locate the main impetus of the threat in the struggle for global hegemony between the United States and the Soviet Union. Segments of the movement have laid the blame on the U.S. alone, contending that the U.S. has been the leader in accelerating the nuclear threat and that the Soviets have merely attempted to match U.S. strategic escalations. In sum, a variety of general and specific factors have been offered by disarmament advocates as the single most important cause of the threat, and each factor has implications for the prognostic aspect of consensus mobilization.

B. Prognostic Framing

The purpose of *prognostic framing* is not only to suggest solutions to the problem but also to identify strategies, tactics, and targets. What is to be done is thereby specified. While proposed solutions to the problems may not necessarily follow directly from the causal attributions offered by a particular segment of a movement, more often than not there is a direct correspondence between diagnostic and prognostic framing efforts.

Continuing with the illustrations employed above, we find that those who see technology as the main cause of the nuclear threat tend to focus upon technology in their prognoses. At one extreme are those who propose a rejection of technology and a return to nature, holistic lifestyles, rural communal living, and the like. The antitechnologists, who are basically retreatist, constitute a relatively small portion of the nuclear disarmament movement. At the other extreme are those who advocate technological solutions for what they see as primarily a technological problem. Groups such as the Union of Concerned Scientists, for instance, have focused their attention on "stopping hardware," that is, on preventing the production and deployment of particular weapon systems that they view as most dangerous, destabilizing, or likely to increase the probability of nuclear war. We are not suggesting that this wing of the movement has altogether avoided advocating political solutions but, rather, that proposed technical solutions tend to be preeminent in their framing efforts and public discourse.[8]

Those who diagnose the nuclear threat as a symptom or manifestation of political factors tend to advocate predominantly political solutions. One of the movement's wings has proposed a variety of globalistic treatments, all of which have to do with shifting the focus of political power from sovereign states to international institutions. These suggestions include proposals for establishing world federalism, strengthening international institutions, challenging the legality of nuclear weapons in the World Court, and so forth. Other segments of the movement, such as the U.S. Freeze Campaign, have focused advocacy on bilateral arms control negotiations and treaties. Still other groups, such as Britain's Campaign for Nuclear Disarmament (CND) or the Dutch Inter-Church Peace Council (IKV), have proposed mobilizing citizens to pressure their governments to initiate unilateral steps toward total nuclear disarmament or to declare their political jurisdictions "nuclear free zones."

C. Motivational Framing

Variation in the content of prognostic frames within the peace movement could be elaborated in much greater detail. The foregoing discussion suffices to illustrate, however, that consensus mobilization is not only multifaceted but that its several dimensions are interconnected such that each successive dimension is constrained by the preceding ones. This interconnection is further illustrated by consideration of the third mobilizing framing task or function: the elaboration of a call to arms or *rationale for action* that goes beyond the diagnosis and prognosis. Since agreement about the causes and solutions to a particular problem does not automatically produce corrective action, it follows that consensus mobilization does not necessarily yield to mobilization. Participation is thus contingent upon the development of motivational frames that function as prods to action. The substance and mobilizing potency of these frames, which consist essentially of a vocabulary of motives (Mills 1940), are obviously constrained by the diagnostic components of movement ideology, but not always in ways that are suspected or intended.

That action mobilization does not necessarily follow on the heels of consensus mobilization is particularly evident in the case of movements that seek goals that constitute what Olson (1965) calls "public goods" (i.e., indivisible, nonexcludable benefits). With its goal of a nuclear-free world, the peace movement is of that genre. It is consequently confronted with the task of convincing particular participants of both the need for and the utility of becoming active in the cause. The solution, according to Olson and the resource mobilization perspective, resides in the generation of "selective incentives" for participation. These incentives, generally speaking, encompass material, status, solidary, and moral inducements.[9]

In the case of the peace movement the rationale for participation is framed most generally and pervasively in terms of moral considerations. This moral element is reflected most clearly in Jonathan Schell's best-seller, *Fate of the Earth,* which provides not only an elegant diagnosis of the nuclear problem confronting humankind but also a clarion call for action. The moral implications of this assessment of the problem are captured by Schell's (1982, p. 116) discussion of what he refers to as "the second death."

> The possibility that the living can stop the future generations from entering into life compels us to ask basic new questions about our existence, the most sweeping of which is what these unborn ones, most of whom we will never meet if they are born, mean to us. No one has ever thought to ask this question before our time, because no generation before ours has ever held the life and death of the species in its hand.

Given this moral dilemma, it follows that we have a moral imperative to do something about it. Thus, in the book's last sentence, Schell (1982, p. 231) issues what is clearly interpretable as a moral call to action:

> Either we will sink into the final coma and end it all or, as I trust and believe, we will awaken to the truth of our peril, a truth as great as life itself, and, like a person who has swallowed a lethal poison up, we will break through the layers of our denials, put aside our fainthearted excuses, and rise up to cleanse the earth of nuclear weapons.

Movement handbooks or "bibles" such as Schell's, Thompson and Smith's *Protest and Survive,* (1981), and Keyes's *The Hundredth Monkey* (1982) function to supply a vocabulary of moral rationales for action that routinely are given expression, in distilled fashion, within movement circles and at rallies. There are other inducements, as well, although perhaps less general and persuasive; but we need not articulate them here since our aim is only to illustrate that the generation of motivation constitutes a framing problem related to, but distinctive from, the diagnostic and prognostic components of consensus mobilization.

In some instances these components unwittingly render existing frames impotent or the development of new ones particularly difficult. This framing dilemma may occur in several ways. The problem may be framed so cataclysmically and hopelessly, for example, that ameliorative action seems highly improbable. Such a framing gives rise to a sense of fatalism. This tendency is manifest in peace movement framings that highlight and embellish the doomsday possibilities of nuclear confrontation. One of the most graphic examples of this tendency is provided by the Physicians for Social Responsibility (PSR) whose framings, until recently, focused solely on the horrifying consequences of nuclear weapons and their claim that "there is no medical response to nuclear war." These "bombing runs" or "apocaporn" framings, as they were dubbed within movement circles, were subsequently called into question precisely because of their numbing effects. They were seen to function as impediments rather than prods to mobilization.

Attention may also be focused so singularly on problem diagnoses that the prognostic considerations are neglected. The unintended consequence is that guidelines for action are unclear. Concern and consensus with respect to the nature and the causes of the problem may be widespread, but questions of what should be done and why may have received only the most ambiguous answers. This framing problem was eventually recognized by PSR leaders as an encumbrance to their action mobilization interests. As a former director of PSR noted:

> It has gone beyond the point where we can not responsibly sound the alarm without prescribing therapy. . . . We have an obligation to go one step further (Rizzo 1983, p. 11).

In January 1983, in an attempt to overcome this framing problem, PSR, for the first time in the group's history, recommended four specific ways of "halting and reversing the arms race."[10] In due time, then, PSR came to recognize what many movement activists and analysts tend to gloss over: that diagnostic frames alone, no matter how richly developed, do little to affect action mobilization and that, the more highly integrated the diagnostic, prognostic, and action frames, the higher the probability of becoming active in any particular cause.

A third way in which antecedent framing efforts may inadvertently stifle action is that both diagnosis and prognosis may be framed in such a way that public debate is rendered superfluous and the prospect of rank-and-file participation is undermined. This framing dilemma is evident in those wings of the disarmament movement in which the problem and solutions are framed largely in technological terms. The issue is defined as a problem for experts, a definition that forecloses public debate. The frequent use of technical terms and acronyms (e.g., throw weights, circular error probable, electromagnetic pulse, SLBMs, MIRVs), as well as discussions focused on the characteristics of particular weapons systems, not only provide a vocabulary that is foreign to all but the technically trained but also underscore the technical nature of the problem. The point is that to frame any issue in terms that are inaccessible to all but a select few, as is the case with technologically framed issues, is to reduce potential participants to spectators and so make the issue nonparticipatory.

To summarize the foregoing observations: we have shown that consensus mobilization is multidimensional and that agreement on one dimension does not ensure unanimity with respect to other dimensions. We have also emphasized the fact that action mobilization does not automatically follow from consensus mobilization, and so the development of motivational frames that function as prods to action are often required. To focus only on the substantive content of the movement's framing efforts, however, runs the risk of creating a picture of frame alignment as an overly mechanistic, nondialectical process whereby mobilizing ideas are poured into or diffused among a passive, nonsuspecting population. Clearly that is an erroneous picture of the alignment process and one that we do not wish to portray.

In his discussions of hegemony and revolution, Gramsci (1971) recognized the importance of "political education" and the development of a counter-ideology or framing as an antidote to ruling class hegemony. But with his distinction between "organic" and "nonorganic" ideology he realized that any successful political education must begin with and be linked to the nature and structure of the belief system that is the objective of transformation. Building on Gramsci, Rude (1980) has argued that the mobilizing potential of protest beliefs and ideas, which he categorizes as a variant of "derived ideology," is partly contingent on the degree to which it is built upon the stock of folk ideas and beliefs he refers to as "inherent ideology." The point is that the relationship between the framing efforts of movements and the mobilization of potential constituents is highly dialectical, such that there is no such thing as a *tabula rasa* or empty glass into which new and perhaps alien ideas can be poured. Neither Gramsci nor Rude clearly specify the ways in which "nonorganic" or "inherent ideologies" constrain the proffered framings of social movements, however. We thus turn to an elaboration of those considerations.

II. INFRASTRUCTURAL CONSTRAINTS OF BELIEF SYSTEMS

Whatever the substance of any particular framing, its appeal and mobilizing potency are affected by several sets of constraints that are external to it. One set concerns the internal structure of the larger belief system or ideology with which the movement seeks to effect some form of alignment. Another pertains to the extent to which the framing effort is relevant to or resonates within the life world of potential participants. In this section we attend to the infrastructure constraints.

Previous work (Borhek and Curtis 1975; Converse 1964) on the nature of belief systems suggest at least three core components: (1) the *centrality* or hierarchical salience of any particular ideational element in relation to other such elements within the belief system as a whole; (2) the *range* of the central ideational elements or the domains of life they encompass; and (3) the degree of *interrelatedness* among the various ideational elements within the belief system.

Belief systems can vary considerably in terms of these characteristics. At one extreme are those based upon a core principle or value wherein the range of elements is highly interconnected with other elements of the system, as in the case of scientific theory. At the other extreme are systems with a number of equally salient principles or beliefs, each of which is related to a particular domain of life but in a highly compartmentalized fashion, as with polytheistic religions of the kind that flowered in classical Greece. In the case of the former, the viability of the entire system rests on the continued salience and credibility of the core principle; in the case of the latter, individual salient elements can be chipped away without the entire corpus of beliefs crumbling (Borhek and Curtis 1975; Snow and Machalek 1982). Most beliefs fall somewhere between these two extremes. Regardless of where the target constituency's belief system falls between these two extremes, however, the three components noted above function to constrain or affect the efficacy of a movement's framing efforts and mobilization campaigns.

A. Centrality

Turning to the first constraint, we see that if the values or beliefs the movement seeks to promote or defend are of low hierarchical salience within the larger belief system, the mobilizing potential is weakened considerably and the task of political education or consciousness raising becomes more central but difficult. It is axiomatic that the greater the correspondence between values promoted by a movement and those held by potential constituents, the greater the success of the mobilization effort, as measured by the number of contributors to or participants in the movement. Things are seldom that simple, however. Individuals routinely hold numerous values that not only are arrayed hierarchically but also vary in terms of the intensity with which they are held.

Values promoted by the peace movement, for example, such as sanctity of human life, preservation of the species, and peaceful coexistence, are those with which most citizens would agree, but the questions of how intensely they feel about the values and of how salient they are in relation to other values are problematic. We suspect that the mobilization difficulties encountered by peace activists in the United States are due in part to the relatively low hierarchical salience of the issues and values promoted by the movement. This hypothetical disjuncture was clearly recognized by the former national coordinator of the Freeze Campaign following the 1984 election:

> The important message [of the election] is that the American people are in favor of a freeze but they don't feel the freeze is an urgent necessity. To them it's not more important than short-term economics or personalities.

A similar conclusion was reached by a movement analyst regarding arms control in general:

> The movement, despite the hoopla and energy exhibited by some activists, was just not able to push the arms race to the center stage in the national political debate (Corn 1984, p. 12).

Public opinion survey results suggest that these observations are empirically on target. For example, a pre-1984 election poll found that over two-thirds (68%) of Americans who thought Mondale would be more likely to reduce the threat of nuclear war than Reagan still preferred Reagan because they felt they would be better off financially with Reagan in the White House (*Washington Post*/ABC News Poll, September 6-11, 1984).

B. Range and Interrelatedness

The second two sets of internal structure constraints of belief systems—range and interrelatedness—present movements with additional framing dilemmas in the course of their mobilization campaigns. If the framing effort is linked to only one core belief or value that is of limited range, then the movement is vulnerable to being discounted if that value or belief is called into question or if its hierarchical salience diminishes within the entire belief system. In order to deal with this dilemma, as well as expand their potential constituency, movements may extend the boundaries of their primary framework by incorporating values that were initially incidental to its central objectives. In doing so, movements often find themselves confronted with the problem of frame overextension. This framing hazard has been frequently encountered by the peace movement.

A 1982 California freeze referendum, for example, represents an unsuccessful attempt to extend the movement's values beyond reducing the nuclear threat. The initial petition proposed not only that the state endorse the freeze but additionally that the funds saved from such an arms control measure would be utilized to "meet human needs." When polls indicated that this two-pronged referendum would fail at the ballot box, freeze organizers decided to drop the welfare component, and the initiative subsequently passed by a substantial margin.

Problems of frame overextension may also arise when several movement organizations establish coalitions and pool their resources to organize an event. To illustrate: in 1983 simultaneous demonstrations were organized throughout the United States and Western Europe to protest the pending deployment of cruise and Pershing II missiles. Yet, as is often the case with movement coalitions, the number of goals and values being promoted extended well beyond the "Euromissile" issue to encompass gay rights, feminist concerns, Palestinian liberation, antiinterventionism, and a host of other causes associated with the Left. A statewide peace coalition organized as part of this mass mobilization effort similarly attempted to extend its focus beyond the Euromissile issue to include opposition to the U.S. involvement in Central America. One advocate of broadening the frame in this fashion explained:

> There is a problem with getting people involved in this because the threat is in Europe. We need to bring in the intervention issue because it is closer to home.

While the coalition's decision to broaden its agenda to include opposition to U.S. foreign policy may have engendered support from persons who might not have otherwise participated, our research indicates that this frame extension led others to reject opportunities to participate in movement activities—or at least provided them with rationales for doing so. This reaction was evident in the case of several freeze supporters, as one commented upon being solicited by a peace coalition member for assistance with the event:

> If your goal was still just "stop the missiles," I'd help. But now you've gone and confused the issue by including Central America. You've muddied up the waters so much that it would be a waste of my time to contribute anything to your march.

III. PHENOMENOLOGICAL CONSTRAINTS

A third set of factors affecting the mobilizing potency of proferred framings is the phenomenological life world of the targets of mobilization. Does the framing strike a responsive chord with those individuals for whom it is intended? To what extent does it inform understanding of events and experiences within the world of potential constituents? Is it relevant to their life situations? There appear to be three interrelated but analytically distinct constraints that bear upon this relevancy issue: (1) empirical credibility, (2) experiential commensurability, and (3) narrative fidelity.

A.   Empirical Credibility

By *empirical credibility* we refer to the fit between the framing and events in the world. Is the framing testable? Can it be subjected to verification? Are there events or occurrences that can be pointed to as evidence substantiating the diagnostic, prognostic, or motivational claims of the movement? Of course, what is constitutive of evidence for any particular claim is itself subject to debate.

One of the central claims of the nuclear disarmament movement, as articulated most vividly by Schell (1982), is that not only are individual lives threatened by the nuclear arms race but the entire human species and perhaps most life on the planet would not survive a nuclear war. As is typically the case with most doomsday framings, Schell's warnings provoked virulent argumentation and discounting. The substance of Schell's claims was attacked on several fronts. The most general counterclaim was that such doomsday fears were unwarranted because of the improbability of nuclear confrontation. Furthermore, nuclear defense proponents argued that, even if such a confrontation were to occur, it was far more likely to be a limited rather than a global nuclear cataclysm. Additionally, some proponents countered that the doomsday claims of the nuclear disarmament movement were without empirical substance and thus existed merely at the level of speculative hypothesis. These countervailing framings in turn engendered more empirically concrete reframings by disarmament proponents. The nuclear winter thesis, as publicly disseminated by Sagan, is a case in point. Drawing on varied research that ranges from Hiroshima and Nagasaki to the effects of volcanic eruptions, proponents attempted to strengthen the empirical credibility of the movement's claims (Turco et al. 1983).

B.   Experiential Commensurability

In an area of competing frames and frame disputes, the question arises as to what determines whether one set of claims is found to be more credible than the others. The answer depends in part on the interpretive screen through which the "evidence" is filtered. One such important screening mechanism is the personal experience of the targets of mobilization. Does the framing have what we call *experiential commensurability?* Does it suggest answers and solutions to troublesome events and situations which harmonize with the ways in which these conditions have been or are currently experienced? Or is the framing too abstract and distant from the everyday experiences of potential participants?

We think this variable of experiential commensurability is perhaps one of the most important determinants of individual and cross-cultural variations in the mobilizing potency of peace movement framing efforts. Although we have not aggregated systematically derived comparative data pertaining to support for and participation in the peace movement, perusal of the popular press, media displays, and peace movement literature suggests three general cross-national observations. First, while there is widespread global consensus regarding the nuclear threat and the need to do something about it, there is disagreement over what should be done. In Japan and Western Europe there appears to be considerable support for unilateral and total nuclear disarmament; in the United States, on the other hand, the prevailing sentiment favors a bilateral freeze. A second general observation is that the proportion of the population participating in peace movement activities appears to be greater in Japan and Western Europe than in the United States. The third observation pertains to differences in the nature and level of movement activity. In Western Europe, in contrast to the United States, for example, movement activity appears to be more constant and intense.

To the extent that these observations are empirically accurate, we think they can be explained in part by differences in the nature of cross-national experience with warfare and nuclear weaponry. Experience with warfare and nuclear weapons has been less direct and immediate in the United States than it has in Japan and Europe. Although the United States has been involved in numerous wars and skirmishes, none have taken place on its soil since the mid-1800s. Additionally, U.S. nuclear weapon installations tend to be located greater distances from dense population settlements than is the case in Western Europe. Given the Europeans' direct experience with warfare and the closer proximity of nuclear weapons installations to population masses, it follows that the threat of nuclear war has far greater experiential commensurability for citizens of European countries than for Americans. And this proposition would appear to be even more relevant to the Japanese, who are the only people to have directly experienced the horrors of nuclear weapons.

Taken together, these observations help to explain our research findings regarding the difficulties faced by U.S. peace activists in concretizing the nuclear threat. In the case of the U.S., the difference in mobilization rates does not appear to stem merely from the way in which the problem is framed; it also lies in the commensurability of the frames with what most citizens have experienced. In short, the doomsday frame does not resonate experientially to the same degree within U.S. citizens that it does with citizens of European countries and Japan, and, as a consequence, it does not function as successfully in the United States as a prod to action.

C. Narrative Fidelity

Such differences can also be explained in part by the degree to which proffered framings resonate with cultural narrations, that is, with the stories, myths, and folk tales that are part and parcel of one's cultural heritage and that thus function to inform events and experiences in the immediate present. When such correspondence exists, framings can be said to have what Fisher (1984) has termed *"narrative fidelity."* In other words, the framing strikes a responsive chord in that it rings true with existing cultural narrations that are functionally similar to what Gouldner (1970, pp. 29-36) calls "domain assumptions."

The importance of narrative fidelity to the success of any kind of framing effort has been recognized in different quarters. In the theological realm, for instance, Goldberg (1982, p. 35) notes that:

> a theologian, regardless of the propositional statements he or she may have to make about a community's convictions, must consciously strive to keep those statements in intimate contact with the narratives which give rise to those convictions, within which they gain their sense and meaning, and *from which they have been abstracted.*

Rude's (1980) linkage of inherent and derived aspects of ideology seems to make a similar point, as does Geertz's (1973) conception of ideology as a cultural system. Geertz's discussion of organized labor's designation of the Taft-Hartley Act of 1947 as a "slave labor law" provides a particularly elegant example of the linkage between cultural narratives and the efficacy of the way in which events or issues are framed. Geertz notes that, although the intent of the "slave labor" framing was to mobilize opposition to the act by suggesting that the labor policies of the Republican Party and the Bolsheviks were analogous, the framing effort fell on deaf ears and thus misfired. The reason, he suggests (1973, p. 211), was that "semantic tension between the image of a conservative Congress outlawing the closed shop and of the prison camps of Siberia was— apparently—too great." Geertz (1973, p. 212) thus concluded that if the Taft-Hartley Act were to be seen as a mortal threat to organized labor, "one must simply frame the argument . . . in some other way."

It is our contention that this variable of narrative fidelity similarly affects the mobilizing potency of movement framing efforts. Again, this connection can clearly be seen in the case of the peace movement. Internationally, two issues have been the object of intramovement debate regarding how best to reduce the threat of nuclear confrontation. One concerns arms control versus total disarmament. The other concerns the question of whether control or disarmament should be pursued unilaterally or bilaterally. In the United States there has been considerable support for a bilateral freeze but relatively little enthusiasm for either complete nuclear disarmament, however it might be pursued, or unilateral arms control.

We think these observations can be partly explained in terms of two factors. The first is grounded in the common sense understanding that all U.S. military ventures are defensive in nature, as reflected in a recent public opinion poll indicating that 81% of Americans believe it is current U.S. policy to use nuclear weapons "if and only if" its adversaries use them first (Yankelovich and Doble 1984, p. 45). The second pertains to the prevailing view among Americans that the Soviet Union is a distrustful aggressor on the world stage or "the bear in the woods" depicted in Reagan's 1984 reelection campaign commericals. The conjunction of these two strands of American folk ideology or common sense render the ideas of unilateral initiatives or total disarmament foolhardy. In the language of political analysts, such a view "would not play in Peoria." That is to say, it lacks narrative fidelity. Among U.S. peace activists recognition of this framing constraint has been widespread and has prompted them to support the freeze, irrespective of their personal beliefs. In Europe, on the other hand, where views of the Soviet Union tend to be less xenophobic, there is greater latitude, wherein both the arms control versus disarmament and the bilateral versus unilateral issues generate considerable public discussion and debate.

To summarize this section: we have suggested that the mobilizing potency of movement framing efforts is partly contingent upon the extent to which they have empirical credibility, experiential commensurability, and narrative fidelity. We suggest that at least one of these relevancy variables is a necessary condition for consensus mobilization and therefore enhances the probability of action mobilization. Hypothetically, if a frame is empirically credible, experientially commensurable, and narratively resonant, the stronger the consensus mobilization and the more fertile the soil for action mobilization.

IV. CYCLES OF PROTEST

A final possible constraint affecting both the substance and mobilizing potency of a movement's framing efforts is the existence of cycles of protest or general movement activity within which specific movements are frequently embedded. Tarrow (1983 a, pp. 38-39; 1983b, p. 11) has conceptualized cycles of protest in terms of five characteristic features, one of which is "the appearance of new technologies of protest" that "spread from their point of origin to other areas and to other sectors of social protest." Cycles of protest thus add to or delimit what Tilly (1978) refers to as the "repertoire" of protest tactics and activities.

Cycles of protest do not function only as crucibles out of which new technologies or repertoires of social protest are fashioned, however. Following our earlier work (Snow et al. 1986) and Turner's (1969, p. 392) contention that within each historical era there are typically "one or two movements that colour the preoccupations and social change effected during the era," we would expand the conceptualization of cycles of protest to include a sixth characteristic feature: that they also generate interpretive frames that either cognitively align structural/material conditions with latent mobilizing strands of "folk" (inherent or organic) ideologies or transform the meaning or significance of those conditions for the aggregations effected by them. In both cases, collective protest is inspired and justified, the tactics that evolve are given meaning and legitimated, and, as a result, structurally based protest potentials become manifest.

If we accept this general proposition as given, all else being equal, then several corollary propositions follow with respect to the nature and efficacy of movement framing activities. First, the point at which a movement emerges within a cycle of protest affects the substance and latitude of its framing efforts. Second, movements that surface early in a cycle of protest are likely to function as progenitors of master frames that provide the ideational or interpretive anchoring for subsequent movements within the cycle. And third, movements that emerge later in the cycle will typically find their framing efforts constrained by the previously elaborated master frame. Such movements may add to and embellish that master frame, but rarely in ways that are inconsistent with its core elements, unless events have discredited it and undermined its mobilizing potency.

Our research provides some illustrative observations which suggest that this line of reasoning is empirically on target. When considering peace movements historically or at a particular point in time, one can find numerous events or issues that might function as the pivotal foci for peace movement initiatives. These include, among others, international confrontations, border disputes, interventionism, weapons stockpiling, and institutional and structural violence. The 1980 election of Ronald Reagan, with his strident and bellicose rhetoric, and, simultaneously, the heightened tensions in various hot spots throughout the world (e.g., the Middle East, Central America, and Africa), provided any number of events and issues around which peace activists might rally. Yet, with the revival of the peace movement in the 1980s, attention was focused almost singularly on the nuclear threat.[11]

The intriguing question thus arises as to how this highly limited focus might be explained. While undoubtedly a number of factors were at work, we think a particularly prominent role was played by the emergence of the freeze initiative and the way in which it framed the problem and solution. We previously noted some of the reasons the freeze seemed to resonate well among many Americans and how it tended to undermine the degree to which other events and values could be seen as interconnected. Because the freeze initiative framed the problem in a narrow and highly compartmentalized fashion, subsequent attempts to encompass other peace issues and link them to the nuclear threat were exceedingly difficult, as illustrated by our earlier discussion of the dilemma of frame overextension. Peace organizations—such as the Mobilization for Survival—that attempted to extend the parameters of the frame to incorporate other events and issues were not able to engender broad-based support, in part because of the way in which the problem was initially framed in the early 1980s.

This initial framing also had implications for the tactical repertoire deemed appropriate. Consistent with the Freeze Campaign's goal of pressuring Congress to pass a resolution freezing the arms race, traditional political tactics such as petition drives, referenda, and other lobbying efforts were utilized. Direct action and civil disobedience were thus regarded as inappropriate and illegitimate by many sectors of the movement. Although the freeze initiative has more recently been called into question by virtue of the fact that it has made little headway in achieving its objectives, it still functions as a springboard for much discussion and debate within the peace movement in the United States.

CONCLUSION

Viewing movements as signifying agents actively involved in the framing of events and conditions, and thus in the production of meanings and ideas, we have attempted in this chapter to identify and elaborate the factors that affect the mobilizing potency of movement framing efforts and activities. Four sets of factors were enumerated and discussed. The first concerns the degree to which core framing tasks—diagnostic, prognostic, motivational—are richly developed and interconnected in a complementary fashion. The second addresses the internal constraints of belief systems with which a movement attempts to affect alignment. The third involves the relevance of proffered framings to the phenomenological life world of potential participants. And the fourth concerns the cycle of protest in which movements are embedded. The underlying thesis prompting this expository effort is that mobilization depends not only on the existence of objective structural disparities and dislocations, the availability and deployment of tangible resources, leaders' organizational skills, political opportunities, and a kind of cost-benefit calculus engaged in by prospective participants but also on the way these variables are framed and the degree to which they resonate with the targets of mobilization.

The factors constraining framing efforts and effecting their mobilizing potency may well go beyond those we have identified. Clearly, we do not assume that our expository effort has been exhaustive. Rather we see the four sets of constraints we have examined as constituting the conceptual scaffolding upon which subsequent research and theorizing might build.

However partial and incomplete this scaffolding, we think it suggests several important conceptual and theoretical implications. The first concerns the tremendous complexity of participant mobilization. To the extent that our observations are on target, the business of convincing and activating prospective participants is far more interactive, dynamic, and dialectic than generally appreciated in the contemporary literature. A second implication, following from the first, is that consensus mobilization is multidimensional and that the ways in which its dimensions are framed may inadvertently impede, as well as facilitate, action mobilization. A third implication is the possibility of answers to a number of vexing questions regarding the relationship between structure and collective action: the failure of mobilization efforts when structural conditions seem otherwise ripe may be attributable in part to the absence of resonant mobilizing frames; or a decline in social movement activity when the structural conditions remain fertile may be due to the failure of movements to frame chancing events and conditions in relevant ways. In both cases, latent structural potential fails to manifest itself fully.

A final implication of our observations is that they direct attention to a side or face of movement activity that has rarely been explored. The most visible side of social movements is their public side, the one that is constituted by confrontational and obstructionist activities such as marches, rallies, boycotts, strikes, and sit-ins. Since this is the side that is captured, catalogued, and archived by the media, and since many researchers today have a penchant for examining collective action via such data sources, it is not surprising that it is the side which is featured most prominently in the literature. Social movements, however, have another side, one that is not clearly understood. It is on this side that one finds the framing efforts, negotiations, and disputes that we have discussed and that are part and parcel of the signifying work of such movements. However, these activities are fully accessible only through ongoing encounters with participants in movement activities and by firsthand contact with the international workings and operations of movement organizations as they unfold and evolve over time.

NOTES

1. For overviews of this perspective, see Klandermans (1986), Melucci (1980), and Tarrow (1986).

2. For critical overviews and discussions of this perspective, see Jenkins (1983), Klandermans (1986), Tarrow (1986), and Zurcher and Snow (1981).

3. The term "frame" is borrowed from Goffman (1974, p. 21) to denote "schemata of interpretation" that enable individuals "to locate, perceive, identify, and label" occurrences within their life space and the world at large. By rendering events or occurrences meaningful, frames function to organize experience and guide action, whether individual or collective.

4. The four frame alignment processes include: (1) frame bridging, which involves "the linkage of two or more ideologically congruent but structurally unconnected frames regarding a particular issue or problem" (Snow et al. 1986, p. 467); (2) frame amplification, which refers to "the clarification and invigoration of an interpretive frame that bears on a particular issue, problem or set of events" (1986, p. 469); (3) frame extension, which involves the expansion of the boundaries of a "movement's primary framework so as to encompass interests or points of view that are

incidental to its primary objectives but of considerable salience to potential adherents" (1986, p. 472); and (4) frame transformation, which refers to the redefinition of "activities, events, and biographies that are already meaningful from the standpoint of some primary framework, such that they are now seen by the participants to be quite something else" (1986, p. 474).

5. It is important to keep in mind that framing efforts can vary considerably depending on the target of mobilization or influence. Perusal of the literature suggests that there are at least seven target groups that are relevant to the life histories of movements: adherents, constituents, bystander publics, media, potential allies, antagonists or countermovements, and elite decision makers. As we have indicated, our focus is on the participants, who include adherents (those who subscribe to movement objectives but do not contribute resources) and constituents (those who devote resources and are thus activated on behalf of the cause).

6. This research, which has focused primarily on the peace movement in the United States, entailed the following data gathering techniques: extensive ethnographic participation in local and regional peace movement activities and organizations; formal and informal interviews with local participants and local and national-level activists; and analyses of movement-generated documents and periodicals. The research was conducted over a four-year period by the second author (see Benford 1984; 1987; 1988) under the supervision of the senior author, among others.

7. A recent Public Agenda Foundation study (Yankelovich and Doble 1984, p. 33) that was based upon several national surveys of public attitudes concluded that an overwhelming majority of Americans (89%) agree that "there can be no winner in an all-out nuclear war." Similarly, 83% believe that "we cannot be certain that life on earth will continue after a nuclear war" (1983, p. 34). Moreover, a smaller but still sizable majority (68%) agree that if current trends in the nuclear arms race continue, "it is only a matter of time before they [nuclear weapons] are used." When the first item is compared to a 1955 survey in which only 27% of the U.S. public agreed that "mankind would be destroyed in an all-out atomic or hydrogen bomb war," the size of the 1984 majority is all the more dramatic. While it would be erroneous to credit the peace movement alone for this shift in reported attitudes, these data support our contention that the diagnostic task of problem identification is not particularly problematical for disarmament activists.

8. It is interesting to note that even opponents of the nuclear disarmament movement frequently espouse technological solutions, such as achieving a more stable nuclear deterrent by improving certain technical aspects of the weaponry or, as in the case of the Strategic Defense Initiative proponents, by developing an impenetrable shield that could destroy enemy missiles before they reached their intended targets.

9. For an insightful and critical discussion of the selective incentive concept and the logic of the rational calculus model see Fireman and Gamson (1979).

10. PSR's recommendations included "support for a bilateral nuclear weapons freeze and a comprehensive test ban, and opposition to destabilizing first strike weapons and civil defense plans against nuclear attack" (Rizzo 1983, p. 11).

11. These observations perhaps suggest, to borrow Althusser's (1970) terminology, that most movements are structurally or materially overdetermined, a situation which for us underscores all the more the importance of framing.

REFERENCES

Althusser, Louis. 1970. *For Marx*. New York: Vintage.

Benford, Robert D. 1984. "The Interorganizational Dynamics of the Austin Peace Movement." Unpublished M.A. Thesis, University of Texas, Austin.

Benford, Robert D. 1987. "Framing Activity, Meaning, and Social Movement Participation: The Nuclear Disarmament Movement." Ph.D. dissertation, University of Texas at Austin.

Benford, Robert D. Forthcoming. "The Nuclear Disarmament Movement." Chapter 14 in Lester
    R. Kurtz, *The Nuclear Cage: A Sociology of the Arms Race*. Englewood Cliffs, N.J.:
    Prentice-Hall.
Blumer, Herbert. 1969. *Symbolic Interactionism: Perspective and Method*. Englewood Cliffs, N.J.:
    Prentice-Hall.
Borhek, James T. and Richard F. Curtis. 1975. *A Sociology of Belief*. New York: Wiley.
Converse, Phillip E. 1964. "The Nature of Belief Systems in Mass Publics." Pages 206-61 in David
    Apter (ed.), *Ideology and Discontent*. New York: Free Press.
Corn, David. 1984. "Election Issues to Build On." *Nuclear Times* 3 (December):12-15.
Ferree, Myra Marx and Frederick D. Miller. 1985. "Mobilization and meaning: Toward an
    integration of social psychological and resource perspectives on social movements."
    Sociological Inquiry 55:38-51.
Fireman, Bruce and William A. Gamson. 1979. "Utilitarian Logic in the Resource Mobilization
    Perspective." Pages 8-45 in Mayer N. Zald and John D. McCarthy (eds.), *The Dynamics
    of Social Movements*. Cambridge, Mass.: Winthrop.
Fisher, Walter R. 1984. "Narration as a human communication paradigm: The case of public
    moral argument." *Communication Monographs* 51:1-23.
Geertz, Clifford. 1973. "Ideology as a Cultural System." Pages 193-233 in Clifford Geertz, *The
    Interpretation of Cultures*. New York: Basic Books.
Goffman, Erving. 1974. *Frame Analysis*. New York: Harper Colphon.
Goldberg, M. 1982. *Theology and Narrative*. Nashville, Tenn.: Parthenon Press.
Gouldner, Alvin W. 1970. *The Coming Crisis in Western Sociology*. New York: Basic Books.
Gramsci, Antonio. 1971. *Selections from the Prison Notebooks of Antonio Gramsci*. Edited by
    Q. Hoare and G.N. Smith. New York: International Publishers.
Hall, Stuart. 1982. "The Rediscovery of Ideology: Return of the Repressed in Media Studies."
    Pages 56-90 in M. Gurevitch, T. Bennett, J. Curon, and J. Woolacott (eds.), *Culture, Society
    and the Media*. New York: Methuen.
Jenkins, J. Craig. 1983. "Resource mobilization theory and the study of social movements." *Annual
    Review of Sociology* 9:527-53.
Keyes, Ken, Jr. 1982. *The Hundredth Monkey*. Coos Bay, Ore.: Vision Books.
Klandermans, Bert. 1984. "Mobilization and participation: Social-psychological expansions of
    resource mobilization theory." *American Sociological Review* 49:583-600.
Klandermans, Bert. 1986. "New Social Movements and Resource Mobilization: The European
    and the American Approach." *International Journal of Mass Emergencies and Disasters*.
    Special issue, *Comparative Perspectives and Research on Collective Behavior and Social
    Movements* 4:13-37.
Mead, George H. 1934. *Mind, Self, and Society*. Chicago: University of Chicago Press.
Melucci, Alberto. 1980. "The new social movements: A theoretical approach." *Social Science
    Information* 19:199-226.
Mills, C. Wright. 1940. "Situated action and the vocabulary of motives." *American Sociological
    Review* 6:904-13.
Newman, Barrie. 1986. "Peace movement imagery." *Transaction Social Science and Modern
    Society* 23:23-29.
Olson, Mancur, Jr. 1965. *The Logic of Collective Action: Public Goods and the Theory of Groups*.
    Cambridge: Harvard University Press.
Rizzo, Renata. 1983. "Professional Approach to Peace." *Nuclear Times* 1:10-13.
Rude, George. 1980. *Ideology and Popular Protest*. New York: Knopf.
Schell, Jonathan. 1982. *The Fate of the Earth*. New York: Knopf.
Snow, David A. and Richard Machalek. 1982. "On the presumed fragility of unconventional
    beliefs." *Journal of the Scientific Study of Religion* 21:15-26.

Snow, David A., E. Burke Rochford, Jr., Steven K. Worden, and Robert D. Benford. 1986. "Frame alignment processes, micromobilization, and movement participation." *American Sociological Review* 51:464-81.

Tarrow, Sidney. 1983a. *Struggling to Reform: Social Movements and Policy Change during Cycles of Protest.* Western Societies Paper No. 15. Ithaca, N.Y.: Cornell University.

Tarrow, Sidney. 1983b. "Resource Mobilization and Cycles of Protest: Theoretical Reflections and Comparative Illustrations." Paper presented at the Annual Meeting of the American Sociological Association, Detroit, August 31-September 4.

Tarrow, Sidney. 1986. "Comparing Social Movement Participation in Western Europe and the United States: Problems, Uses, Examples, and a Proposal for Synthesis." *International Journal of Mass Emergencies and Disasters.* Special issue, *Comparative Perspectives and Research on Collective Behavior and Social Movements* 4:147-70.

Thompson, E.P. and Dan Smith (eds.). 1981. *Protest and Survive.* New York: Monthly Review Press.

Tilly, Charles. 1978. *From Mobilization to Revolution.* Reading, Mass.: Addison-Wesley.

Turco, R.P., O.B. Toon, T.P. Ackerman, J.B. Pollock, and Carl Sagan. 1983. "Nuclear winter: Global atmospheric consequences of multiple nuclear explosions." *Science* 222:1283-92.

Turner, Ralph H. 1969. "The Theme of Contemporary Social Movements." *British Journal of Sociology* 20:390-405.

Turner, Ralph H. and Lewis M. Killian. 1972. *Collective Behavior.* 2d ed. Englewood Cliffs, N.J.: Prentice-Hall.

Wilson, John. 1973. *Introduction to Social Movements.* New York: Basic Books.

Yankelovich, Daniel and John Doble. 1984. "The Public Mood: Nuclear Weapons and the U.S.S.R." *Foreign Affairs* 63:33-46.

Zurcher, Louis A., Jr. and David A. Snow. 1981. "Collective Behavior: Social Movements." Pages 447-82 in Morris Rosenberg and Ralph H. Turner (eds.), *Social Psychology, Sociological Perspectives.* New York: Basic Books.

POLITICAL DISCOURSE AND COLLECTIVE ACTION

William A. Gamson

I. INTRODUCTION

Sustained collective action involves a symbolic struggle. In the broadest sense, it is a struggle over the legitimacy of a regime and trust in the incumbent political authorities. Every regime has a legitimating frame that provides the citizenry with a reason to be quiescent. It is a constant, uphill struggle for those who would sustain collective action in the face of official myths and metaphors.

At a more contextual level, collective action focuses on particular historical conditions and policies. It has a substantive content. It takes place in some issue arena, however broadly or narrowly defined. People act on the basis of some meaning system, and the definition of issues, actors, and events is a matter of constant contention. A central part of the symbolic struggle, then, is about the process of constructing specific meanings.

As theories about ideological hegemony and false consciousness have emphasized, challengers face a formidable task. But the difficulty varies over time for all challengers and, at any single moment, among them. For some, the official meanings with which they must contend are deeply embedded and well-defended; for others, official meanings are in crisis and disarray or perhaps

International Social Movement Research, Vol. 1, pages 219-244.
Supplement to Research in Social Movements, Conflicts and Change
Copyright © 1988 by JAI Press Inc.
All rights of reproduction in any form reserved.
ISBN: 0-89232-955-6

even discredited. Such moments offer opportunities for challengers that may not last.

Mobilization potential has, then, a strong cultural component. To understand it, we need to assess not only structural conduciveness but cultural conduciveness. Unfortunately, we find the analytic tools for assessing the latter comparatively sparse and undeveloped compared to those available for the structural side. This paper attempts to further that development.

A. Political Culture and Issue Cultures

The concept of "political culture," once quite fashionable in American social science, has languished in recent years. As it came to be used under the influence of Almond and Verba's influential book, *The Civic Culture* (1963), it suffered badly from psychological reductionism. Rather than examining culture, American social scientists, in the thrall of the sample survey, focused their attention on psychological orientations toward political objects. Political culture, from this perspective, turned out to be nothing more than a particular type of political attitude. But then, why introduce an additional, redundant concept such as political culture?

A nonredundant concept of political culture refers to the meaning systems that are culturally available for talking, writing, and thinking about political objects: the myths and metaphors, the language and idea elements, the frames, ideologies, values, and condensing symbols. But this description is much too vague. To be useful, such an unwieldy concept needs unpacking.

Cultural Themes

An analysis of political culture requires at least two levels of generality. At the most basic level, there are "cultural themes," by which I mean frames and related symbols that transcend specific issues and suggest larger world views. It is a concept akin to such terms as ideology, values, belief systems, and *weltanschauung*. I prefer a term that makes as few assumptions as possible about the tightness of organization or connections among ideas.

Examples of such politically relevant themes in American society include *technological progress* and *self-reliance*. These terms are mere labels or condensing symbols to suggest the theme and should not be confused with the thing itself. It is more useful to think of themes as packages of idea elements. The package includes *core* elements that provide an underlying framework and are largely taken for granted, plus *condensing symbols,* which are used to express or suggest the package in some form of shorthand. The catchphrase "self-reliance" is an example of the latter and, as such, makes a convenient label for the package.

It is useful to think of themes dialectically. There is no theme without a countertheme. The theme is conventional and normative; the countertheme is adversarial and contentious. But both have their own cultural roots and both can be important in assessing any specific symbolic struggle.

Take the technological progress theme as an example. Few would question the appeal of a technofix for a wide variety of problems in American society. As Williams writes in commenting on American values, "'Efficient' is a word of high praise in a society that has long emphasized adaptability, technological innovation, economic expansion, up-to-dateness, practicality, expediency, 'getting things done'" (1960, p.428). The inventor is a central cultural hero— embodied in the myths of Benjamin Franklin and Thomas Edison. Mastery over nature is the way to progress: good old American know-how.

This theme is reflected in a view of politics. How can we solve the problem, how much is it going to cost, and is it worth it? On the surface nonideological, it presents itself as pragmatic, willing to try whatever is needed to do the job. Issues present technical problems to be solved and one ought to get the best expertise available to help overcome the problems that the country faces.

American culture, however, also contains a countertheme, skeptical of, or even hostile to, technology. To quote Emerson, "Things are in the saddle and ride mankind." Harmony with nature rather than mastery over it is stressed. We live on a "small planet." Our technology must be appropriate and in proper scale. There is an ecosystem to maintain and the more we try to control nature through our technology, the more we disrupt its natural order and threaten the quality of our lives. Thoreau at Walden Pond is also part of American culture.

Much American popular culture features the countertheme: Chaplin's *Modern Times,* Huxley's *Brave New World,* Kubrick's *2001,* and countless other films about technology gone mad and out of control, a Frankenstein monster about to turn on its creator.

The lesson for challengers is to keep this cultural ambivalence or tension in mind. While authorities may attempt to exploit particular cultural themes in any struggle, one cannot invoke the theme without making the countertheme relevant as well, and therein may lie opportunity.

Issue Cultures

Each struggle takes place in a particular issue arena. For every challenge, there is a relevant discourse—a particular set of ideas and symbols that are used in the process of constructing meanings relevant to the struggle. To achieve and sustain mobilization, a challenger must participate in such discourse.

As with themes, the idea elements are organized and clustered into more or less harmonious sets, and we encounter them as packages. By an *issue culture* I mean the set of culturally available packages for carrying on such discourse.

As with theme packages, issue packages have a core frame, largely taken for granted, and condensing symbols that suggest the frame and the package as a whole.

A package has an internal structure. At its core is a central organizing idea or *frame* for making sense of relevant events. As Snow et al. (1986) put it, "By rendering events . . . meaningful frames function to organize experience and guide action, whether individual or collective." The frame suggests what the issue is about.

A frame typically implies a range of positions, rather than any single one, thus allowing for a degree of controversy among those who share the same package. Besides these core elements, a package also offers a number of different condensing symbols that suggest the core frame and positions in shorthand, making it possible to display the package as a whole with a deft metaphor, catchphrase, or other symbolic device. More specifically, five framing devices serve to define the issue and three reasoning devices to justify its general policy line.[1]

To illustrate, consider a package about the use of nuclear power to generate electricity, one we label *Faith in Progress.*

> If the electric chair had been invented before the electric light, would we still be using kerosene lamps? There has always been resistance to technological progress by nervous nellies who see only the problems and ignore the benefits. Resistance to nuclear energy development is the latest version of this irrational fear of progress and change. Of course nuclear energy development is not free of problems, but problems can be solved as the history of technological progress shows. The failure to develop nuclear power will retard our economic growth and renege on our obligation to the poor and to future generations. If we do not move ahead now with nuclear energy, the next generation is likely to be sitting around in the dark blaming the utilities for not doing something this generation's officials would not let them do. [2]

This package frames the nuclear power issue in terms of the society's commitment to technological development and economic growth. Frames should not be confused with positions for or against some policy measure. While this package is clearly pro-nuclear, there is ample room for disagreement within the overall frame—for example, on what type of reactors should be built. Not every disagreement is a frame disagreement; differences between (say) Republicans and Democrats or "liberals" and "conservatives" on many issues may reflect a shared frame. Nor can every package be identified with some clear-cut policy position. On almost any issue, there are packages that are better described as ambivalent than as either pro or con.

The description of *Faith in Progress* above contains a number of catchphrases, metaphors, and other symbolic devices to suggest the frame. Additional examples of condensing symbols include depictions of antinuclear activity as "the rape of progress" and of the activists as "nuclear Luddites," "modern pastoralists," and "coercive utopians."[3]

Packages, if they are to remain viable, are faced with the task of constructing meaning over time, incorporating new events into their interpretive frame. In effect, they contain a story line or, to use Bennett's (1975) term, a scenario. The *Faith in Progress* package, for example, must be able to deal with the accidents at Three Mile Island (TMI) and Chernobyl, providing them with a meaning that is plausible and consistent with the frame. If the event isn't one that the scenario predicts or expects, the anomaly only challenges the ingenuity and suppleness of the skillful cultural entrepreneur.

An arena of contesting packages, then, is the battleground for forming mobilization potentials, the process that Klandermans (1986) labels "consensus mobilization." Themes and counterthemes are relevant since their resonances with issue packages provide constraints and opportunities. But issue cultures are the level at which collective actors can have an impact. Political symbolism can be used more or less effectively by challengers to promote their preferred package, and, in the long run, issue cultures can be permanently altered.

B. General Climate and Issue Climate

Tarrow (1983) analyzes the cyclical nature of protest. Some times provide a general cultural climate that is conducive to many different mobilization efforts; other times, characterized by repression, apathy, or complacency, are inhospitable to such efforts.

This general cultural climate is, of course, affected by many exogenous factors—external crises produced by broad social and economic forces, for example. But this climate is partly a direct product of the interaction between challenging groups and authorities. There is clear evidence in the American case that progressive national administrations help, sometimes inadvertently, to foster and maintain a climate that aids the process of mobilization. The re-election of Roosevelt in 1936 as well as the accession of relatively progressive administrations in states such as Michigan created a favorable general climate for the major CIO organizing drives of the 1930s. Similarly, the mobilizing language of the Kennedy administration and its rhetoric on civil rights helped create a climate conducive to mobilization in the 1960s.

Challenging groups not only thrive in a conducive climate: through their collective action they are important creators of mobilization potential. The civil rights mobilization, for example, preceded the Kennedy Administration, and such direct actions as freedom rides, lunch counter sit-ins, boycotts, and mass demonstrations stimulated the production of a particular kind of official rhetoric. The general climate, then, to the extent that it can be influenced by political actors, arises from an interactive process between challengers and authorities.

General climate is relevant in assessing mobilization potential. But if one is interested in the consensus mobilization process, the climate of a particular mobilization effort is a more useful level of analysis. The culture of an issue changes over time as packages and their elements ebb and flow in prominence. Certain elements become, to use Donald Schon's phrase, "ideas in good currency"; others become stale and redolent with the failures of the past.

Packages vary in their implications for collective action. Some promote passivity, restraint, and quiescence; others imply the need and opportunity for action in varying degrees. Cultural conduciveness, then, is a matter of the relative ascendancy of mobilizing packages in political discourse.

C.   The Role of the Mass Media

General audience media are only one forum for political discourse on an issue. It is useful to think of a set of discourses that interact in complex ways. On many issues, there is a specialist's discourse, using journals and other print media aimed at those whose professional lives involve them in the issue. There is a largely oral discourse used by officials who are directly involved in decision-making roles on the issue and by those who attempt to influence them directly. Finally, there is a challenger discourse, providing packages that are intended to mobilize their audience for some form of collective action. Ascendancy in one of these forums is no guarantee of ascendancy across the board.

For consensus mobilization, we should be concerned with the discourse of relevance to the target of a challenger's mobilization effort. Much of what adherents see, hear, and read is beyond the control of any movement organization. One may read newsletters, receive direct mailing, and hear movement speakers at a rally but these sources are likely to offer only a small fraction of the discourse to which any potential participant is exposed.

Movement adherents also absorb the discourse that broadcast and print media aim at a general, undifferentiated audience. Nothing that they receive from such sources is simply raw information. Although this discourse may contain many facts and details, these are always presented in some context of meaning. In short, they are framed and packaged. This mass media discourse is, in most cases, likely to overwhelm in sheer volume anything that movement sources try to communicate.

I do not mean to imply that such mass media discourse is necessarily monolithic or that it has any particular bias—these are separate and complex questions. My point is merely that understanding the nature of media discourse and how it changes over time is crucial to understanding how mobilization potential is formed and activated.

Media discourse, then, is one part of a larger issue culture, both reflecting it and helping to create it. Journalists may draw their ideas and language from any or all of these other forums, frequently using the language and frames of their sources. At the same time, they contribute their own frames and invent their own clever one-liners, drawing on a popular culture that they share with their audience. Because media discourse is so central in framing issues for the attentive public, it becomes, to quote Gurevitch and Levy (1985, p. 19) "a site on which various social groups, institutions, and ideologies struggle over the definition and construction of social reality."

D. The Role of Collective Action

It is useful to think of media prominence as the outcome of a value-added process. To illustrate this process, we can turn to the example of automobile production. Each stage—the mining of iron ore, smelting, tempering, shaping, assembling, painting, delivering, selling—adds its value to the final product. Furthermore, these stages may be thought of as determinants that, in combination, specify the final outcome. In this sense, they "explain" or account for whatever it is that is finally produced.[4]

The production of issue cultures can be thought of as such a process. The model postulates three broad classes of determinants which combine to produce particular package careers: sponsor activities, media practices, and cultural resonances.

Sponsor Activities

Much of the changing culture of an issue is the product of enterprise. Packages frequently have sponsors interested in promoting their careers. Sponsorship is more than merely advocacy; it involves such tangible activities as speech making, advertising, article and pamphlet writing, and the filing of legal briefs to promote a preferred package.

These sponsors are usually organizations that employ professional specialists whose daily job involves interacting with journalists. Their job breeds sophistication about the news requirements of the media and the norms and habits of working journalists. Indeed, many of these professionals began as journalists before moving to public relations jobs. As Sigal (1973, p. 75) points out, professional sponsors adjust "their thinking to newsmen's conventions. They talk the same language."

The sponsor of a package is typically an agent who is promoting some collective rather than personal agenda. These agents frequently draw on the resources of an organization to prepare materials in a form that lends itself to ready use. Condensing symbols is the journalist's stock and trade. Smart sources are well aware of the journalist's fancy for the apt one-liner and so provide suitable quotations to suggest the frame they want.

Social movement organizations are one important sponsor in this framing process. Snow and Benford (1987) point out the role of these organizations as "signifying agents" who are actively engaged in the production of meaning. "They frame . . . relevant events and conditions in ways that are intended to mobilize potential adherents and constituents, to garner bystander support, and to demobilize antagonists."

Media Practices

That sponsors are active does not imply that journalists are passive. Journalists' working norms and practices add considerable value to the process. A number of students of American news organizations have argued that journalists unconsciously give official packages the benefit of the doubt. In some cases, official assumptions are taken for granted; but even when they are challenged by sponsors of alternative packages, it is these competitors who carry the burden of proof. In a weaker form of this argument, journalists make official packages the starting point for discussing an issue.

Various observers have noted how subtly and unconsciously this process operates. Halberstam (1979, p. 414) describes how Walter Cronkite's concern with avoiding controversy led to his acceptance of the assumptions underlying official packages. "To him, editorializing was going against the government. He had little awareness, nor did his employers want him to, of the editorializing which he did automatically by unconsciously going along with the government's position."[5]

In addition to this tendency to fall into official definitions of an issue, journalists are especially likely to have routine relationships with official sponsors. Most American reporting is the product of ongoing news routines. Sigal (1973) examined over a thousand stories from the *New York Times* and the *Washington Post* and classified the channels by which the information reached the reporter. *Routine* channels included official proceedings, press releases, press conferences, and scheduled, official events. *Informal* channels included background briefings, leaks, nongovernmental proceedings, and reports from other news organizations. Finally, *enterprise* channels included interviews conducted at the reporter's initiative, spontaneous events that a reporter observed firsthand, independent research, and the reporter's own conclusions or analysis. He found that only about one-fourth of the stories came from enterprise channels, while routine channels accounted for almost 60%.

Other media norms and practices in the United States—particularly the balance norm—favor certain rivals to the official package. In news accounts, interpretation is generally provided through quotations. Balance is provided by quoting spokespersons with competing views. In the commentary provided by syndicated columnists and cartoonists, norms of balance generally prevail at the aggregate level. Although an individual columnist is not expected to provide more than one package, a range of "liberal" and "conservative" commentators are employed to achieve this norm.

The balance norm is, of course, a vague one, and the practices it gives rise to favor certain packages over others. There is a strong tendency to educe controversy to two competing positions—an official one and (if there is one) the alternative sponsored by the most vested member of the polity. In many cases, the critics may share the same unstated, common frame as officials.

The balance norm, however, is rarely interpreted to include challenger packages, even when no other alternative is available. Tuchman (1974, p. 112) argues that balance in television news "means in practice that Republicans may rebut Democrats and vice-versa" but that "supposedly illegitimate challengers" are rarely offered the opportunity to criticize governmental statements. Instead, she suggests, reporters search for an "establishment critic" or for a "'responsible spokesman' whom they have themselves created or promoted to a position of prominence."

Cultural Resonances

Not all symbols are equally potent. Certain packages have a natural advantage because their ideas and language resonate with larger cultural themes. Resonances increase the appeal of a package; they make it appear natural and familiar. Those who respond to the larger cultural theme will find it easier to respond to a package with the same sonorities. Snow and Benford (1987) make a similar point in discussing the "narrative fidelity" of a frame. Some framings "resonate with cultural narrations, that is with the stories, myths, and folk tales that are part and parcel of one's cultural heritage."[6]

Since cultural themes remain constant, it may be unclear how they can help us to explain changes in the ebb and flow of packages in media discourse. Resonances are the earliest stage in the value-added process. A package's resonances, we argue, facilitate the work of sponsors by tuning the ear of journalist's to its symbolism. They add value to package careers by amplifying the impact of sponsor activities and media practices.

I suggested earlier that themes exist in a dialectic relationship with counterthemes. Both have cultural roots. If we assume that most members of a culture internalize *both* themes and counterthemes, resonance with either is helpful. Since themes are dominant, the value added should be greater here. But given the above assumption, we expect resonances to have additive effects even when theme and countertheme are in tension.

What value do challengers add to this process? Clearly, they have several disadvantages when it comes to direct influence on media discourse. They frequently lack the resources, professional skills, and routine relationships with journalists that officials or more established sponsors take for granted. When they challenge deeply entrenched ways of thinking, they must confront journalistic norms and practices that make it difficult to be taken seriously. And their alternatives frequently challenge official packages that resonate with long-established and deeply embedded cultural themes. They face an undeniably formidable task and, not surprisingly, media discourse is rarely dominated by mobilizing packages.

Nevertheless, challengers are sometimes able to succeed through collective action that indirectly alters media discourse. Actions by challengers may help to stimulate media discourse where no discourse would have otherwise taken place. In the process, they may provide opportunities for successful sponsor activities both by the group conducting the action and by allies who may have greater access to and legitimacy among journalists.

The absence of discourse generally implies the hegemony of a dominant package that promotes quiescence on the issue. Collective action is a vehicle for creating a contested discourse. At the very least, a vigorous challenge to the offical package will force its taken-for-granted assumptions into the open, necessitating their justification and defense. At best, mobilizing packages may become serious competitors in media discourse and, through this forum, in the minds of movement adherents.

Finally, a contested discourse exposes frame vulnerabilities in the official package. Unfolding events that otherwise might have been ignored may instead be used to discredit and embarrass official packages. In the process, rival, mobilizing packages that have anticipated such events may be elevated to prominence in media discourse in spite of their normal handicaps.

II. THE CASE OF NUCLEAR POWER

Consider the case of the movement against nuclear power in the United States. The nuclear power issue is an apt choice for analysis for several reasons. First, it is a limiting case of an issue that one experiences secondhand. Normally, when we approach media discourse on an issue, we do so with a range of personal experiences from which we also draw meaning. Ball-Rokeach and Defleur's "dependency theory" (1976; 1982) suggests that the role of the media in the process of constructing meaning will vary from issue to issue. On some issues, the audience has no experience or personal history to interpose upon media packages. On other issues, they have a great deal.

Except for those unfortunate people who live or work near Chernobyl and experienced immediate radiation sickness, or the handful of people who work in nuclear power plants, no one has a direct experience of nuclear power. Even those who may suffer long-term personal consequences from radiation fallout must rely on media interpretation about how they may have been affected. For most of us, there is no unmediated experience on which to draw and, hence, the centrality of media discourse in constructing meaning seems especially clear in this limiting case.[7]

Second, the nuclear power issue lends itself to comparative analysis. The huge variation in the degree of nuclear power development and in the strength of the antinuclear movement among European countries is itself a striking phenomenon to be explained. Differences in national culture, in energy dependency, in the organization of the mass media, as well as a host of other structural factors certainly should produce many differences in media discourse. Yet, in spite of these differences, there are striking parallels between the shifts in American media discourse discussed here and the French and German discourse analyzed by Nelkin and Pollak (1981) in their study of the antinuclear movement in those countries.

Finally, I have available an extensive and systematic sample of mass media discourse on nuclear power, beginning in the 1950s.[8] Thus, I have no need to rely on mere impressions or idiosyncratic memories in analyzing media discourse on this issue. More specifically, I have at hand samples of editorial cartoons, syndicated opinion columns, newsmagazine accounts, and (after 1970) television network news coverage.

A. American Nuclear Power Discourse

The culture of nuclear power has been indelibly marked by Hiroshima and Nagasaki. Public awareness begins with these images of sudden, enormous destruction, symbolized in the rising mushroom cloud of a nuclear bomb blast. Even when discourse focuses on the use of nuclear reactors to produce electricity, the afterimage of the bomb is always in the back of one's mind.

Boyer's rich analysis of American nuclear discourse from 1945 to 1950 shows how rapidly these images of unlimited destruction became central. H. V. Kaltenborn, in his NBC evening news broadcast reporting on the first atomic bomb, told his radio audience that "For all we know, we have created a Frankenstein! We must assume that with the passage of only a little time, an improved form of the new weapon we use today can be turned against us" (Boyer 1985, p. 5). *Life* magazine, with a circulation of over five million, devoted much of its August 20, 1945, issue to the Bomb, presenting full-page photographs of the towering mushroom clouds over Hiroshima and Nagasaki. The language that accompanied these frightening images was equally ferocious. Today, fears of extinction seem, as Boyer points out, "so familiar as to be almost trite, but it is important to recognize how *quickly* Americans began to articulate them" (1985, p. 15).

The *Faith in Progress* package on nuclear energy, described above, was just as quick off the mark. A dualism about nuclear energy is part of its core. Boyer points to the "either/or" structure of so many post-Hiroshima pronouncements.

The official platitude about Atomic Fission is that it can be a Force for Good (production)
or a Force for Evil (war), and that the problem is simply how to use its Good rather than
its Bad potentialities (Macdonald 1945, p. 58).

Boyer argues that the faith expressed in the atom's peacetime promise was
"part of the process by which the nation muted its awareness of Hiroshima
and Nagasaki and of even more frightening future prospects" (1985, p. 127).
Not only was it an "anodyne to terror" but it also helped to assuage any
lingering discomfort over the destruction that America had already wrought
with the fearful atom. A peace-loving America should embrace the challenge
of making the atom "a benevolent servant" to produce for humankind "more
comforts, more leisure, better health, more of real freedom [and] a much
happier life" (Waymack 1947, p. 214).

Not all the discourse that Boyer reviews was equally optimistic. There were
certainly cautious skeptics challenging the utopian claims. But this
disagreement is a debate within a frame, a disagreement over how fast and
how easily the promise of nuclear energy will be realized. As long as the issue
is framed as a choice between atoms for war and atoms for peace, it is hard
to see who could be against nuclear power development.

Over the next four decades, the discourse on nuclear power underwent
dramatic changes. In reviewing different periods, I will consider the role of
collective action in adding value to the production of its characteristic discourse.

The Age of Dualism (the 1950s)

Nuclear dualism remained essentially unchallenged for the first quarter
century of the nuclear age. On December 8, 1953, President Eisenhower
addressed the United Nations on nuclear power, presenting what media
discourse labeled his "Atoms for Peace" speech. In it, he proposed to make
American nuclear technology available to an international agency that would
attempt to develop peaceful uses of nuclear energy.

The discourse on Eisenhower's speech further entrenched the dualism
between atoms for peace and atoms for war. The *Faith in Progress* package
remained unchallenged throughout. Atomic Energy Commission (AEC)
Chairman Lewis Strauss set the tone for the decade with a phrase that became
a permanent part of the issue culture when he told the National Association
of Science Writers in 1954 that "It is not too much to expect that our children
will enjoy in their homes electrical energy *too cheap to meter.*"

The either/or structure of nuclear dualism continues to be strongly
represented. The dominant metaphor is a road that branches into two
alternative paths—one leading to the development of weapons of destruction,
the other to the eradication of human misery. Again, there are optimists and
cautious skeptics who warn that the technological problems in tapping this

energy source for human betterment are formidable and far from solved. But no opposition to nuclear power development is presented, and no alternative package is ever offered.

The Role of Collective Action

The first opposition to nuclear power did surface during this period, but its source was, to quote Mitchell (1981), an "elite quarrel" rather than a mass movement. The Joint Congressional Committee on Atomic Energy and the AEC fell out over the latter's construction permit for the Enrico Fermi breeder reactor, 30 miles south of Detroit. In August, 1956, Joint Committee leaders encouraged the United Auto Workers to oppose the reactor at public hearings and in court. But there was no movement effort during this period to mobilize even a local constituency to take some form of collective action.

The Dog that Didn't Bark (the 1960s)

The UAW, later joined by two other unions, was unsuccessful in blocking the construction of the Fermi reactor. By October, 1966, it was going through its final tests prior to going on-line. There were only four other reactors in the United States then operating, but, unlike the others, Fermi was scheduled to be the first breeder reactor. It would not only generate electricity but, in the process, produce plutonium-239, a highly radioactive material with an enormous half-life. To add to the dangers, the Fermi reactor was cooled by liquid sodium, a dangerous and volatile substance in the event of an accident.

On October 5, the cooling system failed and the fuel core experienced a partial meltdown.[9]

The automatic shut down or "scram" system failed to operate and, alerted by alarms signaling the leak of radiation into the containment building, operators shut the plant down manually. The containment building was sealed off.

As far as we know, there was no radiation leak into the atmosphere, but the shutdown did not remove the major threat of a disastrous secondary accident during the following six months as officials tried to figure out what had happened and the damaged fuel was removed. Fuller (1975) likens the process to "look[ing] inside a gasoline tank with a lighted match." During the danger period, plans for the evacuation of a million or more people were discussed by officials but deemed impractical and unnecessary. By almost any reckoning, the Fermi accident was extremely serious. The mystery of Fermi, then, is why it didn't become the center of media discourse and the symbol that TMI became.

Were these events so hidden that extensive media coverage was impossible? A plant official called the sheriff of the county in which the plant was located as well as officials in the state capital to alert them that something was amiss at Fermi. The plant official played down the danger and promised to keep them informed of further developments, asking them not to alert the public for fear of causing undue alarm and panic—a judgment the public officials apparently shared. Furthermore, another plant official called the local newspaper with a brief, somewhat ambiguous, statement informing them that something was wrong at the plant.

There the story sat, unreported. More than five weeks after the accident, the *New York Times* carried a story on what it labeled a "mishap" at the Fermi reactor.[10] There was nothing in the least alarming in the *Times* account. Walker Cisler, the president of Detroit Edison and the leading force behind the construction of the Fermi reactor, was quoted as saying "If all goes well . . . we could start again shortly after the first of the year."[11] A General Electric official classified what happened as "a minor perturbation," and a reassuring report from the Atomic Industrial forum was duly noted.

No critic of nuclear power was quoted in the belated *Times* report on the Fermi accident. Indeed, it would have taken great enterprise to have found such a critic in 1966. In effect, there was no significant antinuclear-power discourse during this era. Nuclear power was, in general a nonissue. *Faith in Progress* remained the dominant package, so taken-for-granted in the little discourse that existed that it required no explicit defense.

The Role of Collective Action

In the late 1950s and early 1960s, a movement against the atmospheric testing of nuclear weapons called public attention to the long range dangers of radiation. Milk, "nature's most nearly perfect food" as the dairy industry advertised it, was found to contain Strontium-90. A famous SANE ad warned the public that "Dr. Spock is worried."

Some of this increased awareness about radiation dangers spilled over into concern about nuclear reactors. Local controversies developed over the licensing of a few reactors. Perhaps the most striking evidence for the impact of the movement against atmospheric testing can be found in the disappearance of any controversy about the licensing of nuclear power plants after the Limited Test Ban Treaty of 1963. With it, radiation concerns receded from media discourse. By the mid-1960s, the nuclear energy industry was enjoying a wave of new orders and no public opposition.

The Rise of an Antinuclear Discourse (the 1970s to TMI)

By the time of the Three Mile Island accident in 1979, media discourse on nuclear power reflected an issue culture in flux. *Faith in Progress* was still the most prominent package but its earlier hegemony had been destroyed.

Nuclear power advocates were finding themselves increasingly on the defensive in spite of events that might appear to have strengthened support for it. The much publicized "energy crisis" of the 1970s stimulated the articulation of a second major pro-nuclear package, *Energy Independence.* This package drew a pro-nuclear meaning from the Arab oil embargo of 1973:

> The lesson is how dependence on foreign sources for vitally needed energy can make the U.S. vulnerable to political blackmail. Nuclear energy must be understood in the context of this larger problem of energy independence. To achieve independence, we must develop and use every practical alternative energy source to imported oil, including nuclear energy. Nuclear energy, plus domestic oil, natural gas, and coal remain the only practical alternatives to a dangerous and humiliating dependence on foreign and, particularly, Middle Eastern sources. These foreign sources are unstable and unreliable and are likely to make unacceptable political demands. Do we want to be dependent on the whims of Arab sheiks? Ultimately, independence is the cornerstone of our freedom.

This addition to the pro-nuclear arsenal was more than offset by other developments that stimulated the rise of an antinuclear discourse. By the 1970s, nuclear dualism had been seriously eroded even among many keepers of the faith. With the advent of the Carter administration, proliferation of nuclear weapons became a presidential priority issue. To deal with the proliferation problem, Carter tried to promote stronger international control of the spread of nuclear technology, including reactor technology. Although a strong supporter of nuclear power generally, Carter turned against the breeder reactor lest the plutonium it produced be diverted to weapons use. Atoms for peace or atoms for war no longer appeared to be such separate paths. Subliminal mushroom clouds had begun to gather over even official discourse on the issue.

More importantly, the dualism was being undermined because of the safety issue. If a serious accident that releases large amounts of radiation into the atmosphere is possible at a nuclear reactor, then the destructive potential of this awesome energy is not confined to bombs.

A broad coalition of antinuclear-power groups raised the safety issue but as part of a number of different packages. The environmental wing, epitomized by Friends of the Earth, offered a *Soft Path* package:

> Split wood, not atoms. Nuclear energy presents us with a fundamental choice about what kind of society we wish to be. Do we wish to continue a way of life that is wasteful of energy, relies on highly centralized technologies, and is insensitive to ecological consequences? Or do we want to become a society more in harmony with its natural environment? Nuclear energy relies on the wrong kind of technology—centralized and dangerous to the earth's long run ecology. We need to pursue alternative, soft paths. We should change our way of life to conserve energy as much as possible and to develop sources of energy that are ecologically safe, renewable and that lend themselves to decentralized production—for example, sun, wind, and water. Small is beautiful.[12]

Other groups, epitomized by the Ralph Nader organization, Critical Mass, offered a more political, anticorporate package, *Public Accountability:*

If Exxon owned the sun, would we have solar energy? The root of the problem is the organization of nuclear production by profit making corporations, which minimizes accountability and control by the public. Spokesmen for the nuclear industry are motivated to protect their own economic interests, not the public interest. One cannot rely on what they say. Company officials are frequently dishonest, greedy, and arrogant. Who killed Karen Silkwood? The nuclear industry has used its political and economic power to undermine the serious exploration of energy alternatives. Public officials, who are supposed to monitor the activities of the industry, are all too often captives of it. They function more to protect the industry, than to protect the public.

Finally, the antinuclear movement, through organizations such as the Union of Concerned Scientists, offered a more pragmatic, cost-benefit package, *Not Cost-Effective*. A litany of unsolved problems and delays are cited, leading to the conclusion that:

When one compares the costs and benefits of nuclear energy with the alternatives, it makes a poor showing. Nuclear power, through nobody's fault in particular, has turned out to be a lemon and it is foolish to keep pouring good money after bad by supporting the continued development of nuclear energy.

Media coverage of nuclear power accelerated rapidly in the mid-1970s. The Media Institute study (1979) of network television news reveals a burst of coverage at the time of Earth Day in 1970, followed by very little through 1974. Coverage then tripled in 1975 and doubled again the following year. Except for a temporary decrease in 1978, it continued to increase up to the time of TMI. In the first three months of 1979, before TMI, the networks ran 26 stories related to nuclear power.

A review of media discourse prior to TMI provides a mixed picture. With the exception of cartoons, there is little display of any antinuclear package, but the confident dualism of an earlier era has become uneasy at best. *Faith in Progress* is represented in the acceptance of nuclear power development as necessary and inevitable. But the discourse clearly recognizes it as controversial, even if one can gain only a vague awareness of how nuclear opponents think about the issue.

The apogee of antinuclear discourse in terms of impact on popular consciousness came with the release, a few weeks before TMI, of a major Hollywood film, *The China Syndrome*. The film numbered among its stars Jane Fonda, an actress so closely identified with the antinuclear movement that pro-nuclear groups used her as a symbol of that movement. The film's most important achievement was to provide a concrete, vivid image of how a disastrous nuclear accident could happen. But, of course, it was just a movie.

The Role of Collective Action

How important was the antinuclear movement in opening the discourse on nuclear power to a range of packages and preparing the ground for a critical interpretation of the TMI accident? The process was sometimes subtle and indirect but, I will argue, collective action through noninstitutional channels was a crucial catalytic ingredient in the change.

The single most significant direct action was the site occupation of the Seabrook, New Hampshire nuclear reactor site by a group of over 1,400 demonstrators under the banner of the Clamshell Alliance. New Hampshire Governor Meldrim Thomson blessed the Clam with a major social control error. The 1,414 demonstrators who were arrested were not, as expected, released on their own recognizance. Instead, they were charged with criminal trespass and asked to post bail, ranging from $100 to $500, which they refused to do. They were then held in five national guard armories for 12 days, and their situation became a continuing national story. Each of the 3 major television networks ran segments on 5 different days, although sometimes merely a short update.

The direct coverage of Seabrook in itself contains little discourse about nuclear power. Most media coverage treated the incident as a story about a dyadic conflict between Governor Thomson and the Clam over whether or not the Seabrook reactor will be completed. The central question in this frame is "who will win?" and not "what about nuclear power?" But the action succeeded in gaining broad media recognition that there is a serious controversy about nuclear power, thereby requiring the application of the balance norm.

The Clamshell Alliance did not succeed through its action in becoming the media-designated "other side" called for by the balance norm. This honor fell to the Union of Concerned Scientists (UCS), which presented all the proper cues for media credibility. A Media Institute study (1979) examined the use of "outside sources" (excluding government officials) in ten years of network coverage of nuclear power and found UCS in front by a large margin, almost doubling its nearest competitor. Part of this finding is testimony to the skill and enterprise of UCS in its sponsor activities and media strategies. But the actions of the Clam plus other antinuclear demonstrations and site occupations across the country helped to create the conditions for media-initiated contacts. When demonstrators are arrested at Seabrook, phones ring at UCS.

In February 1975, some 30,00 farmers, students, and assorted environmentalists occupied the site of a nuclear plant site in Wyhl, a rural area near the Rhine in the Kaiserstuhl area of Southwestern Germany.[13] For the next eight months, they continued, in varying numbers, to occupy the site, in effect creating a local village with a "friendship house" and a "People's High School." Local farmers supported the occupiers with food and in other ways. After eight months, the group agreed to end its occupation, pending a hearing and decision before a panel of judges. The panel ruled against the plant a few months before the Seabrook occupation, providing the antinuclear movement with a clear-cut victory. Wyhl became a potent symbol of successful, nonviolent direct action for American antinuclear activists.

The Wyhl occupation was a nonstory for American national television, never making it into network news coverage. Nevertheless, through movement enterprise, it became an important and inspiring example for the future Seabrook demonstrators. Descriptions and photographs circulated in movement forums, and a movement film company, Green Mountain Post films put together a 15-minute documentary from footage originally shot by participants.

A second action that influenced the Seabrook demonstrators might, at first blush, seem a lonely act of defiance unworthy of the term "collective." In February 1974, a young man, acting alone, toppled a 500-foot weather tower on a planned nuclear site in Montague, Massachusetts. He then turned himself in to police and conducted his own defense at the subsequent trial.[14]

All the symbols surrounding the act resonated with Yankee independence in the spirit of 1776 and the Boston Tea Party: the man's very name, Samuel Holden Lovejoy; the fact that he chose George Washington's birthday to perform his act; his home in the seedbed of the American revolution; his occupation as a farmer. Lovejoy evoked this symbolism in a statement that he released, explaining his act by quoting from the Declaration of Independence and the Massachusetts Bill of Rights.

Lovejoy's act was neither planned nor carried out collectively, but it was collective in a broader sense. He was generally described in the coverage of the event as "a farmer" òr "an organic farmer," and indeed he did earn his living at farming and as a child had spent his summers working on a farm. But Lovejoy was also a social movement activist. In the late 1960s, he had graduated from Amherst, an elite liberal arts college, where he participated in the anti-Vietnam war movement on campus. He had visited Cuba with the Venceremos Brigade and had joined an organic farm collective as part of the "back to the land" movement of the early 1970s. The collective farm where he lived and worked had earlier been associated with the Liberation News Service, part of the movement infrastructure.

After the trial, he worked with some of his movement friends to make a prize-winning documentary film, *Lovejoy's Nuclear War*. Green Mountain Post Films, the same filmmaker that distributed the Wyhl film, produced and distributed it. One of its writers, Harvey Wasserman, later became a leader and spokesman for the Clamshell Alliance. Lovejoy himself traveled around New England speaking at local antinuclear organizing meetings where, in the years leading up to Seabrook, the film was frequently shown.

Lovejoy's original act required individual courage and imagination, but it took place in a movement context. And it was not the act itself but the subsequent collective enterprise based on the act, that influenced the internal discourse of the antinuclear movement.

Events such as the "No Nuke" rock concerts, featuring popular singers Jackson Browne and Bonnie Raitt, helped to create a greater sense of solidarity and collective efficacy on the part of movement participants. By fostering an antinuclear culture, such events helped to create an appropriate climate and national audience for a film such as *The China Syndrome* and helped prepare media discourse for the accident at Three Mile Island. Had the Fermi accident occurred in the culture of 1979 instead of 1966, it would have become as familiar a symbol in media discourse as TMI.[15]

Life Imitates Art (from TMI to Chernobyl)

As events unfold, each package must offer an interpretation that is consistent with its story line. Although it is always possible to do this, the task is sometimes labored, particularly if the event is, from the standpoint of the package, unexpected.

Consider the problem of the *Faith in Progress* package in the face of TMI and Chernobyl:

> TMI showed that the safety systems worked even in the face of a string of improbable errors. A total core meltdown was prevented and most of the radiation released never breached the containment building. Furthermore, we learned from the experience and have improved safety even more. Chernobyl has equally sanguine lessons. It shows the wisdom of the American nuclear industry in building large fortified containment structures as a safety precaution. U.S. nuclear reactors have multiple protective barriers, called "defense in depth." American nuclear reactors cannot be compared with their Soviet counterparts any more than their political systems are comparable. Furthermore, even in this most serious of accidents, it turns out that initial claims of thousands killed reflected mere hysteria, egged on by antinuclear activists.

Events, as the Fermi accident illustrates, do not speak for themselves. By 1979, a *Faith in Progress* interpretation was forced to compete with others that were saying that a serious nuclear accident could and probably will happen. No complicated interpretation is necessary for a prophecy fulfilled.

In media discourse after TMI, *Faith in Progress* had shrunk to a minority position, displayed in less than 25% of media commentary on nuclear power. Furthermore, its displays were often ironical or mocking ones, quoting the utopian vision of electricity that would be "too cheap to meter" to contrast it with the reality of present costs. Even when expressed more positively, the tone is frequently grudging and defensive. For example, NBC quotes Secretary of Energy James Schlesinger conceding that TMI was an "unfortunate occurrence and the reaction to it will not be beneficial, save that it may permit us to better understand some of the plant operations and that the Nuclear Regulatory Commission will be able to institute measures that will reduce risks."[16]

The most striking fact about post-TMI discourse is the emergence into leading prominence of an unsponsored package, *Devil's Bargain*. This package, emphasizing a dilemma, is fundamentally ambivalent about nuclear power, resonating with both the technological progress theme and the soft path countertheme.

So nuclear power turns out to be a bargain with the Devil. We didn't understand what we were getting into. We thought we could harness it to maintain our standard of living. Now we are committed to it and will sooner or later have to pay a price of unknown dimension. We have unleashed it, but we no longer can control it. Nuclear power is a powerful genie that we have summoned and are now unable to force back into its bottle; a Frankenstein monster that might turn on its creator. Nuclear power is a time bomb, waiting to explode. Nuclear energy is not simply one among several alternative energy sources but something more elemental. It defies a cost-benefit analysis. Radiation is invisible and one may be exposed without knowing it; its harmful effects may not show up right away but may strike suddenly and lethally at some later point. Radiation can create grotesque mutants. In a religious version, humans have dared to play God in tampering with the fundamental forces of nature and the universe. He who sows the wind, reaps the whirlwind.

Although the statement above has a negative ring, many expressions of *Devil's Bargain* do not fit comfortably into the category "against." Some who take this position resolve their ambivalence by becoming NIMBYs (Not In My Back Yard). For those embarrassed by such a stance, resignation rather than opposition is the characteristic position. But resignation and nimbyness seem to need no sponsors and, not surprisingly, neither officials nor challengers help this resignation along. Editorial cartoonists are especially likely to feature it, frequently with gallows humor about nasty nuclear surprises. Gallows humor, as Hudge and Mansfield suggest (1985, p. 210), is a way of "distancing the unthinkable so that it can be turned on its head, and subjected to a sense of control."

Among the antinuclear packages, *Public Accountability* is clearly the leader in media discourse. *Soft Paths,* in particular, is rarely displayed, except as generally environmental concern. *Faith in Progress* has slipped to a beleaguered and defensive third, a far cry from the 1950s version. Most important, the most prominent package in media discourse has become an ambivalent one, *Devil's Bargain.* Any overall characterization of media discourse by percentage pro and con necessarily obscures this central fact.

TMI left a permanent legacy of new symbols as a permanent part of the discourse. Three events seem particularly significant in understanding the further evolution of discourse between the events at TMI and Chernobyl.

a.   In 1981, Israel bombed an Iraqi nuclear reactor for fear that the highly enriched uranium it would have used as fuel would be diverted to bomb production—a further reminder of the close connection between nuclear power and nuclear weapons.

b.   *Silkwood,* a second major Hollywood movie with a strong anticorporate theme was released in 1982, greatly broadening the recognition of this symbol of *Public Accountability.*

c.   The collapse of OPEC and the decline in oil prices undercut fears about exploitation and blackmail through dependence on imported energy, lessening the potential salience of *Energy Independence.*

All these developments were bad news for supporters of nuclear energy but nothing compared to Chernobyl, framed in the media as a nuclear nightmare come true. Whither dualism in the images of an exploding reactor spewing a cloud of radioactivity over half a continent? The best a *Faith in Progress* advocate can hope for in media discourse after Chernobyl is a little benign neglect of the issue.

Role of Collective Action

The nuclear power industry in America is in a defensive position, engaged in damage control. There have been no new orders for nuclear power plants since TMI. Those already under construction but not yet operating are frequently subjected to continuing opposition. An anti-nuclear-power position has become increasingly attractive to politicians, especially in New England.

Demonstrations against nuclear plants at Diablo Canyon in California and a number of other sites continued after TMI but had become an old story to journalists and stimulated very little new media discourse on nuclear power. But little influence on the discourse is needed at this point, as the existing issue culture is already quite conducive to further collective action. Mobilization against the licensing of new plants is a relatively easy task, as both antinuclear and ambivalent constituents can be mobilized around concerns about proximity and safety. Broader antinuclear packages are hardly necessary. And anyone who proposes constructing additional nuclear plants is likely to be deterred by the prospects of a long and bitter struggle.

Mobilization against the operation of plants under construction, or the closing of the 100 or so already operating, is, of course, a considerably more difficult task. Here, ambivalence is more likely to lead to paralysis and inaction as doubters face a Hobson's choice. In this case, the advantages of inertia lie with the supporters of nuclear power.

The discourse after Chernobyl boosted trends already under way and added a new exemplar to the antinuclear arsenal. Antinuclear demonstrators in West Germany added a potent new catchphrase that caught the ears of American journalists: "Chernobyl is everywhere." One can anticipate its further appearance at future demonstrations in the United States or Europe.

B. French and German Nuclear Discourse

France and Germany offer sharp contrasts on almost any dimension that one could suppose relevant for political discourse on nuclear power. France is heavily dependent on nuclear energy, drawing almost two-thirds of its electricity from this source. Germany is only moderately dependent, drawing less than one-third of its electricity from nuclear energy. France has one of the weakest antinuclear movements in Europe, Germany one of the strongest. Their national cultures are profoundly different. Yet Nelkin and Pollak's fine study (1981), *The Atom Beseiged,* reveals basic similarities in their discourse, with changes paralleling those in the United States.

Nelkin and Pollak emphasize the same "apocalyptic images of extinction" rooted in images of Hiroshima and Nagasaki. In analyzing the discourse of the "nucleocrats" who manage each country's nuclear reactor program, they find the same *Faith in Progress* characteristic of their American counterparts. This discourse, they suggest, is pervaded by a faith in "technological solutions as well as the desire to dominate nature and society" (1981, p. 24).

In the case of France, *Faith in Progress* and *Energy Independence* seem well-integrated into a single pro-nuclear package emphasizing national independence, a definition of progress, and an image of the future. One earns some international prestige points through being technologically advanced in general but even more through an advanced nuclear technology. "Technological strength is a symbol of independent national strength" Nelkin and Pollak observe, "even when it is not profitable—witness the Concorde." There is great sensitivity among French nucleocrats to the heavy French reliance on imports to meet energy needs. "Will we accept bondage under Arab domination?" asked a leading official of the French nuclear program (1981, p. 21)

The same antinuclear packages also seem well represented in European discourse. Nelkin and Pollak suggest the centrality of the *Public Accountability* package when they write of the emphasis on "the complicity among government agencies and nuclear suppliers, utilities, and banks" (1981, p. 147). *Soft Paths* seems to be reflected in the "radical ecologists" allegiance to Illich's concept of conviviality, providing a model of liberation and emancipation.

The authors also provide evidence to support the same synergy between direct action and scientific wings of the movement as in the American case. The ability of the antinuclear movement to present credible scientists as media sources was a crucial resource in all countries. "When a seriously dressed Dr. Engineer with a black attache case comes to the podium in a debate, the ordinary citizen is already more impressed than he would be by someone with a beard or dirty parka," writes *Der Spiegel,* and we know at least what impresses *Der Spiegel.* But Nelkin and Pollak also remind us that "Under politically less favorable conditions—without the backing of a social movement—[the] voices [of critical scientists] can easily be dismissed" (1981, p. 101). Finally, Nelkin and Pollak take note of the ambivalence in some of the imagery linking life and death or hope and fear.

In sum, in comparing discourse in the United States, France, and Germany, one finds enough similarities to suggest an issue culture that transcends national differences. All these countries share, after all, common images of "The Bomb" and the dualism of atoms for war and atoms for peace. They share movements concerned with the environment and the ecology of the planet. They share nucleocrats with similar world views. And their antinuclear movements in particular share an awareness of each other's collective action. If Chernobyl is everywhere, so is Wyhl.

CONCLUSION

This analysis of nuclear power discourse is intended to make broader points about political discourse and collective action. Collective action by challengers can significantly alter issue cultures and thereby contribute to future mobilization efforts. In the case of nuclear power, the struggle over meaning continues, and the antinuclear movement is an important actor in that ongoing symbolic contest.

When official packages are in crisis and disarray, opportunities are created for challengers. An analysis of media discourse on nuclear power in America suggests that such a crisis condition exists today. The once dominant *Faith in Progress* package retains official sponsorship, but it is overwhelmed in media discourse by ambivalent and antinuclear alternatives.

Mobilization potential is also affected by the presence of certain themes and counterthemes in the political culture. Packages on a given issue resonate in varying degrees with these larger themes, thereby providing constraints and opportunities. Themes, I have argued, are paired with counterthemes in a dialectic relationship. Two pairs in particular have special relevance for the nuclear power issue—one dealing with the relationship of society and nature, centering on technology; the other dealing with the role of the state in the international order and centering on issues of national autonomy and global interdependence. On other issues, different themes and counterthemes will be relevant.

Issue cultures are the battleground for converting potential into action and challengers can affect them in significant ways. Unloosening the hold of offically sponsored packages in mass media discourse is a necessary first step in any long-term mobilization strategy. The powerful cultural resonances of packages such as *Faith in Progress* and *Energy Independence* must be understood and neutralized to accomplish this task.

But weakening official packages is only half the task. Collective action also depends on furthering the careers of mobilizing packages. There are different forums for an issue but general-audience mass media are especially important for consensus mobilization. Media discourse is itself influenced by the enterprise of package sponsors, including the activities of social movement organizations.

On many issues, media practices tend to give advantages to officials while creating handicaps and dilemmas for challengers. But these handicaps were successfully overcome in the case of the antinuclear-power movement in America, and media discourse changed dramatically and favorably. This is not the only issue on which officials, regardless of initial advantage, have lost control of the resulting media discourse. Challengers, then, can develop sophisticated strategies that take into account the organization and practices of journalists and can exploit the available opportunities. The synergy between demonstrators occupying nuclear plant sites and concerned scientists is an excellent example.

In emphasizing the role of collective action in altering political discourse, I run the danger of exaggerating it. The antinuclear movement did not create the mushroom clouds of Hiroshima and Nagasaki nor the accidents at TMI and Chernobyl that have left such an indelible imprint on the culture of the issue. But events take their meaning from the discourse in which they are embedded, and collective action helps to shape these meanings for both movement constituents and a larger audience.

GLOSSARY OF ACRONYMS

AEC	=	Atomic Energy Commission
CIO	=	Congress of Industrial Organizations
NBC	=	National Broadcasting Company
NIMBY	=	Not In My Back Yard
TMI	=	Three Mile Island
UAW	=	United Auto Workers
UCS	=	Union of Concerned Scientists

NOTES

1. The five framing devices are: (1) metaphors, (2) exemplars (that is, historical examples from which lessons are drawn, (3) catchphrases, (4) depictions, and (5) visual images (for example, icons). The three reasoning devices are (1) roots (that is, a causal analysis), (2) consequences (that is, a particular type of effect), and (3) appeals to principle (that is, a set of moral claims). A package can be summarized in a signature matrix that states the frame, range of positions, and the eight different types of signature elements that suggest this core in a condensed manner. For a fuller presentation of this part of the model, see Gamson (1982) and Gamson and Lasch (1983).

2. The acid test of a statement of a package should be its acceptance by an advocate that the statement is a fair one. We attempt to meet this test by relying on the language of advocates and sponsors, deriving it from their pamphlets and writings. In this instance, we paraphrase or quote materials from the Atomic Industrial Forum, the Edison Electric Institute, the Committee on Energy Awareness, and the pro-nuclear writings of neoconservatives (see Nisbet 1979 and McCracken 1977, 1979).

3. See, especially, Nisbet (1979) and McCracken (1979).

4. The economic model of value-added has been used most prominently in sociology by Smelser (1963) in his *Theory of Collective Behavior*. In spite of the influence of this work, the general linear model so dominates the thinking of most American sociologists that they find it difficult to think in value-added terms, immediately attempting to translate such models into the language of dependent and independent variables. But it is confusing rather than helpful to think of an automobile as the dependent variable, while mining, smelting, painting, and delivery are considered independent variables.

5.   Additional examples and a more extended discussion of this value-added model can be found in Gamson and Modigliani (1987).

6.   They also use the term "frame resonance," but this phrase refers to the connection between the content of a frame and the response of an audience member. In contrast, cultural resonance and narrative fidelity connect symbols on a specific issue with more enduring cultural themes.

7.   To qualify this statement a bit: there are alternative, more specialized, media that movement adherents may be exposed to, and some may number movement activists among their friends and acquaintances. The experience of nuclear power for these sources, however, is equally second hand. Peer group conversations that we are conducting show that many people show some awareness that their electricity bills may reflect the costs of accidents, delays, and cost overruns in nuclear power plant construction and operation. But this proximate meaning is again mediated and not something most people can construct through their own experience.

8.   A full report of this data on nuclear power, with appropriate methodological details, appears in Gamson and Modigliani (1986). In the present paper, I report selected findings and conclusions, but the reader is referred to the earlier paper for full information.

9.   I rely here on the detailed account of the Fermi accident by Fuller (1975).

10.   *New York Times*, November 13, 1966.

11.   The breeder reactor at Fermi was eventually abandoned, although a conventional light water reactor (Fermi 2) was later built next to it.

12.   See Lovins (1977) for a particularly influential articulation of this package.

13.   I rely here on the account in Gyorgy (1979).

14.   The trial ended with a judge-oriented verdict of acquittal on a technicality, somewhat to the disappointment of Lovejoy, who would have preferred acquittal by jury. A posttrial survey of the jurors showed that he probably would have received it.

15.   In emphasizing collective action, I do not mean to diminish the importance of actions by local citizen groups and public-interest organizations working through such institutional channels as public hearings and informal lobbying. Very few planned nuclear plants went unopposed during the 1970s, and this opposition activity contributed in major ways to an antinuclear discourse. My argument is for the synergy of conventional activity and direct action by movement organizations, not for the exclusive importance of the latter.

16.   NBC News, March 30, 1979

REFERENCES

Almond, Gabriel A. and Sidney Verba. 1963. *The Civic Culture*. Boston: Little Brown.

Almond, Gabriel A. and Sidney Verba. 1982. *Theories of Mass Communication*. 4th Edition, New York: Longman

Ball-Rokeach, Sandra J. and Melvin DeFleur. "A dependency model of mass media effects." *Communication Research* 3:3-21.

Bennett, W. Lance. 1975. *The Political Mind and the Political Environment*. Lexington, Mass.: D.C. Heath.

Boyer, Paul. 1985. *By the Bomb's Early Light*. New York; Pantheon.

Fuller, John G. 1975. *We Almost Lost Detroit*. New York: Thomas Y. Crowell.

Gamson, William A. 1982. "The political culture of Arab-Israeli conflict." *Conflict Management and Peace Sciences* 5:79-93.

Gamson, William A. and Kathryn E. Lasch. 1983. "The Political Culture of Social Welfare Policy." Pages 397-415 in Shimon E. Spiro and Ephraim Yuchtman-Yaar (eds.), *Evaluating the Welfare State: Social and Political Perspectives*. New York: Academic Press.

Gamson, William A. and André Modigliani. 1986. "Media Discourse and Public Opinion on Nuclear Power." Working Paper No. 5, Boston College Program in Social Economy and Social Justice.

Gamson, William A. and André Modigliani. 1987. "The Changing Culture of Affirmative Action."
    In Richard G. Braungart (ed.), *Research in Political Sociology*. Vol. 3. Greenwich, Conn.:
    JAI.
Gurevitch, Michael and Mark R. Levy (eds.). 1985. *No Nukes: Everyone's Guide to Nuclear Power*.
    Boston: South End Press.
Halberstam, David. 1979. *The Powers That Be*. New York: Knopf.
Hodge, Bob and Alan Mansfield. 1985. "'Nothing Left to Laugh At': Humor as a Tactic of
    Resistance." Pages 197-211 in Paul Chilton (ed.), *Language and the Nuclear Arms Debate:
    Nukespeak Today*. London: Frances Pinter.
Klandermans, Bert. 1986. "New Social Movements and Resource Mobilization: The European
    and the American Approach." *International Journal of Mass Emergencies and Disasters*.
    Special issue, *Comparative Perspectives and Research on Collective Behavior and Social
    Movements* 4:13-27.
Lovins, Amory. 1977. *Soft Energy Paths*. New York: Harper.
McCracken, Samuel. 1977. "The war against the atom." *Commentary* 64:33-47.
McCracken, Samuel. 1979. "The Harrisburg Syndrome." *Commentary* 67:27-39.
Macdonald, Dwight. 1945. "The bomb." *Politics* 2 (September):257-60.
Media Institute. 1979. *Television Evening News Covers Nuclear Energy: A Ten-Year Perspective*.
    Washington, D.C.: Media Institute.
Mitchell, Robert C. 1981. "From elite quarrel to mass movement." *Society* 18:76-84.
Nelkin, Dorothy and Michael Pollak. 1981. *The Atom Beseiged: Extraparliamentary Dissent in
    France and Germany*. Cambridge, Mass.: MIT Press.
Nisbet, Robert. 1979. "The rape of progress." *Public Opinion* 2:2-6, 55.
Sigal, Leon V. 1973. *Reporters and Officials*. Lexington, Mass.: D.C. Heath.
Smelser, Neil J. 1963. *Theory of Collective Behavior*. New York: Free Press.
Snow, David A., E. Burke Rochford, Jr., Steven K. Worden, and Robert D. Benford. 1986. "Frame
    alignment processes, micromobilization, and movement participation." *American
    Sociological Review* 51:464-81.
Tarrow, Sidney. 1983. *Struggling to Reform: Social Movements and Policy Change during Cycles
    of Protest*. Western Societies Paper No. 15. Ithaca, N.Y.: Cornell University.
Tuchman, Gaye. 1974. *The TV Establishment*. Englewood Cliffs, N.J.: Prentice-Hall.
Waymack, W.W. 1947. "A Letter to Judith and Dickie." *National Education Association Journal*
    36:214.
Williams, Robin M., Jr. 1960. *American Society*. New York: Knopf.

PART III

THE CREATION AND CAREERS
OF COLLECTIVE ACTORS

FROM PEACE WEEK TO PEACE WORK:
DYNAMICS OF THE PEACE MOVEMENT
IN THE NETHERLANDS

Ben Schennink

I. INTRODUCTION

In the 1980s the Dutch peace movement experienced a participation explosion. The most visible manifestations of this phenomenon were the demonstrations in Amsterdam (1981) and The Hague (1983) and the people's petition (1985). These actions were directed against the deployment of cruise missiles and Pershing IIs in Western Europe, with particular emphasis on cruise deployment in the Netherlands. Since the 1960s and 1970s, the Dutch peace movement has grown enormously. This development was not unique for the Netherlands; other Western European countries and the United States witnessed a similarly strong revival of the peace movement (Benford 1987; Steinweg 1982). How can this change in participation in the Netherlands best be explained?

Social movement theories suggest answers on three different levels: the level of social movement organizations, the social level, and the political level. Different theories stress different levels. Resource mobilization theories

International Social Movement Research, Vol. 1, pages 247-279.
Supplement to Research in Social Movements, Conflicts and Change
Copyright © 1988 by JAI Press Inc.
All rights of reproduction in any form reserved.
ISBN: 0-89232-955-6

consider the first level as the most important. These theories emphasize the role of movement organizations and their strategies (Klandermans 1986; Jenkins and Perrow 1977). If there is no organization of the resources for protest, or if the organizations do not supply collective actions, no visible form of protest will develop. This means that it is primarily the strategy and organization of a social movement organization which account for growing participation. Resource mobilization theories presuppose the existence of grievances.

New social movement theories stress social factors. Growing participation in the peace movement, like the development of new social movements in general, can be explained on the basis of new values, action forms, and protest potentials that arose as a reaction to the process of modernization in western industrialized societies (Klandermans 1986). These developments created a new culture—a counterculture as Kriesi (Chapter 1) calls it—that provided movements with a mobilization potential, a structural base of people with a predisposition to participate in social movements.

While both these two approaches neglect political factors (Klandermans 1986; Tarrow 1986), such factors do have a clear impact upon one's decision to participate (Tarrow 1983). The political level is emphasized in the political process model that explains growing participation as a combination of the degree of organization of the grievances and the expansion of political opportunities (McAdam 1983; see also Chapter 4). Among the factors that should be taken into consideration at the political level are:

1. extent of political access, i.e., responsiveness of governing bodies;
2. stability of political alignment, i.e., electoral stability;
3. allies and support groups, i.e., support of influential social groups (Tarrow 1983, pp. 26-34).

Walsh (1981) adds to this list "suddenly imposed grievances." These are grievances imposed on a population either as the result of an accident, such as that at Three Mile Island, or by a conscious decision.

The Dutch peace movement organization, the Interchurch Peace Council (IKV), provides a good case study for explaining the low participation in the late sixties and seventies and the high participation in the eighties. Since its founding in 1966 it has actively promoted participation in the peace movement. From 1967 until 1977, IKV organized activities, which intended to raise consciousness on matters of peace and war. In August 1977, IKV changed its strategy drastically. In this year IKV started a long-term political campaign with the slogan "Help Rid the World of Nuclear Weapons, Let it Begin in the Netherlands." From 1977 all IKV activities have been directed toward removing nuclear weapons from the Dutch armed forces and preventing deployment of new nuclear weapons. IKV is generally seen as the central social movement organization in the Dutch protest against the cruise missiles (van Staden 1985b).

Changes in the strategy of a social movement organization, developments in the political opportunity structure, or shifts in the protest potential in society can explain differences in participation between two successive periods. If one looks only for such changes, however, one may neglect the possible influence that activities in the earlier phase of a social movement organization many have on participation in later phases. One should be aware of continuity particularly when the same organization is active in both phases.

What effect can we expect the consciousness-raising activities in the first phase to have on participation in protest in the second phase? Klandermans's (1984) distinction between consensus mobilization and action mobilization activities is useful for answering this question. During consensus mobilization a social movement organization tries to convince people that a certain situation is unacceptable. These efforts result in the development of a mobilization potential, a number of people the organization can call upon for action in organized protest activities. With action mobilization activities a social movement organization motivates these people to participate in organized protest. Consensus mobilization, in other words, is a precondition for action mobilization but is not necessarily followed by action mobilization. The existence of grievances is not enough for successful action mobilization, an organization must define the grievances in a purposeful activity. Social movement organizations are not only mobilizing but also signifying agents. Their signifying work is done in consensus mobilization.

According to Snow and Benford (Chapter 7), consensus mobilization activities may accomplish two signifying or "framing" tasks: the identification of a problem and its causes (diagnostic framing) and the identification of solutions to it (prognostic framing). An organization can restrict itself to diagnostic framing activities. It will then develop opinions and attitudes concerning the definition of the problem. When an organization also proposes a solution and a strategy to implement it, it must elaborate a more extensive system of ideas and must find popular support for this proposal. When in its second phase the same organization tries to motivate people to participate in protest activities (motivational framing), it can and probably will build on these earlier framing activities. Snow and Benford's theory leads one to expect that these earlier framings will foster participation in the later phase particularly when the later framings are related to the earlier ones and especially when the motivational framings that are needed in that later phase are consistent with those earlier framings. These relations suggest that earlier framing activities may also impede action mobilization. Snow and Benford explicitly point to this possibility in the example of a social movement organization that defines the problem as so large that no action would help. The result of such a diagnostic framing will be fatalism. Whether the earlier consensus mobilization activities foster or impede participation is an empirical question.

To mobilize participation in social movement, social movement organizations must pursue three different activities (Klandermans and Tarrow, Introduction; Klandermans andOegema 1987). Besides forming a mobilization potential and motivating people to participate, social movement organizations must also develop recruitment networks. These networks must be developed so that the people who belong to the mobilization potential can be reached during the action mobilization phase. Klandermans and Tarrow's description of mobilization activities (Introduction) implies that the development of such networks must follow the formation of a potential for mobilization. These networks, however, are also important in diffusing the message of the social movement organization; indeed they are built up for this purpose or are naturally inclined to such activities (Mushaben 1986). Networks not only provide bridges between the mobilization potential and the protest participants; during the consensus mobilization period, they also function as messengers from the organization to the people. If in its second phase an organization shifts its strategy to action mobilization, it has these networks at its disposal.

When members of these networks, which are set up to raise consciousness, are asked to take part in action mobilization activities, they may be spurred to increase their activities. Such a change, however, may also create problems, because of the variety of motivations among individual members. This situation is especially typical of church-related social movement organizations. Long-standing ecclesiastic framing efforts have persuaded many church members that obedience to the government is a normal attitude and that protest is forbidden.[1] Similarly, in the peace movement, proponents of conventional, institutional, or democratic means of exerting pressure—such as social discussions and political lobbying for change—are often at odds with advocates of civil disobedience or direct action methods who do not believe in the effectiveness of democratic pressure (Benford 1987; Mushaben 1986). There are, in other words, different protest cultures. Accordingly, during action mobilization, consensus mobilization must continue and must be directed at persuading people that a chosen action is permissible and can lead to results. These framing efforts may diminish the mobilization potential and reduce the networks built up in the consciousness-raising period, since many may not agree with the methods of action. On the other hand, these efforts can stimulate mobilization by attracting new groups and individuals to the networks and to the potentials to mobilize or by furthering the growth of existing networks and potentials, since individuals belonging to them see they can now do something meaningful. Whether there are different protest cultures and along which lines they prevail among the members of the networks and the mobilization potential is another empirical question.

The Peace Research Centre surveyed participation in the peace weeks in the Netherlands in 1969 and 1970. In 1981, Peace Research Centre interviewers questioned a sample of participants in the demonstration in Amsterdam, as they did again during the 1983 demonstration in the Hague. In 1985 the Centre organized a nationwide telephone survey to see who signed and who did not. The information gathered in all these interviews makes it possible to compare participation in the peace movement in the 1960s and 1970s with participation in the 1980s. By combining the Centre data with data on developments in Dutch society and politics during the same period, I will try to describe which variable in the three different levels contributed to the participation explosion in the 1980s.

In the following section the consciousness-raising period (1967-1976) will be described and analyzed. Section III concentrates on the action-stimulating period (1977-1986) and will also assess the influence of the first period on participation in that phase. In Section IV the question of different protest cultures will be analyzed. The last section summarizes the main conclusions.

II. CONSCIOUSNESS-RAISING STRATEGY: THE PEACE WEEK, 1967-1976

A. The Organization and its Consensus-Building Strategy

IKV was founded in 1966 by the two major Protestant churches—the Dutch Reformed Church and the Reformed Churches—and the Roman Catholic Church, at the suggestion of the Roman Catholic peace movement (Pax Christi) in the Netherlands. In 1966 and 1967 six smaller denominations joined.[2] Following a period of concern in the early 1960s, public concern for issues of war and peace had, it felt, begun to fade, and thus it was likely that official Church documents on these issues, which criticized the ongoing arms race and the possible use of nuclear weapons, would be deprived of any public or political impact. IKV was founded to stimulate interest—especially among Church members—in this matter. The IKV council members were nominated by the churches, which also provided the financial means for setting up a small professional secretariat (two to three people). At the same time, however, IKV was not accountable to the churches for its activities (IKV 1977).

In 1967, IKV chose the peace week as the operational definition of its task. From 1967 on, peace weeks have been organized every year. In its first ten years, IKV chose a new theme every year, and, in doing so, emphasized a variety of issues. According to the organizers of the peace week, the object of the event was to interest a growing number of people, especially church members, in the problems of war and peace, to educate them, and thus to give them an opportunity for political action.

For every peace week IKV prepared a peace week journal (100,000-200,000 copies) and a documentation set. These were prepared by council members and other specialists, most of them from universities, who had been approached to treat specific themes. In the peace week journal IKV would inform the public about possible potential actions, but IKV would not organize them (Schennink 1975).

Each year the peace week was announced both at a specially organized press conference and via the normal church communication channels. The Roman Catholic bishops, for example, announced the peace week to their parishes and asked their priests to focus on the theme during that week. The announcements led to many individual requests for more material. The following year, IKV would inform those individuals about the peace week directly. It was from these requests that IKV built up its network of *core activists*. These core activists were asked to form new *local groups* in order to organize local activities during the peace week and to stimulate already existing local peace or Third World groups to participate in the events.

Neither the church authorities, the core activists, nor the local groups, however, had any direct influence on the choice of theme of the peace week or on the materials that were prepared. On the other hand, IKV had no direct influence on the way core activists or local groups presented the peace week or set up local activities. Coordination and communication occurred only at the training weekends for local peace week activists which IKV organized in the first years.

In its first ten years, IKV restricted its lobbying efforts to political parties and government. It produced five statements on security issues, two statements on Third World development issues, and three statements on human rights and conscientious objection, all directed at government and parliament (IKV 1977). Most of this lobbying was carried out in cooperation with Pax Christi.

From the description so far, one can conclude that IKV had a consensus-building strategy in this period. No collective actions were organized, education and consciousness raising were stressed, and political demands were restricted. Core activists agreed with this strategy, as our 1969 survey among them

Table 1. IKV's Goals, Core Activists' Goals, and the Main Effect of the Peace Week, According to Core Activists in 1969 (in percentages)

	IKV's goals	Own goal	Main outcome
Consensus-building[1]	72	61	79
Participation[2]	24	34	10
Other, don't know	4	5	11
Total %	100	100	100
Total N	540	540	540

Notes:
[1]Includes the pre-coded categories: change of attitude, information, and activating the churches.
[2]Includes the pre-coded categories: change the existing structures and influence government.

Table 2. Peace Week Slogans From 1967-1976

Year	Slogan	(theme)
1967	"Proliferate Wealth, not Nuclear Weapons"	
1968	"Europe: Peace, Reconciliation, Security"	
1969	"Don't Give Charity, Give Justice" (Third World poverty)	
1970	"World in Scaffolding: Unite the Nations"	
1971	"Peace: By All Means?" (violence vs. nonviolence)	
1972	"The Future of Europe"	
1973	"Peace at Home" (Everyone is involved in peace and security issues)	
1974	"Peace Work: Quite a Feat" (The power of small-scale initiatives)	
1975	"Away from Hunger and Violence"	
1976	"Endangered Existence" (Poverty and War)	

Source: IKV, 1977: 29-31. When the theme is not evident from the slogan it is added in parentheses.

indicates. They viewed consensus building as both their main goal and the main goal of IKV. Consensus building was also perceived as the main outcome of the peace week.

The consensus-building strategy is also evident from the peace week slogans that were chosen. Most of them were directed at one or more central issues in the field of war and peace. A few slogans (see 1973 and 1974 in Table 2) focused on the powerlessness of ordinary people to influence peace issues. These slogans tried to convey the message that peace is not a remote problem and that few people have an impact on policy. From Table 2 it follows that IKV's main work was in diagnostic framing. The organization provided no prognostic framing and thus suggested no solutions, not to mention strategies for achieving them. As for motivational framing, by providing examples of possible actions, IKV tried to motivate people to choose one of these alternatives, but it rarely organized collective action. On those occasions when it did so, such actions were given very little emphasis. Actions were used to support consciousness raising, not the other way around. Therefore one can conclude that the activities IKV organized during this period were aimed at consensus mobilization. Most core activists (88%) engaged in these activities: in 1969, 47% gave peace week sermons; 50% participated in, and 37% organized, discussion groups; 32% wrote articles in parish newsletters; and 59% undertook other activities, such as teaching at schools or organizing local peace week manifestations.

The emphasis on consensus building is also reflected in the kinds of organizations and institutions at which local peace groups directed their efforts in 1970. Of the local groups, about 75% targeted newspapers. Business firms, unions, political parties, and civil servants were seldom mentioned. The activities of local groups were directed primarily at those institutions which can reach the general public and church members in particular and which can be seen as signifying organizations.

B.   Networks and Mobilization Potential

IKV tried to use its peace week to build a bridge between the activist element in Dutch society and the center, especially the churches. IKV hoped to win support from church members and, indirectly, from Christian Democratic constituencies for views, activities, and policies normally advocated by Radical Democratic or Pacifist Socialist constituencies. At the same time, IKV tried to bring radical or pacifist groups and networks to the traditional church audience.

To reach these potential constituencies IKV built on already existing networks of: national and local church professionals, journalists working in the field of church and society, and peace and Third World organizations and action groups. By informing the public about possible actions organized by these organizations and action groups, IKV motivated individuals to participate in the peace week. Publishing this information brought many of these groups and organizations into contact with the churches.

With the existing networks that IKV had further developed, both direct (local networks) and indirect (mass media) communication channels could be used to draw public attention to the peace week and its message. From research at the Institute for Mass Communication and from our surveys, we can see that IKV succeeded in mobilizing these networks and building new ones as a contribution to its consciousness-raising campaign.

Many journalists became involved and wrote articles or made television or radio programs about the peace week. From Debeuckelaere's (n.d.) extensive research on coverage of IKV in the newspapers during this period, it follows that about two-thirds or more of the 80 to 90 articles written in 1967 and 1968 appeared in newspapers with a Christian or progressive identity.

Did these articles and the television and radio programs inform the public about the peace week, or did the public gain most of its information from the local networks? An answer to this question can be derived from a survey conducted in 1969 in Arnhem, a middle-sized town in the eastern part of the country. We interviewed a random sample (N=488) of the population of those residents 18 years and older. We asked our respondents if and how they had heard about the peace week. Of the total sample, 26% were not informed at all, 25% had heard about it through television, 16% via radio, 36% read about it in newspapers, and 28% were informed by local groups or core activists. These figures confirm that IKV had gained access to the communication channels provided by the mass media and had developed a network in these different media forms.

Although this response to mass media was good, IKV put greater emphasis on direct communication in the peace week by building up a network of core activists and local groups. In 1970, 220 local groups were known to IKV and about 4,500 core activists were listed in the files. In 1969 we asked the core activists if peace week actions had been organized in their town or village. Their reports reveal that activities were organized in 50% of the smaller communities, in 74%

of the towns of 10-50,000 inhabitants, and in 90% of the town of more than 50,000 inhabitants. Thus IKV succeeded in building a network through which it could reach its potential public directly, that is, via local activities. These networks were not restricted to the cities but developed in the country as well.

Our 1969 Arnhem study compared the impact of mass media channels for the peace week publicity with the impact of direct channels. Of the total sample, 29% were well informed about the peace week. Of those who had heard of the peace week via television, 5% were well informed; of those who read about it in the newspaper, 20%. Of those who learned about the peace week from local activists, 39% were well informed: and of those who were informed directly and indirectly, 47%. The better informed people were about the peace week, the more they participated in peace week activities, and the greater the insight they gained into the problems of war and peace. Information from the mass media alone produced mainly superficial knowledge for a large part of the population. Local networks seem to be a precondition for increasing insight and stimulating participation; once reached by these networks people then use mass media to become better informed.

To get an impression of the composition of local peace week networks let us look at some background characteristics of their members. Almost all core activists and members of local peace week groups are active church members. The daily work of the core activist illustrates the consciousness-raising characteristics of the network; 41% did pastoral work, 18% taught, 5% worked in adult education, 12% studied, 21% had other work. The pattern of social characteristics of members of local peace week groups is similar to that evident among the core activists, except that group members tended to be younger, and more of them were students. Table 3 shows that the core activists and members of local peace week groups are perfect examples of what Parkin, in his study of British peace activists in the sixties, called young "educated middle-class" radicals who are engaged primarily in welfare and creative professions (Parkin 1968, p. 177).

Gradually the networks of core and local activists began to fall into two categories: the first, church professionals and active laypeople, the second, members of action groups. It could be expected that the public reached by these local peace week networks would consist primarily of church members and Christian Democratic voters, on the one hand, and supporters of radical left-wing parties, on the other. Most action groups found strong support from the Pacifist Socialists Party (PSP) and the Radical Democratic Party (PPR). People who were not reached by these networks but were nevertheless interested in the problems of war and peace found to be reached by the network of journalists. Because these people were not motivated (or less strongly motivated) by local networks, one would expect them to be far less active than people motivated by local networks. Such was the case among the constituencies of the other progressive parties, the Social Democrats (PvdA), the Liberal Progressives (D'66), and the small Communist Party (CPN).

Table 3. Social Characteristics of Core Activists (1969),
Members of Local Groups (1970), and the General Public Visiting
Peace Week Activities in 1970 (in percentages)

	Core activists	Group Members[1]	Public
Younger than 35	41[2]	72	61
Higher education[3]	74	47	34
Higher-level employment or profession[4]	89	90	65
Students	12	42	43
Church members	94	84	76
Total N	540	106	398

Notes:

[1]Group members include the members of four groups (37) and coordinators of local groups (69).

[2]Only the percentage of those younger than 35 is given in this table. The 59% core activists older than 35 are not included. The same applies to all other percentages in this table.

[3]Higher professional education and/or university education.

[4]The percentages presented in this category are based on those who had an occupation: 458 of the core activists, 62 members of local groups, and 228 visitors to the peace week activities. Because a different coding scheme was used in 1969 and 1970, the number of people in this category, who belonged to a welfare or creative profession cannot be determined. A figure can be supplied only for the core activists: at least 75% of those who had an occupation were employed in a welfare or creative profession.

Within the local networks of core activists and local groups, the two political tendencies—Christian Democratic and radical pacifist—were reflected only in the network of core activists. The local group members had a predominantly radical pacifist orientation, as could be expected given the strong links between PPR and PSP and action groups. The access of local groups to more moderate constituencies was facilitated by the core activists. They could function as a bridge between the radical pacifist local groups and the more moderate constituencies, especially within the churches. Among the core activists, Christian Democratic parties and radical pacifists parties found the same amount of support.

The diverging political tendencies in the local networks were confirmed by our survey among church officials in 1969. The active priests and ministers (24%), who organized or participated in four or more activities during the peace week, can be counted among the members of IKV's networks. They showed a pattern of potential preferences similar to that of the core activists: 33% preferred a radical left-wing party (PPR or PSP), 48% a Christian Democratic party, 12% PvdA, and 7% D'66 (percentages based on those with a preference). The less active (67%) or nonactive (9%) ministers and priests were not only less deeply involved in the peace week networks—although most of them organized or participated in some activities—they were also less strongly interested in the problems of war and peace. They preferred Christian Democratic parties to a very high degree (77%) and showed much less preference for the radical left (10%); 7% preferred D'66, 4% PvdA, and another 2% VVD. When IKV moved

Table 4. Political Preference of Core Activists (1969), Vote in 1970 Provincial Election of Members of Local Groups (1970), Vote of the Public Visiting Peace Week Activities (1970), and the Result of the 1971 National Election (in percentages)

	Preference core activists	Vote group members[1]	Vote peace week public	Vote 1971 national election[2]
Lib. Cons. (VVD)	2	1	6	10
Christ. Dem. (KVP, ARP, CHU)	35	10	39	37
Lib. Progr. (D'66)	10	11	12	7
Soc. Dem. (PvdA)	13	9	11	25
Rad. Left (PPR, PSP, CPN)[3]	39	63	32	7
Other parties	1	7	0.4	14
Total N	100	100	100.4	100
N	479	86	257	6,318,152
No pref., not voted, n.a.	61	20	143	

Notes:
[1]Group members include the members of four groups (N = 37) and coordinators of local groups (N = 69).
[2]*Source:* Daalder and Schuyt (1906. A 1300, 25-27); in 1971, all citizens 21 years and older had the right to vote
[3]CPN was slightly represented; core activists, 0.2%; group members, 1%; peace week public, 2%, national election, 4%.

more in the direction of action mobilization, this part of the network, that is, the less active or nonactive ministers and priests, was one of the first groups to drop out. During the consciousness-raising period, however, IKV could still count on them.

Which mobilization potential was developed by these local networks? Were the social and political characteristics among the core activists and members of local groups reflected among the public that visited peace week activists? In 1970 we interviewed 400 people who attended the peace week activities of four selected groups (for every group 100 people were randomly selected). The third columns of Tables 3 and 4 show the social and political characteristics of these people. The data contained in these tables confirm our expectations. IKV and its network succeeded in reaching church members primarily, as well as a part of the Christian Democratic constituencies and an important part of the radical and pacifist constituencies. They were, however, much less successful in mobilizing Social Democrats and people from the lower and middle socioeconomic levels.

C.   Political Opportunity Structure and Protest Potential in Society

Political opportunities were not unfavorable during the first decade of the peace week's existence. Electoral instability, radicalization of the Social Democratic Party, influential allies, and grievances contributed to a political climate that could have worked favorably for action mobilization.

The main source of the electoral instability was the depillarization of Dutch society.[3] This phenomenon affected primarily the three Christian Democratic parties. From 1945 to 1963 these parties had a stable electorate of about 50%. After 1963 voter support dropped steadily to 32% in 1977. Voter support stabilized after 1977 to around 30% (Everts, 1985). This percentage remained stable up to the last election (1986), when it grew to 35%.

The Social Democrats did not gain very much from the depillarization. Support for the party averaged about 30% in the fifties. Figures for the period 1963-1977 remained about the same: in 1963, 28%; in 1977, 34%. This party, however, went through a process of radicalization that turned it into a potential ally of the peace movement. In this period the party shifted from unconditional support for NATO and U.S. foreign policy to a much more critical position (van Staden 1985a). During this period too, influential allies, such as trade unions and churches, were not asked by IKV to voice their concerns, although they were offered ample opportunity to do so.

Several governmental decisions on security issues could have spurred mobilization for action during this period from 1967 to 1976. In 1968 the Christian Democratic Liberal Conservative coalition government, in reaction to the Soviet invasion of Czechoslovakia, decided to spend an extra 225 million Dutch guilders on defense. In 1974 the Radical Democratic Liberal Progressive/Social Democratic/Christian Democratic coalition government decided to replace the Star-fighter bomber with the F-16. IKV protested but did not organize actions.

IKV had chosen to pursue a consciousness-raising strategy and did not show interest in exploiting the opportunities raised by its consciousness-raising activities. The participation possibilities provided by IKV—in educational work—were useful for teachers, students, and clergymen, but they were not very suitable for other professional groups. And while they were helpful for people in action groups and for the radical left in general, they were not so suitable for the rank-and-file supporters of the main political parties.

IKV showed the same lack of interest in using the growing protest potential in Dutch society for action mobilization. The depillarization of Dutch society and politics which took place in the 1960s was accompanied by the emergence of many action-oriented groups. The Provo movement and, later, the student movement helped to introduce many new types of protest actions. Sit-ins, blockades, and boycotts, in addition to demonstrations and petitions, became "normal" protest methods. It should also be noted that the Vietnam movement

particularly influenced the peace movement. Many demonstrations and petitions were organized, and many people participated in these activities (Barnes,
Kaase, and Allerbeck 1979). This public support for protest was not equally
divided across the political spectrum and society. The center and right voters
in particular were less inclined to support protest activities. The left-wing or
right-wing vote was the best indicator of protest potential in the Netherlands
(Farah et al. 1979). The public support for conventional participation was
evenly divided in society and among the constituencies of the different parties.[4]

To summarize, the peace week strategy was a consensus-building strategy.
It created "networks, arenas and mentalities in which predispositions favorable
to action mobilization" were formed, to use Tarrow's description of consensus
mobilization (1986). It framed oppositional views to the traditional peace and
security positions of Dutch polticians which had been mainly pro-NATO and
pro-nuclear weapons. In doing so it contributed to the shrinking consensus
on foreign policy in Dutch society.

With these framing activities IKV built a new network linking church people
with the protest movements in an ideological sense. By refraining from
mobilization for specific actions and motivating people to join actions of other
peace and Third World organizations, and by concentrating on consensus
mobilization, IKV tried to provide a bridge between the protest culture of the
radical left and the conventional persuasion and discussion culture of the
churches.

III. PARTICIPATION-STIMULATION STRATEGY: NUCLEAR DISARMAMENT CAMPAIGN 1977-1986

A. A New Strategy in A New Political and Social Context

In 1977, after ten annual peace weeks, IKV changed its strategy. The main
reason for the change was the council members' concern that "protest against
the bomb" seemed to be heading down a dead-end street (Everts and ter Veer
1981). Almost no one was concerned about the nuclear weapons issue anymore.
In 1972 the council observed that "the period of grace" mentioned by the Synod
of the Dutch Reform Church in 1962 had not been used to stop the expansion
of the nuclear arms race. The council had at that time already decided that
the Dutch armed forces should abandon nuclear weapons as a step toward
the creation of a nuclear-free Europe and as a stimulus to the process of general
nuclear disarmament (IKV 1972). Their decision received little public attention
until 1977, when IKV started a long-term political campaign to implement its
proposal. In announcing its campaign, IKV departed from its strategy of
abstaining from political action.

In 1977 IKV asked the peace week groups to commit themselves to a ten-year campaign. The peace week theme was set for the next decade and activities in the intervals between peace weeks increased from what had been usual in the first decade. All activities were to be aimed at helping to realize the slogan of the campaign: "Help Rid the World of Nuclear Weapons. Let it Begin in the Netherlands."

Activities were not directed primarily to the political elite but at public opinion. Two council members explained the need for this strategy as follows: "Politicians . . . are apparently unable to extricate themselves from the arms race, unless . . . domestic pressures . . . help them to overcome the pressures and vested interests behind established policies" (Everts and ter Veer 1981, p. 159). IKV expected if its campaign could produce a change in policy in the Netherlands that change could function as a catalyst for policy change in other countries.

Domestic pressure was to be manifested in public opinion and in social and political institutions through a combination of national and local activities. Nationally, the issue was to be put on the agenda of different institutions. At the local level, core activists and local groups were to urge members of these institutions to take an active part in discussions within their institutions. Using this tactic, IKV hoped to gain support from churches, trade unions, and political parties and to give local members of those institutions possibilities for meaningful participation.

IKV started with its existing networks of core activists and local groups but now put greater emphasis on the importance of local groups than it had in its earlier period. These groups were asked not only to devote their energies exclusively to the campaign but also to strengthen their local organization. The core activists were stimulated to build new groups.

IKV set up a campaign assembly in which council members and representatives of the local groups met on a regular basis (about six to ten times a year). In the first years of the campaign this assembly had an advisory position within the IKV structure: IKV's council of church representatives made the decisions. It was necessary for these representatives to consult the assembly, however, since the latter group was of vital importance for the success of the local-level campaign. In 1982, IKV's decision-making structure was changed so that, in matters pertaining directly to the campaign, local groups were given decision-making power, together with the council members. Communication between the central organization and the local groups was strengthened by the publication of a campaign journal (3,000 subscribers). Since 1980 IKV had developed a local group guidance structure consisting of volunteer coordinators for each region who are guided by a professional staff member at the national office. By the early 1980s there were 400 local groups; by 1985 the number had grown to 450. The number of core activists also grew from 4,500 in 1969 to about 20,000 in the 1980s (Everts 1983; Kriesi, Chapter 1). Just as the communication between IKV and the local groups was tightened, so was the communication between IKV and social and political organizations. IKV made use of double memberships in particular.

IKV could also mobilize scientific resources easily. In its first ten years it had developed good contacts with university researchers in different fields. After 1977 some of these people were asked to contribute to the campaign's diagnostic and prognostic framing efforts. These people were mainly peace researchers and political and social scientists. Others—mainly theologians and philosophers—were asked to support IKV's moral claim that the use and possession of nuclear arms must be condemned. Support from the university world contributed a great deal to the "empirical credibility" and "narrative fidelity" (Snow and Benford, Chapter 7) of the campaign.

Financially, IKV was supported in the same way as it was in the first ten years: by a subsidy from the churches and profits from the sale of peace week materials. This support, however, was not enough to cover the demand of the campaign. Therefore IKV asked its friends (core activists) to provide extra support and to ask their friends to also support IKV. This additional support from the network allowed IKV to expand its professional secretariat from two to three people in the 1970s to eight to eleven full-time staff members in the 1980s.

The participation of many church members in the campaign produced positive results. In 1980 the Synod of the Dutch Reformed Church supported IKV's proposal of Dutch unilateral nuclear disarmament as a first step toward multilateral nuclear disarmament. Smaller member churches also supported IKV's proposal in 1980, as they had in 1978 and 1979. IKV's campaign led to long internal discussions, in nationally and locally, in the other, more orthodox, Reformed Churches and to an internal discussion in the Roman Catholic Church in 1981 (Everts 1983).

From 1978-1980 the same kind of discussions were on the agenda of the political parties and, from 1979-1981, on the agenda of the trade unions. D'66 and the PvdA were the first two parties to change their policy as a result of these discussions. D'66 (Liberal Progressive) opposed the NATO double-track decision, although not unconditionally. In the PvdA (Social Democrats) a majority of members favored IKV's goal but failed to gain the support of the party leader. The Social Democrats, however, opposed the NATO double-track decision unconditionally. In 1981, after a long internal debate, the Federation of Trade Unions (FNV) accepted a memorandum opposing modernization of nuclear weapons.

Although no one concrete political decision sparked IKV's campaign, shortly after the campaign began in August 1977, it gained impetus from the U.S. government's decision to produce neutron bombs and deploy them in Europe. In the Netherlands this decision provoked a protest, carried out by a small group from the Communist youth organization on August 12-13, 1977. On August 18 of that same year, the "Stop the Neutron Bomb" campaign was founded by members of the Communist party. A committee of well-known people from different parties and different social backgrounds was formed by the initiating group. These people were asked to write an open letter to the Dutch government and Dutch people requesting the government to protest the production of the neutron bomb and asking the public for actions and demonstrations against it. Soon afterward, the Stop the Neutron Bomb campaign began a signature action and asked local groups to collect signatures. In six months, 1.2 million signatures were collected.

Nationally and locally other people were also asked to support the new protest initiative (Maessen 1979). IKV joined in October 1977, shortly after the start of its own campaign, although with some hesitation, since, first, the initiative came as a complete surprise and, second, it had the backing of the Communists. It is not known how many signatures were collected by local IKV groups or Stop the Neutron Bomb groups. But according to Maessen, IKV, together with the Catholic peace movement Pax Christi, had a decisive influence on the outcome of the Stop the Neutron Bomb campaign: the Dutch Parliament voted against the production of the neutron bomb (Maessen 1979). These two organizations wrote letters to Christian Democratic politicians in government and parliament and encouraged the Dutch Council of Churches and its affiliate churches to do the same, and they did.

Christian Democrats opposed to the further development of nuclear arms capitalized on the signal that these groups were sending. Division in the Christian Democratic party was even reflected in the newly formed government of Christian Democrats (CDA) and Liberal Conservatives (VVS). The minister of defense, a Christian Democrat, strongly opposed the introduction of the neutron bomb. When, in February 1978, the Christian Democratic faction in parliament supported his position, the government had to take a stand on the issue. But the government and the Christian Democratic party were saved the necessity of making troublesome decisions when, in March 1978, President Carter decided to defer the production of the neutron bomb. The minister of defense, however, was forced to resign.[5]

A second, even more hotly debated, issue was the so-called NATO double-track decision of December 1979. This time IKV was not taken by surprise and from the start took the initiative to oppose this decision. Again IKV managed to take advantage of the division within the political elite on cruise-missile deployment in the Netherlands, and strengthening this decision produced a long political stalemate. Because about ten Christian Democratic members of parliament opposed deployment, the government was not able to agree to the NATO decision. Heavy pressure from NATO allies prevented them from opposing the decision outright. These pressures, combined with an impending governmental crisis, produced a kind of double-face decision, which gave the peace movement the opportunity for further mobilization in the years after 1979. The government did not agree to deployment in the Netherlands but did not disapprove of the NATO double-track decision as such.[6]

As to the other elements of the political opportunity structure, it is clear from the description so far that the Christian Democratic party, the central political party in Dutch coalition-governments, was divided. IKV exploited this division. In the seventies the three main Christian Democratic parties merged into one Christian Democratic party (DCA), which took part in national election for the first time in 1977. Its presence reversed the process of diminishing voter support. The memory of the difficult birth process that the new Christian Democratic party had gone through proved a strong force to curb inside opposition to the government's nuclear weapons policy.

Opposition to the neutron bomb was the basis for a coalition platform of peace movements and left and center political parties dedicated to banning nuclear weapons. Formed in 1978, this coalition included Stop the Neutron Bomb, Pax Christi, IKV, and small left-wing parties, D'66, PvdA, and DCA. The Federation of Trade Unions (FNV) informally participated from the beginning and formally joined the coalition in 1981, after the unions had officially decided to oppose modernization of nuclear weapons. The platform was set up mainly as a discussion forum through which peace movement organizations and the political parties could inform each other of their work. It also functioned as a coordination point for organizations taking the initiative to organize demonstrations or other activities protesting the further proliferation of nuclear weapons.

After the 1981 elections a new government was formed, composed of DCA, PvdA, and D'66. This government was to decide whether nuclear weapons would be deployed in the Netherlands. Therefore in 1981 IKV took the initiative for a demonstration in Amsterdam in order to put pressure on the new coalition for a clear "no." This initiative was first discussed in the coalition platform. CDA was willing to participate but could not agree with the slogans of the other participants in the coalitions. Thus the actual organization of the demonstration was done by an ad hoc committee (the November 21st Committee) consisting of all the members of the platform, except CDA, and joined by the Union of Conscripts and the Platform of Radical Peace Groups. Four hundred thousand people were motivated to participate, a number that impressed the government, which, some time earlier, had already announced that the decision would be postponed. Because the coalition of peace movement organizations and political parties, encountered difficulties with cooperation during the protest against the cruise missiles, after the 1981 demonstration a new coalition was formed, the Committee against Cruise-Missile Deployment (KKN).[7] The newly formed peace movement organization; Women for Peace and Women against Nuclear Weapons, entered this coalition (Langhorst-Potma and Smid 1986).

In 1983, shortly before the first deployments in Europe were scheduled, KKN organized another demonstration, this time in The Hague, attended by 550,000 people. By that time a new government coalition was in office: Christian

Democratic/Liberal Conservative coalition. The earlier coalition had resigned in 1982 because of an internal crisis stemming from socioeconomic issues. The newly formed government still had to take a decision on cruise missiles. It finally did so in 1984—by officially deciding to postpone the decision until November 1985. At that time the government would decide against deployment if the Soviets had deployed no additional SS-20s in the intervening year. A positive decision would be made if the Soviet Union continued to deploy SS-20s. This postponement provided the peace movement with a new opportunity to display its opposition. KKN did just that in 1985 by organizing a people's petition action (Krieisi, Chapter 1). About one-third of the electorate (3.75 million people) signed the petition. This impressive number did not prevent the government from agreeing to deployment in November 1985. In a later vote, parliament supported the decision despite opposition from the left and from six Christian Democrats. The government needed and got the support of the small right-wing parties to obtain majority support.

Of the new peace movement organizations that came into existence during 1977 to 1979, the first and foremost was Stop the Neutron Bomb, which appeared in 1977. This organization was important because it orchestrated the first success on the base of which further mobilization occurred and because it developed a new network of about 200 local groups (Maessen 1979). The second important organization that built a new network (of about 200 groups) was Women for Peace (Langhorst-Potma and Smid 1986.)[8] Since 1981, local IKV groups, local groups of Stop the Neutron Bomb, Stop the Nuclear Arms Race—as it has been called since 1978—as well as Women for Peace groups and local branches of both the left-wing parties and the Federation of Trade Unions have formed local platforms to organize demonstrations and petitions.

Generally the protest potential has declined somewhat. On the basis of a 1979 follow-up study of the previously cited 1974 political action study, Heunks (1983) showed that actual protest behavior became less frequent in Dutch society in the late 1970s. From this decline of the general protest potential, however, it does not follow that the specific mobilization potential for the peace movement also declined. As Kriesi and Castenmiller (1987) have shown, this specific potential did not diminish during the seventies.

B.   Who Participated?

Participation in peace movement actions in the eighties was studied in surveys organized by the Peace Research Centre. The subjects of these surveys were the demonstrations in 1981 and 1983 and the petition in 1985.

As Table 5 shows, the 1983 demonstration was much more of an action of young educated middle-class radicals than was the people's petition. There were fewer differences between signers and nonsigners than between signers and demonstrators on all points except membership in churches and unions.

Table 5. Social Characteristics of Peace Demonstrators in 1983, of Signers of the Petition of 1985, and of Those who Purposely did not Sign in 1985 (in percentages)

	Demonstrators[1]	Signed[2]	Refused to Sign[3]
Younger than 35	62[3]	43	40
Higher education[4]	52	32	28
Welf. and creat. prof.[5]	51	35	22
Students	27	9	6
Church members	23	36	57
FNV members	20	19	7
Total N	392	348	235

Notes:

[1] In The Hague a quota-sampling method was used and we organized a random sample mini-survey (N = 320). This random sample was used to weigh the quota sample of 923. These figures are weighted.

[2] Only respondents who had signed at the time of the interview during the last week of the people's petition and the respondents who were sure that they would not sign are presented in this table: 121 respondents who had not decided about signing are omitted.

[3] Only percentages with this characteristic are mentioned.

[4] Higher professional education and/or university.

[5] This category includes all individuals who had or have had an occupation in the educational sector, the welfare and medical sector, and the science and arts sector. The presented percentages included here are based on those who had or have had any occupation: 558 demonstrators, 274 signers, and 201 nonsigners.

Relatively few church members participated in the demonstration and the people's petition; compared with the number that participated in the consciousness-raising activities of IKV (Table 3). The mobilization of new potentials outside the churches by the organization in the KKN coalition only partly explains why fewer church members participated in protest activities. The proportion of church members, both of signers and of those who explicitly refused to sign, also leads to the conclusion that changing its strategy did not enable IKV to produce consensus in the churches and to mobilize a clear majority of church members to participate in protest activities. The change in strategy made the existing dissent within the churches more visible: of the signers of the petition, 36 percent were members of a church, compared to 57 percent of those who refused to sign. By changing its strategy from consensus mobilization to action mobilization, IKV emphasized, first, much stronger prognostic framings, and, second, motivational framings. IKV was now sending a much clearer message to church members to take a stand and to voice concern. The response to this clearer message brought to light the existing dissent within the churches concerning nuclear policies (Everts, 1983), and it also revealed the more obedient attitude of church members toward government. IKV's concentration on diagnostic framing during its first decade had hidden this dissent as refraining from collective action had hidden those barriers against participating in protest which existed within the churches.

Further analysis of the petition survey reveals that both factors—dissent and disapproval of protest activities—had an impact on the participation of church members in demonstrations. In 1985 fewer church members supported the KKN's demand than did people outside the churches, and the support they did give was not as strong as that of nonchurch members.[9] Of the church members, 59% supported the demand and half of this number gave strong unconditional support; of the nonchurch members, 73% gave support and three-quarters of them did so strongly. It follows that, because of the greater dissent in the churches, the mobilization potential within the churches was relatively smaller, and because church members supported the demand less strongly, it was more difficult to call them into action.

The barrier for participating in protest activities was higher in the demonstration of 1983 than in the people's petition in 1985, as Table 5 illustrates. We asked the respondents in the petition survey if they had participated in demonstrations against nuclear weapons since 1979 and also if they had participated in discussions about nuclear weapons in their own social or professional environment. Analysis of the participation behavior of members of the mobilization potentials within and outside the church reveals the reservations church members had about protest activities: 16% of the church members had demonstrated versus 37% of the nonchurch members. These differences are not caused by a difference in strength of support. That church teachings made it especially difficult to mobilize church members for protest activities is also evidenced by the fact that participation in discussions— a conventional type of activity that is not negatively framed by the churches— was the same for church and nonchurch members at all three levels of support for the KKN demand. Within and outside the churches, a total of 42% of the mobilization potential had participated in discussion. When the figures for participation in these two types of activities—protest and discussion—are combined, it becomes clear that the church reservations about protest lead not only to less active participation in protest by church members but also to a different pattern if they do protest. Of those in the mobilization potential outside the churches who had demonstrated, 48% had, in addition to demonstrating, participated in discussions about nuclear weapons; of the KKN-supporting and demonstrating church members, 72% had participated in such discussions. Participation in conventional persuasion activities thus seems to function as a precondition for most of the church members before they can be motivated to participate in a demonstration.

This difference in the motivation to participate in protest activities did not show up in data for the people's petition. If one controls for the strength of support for the KKN demand by church and nonchurch members of the mobilization potential, it appears that church members and nonchurch members signed or would sign to the same degree.[10] This result means that the failure of IKV to motivate the majority of church members to sign was

Table 6. Vote in 1982 National Election of Peace Demonstrators in 1983, of Signers of the Petition in 1985, of Those Who Purposely did not Sign, and the Result of the 1982 National Election (in percentages)

	Demonstrators[1]	Signed [2]	Refused to sign	National election[3]
Small right-wing	0.4	—	6	5
Liberal Conservative (VVD)	0.4	5	44	23
Christian Democratic (CDA)	3	9	36	29
Liberal Progressive (D'66)	5	7	7	4
Social Democratic (PvdA)	42	61	6	29
Radical Left[4]	48	17	0.5	7
Other small left-wing	1.2	1	—	2
Total %	100	100	99.5	99
Total N	792	284	194	9,172,159
Did not vote, unknown	137	74	39	

Notes:

[1]Weighted, see Table 5, note 1.

[2]Only the figures for respondents who had signed or were sure that they would not sign at the time of the interview are included.

[3]*Source:* Daalder and Schuyt (1986; A 1300-25-27): in 1982 all citizens 18 years and older had the right to vote

[4]Figures represented here are for those radical left-wing parties which were represented in parliament from 1982-1986: PPR, PSP, CPN, EVP.

caused by the greater dissent about nuclear weapons that seems to exist within the churches than outside the churches, not by differences in protest predispositions. Apparently, signing a petition seems to be much less an act of protest than a conventional activity like discussion, in which church and nonchurch members participated to the same degree. It follows from this analysis that the smaller number of church members who participated in the demonstration, as compared to the people's petition, is a result of their reservations about participating in protest activities. When in 1985 the more conventional activity of the people's petition was used, the participation of church members grew and the difference between church and nonchurch members in motivation to participate disappeared.

The political preferences among the public attending peace week activities in the first decade (see Table 4) are less left-wing-oriented than were the preferences among the demonstrators in 1983 and the signers in 1985 (Table 6). The proportion of Christian Democrats participating in both the 1981 and 1983 demonstrations was minimal to absent—compared to the percentage participating in peace activities in sum—and it was significantly lower in the people's petition. The participation, both relative and absolute, of Social Democrats grew enormously, whereas the proportion of radical left constituencies was larger in the demonstration but diminished in the people's petition, again in comparison with the figures for 1970. It seems easier to motivate Christian Democrats to attend consciousness-raising actitivies than to mobilize them for protest activities. This finding supports the proposition that, by changing its strategy and organizing protest activities, IKV alienated a part of its mobilization potential. Together with the other forces in the peace movement, it attracted a new potential within the constituency of the Social Democrats, and as in its first decade, it could still count on the radical left-wing voters.

The share of PvdA voters grew in 1983 and increased further in 1985, in comparison not only to 1970 but also to the 1981 demonstration. One should keep in mind, however, that the Social Democrats were in power in 1981 and in opposition in 1983 and 1985. The PvdA's growth in participation from 1981 on can also be explained by successful mobilization in 1983 and 1985 and by the low cost of participating in the people's petition. The mobilization of PvdA voters became much more intense because PvdA was a member of the KKN coalition that organized the 1983 demonstration and the people's petition. Of the Social Democrats who supported the KKN demand—a total of 91% did so—43% were not active in demonstrations or discussions before they signed or would sign the petition. This is the highest percentage for the mobilization potentials of all political parties, except the Liberal Conservatives, of whom 55% only signed or intended to do so. However, 19% of them belonged to the mobilization potential, so they contributed little to the number of signers.

The percentage of radical-left voters declined from 1983 to 1985, not because they were less inclined to protest, but because the overall number of protesters increased. In all three cases—the demonstrations of 1981 and 1983 and the people's petition in 1985—almost all radical left-wing voters who could participate did so. This fact is reflected in their participation history. Of the radical left only 12% signed, another 14% only discussed before signing, and the remaining 76% had demonstrated before the people's petition.

CDA and VVD participation was minimal to absent in the 1983 demonstration, as it was in the 1981 event, and it was restricted in the people's petition. The increase in CDA and VVD participation from the earlier demonstrations to the 1985 petition was slight.

C.   The Campaign Evaluated

The campaign of 1977-1986 presents a perfect example of consensus mobilization combined with action mobilization. Concerned about neglect of the nuclear weapons issue, IKV started its campaign on its own. It capitalized on the existing peace week networks that, because of the peace week, were directed mainly toward consensus mobilization. These networks were predisposed to discussion and persuasion activities. IKV conducted discussions within social institutions and political parties, and these discussions led to changes in the organizations. Strengthening existing networks and improving communication contributed to these changes. The framing efforts became more sophisticated. A clear-cut prognosis was proposed for unilateral initiatives and, using much stronger motivational framing, IKV began to stimulate people to take part in discussions in their organizations. A competing social movement organization, Stop the Neutron Bomb, provoked IKV into more direct protest activities such as collecting signatures and organizing demonstrations. After some hesitations, IKV stepped into this campaign. IKV's networks were used for the Stop the Neutron Bomb signature campaign and the demonstrations against the neutron bomb. Nevertheless, until the first big demonstration in 1981, IKV's main activities involved persuasion and lobbying.

The double character of its networks and mobilization potential was revealed most clearly when IKV together with other organizations, decided to take the initiative to organize a demonstration in 1981. Our data show that many church members were opposed to this kind of protest. The protest was supported mainly by the radical left, the Social Democrats, and members of the FNV trade union. The same pattern revealed itself in our research of the 1983 demonstration and of the 1985 signature campaign. Reservations about protest made it especially difficult to mobilize church members for participation in the demonstrations. Activists attracted by persuasion activities—mainly church members—were more or less alienated when IKV joined in the protest activities. Their alienation may explain why church members and Christian Democratic voters who were opposed to cruise-missile deployment participated to a lesser extent in actions against it. The number of protest opportunities seems to have appealed primarily to the left-wing members of the networks and the mobilization potential.

IV. PARTICIPATION IN PROTEST ACTIVITIES AND DIFFERENCE IN PROTEST CULTURE

From 1981 on, planning future protest activities was an important theme for discussion in peace movement organizations, local peace groups, and within radical-left parties. Many people had the feeling that the time had come for more radical actions, such as strikes, boycotts, blockades, and tax resistance, in order to press the government to make a nondeployment decision. Both the massive participation in the demonstration and the unresponsiveness of the government to the demand of the peace movement contributed to the feeling that it was necessary and proper to go one step further and organize civil disobedience actions. To take such actions would mean crossing the borderline between legal and illegal protest. But as the previous section shows, the peace movement organizations and IKV especially had difficulty in motivating its mobilization potential to take part in demonstrations, because of differences in opinion about the acceptability for effectiveness of protest. The different protest cultures in the peace movement seem to create different motivational predispositions toward protest activities.

This difference in protest predisposition did not show up in the people's petition because that event involved a conventional type of participation and could be seen as a kind of persuasion activity. Besides, as already noted, the costs of participation were very low. This difference in protest predisposition, however, was reflected in participation in the demonstrations. Cultures that create different predispositions to participate in demonstrations should produce even greater differences when more radical, illegal forms of protest are involved.

At the time of the people's petition the government decision on cruise-missile deployment was imminent. People were asked which kind of action they would approve or disapprove should the government decide to deploy the missiles. If for the different members of the mobilization potential we compare the approval rate for massive demonstrations, a legal type of action, with the approval rate for an illegal blockade of nuclear weapon sites, the differences in protest culture should become more visible. Of course one should control for the strength of support for the KKN demand, so we will look only at those members of the mobilization potential who supported the demand most strongly. It appears that church members among this part of the mobilization potential were more reluctant to approve a blockade (56%) than were nonchurch members (76% approval). A massive demonstration was approved to almost the same degree by church members (89%) and nonchurch members (96%). All the radical left approved a demonstration, and 92% of them approved a blockade. These figures indicate the differences between these two protest cultures, but it was also necessary to control for protest experience, because there was the possibility that church members who had demonstrated had lost their reservations. This, however, was not the case, for the differences did not disappear when we controlled for demonstration experience.

The two cultures meet within the moderate left parties. Table 7, which presents the figures only for the members of the mobilization potential who support the KKN demand most strongly, show that church members from the moderate left parties were more reluctant to support a blockade than nonchurch members from these parties, when neither group had any demonstration experience. The demonstrators from the moderate left-wing parties who did not have church ties approved a blockade in almost the same proportion as did the radical left-wing demonstrators.

Table 7.   Degree of approval for a blockade of nuclear weapons sites,
should the government decide to deploy cruise missiles: responses
from voters on center right, moderate left and radical left parties
who support KKN's demand most strongly. (Responses from moderate
left voters controlled for demonstration experience and church
membership). Petition survey, 1985. (Figures given in percentages) [1]

| | Center Right Voters | *Moderate left voters* | | | | Rad. Left Voters | Total |
| | | Church membs. | | Nonchurch membs. | | | |
		ND^2	Dem.[3]	ND	Dem.		
Strong approval	5	38	(38)	42	61	66	46
Moderate appr.	30	18	(12)	26	21	26	24
Mod. disappr.	15	8	(38)	14	7	4	10
Strong disappr.	50	36	(12)	18	11	4	20
Total %	100	100	(100)	100	100	100	100
Total N	20	39	8	73	44	48	232

Notes:
[1] Center right parties include CDA, VVD and small right-wing parties; moderate left-wing parties include D'66 and PvdA; radical left-wing parties include PPR, PSP, CPN, EVP and SP.
[2] ND = had not demonstrated; Dem = had demonstrated.
[3] Percentages in parentheses because of the small absolute number.

Not only type of protest culture but prospects for influencing government policies can contribute to differences in participation rates among different groups. Both factors, different protest culture and availability of other channels for influence, played significant roles. In 1981, when the moderate left parties were in power, IKV took the initiative in organizing a demonstration. Therefore, we could expect these factors to produce differential support for more radical, illegal protest actions among the demonstrators in Amsterdam. In order to reveal such differences we surveyed the opinions of the demonstrators, asking them: "Do you agree that at this stage the peace movement should begin to organize more radical action such as, for example, a blockade of missile sites or a massive tax resistance campaign?" In general, those who were demonstrating for the first time, about one-third of the demonstrators, were more reluctant to support more radical actions than those who had demonstrated earlier against nuclear weapons (Table 8). This general tendency holds for all subdivisions we made for background variables, except for church membership and Social Democratic affiliation.[11]

There was much less support for radical actions among church members than among demonstrators with no church affiliation. Table 8 shows that even church members who were left-wing voters were reluctant to support radical steps. This finding applies equally to moderate left and radical left

Table 8. Support for immediate radical action from demonstrators who had not demonstrated before 1981 and from those who had demonstrated against nuclear weapons before Amsterdam (1981) (in percentages)

	New Demonstrators		Previous Demonstrators	
	%	N	%[3]	N
Church members	35	49	27	37
Rad. left vote[1]	31	16	36	22
Social dem. vote	33	12	(25)	8
Other vote[2]	28	18	(—)	4
Nonchurch members	48	152	71	103
Rad. left vote[1]	50	52	77	94
Social dem. vote	53	51	43	28
Other vote[2]	21	24	(86)	7
Total	45	201	62	190

Notes:
[1]Includes: PPR, EVP, PSP, SP and CPN
[2]Includes: D'66, CDA, VVD, small right-wing parties
[3]Percentages in parentheses because of the small absolute number.

demonstrators within the churches. Church members who had demonstrated against nuclear weapons before the 1981 demonstration gave even less support than did new demonstrators from the churches. Because of their earlier participation in demonstrations and thus, perhaps, in the ongoing discussions about nuclear weapons in the churches, these activists could have been more easily exposed to existing church reservations about radical actions and protest in general than were the demonstrators who in 1981 became motivated to demonstrate for the first time. Their experience may have made the earlier activists more aware of the obstacle these protest-reservations pose for convincing church members.

Social Democrats who had previously demonstrated were also more reluctant to support immediate radical actions than were new demonstrators from this party. As Table 8 shows, this pattern holds when one controls for church membership. Concern about convincing and motivating the rank-and-file PvdA voters may have caused this greater reluctance among previous PvdA demonstrators. These people, like the previous demonstrators within the churches, could have been influenced by the intensive debates within their party in 1979 and 1981 and may have made these activists even more aware of the need to convince their fellow party supporters while at the same time providing conventional possibilities for influencing government. The PvdA demonstrators without church ties who were newly motivated in 1981 were not hampered by past experience or future concerns and so supported immediate radical actions to the same degree as new demonstrators from the radical left who were church members.

One could call the culture of those who support radical actions a struggle culture. The hard core can be found in the radical left-wing political parties and the radical peace movement organizations, which also have strong ties to the countercultural networks (Kriesi, Chapter 1). Those who belong to this culture do not have much confidence in the responsiveness of the political elite. Therefore they promote both a greater number of actions and more radical actions. These radical groups are not burdened by the need to do consensus-building work, because almost all voters of the radical left-wing parties already participate in peace movement activities. They hope to achieve their goals but believe the present political elite will not take the desired stand unless pressed by radical actions from many people. The large demonstrations made these radical groups think that success was close at hand.

The other culture is much more of a discussion or persuasion culture. People and organizations in this culture had more confidence in the possibility of influencing politics by conventional means and also have more channels for such influence. They realize that in their organizational environment it is necessary to avoid radical actions if they wish to motivate new people to participate in protest activities. This is the culture of those in the center of society, of the churches, and to a lesser degree of the Social Democrats, although each group may have different reasons for adhering to this culture. IKV has directed its activities at this latter group, although in the campaign it has also tried to combine the two cultures in common activities.

Although there is a division between these two cultures, it is not a sharp one, for it is not between organizations but within the moderate left constituencies. These parties, and especially the Social Democratic Party, had, in the 1960s, already a part of the counterculture as its social basis alongside its traditional basis in the old social movements, the trade unions. The division is not as sharp, secondly, because of the prominent presence of strong church-related movement organizations in the peace movement. These church organizations brought the counterculture into the environment of traditionally government-supporting social organizations. Both organizational factors contributed to the fact that participation in peace activities became not exclusive but mainly cumulative (Kriesi and van Praag, Jr. 1987).

The absence of a sharp division between the two cultures made it possible to bring them together in a coalition that was able to mobilize mass participation in the major demonstrations and in the people's petition. Those from the struggle culture postponed their direct actions, although some direct actions were organized during this period. A significant number of the people belonging to the persuasion culture, particularly Social Democratic voters, took the step of demonstrating or signing a petition. The reluctance to join protest activities appeared even more strongly among Christian Democratic voters. IKV successfully persuaded a large number of church members and Christian Democrats to share its views on nuclear weapons, but it could not motivate them to participate in demonstrations, nor was it able to muster enough support for its demand that a majority of these individuals sign the petition.

IKV had combined these two protest cultures in its network and mobilization potential since the consciousness-raising period of 1967-1976. This integration of the two cultures made IKV the central organization in the coalition that organized the mass protests during the eighties. But, as a result, some members of its network and its mobilization potential became alienated. These were precisely the members whom IKV deemed essential for political success.

V.   CONCLUSION

Despite expanding political opportunities and a favorable social climate for protest, the Dutch peace movement produced few protests in the period 1967-1976 because it did not mobilize for action. IKV, the central organization in the movement of the 1980s, restricted itself during its first decade to consensus mobilization. As a consequence, it created an opinion climate favorable to the protest activities it sponsored in its second decade. In addition, during the first phase, a network of core activists and local groups was developed which proved of use in the second period. In this network two sectors were combined: the church networks and networks of the radical left.

In the second period the social climate was somewhat less favorable for protest, and electoral instability ended. However, a division in the newly formed Christian Democratic party and decisions by NATO and the U.S. government to deploy neutron bombs, cruise missiles, and Pershing IIs, provided new opportunities leading to the protest activities of the 1980s.

The Dutch peace movement in the 1980s was able to mobilize a broader and more encompassing part of the population for action than were peace movements in other Western countries, because of its consensus mobilization activities in the 1960s and 1970s. These earlier activities contributed to the participation explosion in the 1980s. The history of the Dutch peace movement shows also that action mobilization does not automatically follow consensus mobilization. Networks built for consensus mobilization and mobilization potentials created by consensus mobilization activities became divided in the wake of action mobilization. These findings confirm Snow and Benford's proposition that consensus mobilization not only facilitates action mobilization but impedes it as well.

ABBREVIATIONS

ARP	Anti-Revolutionary Party (Christian Democratic: Protestant)
CDA	Christian Democratic Party
CHU	Christian Historical Party (Christian Democratic: Protestant)
CPN	Dutch Communist Party
D'66	Liberal Progressive Party
EVP	Progressive Christian Party
FNV	Federation of Dutch Trade Unions
IKV	Interchurch Peace Council
KKN	Committee against Cruise Missiles
KVP	Catholic People's Party (Christian Democratic: Roman Catholic)
PPR	Radical Democratic Party
PSP	Pacifist Socialist Party
PvdA	Social Democratic Party
SP	Socialist Party
VVD	Liberal Conservative Party

ACKNOWLEDGMENTS

I would like to thank my colleagues Leon Wecke, Ton Bertrand, and Hans Fun, who helped to collect the data for the demonstration and petition surveys and contributed to the first reports of these surveys, and Wim de Haar, who assisted in data collection and much of the coding work of the petition survey. For the surveys on the peace week in 1969 and 1970, I am much indebted to Roeland Hendrikse, Jan van der Heijden, Cees Beemsterboer, Leon Wecke, and Wim Bartels, who helped with the data collection and reports. Students too numerous to mention have helped with interviewing and coding for all the research. Without their help these surveys would have been impossible.

I am also very grateful to Truus Coenen and Helma Jacobs, who typed different versions of this text; and to Martin Gerritsen, who corrected my original paper; and to Sandra Ball, who corrected my English in this text.

Finally, my thanks to the editors of this volume, whose practical, useful, and insightful comments on an earlier version of this chapter, presented at the International Workshop, Transformation of Structure into Action, in Amsterdam, Free University, June 1986, prompted me to rewrite much of this paper. The contributions of others do not of course make them responsible for what I have written. That responsibility is mine alone.

NOTES

1. Protest behavior is almost forbidden by the Protestant churches because, in their teaching, authority and power are given by God so that sinful human nature may be contained. According to Luther, even a despotic authority has to be obeyed, because God would prefer a bad government to protest of the people (Fromm 1942, p. 70).

In the Dutch Reformed Church this type of framing still exists. Members of more orthodox calvinistic churches, which split from the Dutch Reformed Church during the nineteenth century, were and are educated to believe even more strongly in obedience to government. Article 36 of their Confession states "that God has given the government the sword in order to punish the evildoers and to protect all pious people." Further on, this article declares that everyone must obey authority (Kuyper 1883, p. 26).

Athough Roman Catholic theology traditionally places much greater emphasis on the dignity and equality of human beings, freedom of will, and confidence in God's love than does Protestant theology (Fromm 1942), Roman Catholic church authorities too emphasize the value of obedience. In the Dutch catechism children were taught that "our obligations towards our country are: That we show real love for country and folk; That we obey her lawful authority completely" (de Jong 1948, p. 75). Clearly, then, the dominant attitude for Catholics should be obedience. Only when the authority is unlawful, is protest allowed.

2.   The smaller denominations were: the Remonstrant Brotherhood, the Mennonites, the Moravian Church, the Quakers, the Lutherans, and the Old-Catholics.

3.   For a long time pillarization was a special characteristic of Dutch society and politics. Most societies are segmented horizontally along class lines. Dutch society was, in addition, segmented vertically, along religious lines. Each major religion had its own "pillar" in which its members were organized from top to bottom, socially and politically. There was a Roman Catholic pillar, an orthodox Protestant pillar, and a general or mixed pillar.

Each pillar was socially and politically isolated from the others. There were only frequent contacts at the top level between the elites. In 1960, 80% of the Dutch population had a religious affiliation. Within the general or mixed pillar, horizontal segmentation was possible. This space was used by the Social Democrats and the Liberal Conservatives. Although these parties tried to win voters from the Catholic and Protestant pillars, they failed in this effort until the mid 1960s. Then the process of depillarization began. The result was not only electoral instability but also a decreasing percentage of church members and diminishing participation in church services and activities among the remaining church members.

In our petition survey from 1985 we found—after weighing the sample because of the under-representation of Christian Democrats—that 515 had a religious affiliation. Lijphart (1968) has written an extensive analysis of pillarization in Dutch politics. My description owes much to his work.

4.   Marsh and Kaase (1975, p. 85) operationally defined conventional participation as consisting of the following elements: reading about politics, discussing politics with friends, working on community problems, contacting politicians or public officials, convincing friends to vote as you do, participating in election campaigns, attending political meetings.

Reading, discussing, contacting, convincing, and attending are exactly the type of behaviors which are to be stressed in a consensus-building strategy. Therefore, we also call this type of activity conventional activity. These activities and behaviors are very much unlike unconventional or protesting activities.

5.   See Maessen (1985) for an extensive description of the issue and the public pressure actions organized in the Netherlands. It should be noted, that after President Carter's decision of March 1978, Stop the Neutron Bomb decided to change its name to be more encompassing. It called itself Stop the Neutron Bomb—Stop the Nuclear Arms Race, and continued its activities.

6.   For a detailed description of the issue from 1979 to 1985, just before the final decision and the public pressure actions in the Netherlands, see van Staden (1985b).

7.   See Kriesi's essay in this volume (Chapter 1) for a more complete description of KKN.

8.   Women against Nuclear Weapons did not develop a local network. It was an organization that operated at the national level as a political pressure group, consisting of women who were active in different social and political organizations.

9.   Signing the petition implied that one was personally against nuclear weapons and demanded that the government decide not to deploy cruise missiles around November 11, 1985. The text of the petition could be signed by people who pleaded for a clear decision against

deployment and by those who preferred a further postponement of the decision, if they at least were personally against nuclear weapons. Support for this text was measured by combining the answers on two questions. The first question asked respondents which governmental decision they preferred: deployment, nondeployment, or postponement of the decision. The second question asked respondents to describe their personal attitude toward deployment by choosing among four alternatives: unconditionally in favor of deployment; in favor, but not unconditionally; against, but not unconditionally; and unconditionally against. The mobilization potential is defined as those who preferred a nondeployment or postponement decision and who at the same time were personally against deployment, conditionally or unconditionally. Within this mobilization potential three levels of support are differentiated: the strongest support, given by those who were unconditionally against and preferred a clear nondeployment decision; strong support, given by those who were conditionally against and preferred nondeployment; and the least strong support, given by those who were conditionally against and pleaded for postponement. Few respondents who were unconditionally against preferred postponement; those who gave such answers were counted in the category of strongest support.

10.   Interviews took place during the last week of the campaign for the people's petition. This means that people still had an opportunity to sign. Therefore in the further analysis, those who intended to sign are taken together with those who had already signed.

11.   Members of trade unions were another exception to the general rule that new demonstrators were more reluctant than veteran demonstrators to support radical actions to the same degree—about 63%. The absence in the unions of barriers against protest activities can explain this pattern.

REFERENCES

Barnes, Samuel H., Max Kaase, and Klause R. Allerbeck. 1979. *Political Action: Mass Participation in Five Western Democracies.* London: Sage.

Benford, Robert D. 1987. "The Nuclear Disarmament Movement." In Lester R. Kurtz et al. *The Nuclear Cage: A Sociology of the Arms Race.* Englewood Cliffs, N.J.: Prentice-Hall.

Daalder, Hans and C.J.M. Schuyt (eds.). 1986. *Compendium voor Politiek en Samenleving in Nederland.* Alphen aan den Rijn: Samson.

Debeuckelaere, Godelieve P. n.d. *Het IKV in de Pers: Een Boodschapsanalyse.* Nijmegen: Catholic University, Institute for Mass Communication.

Everts, Philip P. 1983. *Public Opinion, the Churches, and Foreign Policy: Studies of Domestic Factors in the Making of Dutch Foreign Policy.* Leiden: University of Leiden, Institute for International Studies.

Everts, Philip P. (ed.). 1985. *Controversies at Home: Domestic Factors in the Foreign Policy of the Netherlands.* Dordrecht: Nijhoff.

Everts, Philip P. and Ben J. Th. ter Veer. 1981. "Disarmament Education and Peace Action: Report on a Campaign for Unilateral Initiatives Towards Disarmament in the Netherlands." Pages 147-80 in Magnus Haavelsrud (ed.), *Approaching Disarmament Education.* Guilford, Eng.: Westbury House.

Farah, Barbara G., Samuel H. Barnes, and Felix Heunks. 1979. "Personal Dissatisfaction." Pages 409-47 in Samuel H. Barnes, Max Kaase, and Klause R. Allerbeck, *Political Action: Mass Participation in Five Western Democracies.* London: Sage.

Fromm, Erich. 1942. *The Fear of Freedom.* London: Routledge & Kegan Paul.

Heunks, Felix. 1983. "Activisme, Tanend of Ingeburgerd?" Pages 141-63 in J.J.A. Thomassen et al. *De Verstomde Revolutie: Politieke Opvattingen en Gedragingen van Nederlandse Burgers na de Jaren Zestig.* Alphen aan den Rijn: Samson.

IKV. 1972. "De Toekomst van Europa: Een Standpuntbepaling van het Interkerkelijk Vredesberaad." Pages 3-23 in IKV, *Veilig Europa.* The Hague: IKV.

IKV. 1977. *Tien Jaar IKV: Het Interkerkelijk Vredesberaad, 1967-1977.* The Hague: IKV.

Jenkins, J. Craig and Charles Perrow. 1977. "Insurgency of the powerless: Farm worker movements (1946-1972)." *American Sociological Review* 42:249-68.

Jong, Johannes Kardinaal de. 1948. *Katechismus of Christelijke Leer.* Utrecht: van Rossum.

Klandermans, Bert. 1984. "Mobilization and participation: Social-psychological expansions of resource mobilization Theory." *American Sociological Review* 49:583-600.

Klandermans, Bert. 1986. "New Social Movements and Resource Mobilization: The European and the American Approach." *International Journal of Mass Emergencies and Disasters.* Special issue, *Comparative Perspectives and Research on Collective Behavior and Social Movements* 4:13-37,

Klandermans, Bert and Dirk Oegema. 1987. "Potentials, networks, motivations and barriers: Steps toward participation in social movements." *American Sociological Review* 52:519-31.

Kriesi, Hanspeter and Peter Castenmiller. 1987. "De Ontwikkeling van Politiek Protest in Nederland Sinds de Jaren Zeventig." *Acta Politica* 22:61-84.

Kriesi, Hanspeter and Philip van Praag, Jr. 1987. "Old and new politics: The Dutch peace movement and the traditional political organizations." *European Journal of Political Science* 15:319-46.

Kuyper, Abraham. 1883. *De Drie Formulieren van Eenigheid, met de Kerkorde, Gelijk die voor de Gereformeerde Kerken Dezer Landen Zijn Vastgesteld in Haar Laatst Gehouden Nationale Synode.* Amsterdam: Kruyt.

Langhorst-Potma, Loek and Frouke Smid. 1986. "Een Reactie Vanuit Vrouwen Voor Vrede." Pages 158-65 in Dick Benschop et al. *Vredebeweging: Strategie en Effectiviteit; Vredesacties in de Ogen van Wetenschap en Beweging.* Nijmegen: Peace Research Centre.

Lijphart, Arend. 1968. *The Politics of Accommodation: Pluralism and Democracy in the Netherlands.* Berkeley: University of California Press.

McAdam, Doug. 1983. "Tactical innovation and the pace of insurgency." *American Sociological Review* 48:735-54.

Maessen, Pieter J.J. 1979. *Wie Stopt de Neutronenbom?* Leiden: University of Leiden, Institute for International Studies.

Maessen , Pieter J.J. 1985. "The Introduction of the Neutron Bomb (1977-1978)." Pages 115-31 in Philip P. Everts (ed.), *Controversies at Home: Domestic Factors in the Foreign Policy of the Netherlands.* Dordrecht: Nijhoff.

Marsh, Alan and Max Kaase. 1979. "Background of Political Action." Pages 97-136 in Samuel H. Barnes, Max Kaase, and Klause R. Allerbeck, *Political Action: Mass Participation in Five Western Democracies.* London: Sage.

Mushaben, Joyce Marie. 1986. "Grassroots and Gewaltfreie Aktionen: A study of mass mobilization strategies in the West German peace movement." *Journal of Peace Research* 23:141-54.

Parkin, Frank. 1968. *Middle Class Radicalism: The Social Bases of the British Campaign for Nuclear Disarmament.* Manchester: Manchester University Press.

Schennink, Ben. 1975. "Die Friedenswoche in den Niederlanden." Pages 35-59 in Hans-Eckehard Bahr and Albrecht-Sigbert Seippel (eds.), *Soziales Lernen: Gruppenarbeit für den Frieden.* Stuttgart: Kohlhammer.

Staden, Alfred van. 1985a. "The Domestic Environment." Pages 45-67 in Philip P. Everts (ed.), *Controversies at Home: Domestic Factors in the Foreign Policy of the Netherlands.* Dordrecht: Nijhoff.

Staden, Alfred van. 1985b. "To Deploy or Not to Deploy: The Case of the Cruise Missiles." Pages 133-55 in Philip P. Everts (ed.), *Controversies at Home: Domestic Factors in the Foreign Policy of the Netherlands.* Dordrecht: Nijhoff.

Steinweg, Reiner (ed.). 1982. *Die Neue Friedensbewegung: Analysen aus der Friedensforschung.* Frankfurt: Suhrkamp.

Tarrow, Sidney. 1983. *Struggling to Reform: Social Movements and Policy Change During Cycles of Protest.* Western Societies Paper No. 15. Ithaca, N.Y.: Cornell University.

Tarrow, Sidney. 1986. "Comparing Social Movement Participation in Western Europe and the United States: Problems, Uses, Examples, and a Proposal for Synthesis." *International Journal of Mass Emergencies and Disasters.* Special issue, *Comparative Perspectives and Research on Collective Behavior and Social Movements* 4:145-70.

Walsh, Edward J. 1981. "Resource mobilization and citizen protest in communities around Three Mile Island." *Social Problems* 29:1-21.

OLD MOVEMENTS IN NEW CYCLES OF PROTEST:
THE CAREER OF AN ITALIAN RELIGIOUS COMMUNITY

Sidney Tarrow

Today the political arena is being covered with a new flora; later new gardeners will come; we should savour while we can the heady scents of these wild flowers and unruly weeds, so invigorating after so much deodorant and disinfectant (Alain Touraine).

I. NEW SOCIAL MOVEMENTS

"New flora?" "Wild flowers?" "Unruly weeds?" Alain Touraine refers with evocative metaphors to the "new" social movements that arose in Western Europe and the United States after 1968. Like others who have used the term, he is impressed with the new actors, the expressive actions, and the new themes of dissent produced by the movements of the late 1960s and 1970s. Emerging from the new middle class, moved by "postmaterial" values, making transcendent demands, these movements developed informal, decentralized

International Social Movement Research, Vol. 1, pages 281-304.
Supplement to Research in Social Movements, Conflicts and Change
ISBN: 0-89232-955-6

organizations, used radical means of action, and rejected systematic ideologies in favor of a kind of "radical pragmatism." They created a new political paradigm, or so it has been argued (Offe 1985).

Empirical studies of the social movements of the last two decades, usually based on survey methods, provide a more differentiated though less rich account. They show that the supporters of the new movements often do emerge from the new middle class, but, with the partial exception of the labor movement,[1] so do the majority of activists in contemporary interest groups, parties, and "old" movements. The new movements are informally organized, but social movements have always started life in this way and some of the "newest," such as the Greens, quickly developed bureaucratic structures. Finally, while the new movements' use of expressive and confrontational means captured media attention and the imagination of scholars, most used a variety of tactics, some no more radical than those of institutional interest groups (Dalton 1987).

Scholars have long seen social movements in terms of their internal "careers." According to this perspective, movements are born radical and turn conservative as they age (Lowi 1971). But in this chapter, I will argue that the "career" perspective misses both the sources of the "new" movements' radicalism and the reason for their growing institutionalization. The confrontational tactics, the new themes, and the decentralized organizations that marked the new movements of the 1960s and 1970s, I maintain, were more a property of the cycle of protest in which they emerged than of the movements' themes, logics, or actors. For disorderly politics could be found during this period among many collective actors: not only among "new" new movements— ecology, feminism, the peace and student movements—but also among "old" ones such as the labor movement (Regalia, Regini, and Reyneri 1978), and even among the oldest type of movement of all: religious movements.

These religious movements, which began before the cycle of protest began, arose out of a re-interpretation of traditional religious doctrine. During the late 1960s, they were renewed, radicalized, and de-institutionalized in the course of conflicts with church authorities and contacts with a radical subculture. If we can show that even a very "old" movement such as a religious movement was re-"newed" in ways that resembled the new social movements of the decade, we will have shown that the traits of the latter too had more to do with the environment in which they were born than with their social actors, their grievances, or their internal logics.

A. Cycles of Protest

How do ordinary people come together through collective events to create new collective actors? When we recall the major movements of the late 1960s and 1970s, it seems obvious that, like their forebears in the nineteenth century, they develop neither as mechanical responses to social structural changes nor because new social actors appear on the scene but because their members find themselves in a common relationship of solidarity with each other and of antagonism to others (Piven and Cloward 1977; Pizzorno 1978)—and also because appropriate symbols, audiences, and political opportunities are at hand (Snow et al. 1986; Tarrow 1983).

Not every incident of collective action in every period of history gives rise to a social movement, which I, with Charles Tilly, define as a continuing overt relationship of conflict between collective actors and authorities (Tilly 1984). Moreover, movements do not appear with equal frequency in every period of history and in all social sectors; they develop in historic clusters, not only when people have grievances but when these grievances are accompanied by new resources, expanded political opportunities, re-alignments among mass publics, and conflicts among elites. [2] It is these conditions which turn grievances into antagonisms, allow them to be generalized, communicated across sectors and social groups, abstracted into new and expanded ideological packages, and instilled with a general sense of outrage — that is, to undergo what Piven and Cloward (1977) call a process of "transvaluation." When this process occurs, we are in the presence of a general "cycle of protest" like that of the late 1960s and early 1970s (Tarrow 1983).

B.   Movements and Institutions

Within cycles of protest, social movements appear only in some sites and not in others. Many factors—motivational, ideological, and cultural—contribute to their formation, but one characteristic specific to the formation of many movements is that their future members are unified by ties of membership, interest, or common position in the same institutional context (Piven and Cloward 1977) and opposed to some authority that they perceive to be unjust (Fireman et al. 1979). It is through encounters with unjust authority and the use of the resources they find around them that people overcome the normal barriers to collective action.

For this reason, the most conflictual movements often appear within religious institutions. This is so not only because these institutions are inherently rigid but because their members' claims challenge their authority and are far less negotiable than the claims of employees against their firms. Since the members of institutions tend to feel their cause is not only advantageous but just, their sense of injustice can be far greater than that of antagonists in a purely economic relationship.

Institutions not only provide insurgents with causes for insurgency, they also make available the resources—economic, organizational, ideological—that permit them to turn anger and deprivation into mobilization. The solidarities, symbolism, and organization that insurgents use to attack institutions are often provided by the institutions themselves, to be turned against them by those who know them best.

Throughout its history, the Catholic church has been beset by monastic reformers, heretics, evangelical preachers, and antichrists who have insisted on taking literally the Church's own symbolism and values. Within the church-institution, traditional interpretive frames are transformed in the course of conflict into insurgent new ideologies. Such a process of insurgency, stimulated by Vatican II, by liberation theologies, and by the recruitment of new social and ethnic groups, began within the church in the mid-1960s.

But the religious movements of the 1960s and 1970s were also influenced by the cycle of nonreligious protest movements. They enjoyed the support of participants in those movements and shared many features of the generalized disorder that exploded on the industrialized West in the same period. Their creation, their repertoires of action and symbols, and their careers were all affected by this common, extra-religious origin, and were aided by the political opportunities produced by the political movements that preceded them. They grew up as part of a general social movement sector (Garner and Zald 1985), adopting some of its themes and tactics, and ending up with the familiar parabola from movement to institution. But their careers were not internally determined: just as the movements' birth and radicalization were influenced by the general climate of insurgency around them, their institutionalization took forms that were shaped by the decline of mobilization.

We can see all of these components—the production of new out of old interpretive frames, the blending of internal and external symbols and tactics, the shaping of a social movement out of confrontations with unjust authority, and the influence of a general cycle of protest—in the creation and career of a new religious movement in Italy.

II. RELIGIOUS DISSENT AND THE ITALIAN CYCLE OF PROTEST

In 1967 and 1968, in scattered parishes around Italy, ordinary worshipers gathered to demonstrate against the Church hierarchy. Quantitative analysis of protest data recorded many of these events.[3] In Naples, several hundred parishioners prevented a newly appointed priest from entering his church (*Corriere* May 6, 1967). In Milan, numerous cases of neighborhood religious protest occurred. Near Brindisi, a group of women prayed all night to protest the transfer of their priest to another town (*Corriere* Oct. 26, 1968). Why did these neighborhood religious protests appear in the late 1960s?

Catholics had been organizing at the grass-roots level of the Church even before the Second Vatican Council, in *Lumen Gentium,* endorsed a new vision of the Church as a community of believers rather than a hierarchy with its flock. Even before the student movement exploded in 1967-1968, Catholic militants were beginning to grow away from their total dependence on the Church and its secular arm, the Christian Democratic party; they even began to appear within the Catholic workers organizations, the ACLI and the CISL (Lumley 1983, pp. 186-88). On the Catholic, as on the secular Left, there was an explosion of new Catholic publications: *Il Regno* in Bologna, *Rocca* in Assisi, *Il Tetto* in Naples, *Dopoconcilio* in Trento (Sciubba and Pace 1976a, p. 24)

Catholic collective action arose at roughly the same time and in the same places that students were beginning to march, to demonstrate, and to occupy faculties around the country. Events in Milan illustrate this concurrence dramatically. It was mainly in Milan, for example, that the Catholic metalworkers' union, the FIM-CISL, developed an analysis and line of conduct that were radically more innovative than that of its competitors.[4] But the most dramatic conflict pitted students against the Catholic University.[5] In November 1967, between 100 and 200 young activists occupied the university to protest a proposed increase in school fees (*Corriere* Nov. 16, 1967), an issue in both public and private institutions around the country at that time. The bishop, who controls the Catholic University, quickly called in the police, had the occupants removed, and expelled the leaders. The student representatives, using a language and symbolism drawn from their Catholic backgrounds, expressed their "indignation, suffering, and deeply troubled human, civil and Christian feelings in the face of the authorities' behavior" (quoted in Lumley 1983, p.185). By early 1968, conflict had begun to spread from the Catholic University to the Milanese church in general. In April a group of students interrupted a conference of cardinals to protest the Church's resistance to reform (*Corriere* April 1, 1968). In June a fire bomb was set off in the church of San Babila to protest the "criminal activity" of the Church (*Corriere* June 11, 1968). In October a church was occupied to protest the transfer of five local priests to other parishes (*Corriere* Oct. 2, 1968). On December 21, the elegant *Rinascente* department store was blocked by students protesting the commercialization of Christmas (*Corriere* Dec. 23, 1968).

It was the student and worker mobilizations of 1967-1969 that provided the stimulus, the themes, and the political opportunities for dissent within and against the Church. The events of these years provided Catholics throughout Italy with an expanded political opportunity structure, new models of militance, an anti-authoritarian interpretive frame, and political allies that could galvanize latent dissent into collective action. But since our theory holds that collective action will generate a social movement only where political opportunity is linked to both solidarity and confrontation with unjust authority, we will have to look for the rise of a Catholic social movement where these factors appear simultaneously. We shall find such a movement in Florence.

A. The Isolotto Religious Community

In a large, bare, and remarkably ugly piazza on the far side of the Arno
River in Florence is a modern pile of a church which mimics the medieval
city downriver by its ochre coloring but clashes with it by its awkward, barnlike
shape and unwelcoming facade. At the center of the piazza are a newspaper
kiosk and a covered pavement, the *sagrato* of the church, where much of our
story takes place. At the side of the church, in an even more nondescript
building, are the residence and offices of the parish priest.

The Isolotto is no ordinary parish. Like grass-roots Catholics in other cities,
its members have been organizing a *"comunità di base"* since the late 1950s.
They were encouraged to organize by Vatican II and later moved to dissent
by the agitations in the university. Within the neighborhood of Isolotto, the
city and region of Florence, and the Florentine church are both solidarities
and conflicts that are particularly favorable to the formation of a social
movement.[6]

First, the Neighborhood. The Isolotto is a new parish church in a working-
class district that resulted from a rare act of Italian urban planning. In the
mid-1950s, a visionary mayor, Giorgio La Pira, planned a community of low-
cost, low-density public housing with open space and parks built along the
Arno. Soon filled by members of the native Florentine working class, Istrian
refugees, southern immigrants, and former Tuscan peasants, the Isolotto had
few social institutions in the late 1950s, when a progressive cardinal, Elia Della
Costa, built a modern parish church there and asked an energetic young priest,
Enzo Mazzi, to take it over (Comunità dell'Isolotto 1969: Part I: Comunità
dell'Isolotto will hereafter be cited as CdI, 1969).

When Mazzi and two collaborators, Paolo Cacciolli and Sergio Gomito, began
to work in the Isolotto in the mid-1950s, they found a neighborhood with no
political parties, associations, or interest groups, with no community spirit or
identity, and with a school that met in a barracks. In the absence of alternative
social networks, it was natural for the parish church to become a focal point,
and logical that the theme of unity—unity among parishioners, between
southerners and northerners, between former peasants and workers, and
between them all and the Church-institution—would come to typify the teaching
of Mazzi and his associates (CdI, 1969: Part II).[7] As Niebuhr writes of such
movements; "one finds here, more than elsewhere, appreciation of the religious
worth of solidarity and equality, of sympathy and mutual aid" (1957, p. 31).

It was neighborhood interests that first involved Mazzi and his parishioners
in controversy. In 1959 they organized a school strike to dramatize the fact
that the Isolotto's children were being taught in a barracks. In the same year,
they demonstrated in solidarity with laid-off workers of the nearby Galileo
plant and opened the parish house for the workers' use during the strike

(Baldelli 1969, p. 153). In 1963 they declared their solidarity with laid-off workers of another local factory, the Fivre. In 1966, when the Arno flooded, the community participated alongside Communist militants in the grass-roots committees to meet the emergency (Sciubba and Paci 1976a, p. 28; CdI, 1969: Part III).

Second, the City and Region. Mazzi and his associates owed much of their early success to the progressive religious climate they found in Florence in the late 1950s and early 1960s under a Catholic mayor who drew his inspiration from St. Francis. It could hardly be otherwise in a region with a long-standing leftist tradition. The predominance of recent immigrants—many from the South—gave popular Catholicism a chance to take root, provided it kept in touch with its populist roots.

In left-wing Tuscany it was probably inevitable that the community's activities would become more political: activity was first organized in support of the American civil rights movement and against the Vietnam War. In the 1966 elections, lay members of the community created a stir by circulating a document demanding the liberty of Catholics to vote for whom they wanted (Sciubba and Paci 1976, p. 27; CdI, 1969, pp. 34-37). Mazzi and his associates soon jarred the local clergy by refusing to accept payment for officiating at baptisms or weddings, and they offended the church by opening the parish house to homeless orphans. As one observer wrote:

> The call for the "Church of the poor," so frequent in the language of the Isolotto community, shouldn't fool anyone; it is a class political appeal, the identification of the "real" Church with the world of the exploited who are struggling against the world of the rich (Zolo 1970, pp. 17-19).

Third, the Florentine Church. At the same time as La Pira ran the city and the Left ran Tuscany, Florence had a progressive cardinal who was willing to take up the cause of the poor, even when it put him in conflict with the city's bourgeoisie. In Tuscany as in other parts of Italy's anticlerical "Red Belt," the Tuscan Chruch regarded its territory as a *terra di missione*. It was in this climate of progressive Catholicism that experiments such as Don Milani's school of Barbiana had been started, and innovative churchmen such as Giulio Facibeni, Divo Barsotti, and Ernesto Balducci were able to work and publish.[8]

Very soon a network of neighborhood groups began to organize in and around Florence: in Peretola, la Nave di Rovezzano, San Giusto and Le Bagnese, Vignone and Scandicci, and in the Isolotto and the nearby Casella, mainly peripheral or lower class neighborhoods where young priests tried to turn the parish church into a social center. From the start, a key theme of the Florentine groups was to overcome the division between secular and religious citizens, "to stimulate the life of the parish without creating divisions

in the neighborhood on the base of 'who goes' and 'who doesn't go' to mass"
(Sciubba and Paci 1976a, p. 23).

During the 1960s, a network of activists formed around the church of the
Isolotto, drawn both from Florence's progressive Catholic and leftist
communities and from the neighborhood itself. Some of the militants had been
nurtured in the progressive La Pira wing of the Christian Democracy (DC),
while others came from more predictable social movement sources: from
among "elementary and high-school teachers, white collar workers, frustrated
social agitators who had wandered into the 'circle' of the Church" (Baldelli
1969, p. 154)—in summary, the same reservoirs of neighborhood and civic
movements that would appear in "new social movements" across the industrial
West.

In the course of the 1960s the influence of the Catholic Left began to wane,
both in city politics and in the Church. In the bishopric, the aging Della Costa
was seconded—and on his death replaced—by Ermenegildo Florit, a "pre-
conciliar" prelate whose prejudice against politics did not prevent him from
permitting Catholic Action activists to use the churches to publicize their
anticommunist message. Before long, progressive churchmen such as Balducci,
Borghi, and Milani were losing influence and being forced into silence or
semiexile (Baldelli 1969, p. 151).[9]

At the same time, the Catholic Left lost control of the city administration,
for, following the negotiation of a national Center-Left coalition between the
DC and the Socialists, conservative Christian Democrats thought they could
govern without the charismatic La Pira. Thus, precisely as a cycle of protest
was spreading throughout the country, encouraging activism among young left-
wing Catholics, the Florentine hierarchy and the local political class were
closing ranks against progressive currents. It was this combination of political
opportunity on the one hand, and institutional rigidity on the other, which
would produce a confrontation between the Isolotto community and the
Church hierarchy, turning a neighborhood religious group into the center of
a social movement.

III.   THE CATHEDRAL OF PARMA

Parma, September 14, 1968.   Forty Catholic students enter the soaring brick
Romanesque-Lombard cathedral, arrange a group of chairs in a circle, and
begin to hold a discussion on poverty, of the powerlessness of the laity in the
church, and of the authoritarianism of the hierarchy. They have assembled
to protest the transfer of a local priest whose radical ideas have displeased the
bishop and to demand an explanation of the diocese's decision to finance the
construction of a new church with funds from a local bank (*Corriere* Sept.
16, 1968).

They move down into the crypt, where they attempt to participate in the celebration of mass. When the priest in charge refuses to let them intervene, the police are called in and—following a pattern that was becoming familar from university occupations throughout the country—the protesters are carried out. No less an authority than Pope Paul VI denounces their behavior for undermining the Church of God.[10]

Florence, September 22.   Messages of solidarity with the Parma occupiers go out from communities around the country, from "I Tralci" of Bologna, Monsummano Terma near Pistoia, Oregina in Genoa, and from San Giusto and Bagnese, La Casella and the Isolotto in Florence (Sciubba and Paci, 1976a, p. 31). In the Isolotto a group of parishioners meets to discuss the occupation in Parma and the hierarchy's reaction to it. After animated discussion, they decide to send an open letter of solidarity to the occupiers. They not only express their sympathy with the students, they condemn the action of the Parma religious authorities and demand that the Church renounce its ties with "the iniquitous system founded on the exploitation of men by other men" (CdI, 1969, pp. 152-56). One hundred and fifty parishioners agree to sign the letter. Though all three priests co-sign it, it bears the unmistakable imprint of Mazzi's teaching: the Church-institution is accused of separating itself from the people of God and of bowing to the power of lucre.[11]

October 5.   The hierarchy's reaction is immediate and unambiguous. Cardinal Florit, ignoring the other signatures on the open letter, sends a long and offical letter to Don Mazzi criticizing his interference in affairs outside the purview of his parish and demanding either a retraction or his resignation by the end of October. The letter concludes:

> Either you are prepared to publicly retract a statement as offensive to the authority of the Church as was your open letter of September 22nd . . . or else, recognizing that it is absurd to continue to be part of the 'structures' that you so violently condemn, you intend to resign from your position as priest (CdI, 1969, pp. 156-59).

October 9.   An assembly is held in the parish church to discuss the cardinal's letter. The 200-odd people who attend are confused about what line to take and the meeting breaks up in discord. They call a second meeting for October 12, at which a draft of the letter is discussed before a group that has now grown to three hundred people. At a third and still larger meeting on October 19, the final document is approved and is subsequently distributed to all the families of the Isolotto (CdI 1969, pp. 167-70).

A.   Mobilizing a Following

What might have ended with a quiet retraction or with Mazzi's transfer to another parish is made impossible by the events of the next few days. The cardinal's letter is leaked to the press[12] and published in the right-wing local newspaper, *La Nazione,* next to the headline "Don Mazzi disowned (*sconfessato*) by the Cardinal" (CdI 1969, p. 171). The symbolic loading of the term "*sconfessato*" is not lost on this Catholic community, which immediately mobilizes around Mazzi, now no longer only a dissident left-wing priest but a victim of the Florentine establishment.

October 23. The *Nazione* article outrages the new Catholic conscience, not only in Florence. In Parma, a second occupation of the Cathedral takes place, this time to demand the direct participation of the laity in church decision making (*Corriere* Oct. 24, 1968). In the Isolotto, by 4 P.M. on the day the *Nazione* article appears, the church and the piazza are full of neighborhood residents and others—many nonworshipers—who take down the names and addresses of those willing to work in Mazzi's defense. By 8 in the evening, almost 1,000 volunteers have signed up (CdI 1969, p. 171).

October 24. The *Nazione* prints a press release from the Vatican threatening Mazzi with suspension if he fails to retract the letter whose authorship Mazzi has attributed to the people of God. A crowd assembles in the church and decides to begin publishing an alternative *Notiziario* and a wall newspaper, which soon appear all over Florence almost daily.[13] These moves duplicate almost exactly what happened during the early stages of the Catholic University occupation during the previous year.[14]

The Isolotto has by now become a magnet for young people, workers, housewives, dissident Catholics, and disillusioned militants from the Left. The Communist Party (PCI) itself remains silent. As Siedelman observes, the Florentine communists were "unwilling to 'take sides' on an issue that they considered exclusively related to the 'internal politics' of the Catholic Church." However, "party sections surrounding the Isolotto . . . were more willing to explicitly side with the Catholic dissenters, and in fact were frequently involved in the mass meetings and popular assemblies conducted at the various dissenting churches" (1979, pp. 250-51). The PCI-institution was having its own problems with its *base.*

IV. MAKING ALLIES AND ENEMIES

As word of the conflict begins to circulate, hundreds of solidarity messages begin to pour into the Isolotto. Bus drivers who live in the neighborhood organize a meeting for their colleagues at which the problems of the Church are analyzed. Local workers distribute leaflets at factory gates telling of forthcoming assemblies. The workers of the Galileo plant—which the community supported when the factory was threatening to close in the early 1960s—vote support to Mazzi and the community, and the Gover factory goes out on strike in solidarity (CdI 1969, pp. 173-98; *Corriere* Nov. 9, 1968).

October 31.   On the day of the cardinal's deadline, an evening assembly attracts what the community judges to be ten thousand people. The informal, impetuous meetings of the early part of the month have now given way to a well-organized, disciplined assembly, with marshals to keep order, seating by block and workplace, and an agenda of formal speeches. Speakers represent groups of families, factory workers, and individual streets. With an eye to the press as well as its own beliefs, the community assures that lower-class people, housewives, students, and lay people balance its militants in the list of speakers.

Mazzi reads out a cautiously worded letter of sympathy he has received from 93 of his fellow Florentine priests. In his address he returns to the themes of unity and of love that have informed his whole career; "Siamo uniti e ci vogliamo bene perché abbiamo cercato di mettere la nostra vita a servizio degli umili" ("We are united and we love one another because we have sought to use our lives in the service of the humble"), he says (CdI 1969, pp. 198-201). Though in perfect harmony with his faith, the speech is also good politics, for as long as it is the *Popolo di Dio* whose voice is raised against authority, the cardinal's attacks can be read as attacks on the entire community.[15] Like all social movement leaders, Mazzi identifies his fight with that of a solidarity constituency whose rights are being abridged by an unjust authority. The interpretive frame is traditional, but it is being extended to challenge the church-institution.

In addition to generating some classical social movement rhetoric, the October 31 assembly also produces an eight-point resolution, accepted by acclamation. In this document the community takes responsibility for the acts of which Don Mazzi has been accused and underscores the unity of the parishioners with their priests. The resolution goes on to assure the cardinal that it is only his distance from the people that makes it conceivable for him to condemn them, and invites him to come and share their experience, which will surely teach him the error of his ways (CdI 1969, pp. 223-24). The source of truth has shifted from the hierarchy to the base.

November 6.   Florit receives a letter from over a hundred priests of the region, in which they cautiously call the Mazzi case symptomatic of a crisis in the Church and, recalling the language of Vatican II, ask for a broad discussion among all the "members" of the Church before any decision is taken on Mazzi's future (CdI 1969, pp. 227-31). The cardinal ignores the plea but convokes a meeting of the diocesan council to inform them of his decision.

November 14.   In an official letter, Florit, backed by citations from canon law, notifies Mazzi that a bishop *cannot* take the wishes of a community into account in dealing with one of his priests. He rejects not only Mazzi's position but also that of the priests that the "members" of the church are all jointly responsible for its decisions (CdI 1969, p. 233). "The parishioners' request for a meeting with the bishop," writes Florit, "in the present circumstances and in the way it is proposed, is contrary to the good ordering of the ecclesiastical community" (CdI 1969, p. 234). He closes by urging one last time that "his" priest Mazzi reconsider his present attitude (CdI 1969, p. 235).

V. POLARIZATION

Late November—early December.   The community publishes a new catechism, "Meeting with Jesus" (CdI 1968). It is full of references to the "Church of the poor" and to the need to struggle against a world governed by money. Its adoption is immediately banned by the cardinal, but parts of it eventually appear at the *Cattolica,* where it is used to demand the end of church control of the university and the abolition of the requirement that university entrants should be Catholics (Lumley 1983, p. 193).

December 2.   Mazzi and his two assistants, Sergio Gomito and Paolo Caciolli, together with a group of parishioners, visit the Cardinal to attempt a reconciliation, but to no avail. They address the Cardinal in friendship, but they do not fail to make a verbatim record of the conversation, which they will eventually publish (CdI 1969, pp. 243-59).

December 4.   Mazzi receives the curia's Decree of Removal from the post of parish priest. In its *Notiziario* of December 5, the community responds: "The pastor has been attacked to disperse his flock. The flock will not be dispersed" (CdI 1969, p. 262). The attempts of influential local churchmen to mediate have now failed; indeed, as the conflict progresses, positions have become more crystallized, outsiders have chosen sides, and the two actors become more and more polarized. The community and the cardinal move toward confrontation.

A.   Collective Action

December 5.   The community reacts quickly and dramatically to the cardinal's letter with a strike in the elementary and middle schools of the neighborhood. The effort is community-wide: even boy scouts help to ensure participation by offering babysitting services (CdI 1969, p. 263). In the afternoon, the children, their parents, and some of the teachers march through the streets of downtown Florence. They carry posters reading:

> What are the people of the Church—Everything!
> What do we count for—Nothing!
> What should we count for—Something!

They stand in silence in front of the Curia and pray for Cardinal Florit. When the prayer is finished, they deposit their posters in front of the cathedral, recite a *Padre nostro,* and move off toward Santa Maria Novella chanting "You can fire a priest, but not a people" (CdI 1969, p. 265). A new interpretive frame has been invented.

December 6. The cardinal's delegate, Monsignor Panerei, appears in the Isolotto to say mass in response to what he claims is a demand by the faithful. He is greeted by a sullen crowd and placards that read: "To content fifty, you have offended ten thousand of the faithful!" (Baldelli 1969, p. 141). After what the community describes as "a long colloquy of over two hours with the people," Panerei is "convinced" not to continue the mass and he retires (CdI 1971, p. 110).

December 7. At an assembly in the Isolotto church, a group of outsiders is detected. The community forces them to leave and the fact is publicized in a new letter to the cardinal. On December 3, mass is canceled and under a heavy rain a long line of people weaves down the main streets of Florence, after passing through the poorer quarters along the Arno. In front of the curia, another "Our Father" is read. The march is observed by policemen in plainclothes (CdI 1969, p. 276). The outsiders are not mere curiosity-seekers: five of their organizers will eventually be indicted for "promoting unauthorized demonstrations" and accused of "vilification of the state religion" by a group that calls itself the Catholic Anticommunist Movement (*Nazione* May 27, 1968).

December 20. The conflict has not gone unnoticed in the highest places. Don Mazzi receives a letter over the pope's signature calling for a reconciliation with the cardinal before Christmas. The three priests, together with a group of parishioners, go to Rome to seek an audience with the pontiff. They are received by Monsignor Benelli, then substitute Vatican secretary of state, who says the pope is indisposed and asks for a retraction, which the Isolotto delegation still refuses to give (*Nazione* December 22, p. 15; CdI 1969, pp. 281-94).

Christmas eve. Since Mazzi's removal, mass has been offered by a priest from the curia in a small chapel outside the neighborhood (CdI 1969, pp. 279-80). A delegate from the cardinal now arrives in the Isolotto with a functionary from the curia and another from the prefecture (this is the first time the state has been actively involved) to take over the church. Don Mazzi is absent, so the transfer cannot be effected, but they promise to return the next day—which happens to be Christmas (*Nazione* December 27, p. 11).

Christmas day. The church is packed with neighborhood residents, many of whom are not worshipers but have come to support Don Mazzi. Passages from the Bible are read, but, in protest against the hierarchy's actions, no mass is celebrated. That evening, a prayer vigil is held in the piazza in front of the church (Taurini 1968, p. 813).

VI. CONFRONTATION

Sunday, December 29.   Monsignor Alba, who has been sent by the cardinal to celebrate mass, enters a church packed with almost a thousand of Mazzi's supporters. He is accompanied by the cardinal's delegate and, amazingly, by people who appear to be militants of the neofascist party. These people surround the priest protectively and respond to the mass in loud voices, while Mazzi's supporters, who symbolically turn their backs to the altar, read the Bible. Leaders of the community form a kind of *cordon sanitaire* between their followers and Alba's bodyguards to prevent an incident from occurring inside the church. They chant loudly over the voice of the priest: "To celebrate the mass in these conditions is a sacrilege, an offense, a challenge, a provocation" (CdI 1971, pp. 111-14; *L'Unita,* December 30, 1968, p.1). The same day, an official of the neofascist MSI goes to court to denounce the interruption of the mass (CdI 1971, p. 115-16).

The open presence of the extreme Right now makes it impossible for the official Left to keep silent any longer. By the next morning, posters signed by the Communist, socialist, and left-wing socialist (PSIUP) parties appear on the walls of the city denouncing the presence of the police in the Isolotto and warning that the democratic and antifascist forces of the city will not tolerate fascist provocation (CdI, 1971, pp. 120-21).

December 31.   The church is formally transferred to the curia (*Nazione* January 2, 1969, p. 11). This act is followed on New Year's Day by a gathering in Rome outside St. Peter's to protest the hierarchy's action and to demand reforms in the Church (*Corriere* Jan. 2, 1969). The Isolotto has entered a turbulent national conflict structure that divides Left and Right, clerical and anticlerical, and—almost—Church and state. Questions are raised in Parliament, and a long judicial battle begins, a battle that will keep the issue in the news for over a year.

January 4, 1969.   In the presence of representatives of communities in Turin, Ravenna, and other Florentine neighborhoods (Sciubba and Paci 1976a, p. 99), another assembly is held, at which a decision is reached to obstruct future attempts of the Curia to hold mass in the Isolotto (CdI 1969, p. 319). The community maintains that "the people of the Isolotto have been rejected by the bishop and believe that at this point the mass would only serve to hypocritically disguise this rejection" (CdI 1969, p. 277). That night a right-wing group calling itself the "Florentine Action Squad" tears down left-wing wall posters and nails to the door of the church a manifesto ending with the words:

Long live the Army;
Long live the Forces of order;
Long live Italy![16]

Through a sequence of actions and reactions within the community and the Church hierarchy, and by the successive involvement first of the press and then of external allies and enemies who help polarize the struggle and provide an active audience for a broader ideological message, a conflict between a neighborhood church and its bishop has crystallized into a national social movement. Throughout the winter and spring of 1969 action will move to the courts, as the incidents of December and January are adjudicated—to the ultimate satisfaction of the community.[17] But the collective action that will put its permanent stamp on the movement—symbolizing the justice of the people confronted by unjust authority and providing the movement with an organizational form for the future—is still to come.

VII.   THE MASS IN THE PIAZZA

May 1969.   The cardinal now names two new priests to the Isolotto, both to take office the following February. But he does not dare to open the church yet, lest there be a repetition of the events of the previous winter (*Nazione* May 28, 1969, p. 6). One of the new priests, in the foreign accents of the Veneto, remarks that "there is nothing Christian and nothing religious" in the experience of the Isolotto community (Taurini 1969b, p. 531).

July 1969.   The loyalists decide to pray in the public piazza in front of the parish church. They invite a priest from the nearby diocese of Prato to hold a mass there (*Corriere* July 11, 1969; Taurini (1969b, p. 531). The cardinal responds by threatening suspension *a divinis* to any priest who accepts the invitation (Taurini 1969b, p. 532). The community responds that its priests will continue to refuse to celebrate mass but that it will welcome "all those who want to bear witness among us (even if it subjects them to persecution) to the church which has its foundation in the spirit of Christ" (ibid. pp. 533-34).

Negotiations drag on throughout the summer between leaders of the community and the cardinal's representatives. Florit at one point invites Don Mazzi and his assistants to come and live with him in the curia. In early August a group of progressive churchmen meeting at Camaldoli try to effect a reconciliation (ibid. pp. 538-40). "Who is the father," they ask the cardinal, "who, when his sons ask him for bread, gives them a stone?"[18]

August 30.   While these negotiations are going on, the cardinal shocks both supporters and opponents by announcing that the next day he will appear in the neighborhood, reopen the church, and celebrate a mass himself. The community responds at a midnight meeting with a hastily prepared declaration warning the cardinal that his action would be irreversible; they also hold an all-night vigil outside the curia. When, the next morning, the declaration is read to him, the cardinal (according to the memoir published by the community) responds:

> This document is a marxist treatise. You are not a Christian community. . . . You are outside the Church because you are against me. . . . Whoever is against his own bishop is outside the Church. . . . Have the courage to admit that you have left the Church" (Ibid., p. 547).

Sunday, August 31.   At 10 A.M., the piazza in front of the church of the Isolotto begins to fill up. As the cardinal's uncompromising letter is read aloud, the crowd responds with outrage. A unanimous decision is taken not to enter the church during his celebration of the mass. At 11 A.M., the cardinal arrives, protected by both plainclothes and uniformed policemen, and enters the church which, by now, contains several hundred traditional Catholics. When the mass is over and Florit passes through the piazza, he is greeted only by silence. A fast is held until evening (*Nazione* Sept. 1, 1969, p. 1).

The cardinal's *coup de main* is roundly condemned by Florence's Catholic community, including, among others, the influential theologian, Ernesto Balducci (Taurini 1969b, pp. 551-54). The permanent suspension of the three priests has now become inevitable, and they and their loyal supporters move their activities definitively outside the Church. On the following Sunday, in the presence of over a thousand people, a priest from a religious community in Turin performs a baptism and celebrates mass on the piazza (Taurini 1969b, p. 557).

VIII.   THE ISOLOTTO TODAY

The "mass" in the piazza has been held every Sunday morning since 1969 on the Piazza outside the church of the Isolotto. It follows a well-established routine. Enzo Mazzi or his close collaborator, Sergio Gomito, leads off with a general address; then a topic which has been "prepared" and discussed at a regular Thursday evening assembly is presented, often with the participation of friendly and usually highly political outside groups. A discussion is organized. There follow general announcements and, finally, the "religious" part of the assembly, in which the host is offered to all who wish to partake of it.

The mass in the piazza—first celebrated 20 years ago as a deliberate provocation to unjust authority—has become the central symbol and organizing principle of the community's life and meaning. Repeating it every Sunday reconsecrates the group, allows it to continue to attract both disillusioned church members and others, and provides it with a flexible forum in which a variety of issues can be aired. It is participatory, provocative, and expressive; but it is also planned, strategic, and institutionalized. It re-evokes in stylized form the initial encounter with unjust authority, embodies the solidarity of the group, and makes its ritual available to others.

This event takes place in complete indifference to doctrine and to the service being offered concurrently in the church across the street. The meeting in the piazza has taken over the religious significance of the mass; even the group's enemies are invoked not from across the street but from its past. A reference to "all the years that have united us" is more likely to evoke emotion than is the circulation of the wafer and the wine. The solidarity of the people of God in the face of the "abstract, formal, and ethically harmless" church hierarchy (Niebuhr 1957, p. 31) remains the central interpretive frame of the community.

The Isolotto community's indifference to doctrinal niceties should not surprise us; long ago, Niebuhr wrote of such communities:

> the formality of ritual is displaced in such groups by an informality which gives opportunity for the expression of emotional faith and for a simple, often crude, symbolism (1957, p. 30).

But this movement is no "wild flower" or "unruly weed." In the discussions we observed in 1985-1986, there were intense arguments about the meaning of biblical passages, pleas for help by a representative of immigrant workers, a memoir from a married priest, a statement of newly refound faith from a middle-aged woman, and a careful strategy session about a forthcoming meeting with the new cardinal—the first meeting, incidentally, since the events of 1968-1969.

But if the Isolotto community is casual about doctrine, it is scarcely so about organization. Like many new social movements, the community began without a fixed organization, "living in improvisation," as one observer put it. Its major decision-making body, like that of the student movement, was the assembly open to all, "in which spontaneity is the rule." In the words of an activist member of the community, "nothing had an institutional aim; everything was directed at the needs of the moment." [19]

But organizations do not need to look like bureaucracies to have the essential characteristics of organizations: continuity, division of labor, internal rules, and expected roles. The Isolotto community's origins in the Church gave its members a common language and experience that obviated the need for formal organization. Even so, regular procedures and a subtle hierarchy soon came to dominate its activities. For example, the new catechism produced in 1968, though it never became a rigid dogma, involved a regular routine: "Each year we changed the program on the basis of discussions with the childrens' parents. Our goal was to combine their experiences with the word of God." [20]

Moreover, as the struggle with the Church developed, there emerged a clear division between a small group of "lay people" and the mass of the movement's supporters. As Baldelli writes:

Differences soon emerge, for example in the importance of the group of lay members, who soon constitute a kind of small, well-prepared vanguard in relation to the thousands of parishioners. They guide or correct, suggest, invent the vehicles of communication and timing (1969, p. 143).

The insiders, many of whom remain in the community today, became specialists in fashioning the keywords that would eventually be passed on to the mass media (Baldelli 1969, p. 143). The smoothly orchestrated mass meetings held during the winter and spring of 1968-1969, the marches to the steps of the Curia with placards and chants of Our Father, and the slogans combining moral condemnation with quietism reflected anything but spontaneity.

Observing the community 18 years later, we found a similar combination of informality and institutionalization. Discussion is constant, informal, and not always informed. Mazzi inspires the group, Gomito stimulates discussion, but neither lectures the participants—except on the importance of coming to meetings. Everyone—including Mazzi, is called by his or her first name. Outsiders come and go. We could have attended meetings as long as we liked, and no one would have raised an eyebrow.

But as we came to know the group, we saw subtle and not-so-subtle signs of hierarchy and a clear differentiation of roles. As for discussion, it has a clear and important socialization function in a community of low-income people with no "selective" incentives to distribute. As one member put it, the community, in contrast to the sterile ritual of the institutional church, allowed "the people [to] finally speak and not only listen. Enzo taught us about dialogue. People need to talk to each other, even in a family." [21]

At the Sunday assemblies we attended, a small group of lay people would always ask the first questions, keeping them simple and talking as if they were onlookers and not active militants. Outsiders were encouraged to speak, but one or two old-timers were urged to be brief when they began to ride well-worn hobby horses. An observer familiar with the ritual informality of Italian political assemblies would have found nothing unusual here.

Like many of the movements of the 1960s, the Isolotto community soon gravitated toward the party system and the institutional Left. The members of the community claim that they avoid partisan commitments and, like participants in many new social movements today, vigorously deny that their work is in any way political. In our interviews they were at pains to deny that they were allied with the parties of the Left. The critiques of their actions in 1968-1969 from the extreme Left certainly support that claim, but the group gets good coverage in the local left-wing papers. [22]

In at least three ways, the Isolotto community was from the beginning highly political:

First, the issues around which it was organized came to a head when they did because the moment was politically ripe: in the cycle of protest of the late

1960s, there occurred in Italian political culture a process of "frame realignment" in favor of autonomy and against extending an automatic mandate (*la delega*) to organized authority. Even the tactics used against the cardinal—the assembly, the vigil, counter-information—were the same as those which were being simultaneously used against university administrators throughout the country.

Second, both the support gained by the movement and the opposition to it were largely political. In addition to recruiting members of the declining La Pira wing of the DC, the community's protests attracted support from Communist and Socialist party militants, and from small but growing circles of extreme leftists, some of whom would eventually appear in the "extraparliamentary" groups of the early 1970s.[23] Indeed, a major reason for the community's rapid decline in members after 1970 is that a large part of its support had come from the "lay and communist world," much of which returned to its origins in the early 1970s (Barbagli and Corbetta 1978). "The solidarity of these groups was the result of their trust in the movement, but they were not believers and they soon went back into their natural climate."[24]

Finally, the Isolotto community was transformed into a social movement through the political process of interaction between the community itself, its antagonists, and the allies and enemies who flocked to the neighborhood and helped to polarize the conflict. The unintended role of the conservative press, especially the *Nazione,* in diffusing word of the conflict has already been noted. Even more important was the political unity that the community gained from the process of conflict with the Church.[25] Finally, the experience was politicized by the attempts of outside groups to exploit the situation by externalizing the conflict and moving it onto a broader stage.

The Isolotto religious community gave rise to a variety of concrete policy initiatives in the neighborhood—a popular school, a voluntary social work agency, a parents' committee, an after-school program, a social center. But its real importance was in demonstrating that the Church's authority could be challenged and that elements within it were dissatisfied. It stimulated the formation of new religious communities around the country (Sciubba and Paci 1976a, pp. 31-32), giving hope to reformers that, even within the church-institution, "many of the ideas and the needs of the *comunita' di base* could enter the institution and be absorbed by it."[26]

Inevitably, as the hostility of the conflict with the cardinal diminished and the cycle of protest ended, ardor for the rigors of a movement that meets in a windy piazza evey Sunday began to decline. The neighborhood poor, inactive participants at best, were soon wooed back to the Church or relapsed into secularism or the PCI. As for the middle-class ideological recruits, some became more conservative, others became disillusioned with movement politics, while others eventually moved into the institutional Left.

How then did the Isolotto religious community survive the decline of the 1960s social movements and avoid absorption into the institutional Left? The answer to this question emerges from the story told above. When ordinary people come together in extraordinary events that both unite them and set them against the authority in which they have believed, authority is transferred to the group itself, to its unity, and to the critique of authority it embodies. The confrontation with authority gives rise to a new interpretive frame that remains the basis of the group as long as that frame is nurtured and embodied in the group's actions and symbolism.

Over and over in our interviews, and in the assemblies that we observed, the members of the community referred to "the struggle we carried out so many years ago," to the unity of the people represented in the community, and to the horror they still felt that the Church-institution had tried to separate them from their priest. To the evocative force of such themes, many people are immune. But those who are not—like survivors of war, resistance, or personal crisis—are animated by memories of the experience that forged their movement, which is reincarnated each week by the reenactment of their exile and their rebirth.

Such movements do not grow up spontaneously like "wild flowers and unruly weeds," in isolation from politics, institutions, and old interpretive frames. They are produced by solidarities, conflicts, and traditional beliefs and are galvanized by cycles of protest, which both provide their creators with new resources and opportunities and constrain their development. As our story illustrates, even "old" movements within the oldest institutions can be revitalized in such periods. Insurgencies develop out of the interactions between traditional conflicts and interpretive frames and the catalyzing influences in the political system. Through the resulting confrontations, new interpretive frames are constructed, militants are formed, and organizational strategies perfected. Some of these events find an institutional form that will help the movements they embody live to fight again another day, in the next, probably inevitable, cycle of protest.[27]

ACKNOWLEDGMENTS

This paper is a revised version of my paper "You can fire a priest but not a people," presented at the Annual Conference of the Social Science History Association, St. Louis, Mo., October 1986. For comments on the earlier paper, I am grateful to Glenn Altschuler, Peter Hall, Stephen Hellman, Hanspeter Kriesi, John Modell, Susan Tarrow, and Danilo Zolo. My thanks as well to Margherita Perretti, who helped to gather the primary data.

NOTES

1. "Partial" because, even in the labor movement, the only real growth has been in the largely middle-class public sector unions. See Goldfield and Plotkin (1987) for representative American findings.

2. The perspective taken here builds on the "political process model" of collective action found in the work of Lipsky (1968), Eisinger (1973), Piven and Cloward (1977), and McAdam (1982). For a review of research, see Tarrow (1983 and 1988b).

3. The quantitative data were collected for the Cornell Project on Social Protest and Policy Innovation and came from a daily reading of Italy's national newspaper of record, *Corriere della Sera,* from January 1, 1966, to December 31, 1973. In all, 4,980 "protest events" were identified, coded, and recorded. For a technical description of the Cornell study, see Tarrow (1985); for some early results, see della Porta and Tarrow (1987), and Stefanizzi (1986). The complete report will appear in Tarrow (1988a).

4. In these years, the FIM's journal, *Dibattito sindacale,* became a meeting ground for unionists, left-wing sociologists, and radical Catholics. For an analysis of the changes in the union during these years, see Cella, Manghi, and Piva (1972).

5. My account of the events at the Catholic University is dependent on Lumley's sensitive reconstruction in Chapter 9 of his thesis. I am grateful for the reflections on this episode provided me in personal interviews by Bruno Dente, Ida Regalia, and Gloria Regonini.

6. The following section is based on personal interviews with members of the Isolotto religious community (Padre Ernesto Balducci, Danilo Zolo), and on a synthesis of the following published sources: Baldelli (1969), *Il Ponte* (1971), Sciubba and Pace (1976), Seidelman (1979), *Comunita' dell'Isolotto* (1969 and 1971), Taurini (1968, 1969a and b, and 1970), and Zolo (1970).

7. As Baldelli writes: "The city hall was far away and local needs were ignored. . . . The religious assembly thus became the only place in the neighborhood in which people could meet and talk" (1969, p. 152).

8. Milani wrote a book in 1967, *Letter to a Schoolteacher,* which one observer has called "possibly the single most influential text in the student movement" (Lumley 1983, p. 194). Using the experiences of the Tuscan village school in which he taught, Milani "wrote through the voices of the children, who, for him, were excluded not only by economic but by cultural processes" (Lumley, p. 195). At the school of Barbiana, he also tried to link learning to a participatory notion of democracy. Milani was only the most visible of a group of Tuscan clergymen — often from lower-class backgrounds and almost always working in poor neighborhoods — who saw themselves as working for the People of God, and not for the Church of Rome.

9. Balducci did not go very far; he founded a study center at the Badia Fiesolana at nearby San Domenico, outside the diocese of Florence, from which he still publishes *Testimonianze* and works for the international peace movement.

10. *Corriere della Sera,* September 15, 1968, p. 5. For a detailed treatment sympathetic to the students, see the volume by "Protagonisti," *La cattedrale occupata* (1969). See also Sciubba and Pace (1976, pp. 30-31).

11. Sergio Gomito was still outraged eighteen years later: "The People of God were ejected from God's house and the Pope approved!" he said. Interview, Florence, December, 1985.

12. The community claimed that hostile right-wing elements were responsible for the story. If they were, their actions had the worst possible effect on the Church's cause, for in the climate of social mobilization at the time, reporters and left-wing sympathizers flocked to the Isolotto and the affair came to be seen as a litmus test of the power of the hierarchy.

13. The entire collection of the *Notiziario* has been preserved, and may be consulted, in the Marucelliana Library in Florence.

14. Lumley writes:

They (the Cattolica militants) carried out an 'information picket' and distributed a daily bulletin. The main decisions were taken at the general assemblies of all the students, whilst a 'committee of agitation' ran the every day activity. 'Commissions' were formed to hold seminars and organise specific activities (1983, pp. 190-91).

15.   Mazzi says to his supporters, "We are faced with a problem that I could not have solved by myself; I would have betrayed and excluded you (CdI 1969, pp. 198-201).

16.   That the group was clearly of fascist derivation is demonstrated not only by the slogan, but by the name, for no one but fascists would use the Mussolinian term *squadra* (CdI 1971, pp. 123-24).

17.   On January 14 the attorney general sent an indictment to 11 lay people and 5 priests for "istigazione a delinquere" when they "publicly instigated the obstruction of the mass" in early December (*Nazione* January 15, 1969, p. 1). In response, over a thousand people signed a letter claiming co-responsibility for the boycott of the mass (CdI, 1971, p. 133). Though the legal wrangling went on for months, keeping the case in the national news and leading to protests around the country, the Church and its supporters got little satisfaction from the judiciary. The six organizers of the December 5 demonstration were absolved on the request of the Ministry of Justice (*Nazione* May 24, 1969, p. 1). Of the 438 signers of the "co-responsibility" letter, most were amnestied and the rest—5 priests and 4 lay people—were eventually absolved (*Nazione* July 6, 1969, p. 1; *L'Unita* July 6, 1969, p. 5).

18.   But at least one of these distinguished churchmen believes that neither side wanted a reconciliation, since the compromise offered at Camaldoli was rejected by both sides. Interview with Ernesto Balducci, November 18, 1985.

19.   Interview, Florence, Nov. 9, 1985.

20.   Interview, Florence, Nov. 4, 1985.

21.   Interview, Florence, Nov. 9, 1985.

22.   As the furor died down, the community was lectured by the extreme left *Manifesto* party:

The religious movements will have to learn . . . that struggles born under the sign of spontaneism and against immediate repression must be sustained if they are to come to grips with changing situations and with the different ways in which power is organized (*Manifesto* July 7, 1971, p. 3).

23.   Baldelli, for example, on whose *Nuovo Impegno* article I have relied, eventually became part of *Lotta continua*.

24.   Interview, Florence, Nov. 9, 1985.

25.   As one member of the community said, "You have to recognize that the cardinal did all he could to unite us; he smoothed our path" (*Il Ponte* 1971, p. 638).

26.   Interview, San Domenico, Oct. 21, 1985.

27.   On the occasion of a recent visit of Pope John Paul II to Florence, the community sent him an open letter on injustive and poverty in the Third World and on corruption in the finances of the Vatican (*Paese Sera* October 12, 1986, p. 15).

REFERENCES

Alberoni, Francesco. 1979. "Movimenti e istituzioni nell'Italia tra il 1960 e il 1970." Pages 233-270 in Luigi Graziano and Sidney Tarrow (eds.), *La crisi italiana*. Vol. 1. Turin: Einaudi.

Baldelli, Pio. 1969. "Isolotto: esperienza di un quartiere popolare di Firenze." *Nuovo Impegno*, no. 16 (May-July), pp. 141-64.

Barbagli, Marzio and Piergiorgio Corbetta. 1978. "Partito e movimento. Aspetti del rinnovamento del PCI." *Inchesta,* 8:3-49.

Cella, Gianprimo, Bruno Manghi, and Paola Piva. 1972. *Un sindacato italiano negli anni sessanta.* Bari: De Donato.

Cohn, Norman. 1959. *Pursuit of the Millennium.* New York: Harper.

Comunita' dell'Isolotto (CdI). 1968. "Proposta per un nuovo catechismo." *Testimonianze* 11 (August): 527-39.

Comunita' dell'Isolotto (CdI). 1969. *Isolotto 1954/1969.* Introduzione di Don Enzo Mazzi. Bari: Laterza.

Comunita' dell'Isolotto (CdI). 1971. *Isolotto sotto processo.* Bari: Laterza.

della Porta, Donatella and Sidney Tarrow. 1986. "Unwanted children: Political violence and the cycle of protest in Italy, 1966-1973." *European Journal of Political Research* 14: 607-32.

Dalton, Russell et al. 1987. "Environmental Action in Western Democracies." Project Report. Unpublished paper. Department of Political Science, Florida State University, Tallahasse, Fla., March.

Eisinger, Peter. 1973. "The conditions of protest behavior in American cities." *American Political Science Review* 67: 11-28.

Fireman, Bruce, William Gamson, Steve Rytina, and Bruce Taylor. 1979. "Encounters with Unjust Authority." In Louis Kriesberg (ed.), *Research in Social Movements, Conflict, and Change.* Vol. 2. Greenwich, Conn.: JAI.

Garner, Roberta and Mayer N. Zald. 1985. "The Political Economy and Social Movement Sectors." Pages 119-45 in Gerald D. Suttles and Mayer N. Zald (eds.), *The Challenge of Social Control. Citizenship and Institution Building in Modern Society.* Norwood, N.J.: Ablex.

Goldfield, Michael and Jonathan Plotkin. 1987. "Public Sector Union Growth in the United States: Do the Laws Matter?" Unpublished paper, Ithaca: Cornell University, June.

Jenkins, J. Craig. 1983. "Resource mobilization theory and the study of social movements." *Annual Review of Sociology* 9.327-33.

Klandermans, Bert. 1987. "Linking the 'Old' and the 'New': Movement Networks in the Netherlands." Paper presented at the Joint Seminar on New Social Movements, Tallahasse, Fla., April 2-4.

Lipsky, Michael. 1968. "Protest as a political resource." *American Political Science Review* 62:1144-58.

Lowi, Theodore W. 1971. *The Politics of Disorder.* New York: Basic Books.

Lumley, Robert. 1983. "Social Movements in Italy, 1968-1978." Ph.D dissertation, Centre for Contemporary Cultural Studies, University of Birmingham, England.

McAdam, Doug. 1982. *Political Process and the Development of Black Insurgency.* Chicago: University of Chicago Press.

Melucci, Alberto. 1982. *L'invenzione del presente.* Bologna: Il Mulino.

Melucci, Alberto. 1984. *Altri codici. Aree di movimento nella metropoli.* Bologna: Il Mulino.

Niebuhr, H. Richard. 1957. *The Social Sources of Denominationalism.* Cleveland: Meridian.

Offe, Claus. 1985. "New Social Movements: Challenging the Boundaries of Institutional Politics." *Social Research* 52:817-68.

Piven, Frances Fox and Richard Cloward. 1979. *Poor People's Movements; How They Succeed, and Why They Fail.* New York: Vintage.

Pizzorno, Alessandro. 1978. "Political Exchange and Collective Identity in Industrial Conflict." Pages 277-98 in Colin Crouch and Alessandro Pizzorno (eds.), *The Resurgence of Class Conflict in Western Europe since 1968.* Vol. 2. London: Macmillan.

Ponte, Il. 1971. "Il paradosso Isolotto." *Il Ponte,* no. 5-6, (May-June): 633-65.

Protagonisti (ed.). 1969. *La cattedrale occupata.* Parma: La cultura.

Regalia, Ida. 1986. "Evolving Patterns of Participation in the Trade Union Movement: Membership, Strikes, and Militancy in Italy." Paper presented at the International Symposium on New Social Movements, Amsterdam, Free University, June, 12-14.

Regalia, Ida, Marino Regini, and Emilio Reyneri. 1979. "Labour Conflicts and Industrial Relations in Italy." Pages 101-58 in Colin Crouch and Alessandro Pizzorno (eds.), *The Resurgence of Class Conflict in Western Europe since 1968.* Vol. 1. London: Macmillan.

Sciubba, Roberto and Rossana Sciubba Pace. 1976. *Le Comunita' di base in Italia.* 2 vols. Rome: Coines.

Scuola di Barbiana. 1967. *Lettera di una professoressa.* Florence.

Seidelman, Raymond M. 1979. "Neighborhood Communism in Florence: Goals and Dilemmas of the Italian Road to Socialism." Ph.D. dissertation, Cornell University.

Snow, David, Louis A. Zurcher, Jr., and Sheldon Ekland-Olson. 1981. "Social networks and social movements: A micro-structural approach to differential recruitment." *American Sociological Review* 45:787-801.

Snow, David, E. Burke Rochford, Jr., Steven K. Worden, and Robert D. Benford. 1986. "Frame alignment processes, micromobilization, and movement participation." *American Sociological Review* 51:464-81.

Stefanizzi, Sonia. 1986. "Noninstitutional collective action: Women's protests in Italy, 1966-1973." Paper presented at the ECPR International Joint Workshops, Göteborg, Sweden, March.

Tarrow, Sidney. 1983. *Struggling to Reform: Social Movements and Policy Change during Cycles of Protest.* Western Societies Paper No. 15. Ithaca N.Y.: Cornell University.

Tarrow, Sidney. 1985. *Project Manual.* Cornell Project on Social Protest and Policy Innovation. Ithaca, N.Y.

Tarrow, Sidney. 1988a. *Democracy and Disorder: Society and Politics in Italy, 1965-1975.* Oxford: Oxford University Press (forthcoming).

Tarrow, Sidney. 1988b. "National politics and collective action: Recent theory and research in Western Europe and the U.S." *Annual Review of Sociology* 14.

Taurini, Giampaolo. 1968. "Una comunita' in cammino: appunti per una storia della parrocchia dell'Isolotto." *Testimonianze* 11 (Nov.-Dec.):782-816.

Taurini, Giampaolo. 1969a. "Ancora sull' Isolotto." *Testimonianze* 12 (Jan.-Feb.):46-64.

Taurini, Giampaolo. 1969b. "Gli ultimi sviluppi della vicenda dell' Isolotto." *Testimonianze* 12 (July-August):529-60.

Taurini, Giampaolo. 1970. "L'Isolotto un anno dopo." *Testimonianze* 13 (Jan.-Feb.):39-64.

Tilly, Charles. 1984. "Social Movements and National Politics." In Charles Bright and Susan Harding (eds.), *Statemaking and Social Movements.* Ann Arbor: University of Michigan Press.

Touraine, Alain. 1984. *Le retour de l'acteur.* Paris: Fayard.

Walzer, Michael. 1971. *The Revolution of the Saints.* New York: Atheneum.

Zald, Mayer N. and Michael Berger. 1978. "Social movements in organizations: Coup d'état, insurgency, and mass movements." *American Journal of Sociology* 83:823-61.

Zolo, Danilo. 1970. "La formazione dei giovani cattolici fiorentini (1960-1970)." *Rinascita,* 26 June 1970.

THEMES, LOGICS, AND ARENAS
OF SOCIAL MOVEMENTS:
A STRUCTURAL APPROACH

Dieter Rucht

I. INTRODUCTION

Individual and collective action, though caused or shaped by structural factors, is not entirely determined by these factors. This fact is true for social movements as well. The analysis of a structural framework may yield general information on causes, potential for recruitment, strategies, and possible impacts of social movements. But on the level of concrete issues and activities of groups and organizations involved in social movements, we find variations that must be explained by situational factors and events, by the contingent environment of given organizations, by endogenous parameters such as international cleavages and factions, and by the skills of a leadership. To study the range and causes of these variations it is useful to compare different groups and organizations within the same movement.

But in addition to a global framework, which can be conceptualized as a (political) "opportunity structure" (Tarrow 1983; Kitschelt 1986), and beyond

International Social Movement Research, Vol. 1, pages 305-328.
Supplement to Research in Social Movements, Conflicts and Change
Copyright © 1988 by JAI Press Inc.
All rights of reproduction in any form reserved.
ISBN: 0-89232-955-6

the more concrete factors mentioned above, a social movement may have a more hidden feature, one I propose to call the "logic" of a movement. To assess the manner and the extent to which such a "deep" variable shapes a movement's "industry," its strategies and activities, I have chosen for comparative analysis two movements within the same geographical and temporal frame; the women's movement and the environmental movement in West Germany. This comparative approach can demonstrate that the two movements—regardless of some common features—involve characteristic differences in their forms of organization, methods of mobilization, and arenas of conflict. These differences will be explained by the respective logic of each movement, a logic that in turn can be related to basic social changes that produce new expectations, strains, and conflicts. These new developments, in turn, are reflected in global, highly conflictual "themes" that are a focus of social struggles in a given historical period. Depending on the fundamental logic of a movement, certain fields of action, among them public "arenas," crystallize in the course of conflicts. These arenas have a different relevance for both movements, and different forms of action take place within them.

The structural interpretation of social movements suggested here should not be overstretched. Social movements are neither a simple reflex of structural conditions nor a stable agent within a fixed institutional setting. Social movements are at the same time products and producers of societal patterns. Though they act within a historically created and relatively stable frame, they also actively participate in changing political discourses, power constellations, and cultural symbols, and thus in changing their own aims, forms, and identity (Touraine 1973; Japp 1984; Melucci 1985).

II. SOME CROSS-MOVEMENT FINDINGS

At the end of the 1960s and the beginning of the 1970s many advanced capitalist societies experienced the rise of a number of protest movements. At least in Europe, these movements came to be called "new social movements" (NSMs) (for an overview, see Klandermans 1987). This term usually implies two assumptions. First, it is argued that, regardless of the specific issue or cause they represent, the various movements have common features (such as the social bases of recruitment, organizational patterns, general values, etc.). Second, even though these individual movements did not emerge simultaneously and even though their rhythms of activity differ, they belong to an overall movement cycle. This cycle began with the countercultural and emancipatory currents in the 1960s. Via a number of issue cycles and waves of mobilization, this general movement cycle led to the development of an extended activist protest culture, which in recent years, however, seems to have lost its momentum and its clear-cut contours (Brand 1985; for West Germany, see Brand, Büsser, and Rucht 1986).

It is certain that the women's movement and the environmental movement must be counted among the strongest pillars of the NSMs. Moreover, both movements provide an important personal and infrastructural basis for related movements, such as the new peace movement, which experienced its peak in the early 1980s. The protest energies transmitted from one movement to another, overlapping memberships, and occasional mutual support all indicate that these movements occupy some common ground; however they are far from merging into one large movement, as some observers hoped or expected (for such a vision, see Touraine 1981). Consequently these individual movements tend to view themselves as affiliated forces, virtually sharing a kind of division of labor in an admittedly vague project to bring about a "better" society.

If we use the term NSMs as an analytical concept, we should not forget that empirically there are considerable differences between the various groups and movements. Generalizing statements—those asserting that NSMs are a "new middle-class"—phenomena, that they have an "antimodernistic" ideology and a decentralized, informal organizational structure and are inclined to use unconventional, disruptive forms of action—must be qualified. In the following section, I hope to differentiate this general picture by comparing two movements. To be sure, as long as the various tendencies and their development over time cannot be described in detail, this attempt will remain on a very abstract level.

A. Political and Ideological Orientations

Obviously, the women's movement and the environmental movement pursue different objectives: the former seeks to end sexual discrimination against women, the latter tries to arrest the destruction of our natural environment. But beyond these differences, fundamental similarities appear.

The political orientation of the core groups within both movements is definitely leftist. If we look at the whole spectrum, some differentiations have to be made. Although there are some marginal points of agreement between the women's movement and the political right (e.g., the opposition to pornography and the marketing of the female body), the political spectrum of the women's movement includes two major forces: a socialist and a radical-liberal tendency. The composition of the environmental movement, however, is more complex. It, too includes a minor conservative faction, at least in West Germany, even right-wing extremists. But on the whole there is no doubt that the prevailing political tendency of adherents of both movements (Müller-Rommel 1984) and of NSMs in general (Watts 1987) is toward the left.

Furthermore, both movements fundamentally agree on the demand for extensive political participation and a democratically organized society, for a better "quality of life," and for a critique of entrenched bureaucratic powermachines.

The unifying element of the women's and the environmental movement, as well as of NSMs in general, lies beyond the conjunction of emancipatory, radical-democratic demands and a specific antimodernistic attitude. Though both movements may have different sources and points of reference (the subordination of women and the subordination of nature), they nevertheless have an identical target: the primacy of a one-sided, recklessly used technical-instrumental reason, the logic of "conquering," "mastering" and "dominating." No wonder such authors as Herbert Marcuse or Erich Fromm, whose life's work was devoted to a critique of such a rationality, sympathized with both movements.

Especially in the most radical and frequently most naive versions of feminist and ecological antimodernism, the affinity between the two lines of critique becomes obvious: each promotes a holistic worldview and a corresponding way of life, the search for a "gentle" society, and the vision of great, all-encompassing harmony.

Common ends on an abstract level, however, do not automatically create a consensus on concrete methods and practical means to change society. For instance, a movement fighting for self-determination and the development of personality will hardly be compatible with forces that, on the basis of ecological concerns, encourage the restriction of individual freedom. And even different members of the same organization—the German Green Party, for example—differ fundamentally on the issue of abortion: radical feminists struggling for the liberalization of abortion are challenged by proponents of a kind of moral ecologism ("Lebensschützer") whose aim is to save human life under all circumstances. Precisely because the similarities and convergences of both movements are limited, and because each movement has its own profile and its own priorities, the quasi-organic unity of ecologism and feminism has to be proclaimed again and again (for such a voluntaristic attempt, cf. Balbus 1982).

B. Social Recruitment

The available data on the social composition of the women's movement and the environmental movement are unsatisfactory. In fact, apart from conventional surveys, complete or even representative data are hardly to be expected in part because of ubiquitous problems of delimiting social movements, in part because it is so difficult to gain access to certain protest groups. Existing informations, however, does confirm a well-known supposition: the core groups of these movements are relatively homogeneous. Activists are essentially younger middle-class people with an above-average education, among whom are many employees of the social service sector. Comparing the outer circles of adherents, supporters, and sympathizers of both movements, however, we find that the environmental movement again presents a more highly differentiated picture. In addition to the groups of middle-class activists previously described, who are very sensitive to all ecological issues, we find groups of people directly affected by specific institutions and projects that pollute or endanger the natural environment: noise-plagued neighbors of an airport, for example, or fishermen whose subsistence is threatened by water pollution, or forest owners concerned about acid rain. At times such groups constitute the backbone of local protests confined to specific issues. Further, by documenting the authenticity and seriousness of the protest motives, they may play an important legitimizing function. But they play only a subordinate role in the programmatic and strategic decision-making process of the movement. Generally, it holds true that the most dynamic and politically active factions in both the women's movement and the environmental movement are recruited from the same social bases.

C. Forms of Organization and Infrastructure

Usually a loose, decentralized network-organization is considered to be typical of NSMs (Gundelach 1984; Donati 1984; Rucht 1984; Melucci 1985). And the organization of NSMs certainly is decentralized compared to the hierarchical and formal structures of industrial enterprise, public administrations, or large membership associations. But in the case of the two NSMs we are considering, a close inspection reveals significant differences between the organization of the two movements.

The image of a grass-roots movement is fairly accurate for the women's movement. Its base of action and its actual sphere of influence are local and regional. The networks found at this local level are for the most part informally structured, founded on close personal relations and shared experiences. Above all, the principle of autonomy espoused by the radical feminist wing of the women's movement contributes to the stabilization of this internal structure and allows for a relatively clear separation from the movement's social environment—including organizations sympathetic to the women's movement. Because distrust of bureaucratic machines and elitist circles—that are perceived as typically male-dominated—is so widespread, all attempts to create a national feminist party or a traditional pressure group have, up to now, received almost no support.

When actions and campaigns do take place at the national level, they are frequently organized by local groups or loose coordinating committees formed ad hoc and on the basis of personal relationship. On the national level, issue-oriented forms of cooperation rarely become formalized. Large and tightly organized associations are completely lacking in the new German women's movement. The principle of autonomy espoused by the radical wing implies not only distance from organizations dominated by men but also a rejection of all ritualized forms of representation. Consequently an established and formalized umbrella organization such as the "Deutscher Frauenrat" (German Women's Council)[1] exists practically outside of the women's movement (Frevert 1986, pp. 276-77). Interactions between this organization and the movement's groups, as far as they occur at all, are severely strained. Similarly, relations between the autonomous women's movement and women's organizations within the political parties and labor unions tend to be problematic. Even though many of the movement's adherents sympathize with the Green Party—which, unlike other parties, has endorsed many feminist issues, such as an antidiscrimination law, or quotas in economic and political institutions—this sympathy is overshadowed by a fundamental skepticism about the idea of the political party per se. Whenever the women's movement comes into contact with sympathetic groups of mixed gender, demands for autonomy, or at least for the temporary separation of women into their own circles and suborganizations, become audible. Thus the "Netzwerk Selbsthilfe," an organization for the financial support of alternative economic, social, and cultural initiatives, has led to the establishment of a feminist counterpart named "gold rush." For the same reason, specific women's organizations have been founded within scientific associations. Although a small number of specialized and increasingly professional networks have been established on the national level (e.g., houses for battered women, groups focusing on the liberalization of abortion, a feminist initiative promoting women's issues on the occasion of national electoral campaigns), organizations and designated speakers who combine the various concerns and represent them in the national political arena do not exist. Even a temporary semiformal coordinating committee, which plays an important role in the West German peace movement (Leif 1985), for instance, seems to contradict everything the radical wing of the women's movement stands for.

The environmental movement too maintains an image of a grass-roots movement. But in the case of this movement, the image is only partially true to reality. The environmental movement, in fact, has a dual structure (Rucht 1988). On the one hand, it contains an informal network of local, regional, and national organizations. The majority of the antinuclear-power groups, for instance, are organized in this informal manner. Even the movement's national conferences, which are held at irregular intervals, are based on extremely loose organization. Locations, dates, organizers, and topics are fixed at preparatory meetings that are open to everyone who wishes to attend and even to intervene. On the other hand, the environmental movement includes hierarchical and formalized organizations on all levels. In many cases these organizations differ only slightly from traditional pressure groups. In part, these organizations have not grown organically from the grass roots, but were created "from above." Some have been called into existence by officials of preexisting interest groups. Such organizations are the preferred playground for "movement entrepreneurs," those trained in strategic thinking, in collecting and managing resources, eliminating rivals, building coalitions, in short, those pursuing that very power game of which the feminists are so suspicious. The guiding principle of such strategies is not ideological purity but demonstrable success. Thus it is not always easy to determine whether organizational patriotism, altruistic dedication for the common interest, or desire for personal prestige is the driving force behind a specific activity. Here the contours of a protest movement become blurred, for once such organizations become dependent on governmental subsidies, they tend to moderate their demands and policies and to lose their movement identity.

Within the environmental movement the importance of large membership organizations seems to increase steadily, because of their permanent presence, their growing expertise, and their managerial and financial resources. This development is especially evident at the national level of action (Rucht 1987). Local and regional groups cannot cope with complex political issues. Moreover, the formation of a nationwide Green Party has also contributed to shift the political power within the movement to the disadvantage of informal structured and locally based groups.

D. Mobilization, Forms of Action, and Conflict Strategies

The most pronounced differences between the organization of the women's movement and that of the environmental movement are also reflected in their various practices of mobilization and conflict settlement.

The new women's movement tends to pursue a qualitative mobilization. Instrumental calculus does not dominate the forms of action. Communication and solidarity are not only the means to an end but values in themselves. The focus is not so much on the number of activists but on right attitudes. Thus it is not surprising that "no national organization of any duration has ever been established by the women's liberation movement in any country" (Dahlerup 1986, p. 8). More important than sheer numbers are the intensity and authenticity of commitment, the range of alteration of consciousness, and changes in personal behavior. Accordingly, many activities in the women's movement, especially self-help and consciousness-raising groups, remain invisible to the public. On the other hand, problems that are generally considered private (e.g., domestic violence against women, division of labor between couples), are purposely made public in accord with the slogan "the personal is political." So far, conventional, ritualized forms and methods of influencing the political decision-making process have not been pursued. Whenever the women's movement has entered the realm of established politics (e.g., to modify or abolish the abortion law or to promote an anti-discrimination law), it has definitely preferred provocative actions rather than traditional lobbying. The movement symbolically challenged the established tactics of interest-group politics and the persistent games of political bargaining. It is clear that, in doing so, the movement expects changes to arise not so much from institutional policies but from revolutionizing everyday behavior (cf. Schenk 1981, p. 191). This expectation reveals an essential difference between the new women's movement and the old movement, whose struggles focused on the right for the social and political inclusion of women (see Section IV).

The emphasis in the environmental movement is different from that in the women's movement. For the environmental movement, influencing concrete policies is of central importance: members seek to tighten air pollution laws, for example, or stop the nuclear power program or prevent a local construction project from proceeding. In so far as the environmental movement focuses on the established political system, it cannot ignore the mechanisms, rules, and results of that system. But if the opportunities for conventional lobbying either do not exist or are consciously abandoned, the environmental movement is primarily tending to a policy of quantitative mobilization. Quantitative mobilization involves forming large membership organizations and broad coalitions, organizing information and campaigns and petitions, influencing polls, mobilizing for mass demonstrations, and acts of civil disobedience. Compared with these actions, immediate changes in social roles, lifestyles, and consumer behavior are of minor importance. Such behavioral changes may demonstrate the honourable intentions of the environmentalists vis-à-vis the public but will hardly impress the political establishment.

In summary, then, the women's movement and the environmental movement in West Germany do not in fact differ fundamentally with regard to their social basis of recruitment and their global political assumptions. Their forms of organization and mobilization, however, as well as their strategic preferences, are significantly different. Unlike the environmental movement, the women's movement lacks large, representative membership organizations, formal national coordinating committees, and "spokeswomen." Moreover, the women's movement pursues mainly a qualitative rather than quantitative mobilization, and so does not primarily try to influence political institutions directly or to participate in political power play.

How are the similarities and differences between the two movements to be explained? Are the aforementioned differences of a contingent or a structural nature? Are the absence of strong membership organizations and the infrequency of mass mobilizations in the women's movement unintentional, that is, an expression of inability or of internal disagreement?

Answering these questions requires a detour to clarify and differentiate the concept of NSMs for the purpose of a structural analysis.

III. ELEMENTS OF A STRUCTURAL APPROACH

A. Dimensions of a Diachronic Analysis

As mentioned above, social movements do not form stable and clearly definable social entities. They experience cycles of expansion and contraction, and their aims and strategies may change as well. Phases of self-reflection may alternate with spectacular activities. Which phenomena become visible for an external observer depends not only on the methods of investigation but also on the level of abstraction and the angle and time span of analysis. For example, only a broad historical perspective and a comparison of many movements allows us to try to determine whether there is any universal pattern of development, a kind of "natural life cycle" of social movements, as many observers claim (see Mayreder 1925; Dawson and Gettys 1935; Rammstedt 1978).

The following action focuses not on developmental stages of various movements but on the underlying "themes" that correspond to such movements. My analysis is based on the assumption that every movement of historical significance centers around one basic problem of a given society. Even if the concrete issues and organizational forms of a movement vary over time, a movement's theme remains its raison d'être and its Archimedic point of reference (cf. Turner 1969). Only when the historical question embodied in such a theme (e.g., the dispute between absolutism and liberalism about political and economic sovereignty; the struggle between capital and labor over the control of the means of production) is solved or neutralized, can its corresponding movement definitely disappear from the historical stage.

In identifying the theme of a movement, one should be aware that not every possible analytical dimension may provide an adequate answer and that each approach has its own strengths and limitations.

a. The advantage of studies focusing on manifest protest actions is the concreteness of their empirical data. Thus the material manifestations of social movements can be apprehended by a direct and close look at specific groups and protest events. This perspective is provided primarily by case studies. These studies, however, cover only a small part of a social movement's existence; they investigate only the tip of the iceberg. Consequently, other approaches, whether participant observations of the everyday life of these groups, or experimental group analyses, would be a vital complement. At any rate, I am not convinced that the hermeneutic reconstruction of perceptions of artificially composed groups (Touraine 1981) can unveil the historical meaning ("historicité") of a movement. I am also unsure whether in a methodologically more sophisticated research setting, carefully selected "natural" groups can mirror a total movement, as Melucci maintains (Melucci 1986).

b. Studies focusing on the complex institutional setting of a movement (economic background, power constellations, etc.) may reveal general opportunities for and restrictions on social movement activities, as well as the mutual impact of social movements and their environmental structure. Clearly these studies profit from the advantages of "middle-range approaches," that is, surveying many sequences of protest events (without knowing or having to know all the details) and connecting them with the frame of action. But these studies are likely to run the risk of "political overload" (Melucci 1984, p. 822) and to overlook the internal life of organizations and groups.

c.   On a third level of investigation social movements as units of analysis can be related to basic problems and "currents" within a society. These currents are sluggish, and, to contemporaries, usually invisible macrostructural developments. They are reflected solely at an aggregated level and are detectable only by longitudinal diachronical studies of the compound effect of numerous institutional alterations and changes in social values and world-views. Such changes are the macrostructural basis of social movements. They determine three things: the possibility that social movements will come into existence; the general subject of their discourses; and last but not least, diffuse collective moods that become the "sounding board" for particular movements. Studies on social movements which refer to this historical dimension may account for the significance of structural contradictions in a given society (e.g., strain in and between system and social integration; for these categories, see Lockwood 1964). These studies can provide as well—at least ex post facto— an account of the long-range effects of social movements. Only this broad perspective makes it possible to distinguish long-lasting structures from both cyclical and accidental phenomena (Tilly 1983). But this same wide-angle perspective also creates certain problems. Social reality appears as a panorama in which only the most striking phenomena are visible. The broad perspective facilitates the survey, yet at the same time the observer is removed from the microcosmos of social action. Delicate differences and minute facets, overshadowed by the major events of history and never (or not yet) crystallized into structural form, remain hidden. Thus the analysis runs the risk of getting stuck in empty abstractions, of not getting beyond global assumptions and hypotheses on the development and general alterations in the form of social movements. An especially condensed presentation, such as this article, is particularly susceptible to such pitfalls.

B.   Modernization and Social Movements

Moving to the historical level of analysis as a central point of reference, I now wish to draw on a specific concept of modernization.[2] Following Habermas, I use the term "modernization" to designate a historical development in epochal dimensions through which "system" and "life world" become increasingly decoupled and undergo processes of internal differentiation. The definite structural result of these processes is, on the one hand, the establishment of the modern territorial state and the ascendance of a capitalist economy, and, on the other, the splitting up of the once integrated spheres of culture (focused on cultural reproduction), society (focused on social integration), and personality (focused on socialization) (Habermas 1981). Even though Habermas emphasizes the difference between a "developmental logic" and a "developmental dynamics" (i.e., the concrete historical course with all its regional and temporal variations), he himself does not closely look at the real process, nor does he confront it with his evolutionary model (Habermas 1976).

The work of economic and social historians (e.g., Fernand Braudel, Simon Kuznets, Barrington Moore, Charles Tilly, Immanuel Wallerstein) demonstrates that processes of modernization have followed an unsteady course. Qualitative breakthroughs are followed by phases of consolidation which simply complete existing structures. Breakthroughs are connected to social upheavals, economic deprivations of certain strata and classes, the redistribution of power, and the emergence of new cultural patterns. In view of these historical analyses, one could argue that Habermas's vision of modernization processes should be broadened: attention should be paid to the phases of breakthroughs, that is, to the periods of relatively rapid generation of new structures, new values, and new world views. These breakthroughs in the spheres of "system" and "life world"—as well as related crises of systemic control and social integration—are not necessarily synchronic, and thus may not be experienced as a fundamental challenge for a given society as a whole. But should these crises occur simultaneously, their impact would probably be amplified.[3]

I argue that historically significant social movements formed primarily during, or in the wake of, such breakthroughs. This hypothesis does not necessarily imply that a boom in collective violence takes place at these times. Protest events may proliferate rather constantly over long periods (cf. Tilly et al. 1975) and must not be linked to the genesis of a movement.

Social movements can be classified with respect to their attitude vis-à-vis a concrete modernization process. Thus they can have a proactive, reactive, or ambivalent status.[4] Above all, the problems and contradictions in and between the spheres of "system" and "life world" constitute the basic structural parameters for social movements. They determine the general theme, that is, the content of social struggles. It is along these lines that the formation of major historical movements such as bourgeois liberalism or the labor movement have to be interpreted. They have put the fight for a social alternative (against feudalism and absolutism, against bourgeois capitalism) on the historical agenda. They have thus accelerated the process of modernization according to the given opportunities. In their most advanced versions, the utopias of these movements were designed as emancipatory "projects of reconciliation." Systemic and life world rationalization should be conducted simultaneously, taking into account their reciprocal effects. This meant that productive forces could unfold and individual capacities could develop without violating the sensible mechanisms of the reproduction of the external, social, and internal nature.

In the shadow of these large movements and their social opponents, other movements are to be found. These movements too refer to the social process of modernization either in an offensive position (e.g., the "old" women's movement), a defensive position (e.g., the antiurbanist tendencies at the eve of the last century), or a highly ambivalent position (e.g., the fascist movement).

C. New Social Movements

Like their antecedents, the NSMs can be seen as products and in part also as causes of a complex and encompassing breakthrough in the postwar decades, a push leading to the integration of the still existing traditional informal economic sectors into the capitalist mode of production (Lutz 1984), to the dissolution of the proletarian milieus and the growth of the new middle class, to the unfolding of the state-interventionist planning and welfare system, and to the spread of postmaterial values. One major effect of these changes was the narrowing of the dominating cleavage between labor and capital: industrial work lost its importance as a focus for economic conflicts and class identity.

Two other themes became relevant for social confrontations. First, rationalization of the life world produces conflicts centered around democratization, self-determination, and individualization. The countercultures of the 1960s, the student movement and the New Left, and the new women's movement are variations of a militant awakening and outburst that challenges established authorities, values, and social roles. This emancipatory "current" aims at, among other things, the delimitation of individual spaces, the redirection of conventional role patterns and ways of life, as well as the realization of radical-democratic, egalitarian demands in the name of social progress. Clearly these are modern goals, whose sources can be found in the Enlightenment.

In the early 1970s, another current was superimposed on the 1960s emancipatory tendency. This second current favors defensive protest directed at systemic rationalization and related to the unsolved and unexpected side effects of technological, economic, and politico-administrative modernization. Again the vanguard of this process was and is the "new middle class." Not directly involved in the industrial sphere of production, economically secure, sensitive to questions concerning the quality of life, and capable of articulating its views in public, this class is crucial to the promotion of social change. It challenges methods and means—the basic principles of modernization. To many in this new middle class, functional differentiation, calculable formal organization, increased productivity, and administrative centralization appear to be exceedingly inhumane principles, and they oppose these principles with values such as self-limitation, holism, community, and particularity. These values, of course, may also be the reference points for traditional, populist antimodernism. Thus Offe oversimplifies in asserting that the NSMs have a positive attitude toward the values of modernization but reject the means of modernization (Offe 1986).

These two basic currents and their diverse variations combine and form a specific mixture, depending on the matters of conflict, the social prerequisites of protests, and the political socialization of the activists. It is this combination of a proactive, modernist current and a reactive, antimodernist current which accounts for the ambivalent status of NSMs in general. If this global interpretation should prove to be correct, it provides grounds for identifying the "newness" of the NSMs, at least if the characteristics mentioned above are considered together:

- NSMs combine a militant, countercultural, emancipatory, and radical-democratic current with a defensive, antimodernistic current that reacts to the destructive consequences of systemic rationalization.[5]
- Themes and supporters of NSMs are not necessarily defined by class interests, economic deprivation, or political exclusion. In contrast to former versions of modernistic countercultures (the aesthetic avant-garde, or "bohemia") and to antimodernistic currents (agrarian populism in Europe), the social cores of NSMs are neither socially marginal nor economically threatened, nor do they exist in subculture niches.
- Unlike earlier manifestations of antimodernistic currents, NSMs are based upon a self-reflexive critique of reason and rationality. They use scientific arguments and promote an institutionalized "counter-science." In addition, they are highly politicized. They try to influence decisions and cultural modes that concern the whole of society.
- In contrast to the liberal-bourgeois movement and the workers' movement, NSMs do not perceive productivity, division of labor, and economy of time as guarantees of social progress.

Using this interpretation we can classify not only historical social forces (see Table 1) but also contemporary forces. On the two terrains ("system" and "life world") opponents are fighting for formally identical objectives (systemic control and / or autonomy of life world), but they rely on totally different values, perceptions of problems, and propositions for a solution (see Table 2).

In the horizontal direction, overlapping concerns and temporary coalitions may exist.[6] Limited similarities are also to be found in the diagonal direction (e.g., political demands for equality characterize both the women's movement and the neoliberals; the protection of nature is a concern of both the environmental movement and the "old" conservatives). Social democratic

Table 1.   Status of Historical Social Forces

Reactive	*Proactive*	*Ambivalent*
absolutism	liberal-bourgeois movement	petty bourgeoisie
nationalism	workers movement	
conservationism	old women's movement	
agrarian populism (Europe)		agrarian populism (USA)
		life reformers
	bohemia	German Youth Movement
		facism

Table 2.   Status and Constellation of Contemporary Social Forces

Forces/Themes	*Autonomy of "life world"*	*Systemic control*
	proactive:	reactive:
new social movements	women's movement youth protests	environmental movement peace movement
	alternative movement	
	reactive:	proactive:
counterforces	moral majority old conservatism	neoliberals neoconservatism
potential allies	social democrats	

forces, as extremely important allies of both the NSMs and some of the movement's opponents, are nowadays typically hybrids. Depending on the respective wing, Social Democrats tend to form alliances with either NSMs or neoconservatives/neoliberals (cf. Offe 1985).

IV.   THE WOMEN'S MOVEMENT AND ENVIRONMENTAL MOVEMENT: LOGICS, FIELDS OF ACTION, AND ARENAS

This general concept of (new) social movements offers an answer to the initial question—why the forms of organization and mobilization, as well as the strategies, of both movements differ. The answer lies in the respective logics of the two movements, and in their related fields of actions and arenas.

The literature contains various attempts to construct typologies of social movements (for an overview, see Raschke 1985, pp. 105 ff.). Most of these attempts fail to clarify the theoretical background of the typology, its criteria of classification, and its consequences for organizations and activities. For the concept of modernization sketched in this article, two basic types of movements and two respective logics can be distinguished. A movement concerned with the process of cultural rationalization will be termed "expressive" (or identity-oriented), whereas a movement fighting for the control of the systemic steering process will be called "instrumental" (or power-oriented). Obviously this typology is neither original nor sophisticated. It is inspired by Turner and Killian's distinction between power-oriented, value-oriented, and participation-oriented movements. Because it is difficult to separate a struggle for participation from questions of power, I prefer a dual typology (for similar concepts, see Cohen 1985; Raschke 1985, p. 396), which—in further steps not to be taken here—must be "historicized" to give it a more concrete meaning.

Distinct logics of social movements arise from their position in, and in relation to, the process of modernization. A logic is defined as a guiding principle whose recognition (or empirical validity) will elicit certain structural and behavioral consequences. Thus a "logic" signifies not a causal determination but probable results. Here the term logic is applied to social movements as units of analysis. A movement's logic defines a general field of action, the substantive matter of conflict between the movement and its opponents, and the movement's internal "rationale." Depending on the logic, the movement's industry (Zald and McCarthy 1980) will have characteristic features, even if not all concrete social movement organizations and actions must be guided by this logic.

I argue that the women's movement follows primarily an expressive logic, whereas the environmental movement tends toward an instrumental logic. What are the implications of these logics, and how can they be demonstrated?

It has been argued that a movement's logic accounts for its range and the preferred field of action and thus for its strategies and dominant types of action. Expressive movements focus on cultural symbols, and their legitimacy, interpretation, and application. Cultural codes are not to be prescribed and altered by physical force. In modern societies they are rather an option that needs to be permanently interpreted and justified. Cultural patterns are established, confirmed, challenged, and altered in communicative practices. Thus, social movements' resistance to prevailing cultural practices cannot be limited to verbal critique and/or changes of institutions. Resistance will only attain relevance in conjunction with the formation and expansion of dissenting cultural practices. Hence questions of form and identity, the use of symbols, and the reinterpretation of values are key factors in expressive movements.

Means and ends, forms and contents of activities are not perceived as having a hierarchical or instrumental relationship. (What Melucci maintains is characteristic of NSMs in general holds at least for their expressive aspect: "The form of the movement is the message." Melucci 1985, p. 801).

Instrumental movements try to achieve social change by influencing or taking over organized power. For that purpose they have to build up an effective counterforce. Such a force requires powerful organizations designed to collect and mobilize as many resources as possible and to use them strategically. Personal relations as well as subjective sentiments and claims are considered of secondary importance. Means and ends are likely to be separated, and the forms and activities of the movement are perceived as mere tools. This orientation can imply that the movement's aim—even if it is a vision of a peaceful society—may ultimately be pursued through physical defeat of the opponent or by repressing internal critique. The Leninist concept of cadre organization is clearly an outcome of such a pure instrumental logic.

The analytical construct of a movement logic should not blind us to the fact that empirical movements never represent pure forms. Movements with an expressive tendency must confront questions of power, for instance, when countercultural spheres of life have to be defended against administrative intervention and control. Instrumental movements, on the other hand, cannot totally ignore the feelings and values of their supporters and the need to create and maintain a collective identity, for their adherents are not welded together by coercion, and the movement's organizations are not usually able to offer material incentives to their supporters. Depending on the changing conditions of actual conflicts and the internal state of a movement, the prevailing forms of organization and action will alternate between the predominantly instrumental and the predominantly expressive. In practice we have to place movements, their respective movement industry, and individual movement organizations on a continuum between the analytical poles of the expressive and the instrumental dimension. Moreover, a movement that follows an expressve logic may involve some organizations and forms of action that have a prevailing instrumental orientation. I assume that, overall, these are exceptions to the rule, and that these exceptions can be explained by intervening variables, for example, the particular field of action or issue of a movement's organization or the composition of its leadership.

A further reservation must be made: ascribing a dominant logic to a concrete movement does not mean that this movement never shifts toward another logic. A movement's logic depends on a global historical situation, and as this situation may change fundamentally over decades and centuries, the movement's logic may change in turn. The historical course of the women's movement illustrates this phenomenon.

The former (or "old") women's movement followed primarily an instrumental logic. Its most important objective was the social and political inclusion of women: the right of women to participate in political meetings and parties, to have access to all educational institutions and professions, to have an equal and universal right to vote. For these purposes the movement also had to question the existing role of women—a role that clearly was also culturally determined. Nonetheless, the general hope was that, once women had gained access to all institutions, their gender role would be automatically transformed. The preferred focus of action was the public sphere. The movement's most important audience was the political decision-makers. Formalized women's associations and cooperation with sympathetic parties played a decisive role for the movement. Accordingly, once the demands for inclusion were realized step by step, the movement gradually lost momentum and its organizations dissolved.

The new women's movement is preoccupied with the struggle to change culture patterns. Its most important goal is not formal equality with men but liberation, the creation of a self-determined female identity. The field of action, thus defined, encompasses cultural reproduction and socialization as the spheres where gender roles are defined, offered, and overtaken: the marriage bed as well as the factory, the pub and the rostrum, women's groups and the army, the kindergarten and the scientific conference. The realm of institutional politics is just one of these fields of action, though it is certainly not the least important, as political decisions define the premises for many other social areas. Powerful membership organizations, structured like any pressure group, are hardly acceptable in the new women's movement, because they reduce chances for the direct expression of sentiments and hinder immediate self-determination. In addition, such organizations are frequently inadequate to the character and social meaning of feminist concerns. What male chauvinist, for instance, would be persuaded to change his everyday behavior simply by the sheer number of organized and/or demonstrating women? Consequently, the women's movement concentrates its energies on methods of qualitative mobilization:

1.   On the one hand, the creation of autonomous cultural practices and the establishment of a specific feminist infrastructure;
2.   On the other hand, the abolition of sexist institutions and modes of behavior through techniques of provocation and the ironic exaggeration and inversion of connotations (critique of "male" language, symbolic castration, positive evaluation of witches, etc.).

In contrast to the new women's movement, the environmental movement fights primarily for landmark political decisions. Ecological risks and destruction are to be limited, mastered, or, in the future, to be avoided as much as possible. At least at first, the relevant frame of reference encompasses concrete policies. (What is to be decided?) Eventually, however, the movement may challenge the very prerequisites for political decision making. (Who is to decide what, according to what, and according to which rules?) The means and techniques of political intervention may embrace the whole spectrum of political activities: pressure group politics, creating parties, litigation, mass rallies, and civil disobedience. Contrasted with these methods of direct political intervention, changes in individual lifestyles (e.g., restriction of private energy consumption, interaction in small groups) remain of secondary importance. Though the movement's energies focus on quantitative mobilization, this does not necessarily require large and formal membership organizations. Grass-roots groups may have an astonishing capacity to mobilize people. In the long run, however, strong organizations are most likely to be in a position to challenge the established political institutions, to act quickly, permanently, and competently. No wonder that in recent years this kind of organization has become more and more important. And it is not by accident that the environmental movements in various countries have given rise to Green Parties, whereas feminist parties, if they are established at all (as in Belgium, for example), remain totally marginal.

Up to now I have used the term "fields of action" in a very general way. But for conceptual clarity as well as for clarifying my initial question, it seems necessary to differentiate several elements this term embraces. First, one must emphasize that the field of action of social movements is larger and much more complex than the terrain of their manifest struggles. There are "internal" fields of action: organizations and groups within a social movement establish a daily routine that is not at all, or only indirectly, related to external conflicts. There must be an exchange of experiences; information must be collected and evaluated; it is necessary to cope with factionalism and problems of group dynamics; friendship ties are to be maintained, and so on. A closer look at a large field reveals even finer distinctions: fields of action designed exclusively for core activists; other fields reserved for specific tendencies; yet others that are open to every movement adherent; and some fields of action that are semipublic.

On the other hand, the field of action that is visible to a large public can also be qualified. Here I refer to the notion of "arena." Unlike scholars who introduced (Lowi 1964 and 1972) or elaborated and empirically applied this concept (Kitschelt 1980), I do not conceive of an arena as a relatively closed system of bargaining and decision making, generally hidden from the public. My definition is closer to the original meaning of the term: an arena is an action system in which, under the eyes of the public, a major fight between a social movement and its opponents takes place. The basic components of an arena are the conflictual parties and the audience, whose neutrality or support may be a relevant factor in the outcome of the struggle. Thus the opponents are not only engaged with each other, but they devote much of their energy to the public bystanders. The actors in the arena, in contrast to those in the "theater," do not have predefined roles or texts. The object and end of the conflict, the identity of the two opponents, the possibility of coalition building, the partisanship of the uninvolved are variable within certain limits. Moreover, arenas are "organically" embedded in the flow of social changes and events and in an institutional context. Thus the agents mobilize and introduce their past experiences, construct parallels with other arenas and conflicts, and, from time to time, concentrate their energies on other struggles, or retire altogether.

Arenas of the women's movement were opened up by conflicts and campaigns focused on abortion policy, sexism in private and public spheres, physical violence against women, and discrimination at the working place. Relevant arenas of the environmental movement were established by conflicts about the nuclear energy program or policies to reduce air pollution.

Though comparing the arenas of both movements reveals striking formal similarities (e.g., both fight against a federal law), the different logics of the two movements account for differences in the significance of the activities. The existence of the environmental movement, or at least of some of its sectors and components, is intimately linked to the outcome of relevant conflicts. Contingent political decisions (e.g., abandoning nuclear energy production) may bring about the end of the movement. The existence of the women's movement, however, is not endangered by political decisions, although it may be influenced by them. Therefore arenas have a different status for each of the two movements. The environmental movement tends to perceive each major fight as "the last battle;" for the women's movement, political issues are not the raison d'être. Even outstanding political victories and the support of a great majority will hardly result in the "liberation" of women. Thus it is easier for the women's movement than for the environmental movement to maintain some detachment from political conflicts, to revitalize them, to view them as just one link in the long chain of past and future battles in the struggle for women's liberation. Compared to the environmental movement, the women's movement seems to spend much more energies on internal or semipublic fields of action. Moreover, the organizational structure of the women's movement makes any attempt to fight the opponent with his own weapons pointless. This too, encourages the use of symbolic actions and qualitative forms of mobilization in arenas where the women's movement is engaged.

There is at least one significant exception to my view of the women's movement. In contrast to the women's movement in all the West European countries, the women's movement in the USA includes strong, powerful, and nationwide membership organizations (in particular the "National Organization for Women," see Costain 1981; Gelb 1987; Freeman 1981). This fact runs counter to my overall argument and could be raised as an objection to my analysis. In this case, one must examine the weight of various sectors within the U.S. women's movement, the specific character of the political culture (e.g., the strong pragmatic tradition) and of the politico-institutional setting (e.g., the relatively open access to the decision-making system, which encourages lobbying (cf. Kitschelt 1985; Mayer 1985). This exception also demonstrates the need for systematic cross-national comparison (for designs, potentialities, and risks of comparative approaches, see Tarrow 1986). Such a comparison could demonstrate the extent and manner to which national opportunity structure can shape the "logically" given features of a movement.

V. SUMMARY AND CONCLUSIONS

From a problematic centered on how to explain the striking differences between the organization and activities of the women's movement and those of the environmental movement, a macrostructural approach emerges. The general argument underlying this approach is that social movements are linked to deeply rooted structural changes that have been identified as modernization breakthroughs in the spheres of "system" and "life world." These breakthroughs create, on the one hand, extended demands, expectations, and chances for articulation and action. On the other hand, they produce unforeseen and alarming side effects. The new women's movement is proactively concerned with processes of the "life world." The environmental movement reacts defensively to negative outcomes of systemic modernization. These different points of reference each have specific implications: The women's movement is based primarily on an expressive logic. It focuses on cultural codes, gender-specific identity, and role definition. The environmental movement, however, focuses much more on the control and/or improvement of systemic steering mechanisms. For this movement, the struggle for power is a dominant concern. Thus the two movements tend to have different fields of action in which political arenas, as places of public discourse and struggle, have a different status, meaning, and scope.

The field of the women's movement encompasses all places and modes of cultural reproduction and socialization, even some usually considered "private." Objectives such as consciousness-raising, changes in role patterns and sexist language, the questioning of gender-specific discrimination in daily life, and the creation of a female identity are seen as constitutive. Except for its liberal wing, which does not pursue the struggle for formal equality with men, the movement does not assign a privileged role to the fight against representatives of the established political forces per se. Activities primarily follow a course of qualitative mobilization based on symbolic actions and the establishment of a countercultural infrastructure. Most efforts are directed toward changing the behavior in and of small groups.

In contrast, the environmental movement's battleground is essentially the field of institutional politics. Consequently, the politico-institutional setting and the methods of influencing or exercising political power are of prime importance for the movement. Forms of quantitative mobilization—building large membership organizations and broad alliances, lobbying, mass rallies—thus play a decisive role. Except for its radical wing of political ecologists, the environmental movement regards personal problems, questions of identity, and daily life behavior as of only minor importance.

In conclusion, the differences between the two movements mentioned above are due primarily to global structural parameters.

This chapter presents a macrostructural approach applied to an empirical question. The principal strengths and failures of such an approach (as well as competing approaches) are well known. Thus an important task for further research would be not simply to confront macro- and microstructural analysis in isolation (which could lead to a shrugging of shoulders on both sides), but rather to erect conceptual bridges. My proposal—admittedly still fairly unsophisticated—to differentiate several processional levels of analysis and to move from highly abstract to more concrete dimensions is intended as one such "bridging" effort that evaluates themes, logics, fields of actions, arenas, organizations and actions, and asks how these dimensions are related to each other. In a more detailed application of such an approach it would be necessary to assess on each processional level the impact of intervening variables (such as national opportunity structures, the environment and specific issues of various movements components, endogenous parameters of the latter, precipitating incidents, etc.) in order to explain the variety of forms and actions.

Comparing two movements within the same national setting demonstrates that a discussion about the political or cultural significance of the NSMs is of little help as long as the inherent "logics" of individual movements are not sufficiently clarified. Whereas the analysis of a movement that—on the basis of a close empirical investigation—can be classified as predominantly instrumental rightly directs our attention to political factors and corresponding activities, the analysis of an expressive movement must, above all, decipher the movement's cultural practices and codes.

NOTES

1. At present, this league includes 42 membership organizations and claims to represent 10 million individual members. Because of its heterogenity and its internal contradictions, the league is generally handicapped in acting as a powerful political force. Many German women do not even know that the league exists.

2. Unfortunately, the term modernization evokes associations that I want to avoid. Here it means neither the "rationalization" of or within a firm, an industrial branch, or a public administration office, nor the process of adapting "underdeveloped" countries to the "model" of capitalist states, generally advanced as a mode of modernization, the U.S. being the prime "model."

3. In my view, the social conflicts in Central Europe in the first half of the seventeenth century, the revolutionary France in the eighteenth century, and the emergent fascism in Germany could be interpreted as a simultaneous breakdown of system and social integration.

4. Tilly's typology of "proactive," "reactive," and "competitive" action depends on the status and claims of collective actors in concrete situations. In my view, "competitive action" is just one

of several ways to carry out a conflict from a proactive or reactive position. Thus I would advance the term "ambivalent" for cases in which a movement simultaneously takes a proactive position toward modernization in one dimension (e.g., systemic rationalization) and a reactive position with respect to another dimension.

5.   At least to some extent, these characteristics typified various tendencies within the "utopian socialism" in the first decades of the nineteenth century and for communist communitarian projects in the 1920s. But compared to the NSMs, these were marginal experiments.

6.   On the whole, the "alternative movement," which includes the network of cooperatives, self-run service centers, countercultural journals, etc., typically does not clearly emphasize the expressive or the instrumental dimension. Here the aspects of "autonomy of life world" and of "systemic control" are closely interrelated. Of course this interrelation is also characteristic of some groups within the other movements placed in the left or the right column of Table 2.

REFERENCES

Balbus, Isaak D. 1982. *Marxism and Domination: A Neo-Hegelian, Feminist, Psychoanalytic Theory of Sexual, Political, and Technological Liberation.* Princeton: Princeton University Press.

Berger, Peter L., Brigitte Berger, and Hansfried Kellner. 1973. *The Homeless Mind: Modernization and Consciousness.* New York: Random House.

Brand, Karl-Werner. 1985. *Neue Soziale Bewegungen in Westeuropa und den USA. Ein Internationaler Vergleich.* Frankfurt: Campus.

Brand, Karl-Werner. 1983. *Aufbruch in Eine Andere Gesellschaft. Neue Soziale Bewegungen in der Bundesrepublik.* Frankfurt: Campus.

Cohen, Jean L. 1985. "Strategy or identity: New theoretical paradigms and contemporary social movements." *Social Research* 52:663-716.

Costain, Anne N. 1981. "Representing women: The transition from social movement to interest group." *Western Political Quarterly* 34:100-113.

Dahlerup, Drude. 1986. "Introduction." Pages 1-25 in Drude Dahlerup (ed.), *The New Women's Movement: Feminism and Political Power in Europe and the USA.* London: Sage.

Dawson, Carl A. and Warner E. Gettys. 1935. *An Introduction to Sociology.* Rev. ed. New York: Ronald Press.

Donati, Paolo R. 1984. "Organization between Movement and Institution." *Social Science Information* 23:837-59.

Freeman, Jo. 1981. "Resource Mobilization and Strategy: A Model for Analyzing Social Movement Organization Actions." Pages 167-89 in Mayer N. Zald and John D. McCarthy (eds.), *The Dynamics of Social Movements.* Cambridge, Mass.: Winthrop.

Frevert, Ute. 1986. *Frauen-Geschichte. Zwischen Bürgerlicher Verbesserung und Neuer Weiblichkeit.* Frankfurt: Suhrkamp.

Gelb, Joyce. 1987. "Social Movement Success: A Comparative Analysis of Feminism in the U.S. and the U.K." In Mary Katzenstein and Carol Mueller (eds.), *The Women's Movement of the United States and Western Europe: Consciousness, Political Opportunity, and Public Policy.* Philadelphia: Temple University Press.

Gundelach, Peter. 1984. "Social transformation and new forms of voluntary associations." *Social Science Information* 23:1049-81.

Habermas, Jürgen. 1976. "Zum thema: Geschichte und evolution." *Geschichte und Gesellschaft* 2:310-57.

Habermas, Jürgen. 1981. *Theorie des kommunikativen Handelns.* 2 vols. Frankfurt: Suhrkamp.

Japp, Klaus P. 1984. "Selbsterzeugung Oder Fremdverschulden. Thesen Zum Rationalisums in den Theorien Sozialer Bewegungen."

Kitschelt, Herbert. 1980. *Kernenergiekonflikt. Arena Eines Gesellschaftlichen Konflikts.* Frankfurt: Campus.

Kitschelt, Herbert. 1983. *Politik und Energie. Energie-Technologiepolitiken in den USA, der Bundesrepublik Deutschland, Frankreich und Schweden.* Frankfurt: Campus.

Kitschelt, Herbert. 1985. "Zur Dynamik neuer Sozialer Bewegungen in den USA. Strategien Gesellschaftlichen Wandels und 'American Exceptionalism.' "*Neue Soziale Bewegungen in Westeurope und den USA.* Frankfurt: Campus.

Kitschelt, Herbert. 1988. "Political opportunity structures and protest: Antinuclear movements in four democracies." *British Journal of Political Science* 16:57-85.

Klandermans, Bert. 1986. "New Social Movements and Resource Mobilization: The European and the American Approach." *International Journal of Mass Emergencies and Disasters.* Special issue, *Comparative Perspectives and Research on Collective Behavior and Social Movements* 4:13-37.

Leif, Thomas. 1985. *Die professionelle Bewegung. Friedensbewegung von Innen.* Bonn: Forum Europa Verlag.

Lipset, Seymour Martin. 1981. "The Revolt Against Modernity." Pages 451-500 in P. Torsvik (ed.), *Mobilization, Center-Periphery Structures and Nation Building.* Bergen: University Press.

Lockwood, David. 1964. "Social Integration and System Integration." Pages 244-57 in G.K. Zollschan and W. Hirsch (eds.), *Explorations in Social Change.* Boston: Houghton Mifflin.

Lowi, Theodore W. 1964. "Four systems of policy, politics, and choice." *Public Administration Review* 32:298-310.

Lutz, Burkhart. 1984. *Der kurze Traum immerwährender Prosperität.* Frankfurt: Campus.

Mayer, Margit. 1985. "Urban Social Movements and Beyond: New Linkages Between Movement Sectors and the State in West Germany and the United States." Paper presented at the Fifth International Conference of Europeanists, Washington, D.C., October 18-20.

Mayreder, Rosa. 1925. *Der Typische Verlauf Sozialer Bewegungen.* Vienna: W. Braumüller.

Melucci, Alberto. 1984. "An end to social movements." *Social Science Information* 23:819-35.

Melucci, Alberto. 1985. "The symbolic challenge of contemporary movements." *Social Research* 52: 789-816.

Müller-Rommel, Ferdinand. 1984. "The Followers of New Social Movements in Western Europe." Paper presented at the Annual Meeting of the American Political Science Association, Washington, D.C., August 30-September 2.

Nelkin, Dorothy and Michael Pollak. 1982. *The Atom Besieged: Extraparliamentary Dissent in France and Germany.* Cambridge, Mass.: MIT Press.

Offe, Claus. 1982. "New social movements: Challenging the boundaries of institutional politics." *Social Research* 52:817-68.

Offe, Claus. 1986. "Die Utopie der Null-Option. Modernität und Modernisierung als Politische Gütekriterien." Pages 97-117 in Johannes Berger (ed.), *Die Moderne-Kontinuitäten und Zäsuyren. Soziale Welt.* Sonderband 4. Göttingen: Schwarz.

Rammstedt, Otthein. 1978. *Soziale Bewegung.* Frankfurt: Suhrkamp.

Raschke, Joachim. 1985. *Soziale Bewegungen. Ein Historisch-Systematischer Grundriss.* Frankfurt: Campus.

Roth, Orland. 1985. "Neue Soziale Bewegungen in der Politischen Kultur der Bundesrepublik—eine Vorläufige Skizze." Pages 20-82 in Karl-Werner Brand (ed.), *Neue soziale Bewegungen in Westeuropa und den USA.* Frankfurt: Campus.

Rucht, Dieter. 1984. "Zur Organisation der Neuen Sozialen Bewegungen." Pages 609-20 in Jürgen W. Falter, C. Fenner, and M. Th. Greven (eds.), *Politische Willensbildung und Interessenvermittlung.* Opladen: Westdeutscher Verlag.

Rucht, Dieter. 1987. "Von der Bewegung zur Institution? Organisationsstrukturen der Ökologiebewegung." In Roland Roth and Dieter Rucht (eds.), *Neue soziale Bewegungen in der Bundesrepublik Deutschland.* Frankfurt: Campus (forthcoming).

Rucht, Dieter. 1988. "Environmental Movement Organizations in West Germany and France: Structure and Interorganizational Relations." In Bert Klandermans (ed.), *Organizing for Change: Social Movement Organizations Across Cultures*. Greenwich, Conn.: JAI (forthcoming).

Schenk, Herrad. 1981. *Die feministische Herausforderung. 150 Jahre Frauenbewegung in Deutschland*. Munich: Beck.

Tarrow, Sidney. 1983. *Struggling to Reform: Social Movements and Policy Change during Cycles of Protest*. Western Societies Paper No. 15. Ithaca, N.Y.: Cornell University.

Tarrow, Sidney. 1986. "Comparing social movement participation in Western Europe and the United States: Problems, uses, examples and a proposal for synthesis." *International Journal of Mass Emergencies and Disasters*. Special Issue, *Comparative Perspectives and Research on Collective Behavior and Social Movements* 4:145-70.

Tilly, Charles. 1977. "Hauptformen kollektiver Aktion in Westeuropa 1500-1975." *Geschichte und Gesellschaft* 3:153-63.

Tilly, Charles. 1983. "Big Structures, Large Processes, Huge Comparisons." CRSO Working Paper No. 295. Ann Arbor: University of Michigan.

Tilly, Charles, Louise Tilly, and Richard Tilly. 1975. *The Rebellious Century: 1830-1930*. Cambridge: Harvard University Press.

Touraine, Alain. 1973. *Production de la Société*. Paris: Seuil.

Touraine, Alain. 1978. *La Voix et le Regard*. Paris: Seuil.

Turner, Ralph. 1969. "The theme of contemporary social movements." *British Journal of Sociology* 20:390-405.

Turner, Ralph H. and Lewis M. Killian. 1972. *Collective Behavior*. 2d ed. Englewood Cliffs, N.J.: Prentice-Hall.

Watts, Nicholas, S.J. 1987. "Mobilisierungspotential und Gesellschaftspolitische Bedeutung der Neuen Sozialen Bewegungen. Ein Vergleich der Länder der Europäischen Gemeinschaft." In Roland Roth and Dieter Rucht (eds.), *Neue Soziale Bewegungen in der Bundesrepublik Deutschland*. Frankfurt: Campus (forthcoming).

Zald, Mayer N. and John D. McCarthy. 1980. "Social Movement Industries: Competition and Cooperation Among Movement Organizations." Pages 1-20 in Louis Kriesberg (ed.), *Research in Social Movements, Conflict, and Change*. Vol. 3. Greenwich, Conn.: JAI.

GETTING INVOLVED:
IDENTITY AND MOBILIZATION
IN SOCIAL MOVEMENTS

Alberto Melucci

I. COLLECTIVE ACTION IS A SOCIAL CONSTRUCTION

In the traditional analysis of collective phenomena we can find two recurrent orientations. Sometimes the emphasis has been laid on the pure factuality of collective action, which thus appears as *action without actor,* an accidental sum of individual events. Crowd psychology thus emphasizes imitation, irrationality, contagion, or suggestion. In the sociology of collective behavior, collective action has been represented as a reactive response to the crisis or disorders of the social system. Another traditional view has sought the "objective foundations of the observed phenomenon in the social structure, and has derived the action from the analysis of a social condition that the actors would seem to have in common. Here one finds an *actor without action,* as the gap between the objective conditions and the empirically observed collective behaviors always proves impossible to bridge. Marx's old problem (how to pass

International Social Movement Research, Vol. 1, pages 329-348.
Supplement to Research in Social Movements, Conflicts and Change
Copyright © 1988 by JAI Press Inc.
All rights of reproduction in any form reserved.
ISBN: 0-89232-955-6

from class in itself to class for itself, from class condition to class action) remains, unsolved, in the background.

These orientations, part of the traditional studies of collective phenomena which continue to influence contributions in this field to the present day, share two epistemological assumptions that it is useful to make explicit. First, the collective phenomenon—whether a panic, a social movement, or a revolutionary process—is treated as a *unitary empirical datum*. That is, in the first place, it is assumed that the empirical *unity* of the phenomenon, as it is perceived and interpreted by the observer, really exists. The occurrence of certain concomitant individual behaviors forms a unitary *gestalt* that is transferred from the phenomenological to the conceptual level and acquires ontological consistency: the collective reality exists as a thing. At the same time a second assumption insinuates itself into the process of reification of the "collective phenomenon" object: the idea that the collective dimension of social action is an incontrovertible fact, a *given* that does not merit further investigation.

In recent years critical reflection has begun to recognize the questionable nature of these assumptions. Changing historical conditions and the evolution of the theoretical debate have both contributed to this recognition. The conflicts that gave rise to the theory and the analysis of collective action are historically linked to forms of action in which the crisis of the old order, social struggles in the strict sense, and struggles for citizenship all played an important part.

The action of the working class in the phase of industrial capitalism served as a model, now feared, now favored, for the study of collective phenomena. This action combined resistance to the decline of pre- or protoindustrial forms of production, struggles directly connected with the development of the capitalistic factory system, and demands for access to the State and for the extension of citizenship. The industrial conflict was thus inextricably bound up with the national problem and with that of extending political rights to excluded social groups. It was in this historical context that the idea of the social movements as historical agents marching toward a destiny of liberation, or crowds in the grip of suggestion and under the control of a few agitators, developed.[1]

Today we find ourselves at the end of this cycle, not because the struggles for citizenship are over or because there are no democratic spaces left to conquer, but because the different aspects of the social conflicts have increasingly become separated. Conflicts concerning the social relationships constituting a system, on the one hand, and the struggles for extension of citizenship—for granting excluded or underprivileged groups their rights and initiating them in the "rules of the game"—on the other, tend to become distinct and to involve different actors. Different again are the forms of action which express resistance to the process of modernization and its worldwide extension. This differentiation of fields, of actors, of forms of action does not admit the stereotypical image of collective actors moving on the historical stage like the characters of an epic drama; and equally disqualified is the opposite and specular image of an amorphous crowd guided solely by its gregarious instincts.

Changes in the historical frame of reference have been accompanied by a new theoretical awareness, linked to the evolution of the debate within the social sciences. The perception of a collective phenomenon as a unitary empirical datum reveals a very fragile, even nonexistent, analytical foundation. The progress of reflection and research in the sociological and psychological fields leads us to consider the collective phenomena as the result of multiple processes that favor or impede the formation and maintenance of the cognitive frameworks and the systems of relationships necessary for action. What in many analyses of collective action is taken for granted, that is, the existence of a relatively unified actor, is in this view a problem to be explained. The collective phenomenon is in fact the product of differentiated social processes, of orientations of action, of elements of structure and motivation that can combine in a variable manner. The problem of the analysis becomes that of explaining how these elements are held together, how a "collective" actor is formed and maintains itself.[2]

One of the most important corollaries of this evolution of theoretical orientations is the possibility of improving our comprehension of collective phenomena in terms of *action*. The advances in cognitive and constructive theories of human action have helped us consider collective phenomena as processes in which the actors produce meanings, communicate, negotiate, and make decisions. The actors, in other words, are capable of going beyond the linear logic of stimulus-response. Thus collective action cannot be explained either by pure structural determinants (e.g., in terms of suggestion, imitation, or manipulation).

We can now return to the implicit assumptions common to the tradition and examine their consequences for the analysis of collective phenomena. In considering collective action as a datum and an empirical unity, the traditional approaches impeded the formulation of a number of crucial questions, which only today have come to be posed explicitly in the scientific debate and have revealed themselves to be of great significance for any theory of collective action:

- By means of what processes do the actors construct a common action?
- How is the unity of the various parts, levels, and orientations present in an empirical phenomenon of collective action produced?
- What are the processes and relationships through which individuals become involved in collective action?

If we turn to the tradition to find answers to these questions (necessarily only implicit answers, for the questions were never posed as such) we encounter two recurrent orders of explanations: structural contradictions or dysfunctions of the social system, on the one hand, and psychological differences or individual motivations on the other. In any case, none of these factors is in itself capable of satisfactorily answering the questions.

In fact both the macrostructural factors and the individual variables imply an unbridgeable gap between the level of explanation proposed and the concrete process that allows a certain number of individuals to act together. The explanation founded on the common structural condition of the actors takes for granted their capacity to perceive, evaluate, and decide what they have in common; it ignores, in other words, the very processes that enable the actors to define (or prevent them from defining) the situation as susceptible of common action. On the other hand, individual differences and motivations never suffice to explain how certain individuals come to recognize themselves in and become part of a more or less integrated "we."

These impasses can be overcome only by calling into question the "ingenuous" assumption of collective action as a datum and a unity. It is necessary to question the datum in order to ascertain how it is produced and to dissect the empirical unity in order to discover the plurality of analytical elements,—of orientations, significations, and relationships—which converge in the same phenomenon.

In the view I am proposing here collective action is thus considered as the result of purposes, resources, and limits, as a purposive orientation constructed by means of social relationships within a system of opportunities and constraints. It therefore cannot be considered the simple effect of structural preconditions or the expression of values and beliefs. Individuals acting collectively "construct" their action by means of "organized" investments: that is, they define in cognitive terms the field of possibilities and limits which they perceive, while at the same time activating their relationships so as to give sense to their "being together" and to the goals they pursue. Each time we observe a certain number of individuals acting collectively we confront a *multipolar action system*. Collective action is not a unitary empirical phenomenon, and the unity, if it exists, should be considered as a result rather than a starting-point, a fact to be explained rather than evidence. The events in which individuals act collectively combine different orientations, involve multiple actors, and implicate a system of the opportunities and constraints that shape their relationships.

The actors "produce" the collective action because they are able to define themselves and to define their relationship with the environment (other actors, available resources, opportunities and obstacles). The definition that the actors construct is not linear but produced by interaction, negotiation, and the opposition of different orientations. Individuals contribute to the formation of a "we" (more or less stable and integrated according to the type of action) by rendering common and laboriously adjusting at least three orders of orientations: those relating to the *ends* of the actions (i.e., the sense the action has for the actor); those relating to the *means* (i.e., the possibilities and the limits of the action); and finally those relating to relationships with the *environment* (i.e., the field in which the action takes place).

The multipolar action system of a collective actor is thus organized along three axes (ends, means, environment) that can be imagined as a set of interdependent vectors in a state of mutual tension. The "organizational" form of the action is the manner in which the collective actor seeks to give an acceptable and lasting unity to such a system, which is continuously subject to tensions. In fact, the collective action has to meet multiple and contrasting requirements. It is never the simple expression of a purposeful intention but is constructed by means of the resources available to the actors and according to the possibilities/obstacles provided by a certain environment. Ends, means, and environment continually create possibilities of tension: the objectives are not adequate to the means or vice versa, the environment is rich or poor in relevant resources, the means are more or less congruent to the field of the action, and so on. There are continual tensions even within the single axes: for example, in the definition of ends, between short- and long-term objectives; in the choice of means, between the use of resources to achieve efficacy and their use to consolidate solidarity; in relationships with the environment, between internal balance and external exchanges, and so on.

The collective actors continually negotiate and renegotiate all these aspects of their action. The functions of leadership and the forms of organization represent attempts to give a more durable and predictable order to these definitions. When collective phenomena are considered, attention is normally focused on the more visible aspects of the action (events, mobilizations, acts of violence); these visible aspects however, are manifestations of a process working at the analytical level I have outlined, which is normally ignored. Events, mobilizations, forms of discontent or of enthusiasm can occur and can even continue because a collective actor has succeeded in realizing, and in the course of the action continues to realize, a certain integration between those orientations I have indicated. Facilitating factors of a conjunctural type (for example, the opportunity structure, whether political or other; the existence of entrepreneurs; the degree of integration or of crisis of the environment, etc.) certainly contribute to the explosion of collective phenomena. But these factors could not operate without the actor's capacity to perceive and integrate them in an interactive and negotiated system of orientations concerning the ends, means, and environment of the action. This "social construction" of the "collective" is continually at work when a form of collective action occurs. A failure or a break in this constructive process makes the action impossible.

Having clarified the sense in which collective action is a *product,* I can now introduce some distinctions that indicate the existence, in the same empirical phenomenon, of a *plurality* of analytical dimensions. The "collective" character

of an event can be connoted in phenomenological terms by the simple presence
of several individuals who, in contiguity of space and time, manifest common
behaviors. But it is easy to see that this undifferentiated empirical connotation
is subject to at least three analytical distinctions:

1. Some collective phenomena imply *solidarity,* that is the capacity of the
    actors to recognize themselves and to be recognized as part of the same
    social unit. Others have the character of phenomena of *aggregation*
    (Alberoni 1977): that is, they can be reduced to the level of the individual
    without losing their morphological characteristics and have an
    orientation exclusively toward the exterior, rather than toward the
    group. In a strike one will probably find a prevalence of solidarity, while
    a panic will be closer to the pole of aggregative behavior.
2. Some collective phenomena imply the presence of a *conflict,* that is of
    an opposition between two (or more) actors competing for the control
    of resources to which they attribute value. Other collective phenomena,
    however, come into being through the actors' *consensus* on the rules
    and procedures for the control and use of valued resources. An
    antinuclear demonstration will probably imply a conflictual orientation
    and will differ in this respect from a march of enthusiastic football
    supporters after a match.
3. Some collective phenomena involve *transgressing the limits of
    compatibility* of the system of social relationships in which the action
    takes place. I call limits of compatibility the range of variations that a
    system can tolerate without modifying its own structure. Other collective
    phenomena can be described as forms of *adaptation of order* in that they
    are situated within the limits of structural variability of a system of social
    relationships. Many organizational grievances, which affect the simple
    redistribution of rewards within a firm, are good examples of the latter
    situation. But when a struggle aims to change the decision-making
    structure of an organization, the collective action implies a redefinition
    of the present boundaries of the organization itself.[3]

This set of analytical distinctions permits us to separate different orientations
of collective action which can be found in variable combinations in the
empirical phenomena. For example, in the same empirical case one could find
a regulated competition of interests observing the limits of a given social order;
orientations of action that extend the conflict beyond the system's limits of
compatibility; collective behaviors which are the sum of atomized individual
aims (as in some crowd behaviors); deviant behaviors that transgress the shared
rules, without, however, implying conflict; and so on.[4]

Recognition of this plurality of meanings, suggests research questions that
are usually ignored or which receive commonplace answers: how do the actors

"construct" their action so that we can observe an apparently unified empirical behavior? What facilitates or impedes the integration of the different orientations in a given collective phenomenon? How does the involvement or defection of the individual occur, if one takes into account this plurality of meanings? I shall attend to these questions in the following sections, explaining their importance for an understanding of contemporary collective phenomena, and then indicating some elements of an answer.

II. AN EPISTEMOLOGICAL MISUNDERSTANDING: THE CASE OF THE "NEW SOCIAL MOVEMENTS"

A good example of the ambiguities to which the analysis of collective phenomena is subject, in the absence of a clarification of the conceptual problems I have referred to, is provided by the debate on the "new social movements." In the last 25 years, forms of collective action have developed in areas previously untouched by social conflicts; new actors have emerged whose organizational models and repertoires of action differ from those of the earlier social movements.

The sociological significance of these collective phenomena inspired, especially in the second half of the 1970s, a considerable number of studies, both theoretical and empirical, concerning the major western countries. One of the recurrent questions in the debate over these collective phenomena concerns the "novelty" of the modern conflicts: what is "new" in the "new social movements"? This debate constitutes a revealing frame of reference because it exposes epistemological ambiguities that have important consequences for the substantive comprehension of a phenomenon that plays an important part in the more advanced social systems. As one of those who introduced the term "new social movements" to sociological literature (Melucci 1978, 1980), I have observed with embarrassment the progressive ontologization of this expression, which in the course of the debate came to be characterized as a veritable "paradigm." Many recent contributions have reproposed the "paradigm of the new social movements," whether in terms of empirical research or as one of the poles of a comparison of the European and U.S. approaches.[5] The problem of the "novelty" of the "new movements" has been widely discussed and criticized in this literature. To me, however, the debate seems to be centered on a false problem. "Newness" is by definition a relative concept, whose temporary function is to emphasize some comparative differences between classes of phenomena (in this case between the traditional forms of class conflict and the emergent forms of collective action). But if the analysis is incapable of going beyond this conventional definition and cannot determine the specific and distinctive characteristics of the "new" phenomena, the accent on the "novelty" ends up as an easy cover for an underlying conceptual weakness.

Without an awareness of the relative and transitory nature of the concept of "new social movement," critics and analysts run the risk of becoming entrapped in an endless debate. Both the supporters and the critics of the "novelty" of contemporary movements share the same epistemological weakness. Criticism of the "paradigm of the new social movements" is based on the fact that many of the characteristics of the contemporary forms of action appeared as well in earlier historical periods. The claimed novelty would be thus merely the effect of that "myopia of the present" often suffered by sociologists, above all when they are emotionally involved with the object of their study.

In its more radical version ("nothing new under the sun"), this criticism is, however, based on an ingenuous historicism that assumes the substantial continuity of the historical flow; it is therefore incapable of perceiving the different systemic location—that is, the different signification—of events and behaviors that, on the factual plane, may reveal undeniable analogies and similarities. The softer version of this criticism ("not everything under the sun is new") is empirically justified, but in my opinion its justification does not make it any more valid. In fact those who criticize the "novelty" of the "new movements" share with the supporters of this "paradigm" the same epistemological limitation: both sides regard the contemporary phenomena as a unitary empirical object. Starting from this unity, the supporters seek to qualify its novelty, the critics deny or question it. The problem becomes whether the "women's movement" or the "peace movement" is new or is not new: some seek to indicate the differences from the past, others emphasize the continuity and comparability.

The preceding discussion should make it sufficiently clear why a debate of this sort seems to me to be short of breath, for the contemporary collective action, in its empirical unity, combines different orientations and meanings. Unless such components are distinguished and identified, it is impossible to compare different forms of action. One ends up by considering the movements as "characters" moving on the historical scene and affirming a sort of essence.

What, then, is the result of the debate on the "new social movements?"

Paradoxically, and exceeding the intentions of the debaters themselves, the favorable result seems to me to be the exhaustion of the image of movements as "personages." The discussion of what is new and what is not new in the modern phenomena has in fact opened the way to recognition of the plurality of significations and of forms of action present in a concrete collective phenomenon. Going beyond the "ingenuous" consideration of a global empirical object, we can perhaps recognize that the contemporary movements, like other collective phenomena, combine forms of action that: concern different levels or systems of the social structure; implicate different orientations; and belong to different phases of development of a system or to different historical systems. It is a question, therefore, of understanding this multiplicity of elements, synchronic and diachronic, and then of explaining how they are held together in the concrete unity of a collective actor.

This said, it is nevertheless legitimate to ask whether we are observing the appearance of a new paradigm of collective action, not in an empirical sense—referred, that is, to the totality of the phenomenon observed—but in an analytical sense, referred to certain levels, elements, and aspects of the action observed. The problem thus becomes whether there are levels or dimensions of the "new" forms of action that belong to a systemic context different from that of industrial capitalism.

This question is too quickly dismissed by critics of the "paradigm of the new social movements," who end up by throwing out the baby with the bathwater. Political reductionism—which I shall return to shortly—is the predictable result of such a criticism. If contemporary movements are not "new," the main ground for comparison with previous forms of action will be their impact on the political system. They will be relevant for the analyst only as far as they act as political actors. Political reductionism, thus, eliminates the question concerning the systemic change in advanced societies, without supplying an answer. Furthermore, it underestimates the social and cultural dimensions of contemporary collective action, which are, however, particularly significant in the case of the "new movements." The result is a "myopia of the visible" which focuses all the attention on the measurable aspects of the collective action (confrontation with the political system and effects on policies), and ignores the production of new cultural codes that constitute the submerged activity of the contemporary movement networks and the condition for their visible action.[6]

Often observers describe the action of contemporary movements generically as "protest," thus applying the empirical simplification I have criticized to a very wide range of forms of action. The analysis, however, is confined to the political level. [7] In this undifferentiated view the concept of protest is a typical example of what I have called political reductionism. Such reductionism can have a negative version, but it can also represent a conscious methodological choice. If the concept of protest is explicitly limited to the political level, that is, to those forms of collective action which implicate a direct confrontation with authority, then, necessarily other levels of the collective action are not included in that concept. If, however, reductionism is applied implicitly, it tends to eliminate or to deny all those dimensions of the collective action which are not reducible to the political (they are dismissed, as the case may be, as uninteresting, unmeasurable, expressive, folkloristic, and so on).

Political reductionism also affects the levels of observation considered significant by researchers. For example the quantitative research on collective action (Tilly 1975, 1978; and more recently Tarrow 1988) uses events as units of analysis. This methodological choice results in a very effective research strategy and it has sensibly contributed to the renewal of the field, providing a large empirical evidence to the study of collective action and social movements. This approach privileges a factual concept of action as behavior, yet what is observed is actually the product of relationships and orientations that constitute the underlying structure of the action. Events are the "objectified" result (particularly when the sources are newspaper reports and public records) of a fabric of relationships and meanings, of an interactive process which is the basis of the visible action.

A constructivist view cannot limit itself to consider the action as an event. Quantitative studies based on events are concerned with the final effects of the action, not with the manner in which the action itself is produced. An approach of this sort certainly provides important information, but it also requires that the researcher be fully aware of the limitations of his point of view: it concentrates on the collective action as a "fact" and not as a process; for this reason it necessarily tends to privilege the public scene and confrontation with political authorities (the area, that is, in which social relationships are already crystallized as a system of order); and it excludes from the field of analysis the network of relationships that constitute the submerged reality of the movements before, during, and after the events.

This point of view can represent a conscious and legitimate delimitation of the field, a selective choice of a specific level of analysis. It can become a "negative" form of reductionism only insofar as it denies the processes of "production" of the collective action. In denying these processes it ignores some very significant dimensions of the "new movements," those relating to the creation of cultural models and symbolic challenges. These dimensions cannot be perceived at the political level and need a different methodological approach to be detected.

Thus, in the end, the debate on the "new movements" confirms the need to focus theoretical and epistemological speculation on the questions I have formulated above. The possibility of determining in a specific manner what is "new" in contemporary movements largely depends on the capacity of analysis to go beyond the globality of the phenomena observed and to explain how a collective reality is produced by the convergence and integration of the many elements of which it is composed.

III.   INDIVIDUAL INVOLVEMENT:
EXPECTATIONS, IDENTITY, ACTION

Neither the macrostructural models nor those based on individual motivations are capable of explaining the concrete forms of collective action and the involvement of individuals in such action. What is lacking, between the analysis of structural determinants and individual preferences, is the analysis of an intermediate level concerned with the processes by which individuals evaluate and recognize what they have in common and decide to act together.

In recent years critical work has concentrated on this intermediate level in an effort to make the European and U.S. approaches comparable.[8] A first distinction that can usefully delimit this level identifies mobilization potential, recruitment networks, and the motivation to participate (Klandermans 1986).

The concept of *mobilization potential* normally refers to that part of the population which, because of its situation, has attitudes favorable to a movement or a certain issue. In the sense in which the term is used here, however, mobilization potential cannot be considered a subjective attitude based on objective preconditions; in such a case one would be faced with the insoluble problem of the relationship between class condition and class-consciousness that I have already mentioned. If one starts from a dualistic assumption, one must resort to a *deus ex machina* (the intellectuals, the party, the organization) in order to connect the objective preconditions and the subjective attitudes and to transform the latter into action. If unity does not exist as a concept right from the beginning of the process it cannot be found at the end. So the mobilization potential should be conceived from the start as an interactive and negotiated perception of action opportunities and constraints common to a certain number of individuals.

Recruitment networks play a fundamental role in the process of involving individuals. No process of mobilization begins in a void, and, contrary to the claims of the theory of mass society (Kornhauser 1959), it is never the isolated and uprooted individuals who mobilize. The networks of relationships already present in the social fabric facilitate the processes of involvement and make the individual's investment in the collective action less costly.[9]

The now classic Olsonian argument of the free rider (Olson 1965) is a useful term of comparison in this context. As is known, Olson holds that interest in obtaining a collective good is not enough to induce individuals to pay the cost of obtaining it (since the individual will equally enjoy the fruits of an action carried out by others). This argument carries undeniable critical weight vis-à-vis the ingenuous assumption that collective action derives from the "objective" common interests of several individuals. Its substantive contribution, however, does not go beyond this critical function.

In the debate over the Olsonian argument numerous objections were raised. Fireman and Gamson (1979), for example, pointed out that individuals participate in the action to obtain a collective benefit because they are aware that the benefit could not be obtained if each waited for the other to act. Others drew attention to the role played by the individual's perception of the action's chance of success, which is often related to the number of participants, and of the importance of his contribution (Oberschall 1980; Oliver 1984). It was also emphasized that the existence of a collective identity is the condition for the calculation of the costs and benefits of the action (Pizzorno 1983a). In conclusion we can affirm that the networks constitute an intermediate level of fundamental importance for understanding the processes of individual involvement. Individuals interact, influence each other, negotiate within these networks, and produce the cognitive and motivational frames of reference necessary for the action.

Thus the *motivation to participate* cannot be considered as an exclusively individual variable, even though it operates at the level of the individual. Motivation is certainly rooted in individual psychological differences and personality traits but it is constructed and consolidated in interaction. A determinant influence on motivation is exerted by the structure of the incentives, whose value originates at the level of the relationship networks connecting individuals. Incentives are effective in motivating individuals because their value is recognized; but the evaluation criteria are always interactive and they are established by an active exchange within the networks to which individuals belong.

In light of these considerations it is clear that the models that western political tradition provides to explain the involvement of individuals are weak. For simplicity I shall refer to them as "Leninist" and "Luxemburghian." The former is paradoxically common to Leninism, crowd psychology, and the theory of mass society; the common assumption being that involvement is the result of the work of a minority that drags an undifferentiated mass of individuals in the direction of their real interests (in the Leninist version) or in the direction of the purposes of the agitators, by means of suggestion and manipulation (in the case of crowd psychology). The Luxemburghian model is specular to the Leninist one and attributes to individuals the spontaneous capacity to mobilize collectively in the presence of discontent, injustice, and deprivation. What both models ignore is the fact that individuals interact, influence each other, and negotiate in order to define themselves as a collective actor and to define the field of their action.

Let us therefore observe more closely how this process takes place. Individuals construct their orientation and make choices and decisions in an environment that they perceive. In this context the concept of expectation is fundamental in analyzing the connection between an actor and his environment.[10] The expectation is a construction of the social reality that enables an actor to relate to the external world. But on what basis are expectations formed and how can they be compared with reality?

I contend that only if an actor can perceive his consistency and his continuity will he be able to construct his own script of the social reality and compare expectations and realizations. Thus any theory of action that introduces the concept of expectation implies an underlying theory of identity. This dimension, however, is rarely elaborated in an explicit manner. A rapid survey of the models which, in the field of collective action, implicate a theory of expectations reveals the weakness of their foundations and the implicit assumption of a theory of identity. The most common models can be reduced to the following descriptions:

1. *rise and drop:* the cycles of collective protest and agitation occur when a period of increasing well-being is followed by a sharp drop in the capacity of the system to satisfy the needs of the population.
2. *rising expectations:* after a period of uninterrupted growth, which multiplies the common expectations, a gap inevitably appears between the expectation curve and that of real satisfaction of needs, and this gap causes the social turbulence.
3. *relative deprivation:* an actor compares his position and rewards with those of a reference group considered comparable in the stratification scale, and this comparison gives rise to discontent and mobilization.
4. *downward mobility:* this generates a particular form of relative deprivation which occurs when an actor is losing his position on the social scale and when he compares himself with his previous condition and with the relative position of other reference groups.
5. *status inconsistency:* a social actor perceives a difference between the various elements of his status (income, prestige, power) and mobilizes in order to eliminate this discrepancy.

All these models imply a theory of expectations (based on previous experience or on comparison with reference groups) and postulate a gap between expectations and realizations as the basis of the action. As such they are an extension of the frustration-aggression paradigm: a perceived difference between expected gratifications and realizations (frustration) produces an aggressive response (in collective terms, protest, violence, etc.).

The excessive simplification of this model has already been criticized by the authors of the resource mobilization theory (RMT) (McCarthy and Zald 1976; for a review, see Jenkins 1983). The explicit criticism relates to the relative deprivation theory but applies implicitly to the other cases as well. The RMT authors have pointed out that discontent is always present in a system and as such is insufficient to justify the processes of mobilization, and they emphasize the importance of the available "discretional resources" and of the "structure of opportunities" that makes action possible. This criticism certainly reveals the inadequacy of the discontent (frustration) = mobilization (aggression) equation and underlines the importance of certain conditions present in the environment. But the critical argument does not confront the fundamental weakness of the model and does not formulate a proper alternative.

In fact the frustration-aggression paradigm, and in general all the theories based on expectations, must assume the capacity of the actor to (a) maintain a unity and a consistency that enable him to compare expectations and rewards at different times; (b) relate his deprivation to an identifiable agent of the

environment toward which the protest or mobilization can be directed; and
(c) recognize the expected benefit as not only desirable but due.

In the absence of these conditions (i.e., if it is not admitted that the actor
undergoes a process of identity construction), it is difficult to assert that the
simple deprivation of an expected gratification will produce a response of the
"voice" type, in other words, a response with conflictual connotations. Many
other responses are in fact possible in terms of "exit": sublimation, symbolic
flight, search for a scapegoat, and so on.[11]

The criticism expressed by the RMT authors indicates that expectations
are constructed through the evaluation of the possibilities provided by and
the constraints inherent in the environment. Thus the RMT reveals the
importance of an intermediate level completely ignored by the models that
assume a direct relationship between discontent and mobilization. But where
the implicit assumptions about identity are concerned, the RMT has the same
limitations as the theories it criticizes. In fact, such concepts as "discretional
resources" and "structure of opportunities" do not refer to "objective" realities
but imply the capacity of the actors to perceive, evaluate, and determine the
possibilities and limits afforded by the environment. The RMT thus postulates
some process of construction of identity on the part of the actor, without,
however, examining this level of analysis. RMT and the models based on
expectations all presuppose a theory of identity, which can give their
arguments a foundation. Expectations are constructed and compared with
reality (e.g., with the realization, but also with the opportunity structure) only
on the basis of a negotiated definition of the internal constitution of the actor
and of the field of his action. For an actor to elaborate expectations and to
evaluate the possibilities and the limits of the action presupposes a capacity
to define himself and his environment. This process of "constructing" an
action system I call *collective identity*.

Collective identity is an interactive and shared definition produced by several
individuals and concerned with the orientations of action and the field of
opportunities and constraints in which the action takes place: by "interactive
and shared" I mean a definition that must be conceived as a process, because
it is constructed and negotiated through a repeated activation of the
relationships that link individuals.

The process of a collective identity's construction, adaption, and
maintenance always has two aspects: the internal complexity of an actor, (the
plurality of orientations which characterizes him), and the actor's relationship
with the environment (other actors, opportunities and constraints). Collective
identity provides the base for shaping expectations and for calculating costs
and benefits of the action. The construction of a collective identity involves
continual investment and occurs as a process. As it approaches the more
institutionalized forms of social action, an identity may crystallize into
organizational forms, system of rules, leadership relationships. In less

institutionalized forms of action its character is closer to a process which must be continually activated to make the action possible.

Collective identity as a process involves at least three fundamental dimensions that I distinguish analytically, though in reality they are closely interwoven: (1) formulating cognitive frameworks concerning the ends, means, and field of action, (2) activating relationships between the actors, who interact, communicate, influence each other, negotiate, and make decisions, (3) making emotional investments, which enable individuals to recognize themselves.

Collective identity is thus a process in which the actors produce the common cognitive frameworks that enable them to assess the environment and to calculate the costs and benefits of the action; the definitions that they formulate are in part the result of negotiated interactions and of influence relationships; and in part the fruit of emotional recognition. In this sense collective action is never based solely on cost-benefit calculation and a collective identity is never entirely negotiable. Some elements of participation in collective action are endowed with meaning but cannot be reduced to instrumental rationality (they are not ir-rational but neither are they based on calculation logic).[12]

Collective identity thus defined indicates a key analytical dimension to be explored when sociological analysis is concerned with collective phenomena. Stability or variability, concentration or diffusion, integration or fragmentation of such a dimension will vary considerably according to how highly structured the collective phenomenon is (along an ideal continuum that goes from pure aggregation to formal organization).

The propensity of an individual to become involved in collective action is thus tied to the differential capacity to define an identity, that is, to the differential access to resources that enable him to participate in the process of identity building. These differences also influence the quality of the expectations represented by the individuals or the sub-groups participating in a collective phenomenon. An individual's degree of exposure to certain resources (cognitive and relational) makes him more or less likely to enter the interactive process of constructing a collective identity. On this exposure depend the individual chances of participating in the negotiation of that identity and in particular: (a) the intensity and quality of an individual's participation; and (b) the starting point and duration of his involvement. Circumstantial factors can influence the structure of opportunities and its variations. But the way in which the opportunities are perceived and used depends on the differential access of individuals to identity resources.

Studies of militancy and of participation show that the militants and activists in the movements are always recruited from among those who are highly integrated into the social structure, play a central role in the networks to which they belong, and have at their disposal substantial cognitive and relational resources. These studies also clarify the differences between the militants and individuals belonging to marginal, deprived, or declining social groups. The latter become involved at a later stage, for shorter periods of time, and at levels of participation with lower costs.[13]

The comparative empirical evidence contained in the research literature on "new" social movements largely confirms the plural nature of the actors involved. The social base of these movements is located in three main sectors of the social structure: (a) the "new middle class" or "human capital class," that is, those who work in the advanced technological sectors based on information, the human service professions and/or the public sector (particularly in education and welfare), and who have achieved a high educational status and enjoy relative economic security; (b) those in a marginal position in the labor market (e.g., students, unemployed or "peripheral" youth, retired people, middle-class housewives); and (c) elements of the independent "old middle class" (farmers, craftsmen, particularly in regional and environmental mobilizations). The relative weight of each category is different and the core group of activists and supporters is to be found in the first.[14]

The three groups have different structural positions and participate for different reasons. The "new middle class" consists of at least two groups of people: new elites who are just emerging and are challenging the already established elites, and "human capital" professionals, who experience both the surplus of potentialities offered by the system and its constraints. Research has shown that these people appear to be well integrated into social activities and institutions, have previously participated in more traditional politics and social networks, and are highly educated and relatively young. All these characteristics indicate the central position of these individuals, their adherence to the most modern values, and their relation to the core structures of society. Their capacity for building an identity is rooted in an available set of resources and they can perceive these resources because they are well exposed to the knowledge and information available in society. The shift from a position of conflict to a counter-elite role can be very easy for this group of people, since the institutionalization processes occur frequently and rapidly. For example environmental groups with high professional skills can easily become consultant firms working on environmental problems.

The "peripheral" group is also composed of a variety of actors. Some are "affluent marginals," for instance students or middle-class women who experience the gap already mentioned between the surplus of possibilities offered by the system and the actual constraints of their social condition. Others are marginals *strictu sensu* (the elderly or the unemployed) whose action has to be explained in different terms: these people respond to crisis conditions only when an already existing context of mobilization is available.

The "old middle class" groups react to a development that threatens to affect their previous social position. Here the populist or *re*-actionary orientation is dominant.

These three different groups have different capabilities for building and negotiating their identity over time; they therefore have different sets of expectations. Thus the reasons individuals become involved in collective action differ. For the "central" groups or the "affluent marginals" the likelihood of becoming involved is related on the one hand to their degree of "centrality" and the extent of their exposure to the core information and knowledge of the "modern" system, and, on the other hand, to the impact of conjunctural contradictory requirements to which they are submitted. For the marginal or deprived groups, by contrast, the degree of exclusion, combined with the pace of the crisis processes, is the most likely differential dimension.

The stage at which different individuals become involved is also important. Those in the first group are more likely to get involved in the early phases of mobilization because they can count on their identity resources. Individuals in the second group will use the already existing wave of mobilization as a channel for their *re*-action and are likely to drop out sooner.

IV. CONCLUSION

Even at the less structured levels of the collective action the actors "organize" their behavior, produce meanings, establish relationships. Individual involvement thus calls for explanations that imply the capacity of the actors to "construct" their collective action in different ways.

The processes that characterize the construction of a collective identity vary greatly, both in intensity and in the complexity of the dimensions involved, according to the type of collective phenomenon in question. But researchers, when faced by the "collective" dimension of social action, can no longer avoid asking themselves questions concerning the actors' cognitive and emotional investment in this interactive and communicative construction.

NOTES

1. A definitive light was thrown on these aspects by the studies of Tilly (1975, 1986) and Moscovici (1981). See also the classic contributions of Bendix (1964, 1978) that remain of fundamental importance.

2. A variety of studies contributed to the development of this view. I note here the role of cognitive social psychology (see, for example, Eiser 1980); the sociology of action (Touraine 1973); the constructivism of the sociology of organization (Crozier and Friedberg 1977) and of decision-making processes (for a review and a synthesis, see Gherardi 1985). In the field of collective action an important role was played by the resource mobilization theory (for a synthesis, see Jenkins, 1983). In the field of the social movements a constructivist approach has been adopted by Melucci (1984a, 1984b, 1985), Hosking (1983), Brown and Hosking (1984), Donati (1984).

3. A corollary of this distinction is the need to define the system of reference or field of action considered. Any analysis that implicitly or explicity introduces the notion of a breaking of limits implies the definition of a system of reference. Authors are not always aware of this need, when

working with "disruptive" forms of collective action. It could be useful, for example, at least to distinguish the system that ensures the production of the constitutive resources of a society, the system within which decisions concerning the distribution of those resources are made, and the system of roles that permits the exchange and enjoyment of the resources. The meaning of the action will vary according to which system is affected or "disrupted" by collective mobilization.

4.   For a detailed presentation of types of collective action which can be derived from a combination of the analytical dimensions discussed above, see Melucci (1982, 1984a).

5.   For an extensive comparative discussion of the literature concerning the resource mobilization theory and the "new movements," see Klandermans (1986), Tarrow (1986), Cohen (1985). A synthesis of the results of empirical research on the "new movements" is provided by Offe (1985). Other empirical contributions of comparative character are those of Rucht (1984, 1986) and Kitschelt (1985).

6.   For a discussion of these aspects, see Melucci (1984a, 1984b, 1985).

7.   To my knowledge only Tarrow (1983, 1988) has proposed an explicit delimitation of the concept of protest at the political level, as a basis for his model of the "cycles of protest."

8.   I first proposed a comparison between these approaches in Melucci (1984b). For a critical survey, see Klandermans (1986). On the intermediate level see Tarrow (1986), McAdam (1986), Snow and Benford (1986) and Kriesi (1986). A psycho-social extension of resource mobilization theory, focusing on the intermediate level, is proposed by Klandermans (1984).

9.   Among the many contributions of empirical research, see Oberschall (1973), Wilson and Orum (1976), McAdam (1982), Melucci (1984a), Donati (1984), Diani and Lodi (1986).

10.   A critical discussion of expectation models is proposed by Melucci (1982, chap. 2).

11.   On the alternative exit-voice, see Hirschman (1970).

12.   The concept of collective identity was introduced to recent sociological debate by authors such as Touraine (1973, 1978, 1984, 1985) and Pizzorno (1978, 1983a, 1983b, 1986). For a discussion of the theoretical paradigm, see Cohen (1985). With regard to the concept of collective identity I am proposing, these authors fail to clarify the process of construction of the collective actor by means of interactions, negotiations, and relationships with the environment. The identity appears as a datum, a sort of essence of the movement, in the case of Touraine; in the case of Pizzorno, the concept seems to be still founded on shared interest, in accordance with Marxist tradition.

13.   For an extensive survey of the empirical literature, see Grazioli and Lodi (1984), McAdam (1986).

14.   See the review of research in Offe (1985).

REFERENCES

Alberoni, Francesco. 1977. *Movimento e istituzione*. Bologna: Il Mulino.

Bendix, Reinhard. 1964. *Nation-Building and Citizenship*. New York: Wiley.

Bendix, Reinhard. 1978. *Kings or People*. Berkeley: University of California Press.

Brown, Mary H. and Dian-Marie Hosking. 1984. "Distributed Leadership and Skilled Performance as Successful Organization in Social Movements." Paper presented at the Conference of the European Group of Organizational Sociologists on New Social Movements, Aarhus, Denmark, August 27-29.

Cohen, Jean L. 1985. "Strategy or identity: New theoretical paradigms and contemporary social movements." *Social Research* 52:663-716.

Crozier, Michel and Erhard Friedberg. 1977. *L'acteur et le système*. Paris: Seuil.

Diani, Mario and Giovanni Lodi. 1986. "On Participation in the Ecological Movement." Paper presented at the International Symposium on New Social Movements, Amsterdam, Free University, June 12-14.

Donati, Paolo R. 1984. "Organization between movement and institution." *Social Science Information* 23:837-59.

Eiser, J. Richard. 1980. *Cognitive Social Psychology*. New York: McGraw-Hill.

Fireman, Bruce and William A. Gamson. 1979. "Utilitarian Logic in the Resource Mobilization Perspective." Pages 8-45 in Mayer N. Zald and John D. McCarthy (eds.). *The Dynamics of Social Movements*. Cambridge, Mass.: Winthrop.

Gherardi, Silvia. 1985. *Sociologia delle decisioni organizzative*. Bologna: Il Mulino.

Grazioli, Marco and Giovanni Lodi. 1984. "La mobilitazione collettiva negli anni Ottanta: Tra condizione e convinzione." Pages 267-314 in Alberto Melucci (ed.), *Altri codici. Aree di movimento nella metropoli*. Bologna: Il Mulino.

Hirschman, Albert O. 1970. *Exit, Voice, and Loyalty*. Cambridge: Harvard University Press.

Hosking, Dian-Marie. 1983. "Leadership Skills and Organizational Forms." Paper presented at the 6th Conference of the European Group of Organizational Sociologists, Florence, November 3-5.

Jenkins, J. Craig. 1983. "Resource mobilization theory and the study of social movements." *Annual Review of Sociology* 9:527-53.

Kitschelt, Herbert. 1985. "New social movements in West Germany and the United States." *Political Power and Social Theory* 5:273-324.

Klandermans, Bert. 1984. "Mobilization and participation: Social-psychological expansions of resource mobilization theory." *American Sociological Review* 49:583-600.

Klandermans, Bert. 1986. "New Social Movements and Resource Mobilization: The European and the American Approach." *Journal of Mass Emergencies and International Disasters*. Special issue, *Comparative Perspectives and Research on Collective Behavior and Social Movements* 4:13-37.

Kornhauser, William. 1959. *The Politics of Mass Society*. Glencoe, Ill.: Free Press.

Kriesi, Hanspeter. 1986. "Local Mobilization for the People's Petition of the Dutch Peace Movement." Paper presented at the International Symposium on New Social Movements, Amsterdam, Free University, June 12-14.

McCarthy, John D. and Mayer N. Zald. 1976. "Resource mobilization and social movements: A partial theory." *American Journal of Sociology* 82:1212-41.

Melucci, Alberto. 1978. "Dieci ipotesi per l'analisi dei nuovi movimenti." *Quaderni Piacentini* 65-66:3-19. English translation, pages 173-94 in Diana Pinto (ed.). *Contemporary Italian Sociology*. Cambridge: Cambridge University Press, 1981.

Melucci, Alberto. 1980. "The new social movements: A theoretical approach." *Social Science Information* 19:199-226.

Melucci, Alberto. 1982. *L'invenzione del presente*. Bologna: Il Mulino.

Melucci, Alberto. 1984a. (ed.) *Altri codici. Aree di movimento nella metropoli*. Bologna: Il Mulino.

Melucci, Alberto. 1984b. "An end to social movements?" *Social Science Information* 23:819-35.

Melucci, Alberto. 1985. "The symbolic challenge of contemporary movements." *Social Research* 52:789-816.

Muscovici, Serge. *L'âge des foules*. Paris: Fayard.

Oberschall, Anthony. 1973. *Social Conflict and Social Movements*. Englewood Cliffs, N.J.: Prentice-Hall.

Oberschall, Anthony. 1980. "Loosely Structured Collective Conflict: A Theory and Application." Pages 45-68 in Louis Kriesberg (ed.), *Research in Social Movements, Conflict, and Change*. Vol. 3. Greenwich, Conn.: JAI. Press.

Offe, Claus. 1985. "New Social Movements: Challenging the Boundaries of Institutional Politics." *Social Research* 52:817-68.

Oliver, Pamela. 1984. "If you don't do it, nobody else will: Active and token contributors to local collective action." *American Sociological Review* 49:601-10.

Olson, Mancur, Jr. 1965. *The Logic of Collective Action: Public Goods and the Theory of Groups.* Cambridge: Harvard University Press.

Pizzorno, Alessandro. 1978. "Political Exchange and Collective Identity in Industrial Conflict." Pages 277-98 in Colin Crouch and Alessandro Pizzorno (eds.), *The Resurgence of Class Conflict in Western Europe since 1968.* Vol. 2. London: Macmillan.

Pizzorno, Alessandro. 1983a. "Identita e interesse." Pages 139-54 in Loredana Sciolla (ed.), *Identita.* Turin: Rosemberg e Sellier.

Pizzorno, Alessandro. 1983b. "Sulla razionalita della scelta democratica." *Stato e Mercato* 7:3-46.

Pizzorno, Alessandro. 1986. "Sul confronto intemporale delle utilita." *Stato e Mercato* 16:3-26.

Rucht, Dieter. 1984. "Comparative New Social Movements." Paper presented at the Conference of the European Group of Organizational Sociologists on New Social Movements, Aarhus, Denmark, August 27-29.

Rucht, Dieter. 1986. "Themes, Logics and Arenas of Social Movements." Paper presented at the International Symposium on New Social Movements, Amsterdam, Free University, June 12-14.

Snow, David A. and Robert D. Benford. 1986. "Ideology, Frame Alignment Processes and Cycles of Protest." Paper presented at the International Symposium on New Social Movements, Amsterdam, Free University, June 12-14.

Tarrow, Sidney. 1983. *Struggling to Reform: Social Movements and Policy Change during Cycles of Protest.* Western Societies Paper No. 15. Ithaca, N.Y.: Cornell University.

Tarrow, Sidney. 1986. "Comparing social movement participation in Western Europe and the United States: Problems, uses, examples, and a proposal for synthesis." *International Journal of Mass Emergencies and Disasters.* Special issue, *Comparative Perspectives and Research on Collective Behavior and Social Movements* 4:145-70.

Tarrow, Sidney. 1988. *Democracy and Disorder: Society and Politics in Italy, 1965-1975.* Oxford: Oxford University Press (forthcoming).

Tilly, Charles. 1975. *The Rebellious Century: 1830-1930.* Cambridge: Harvard University Press.

Tilly, Charles. 1978. *From Mobilization to Revolution.* Reading, Mass.: Addison-Wesley.

Tilly, Charles. 1986. *The Contentious French.* Cambridge: Belknap Press, Harvard University Press.

Touraine, Alain. 1973. *Production de la société.* Paris: Seuil.

Touraine, Alain. 1978. *La voix et le regard.* Paris: Seuil.

Touraine, Alain. 1984. *Le retour de l'acteur.* Paris: Fayard.

Touraine, Alain. 1985. "An introduction to the study of social movements." *Social Research* 52:749-88.

Wilson, Kenneth L. and Anthony M. Orum. 1976. "Mobilizing people for collective political action." *Journal of Political and Military Sociology* 4:187-202.

THE INTERDEPENDENCE OF STRUCTURE AND ACTION:
SOME REFLECTIONS ON THE STATE OF THE ART

Hanspeter Kriesi

Social movements are both causes and consequences of large-scale processes of social change. The study of the mobilization of social movements is part of the study of social change. Some, Touraine (1978) for example, think that the two terrains are identical. Others, including myself, do not. As Bert Klandermans and Sidney Tarrow point out in the Introduction, the tendency to link social movements to large-scale structural or cultural change has been common above all among European scholars, whereas their American colleagues have tended to be too concerned with analyzing mobilization processes at the group and individual level, showing little regard for structural or cultural change. Although this pigeon-holing of students of social movements from the two continents is something of an exaggeration, it provides a useful starting point for an attempt to bridge the gaps between intellectual traditions that are more compatible than many of the staunch adherents of one or the other might at first think. This book represents a first attempt to integrate approaches that have existed alongside each other without taking

International Social Movement Research, Vol. 1, pages 349-368.
Supplement to Research in Social Movements, Conflicts and Change
Copyright © 1988 by JAI Press Inc.
ISBN: 0-89232-955-6

due notice of each other. All the contributions to this volume try to link the two traditions by focusing on the specific mechanisms that account for the transformation of structure into action. Discussing these mechanisms in the historically specific context of the so-called new social movements provides an opportunity to connect the general theoretical concerns typical of American authors to the preoccupation with historically specific developments typical of European social scientists. In this concluding chapter, I shall try to summarize my view of how links have been made or should be made and to elaborate my interpretation of the ways the terrain of the study of social movements has been (re-)conceptualized by the work of the authors represented here and, of course, by the work of many others who have not directly participated in this endeavor.

I. SOCIAL MOVEMENTS

Social movements are elusive phenomena with unclear boundaries in time and space. As Alberto Melucci points out in his contribution to this volume, what we perceive as a social movement is the result of a process of social construction of reality. The unity of a movement is not given at the outset but is the contested result of mobilization processes in the course of which all those involved try to structure the field in accordance with their perceptions and preferences. What to some are "terrorists," others call "freedom fighters"—a difference in terminology that has nonnegligible consequences for those activists themselves. The unity of a movement emerging from the contest carries the traces of the battle and tells us much about that battle. As social scientists studying social movements, we always encounter preconceptions of the units of analysis to be studied, but, to complicate matters, since we are concerned with (re-) constructing social reality ourselves, we also try to (re-)define the units under study. If we are creative and acute enough, our notions will contribute to the way a particular social movement will be perceived. "The best and most interesting ideas in the social sciences," Giddens (1984, p. xxxiv) maintains, "(a) participate in fostering the climate of opinion and the social processes which give rise to them, (b) are in greater or lesser degree entwined with theories-in-use which help to constitute those processes, and (c) are thus unlikely to be clearly distinct from considered reflection which lay actors may bring to bear insofar as they discursively articulate, or improve upon, theories-in-use."

Social movements are additionally hard to grasp, because their conceptualization requires that we pay attention to at least three analytically distinct dimensions that intersect to constitute a social movement: these three dimensions refer to the actors (groups) involved; to the values, beliefs, and claims (issues) articulated; and to the actions (events) carried out (Tilly 1978,

p. 9). As Tilly points out, change in one dimension may occur independent of change in another one. Thus our reconstructions differ considerably, depending on which of the three dimensions we are focusing our attention on.

Lay people have fewer problems with definitions than do social scientists. When nonspecialists identify specific social movements, they characteristically do not pay attention to all three dimensions just mentioned; they simplify matters. To my great surprise, when asked whether they sympathize with different types of new social movements (NSMs)—peace movement, antinuclear movement, ecology movement—people in different European countries are able to answer the question (see the corresponding questions in the Eurobarometer). In other words, they must have a rather clear conception of these movements. Whether they all have the same conception is quite a different question, and whether these conceptions have anything to do with what the social scientists have in mind is still another matter. What is striking, however, is the fact that the three movements just mentioned are identified by the general public in terms of the issues at stake, or, more precisely, in terms of certain preferences with regard to specific issues. Very loosely speaking, they are identified in terms of the dimension referring to values, beliefs, and claims. Correspondingly, these NSMs are considered "single-issue-movements" that pursue rather narrow kinds of interest. I do not know how these movements have come to be perceived in this fashion, but I venture that this development has something to do with the difficulties that the general public, the challenged authorities, and the social scientists observing these movements have in defining in structural terms the actors who form these movements. Still thinking in terms of traditional political cleavages (of language, religion, and class), these outside observers are at a loss if it comes to pinning down the segments of the population they are in fact concerned with. To talk about these movements as "single-issue-movements," however, can be highly misleading, given the fact that they are all generally rooted in the same social-structural background and often are even formed by the same individual activists (Kriesi 1986, 1987b).

There are, of course, some other new social movements that are identified by their most visible actors: the squatters' movements, women's movements, student movements, and youth movements. Compared to the actors in the previously mentioned group of movements, the actors forming these movements are more homogeneous, at least in one respect (typically in terms of an ascriptive trait, such as sex, ethnicity, or age, which is readily visible to external observers). Again, however, the label given to the movement can be highly misleading, as in the case of the "youth movement," for example. Young people form the majority of the activists in many movements that do *not* articulate age-specific claims. Calling such movements "youth-movements" is often a ploy of their antagonists who thus indicate these movements are not to be taken seriously. (This tactic applies to the label of "single-issue movement" as well.) A case in point is the "Movement of Zurich" at the beginning of the eighties: the challengers considered themselves as "the Movement" or as "the movement of all the discontented," while authorities referred to them as "youth movement" (Kriesi 1984). Social scientists contribute to the confusion by often viewing such movements from the narrow point of view of their own specialty—sociology of youth (subcultures) or urban sociology (calling these very same movements "urban movements"). To account for the complexity of the phenomenon, we need to define social movements in terms of all three dimensions mentioned above. Tilly (1984) proposes a definition that implicitly takes into account all three, although it emphasizes the dimension of action. According to this definition, social movements are to be viewed as "sustained series of interactions" between authorities and challengers making claims on behalf of a constituency with specific preferences. The unity of the "series of challenges to establish authorities" (Tilly 1986, p. 392) is here sought on the level of a series of actions and reactions. The individuals doing the challenging and their particular claims may change in the course of the series, but it is the form and the pattern of interactions which provide the link that accounts for the unity. This definition, however, leaves open the question how we can identify the different instances of interactions as belonging to the same series. To be more specific: in the case of the peace movement, for example, the question is at what point in the series the "new" peace movement starts (Young 1986). Some observers maintain that there is a strong enough continuity in the struggle for peace that we cannot speak of any "new" peace movement in the first place. Other observers, myself among them, point to the substantial shifts in the composition and number of people mobilized, in the type of actions involved, and in the preferences articulated in order to justify the development of a new movement. Ben Schennink in his analysis of a crucial shift in the development of the movement (Chapter 4 in this volume), seems to take a middle position between these two extremes by distinguishing two stages in what he perceives to be one sequence. My point is that there is no ready-made criterion to delimit the sequence of interactions and that, depending on the component of action we focus upon in restructuring the challenge we are studying, we come up with different answers to the same question.

If we stick to the dimension of interaction, we could use a purely quantitative criterion for delimiting the sequence, namely, the magnitude and intensity of conflictual interactions between challengers and authorities. But this approach does not allow us to settle the problem of delineating a movement, because, to do so, we also need a conception of the challenger. Movements, as Melucci again points out, are not "characters," "heroes" acting on a stage, but "multipolar action systems." I take this statement to mean that the entity we finally perceive as a unity—on whatever grounds—is a highly precarious construct made up of different groups with widely different types of beliefs and different strategies for action, groups that join forces at a specific moment in history as a result of specific "conjunctural" circumstances. Movements typically are internally divided into different tendencies—the most obvious and pervasive division being that between reformist and radical tendencies. But where to draw the boundary? What is simply a tendency within a movement, and what should be considered a separate movement forming a Social Movement Industry (SMI) together with other movements? Again, there are no hard and fast criteria to fall back on. Mario Diani and Giovanni Lodi, for example, distinguish between what they call "factions" within the ecological movement in Milan. Their "conservationist" faction, however, is often not considered part of that movement at all. For example, the Eurobarometer (mentioned above) asks separate questions about sympathy for the ecology movement and sympathy for "nature protection associations" (see, e.g., Müller-Rommel 1985). These latter associations are by no means recent phenomena; their origin reaches back many years. Moreover, as Diani and Lodi's data show, they are not particularly "new" with respect to the three components of action either, if we take the political ecologists as typical of what a new social movement is supposed to signify.

On the other hand, Diani and Lodi's data also show a considerable overlap between the three tendencies with respect to participation in each other's activities: two-thirds of the activists have participated in activities of tendencies other than their own. Among the environmentalists, active participation in other groups reaches such proportions (42%) that one might wonder whether the majority have been classified correctly as representatives of this tendency. In the study of the Dutch peace movement, we have also noticed the existence of this overlap. Among the activists we studied, the majority did not identify with any one tendency in particular but sympathized with all three of the major tendencies of that movement (see Kriesi and van Praag, Jr. 1987). All these observations suggest that the different factions may form a unity after all. One explanation for this unification may be that, under the impact of increasing environmental problems, traditional conservationists are undergoing a process of goal-transformation in a direction running counter to the logic implied by the traditional Weber-Michels model (see Zald and Ash 1966). They might become radicalized following the example of the much younger branch of the movement.

Melucci introduces one more complicating factor. He warns that, in identifying the challenger and his challenge, we should also avoid "political reductionism," that is, the tendency to ignore the "specifically social dimension of contemporary collective action" so significant to NSMs. According to Melucci, these movements are submerged in everyday life, and their submerged activity is the production of cultural codes that constitute the condition for visible action. I agree with this view insofar as I too think that the establishment of new cultural codes—and of a corresponding institutional infrastructure I might add—do indeed form a very important aspect of the development of NSMs. These developments in the everyday life of a specific segment of the population should not, however, be considered to be already part of a movement. Rather, they are part of what Bert Klandermans in his essay in this volume calls "consensus formation," "the unplanned convergence of meaning in social networks and subcultures," which is to be distinguished from conscious mobilization attempts by a specific social movement.

Although in studying social movements we should not lose sight of these developments outside the political sphere narrowly conceived, we should not neglect the interaction between challengers and authorities either. Movements build up for a long time before they become visible, but it is only when the mobilization potentials are transformed in events of collective action that we speak of movements. We can, of course, change our conventions for speaking about this subject, but I do not suggest that we do so. The study of movements is, in my view, not identical with the study of social change in general but most generally associated with the study of articulate, explicit collective attempts to defend established positions of power which do not rely on established institutionalized procedures but resort to methods typically used by outsiders of the system.

But why bother about this notion of social movements at all? Why not stick to the simpler notions of events, groups, or actions? Because the concept of social movement is, I think, particularly well suited for the conceptualization of the transformation of structure into action. The notion of the "social movement" provides us with an "intermediary" conceptual tool facilitating the link between the macro- and the micro-levels. If we stick to events, we are bound to be either too microscopic or too macroscopic. The study of single events remains episodic; documenting all events of a specific form of action—for example all protest events involving violence (Tilly, Tilly, and Tilly 1975)— allows us to establish the shape of cycles of protest on an aggregate, macro-level. But in order to account for the dynamics of the cycle, the events must be connected to one another. Let me clarify this point: I am not saying that we should not study events; on the contrary, events are the moments when the elusive entity we are trying to grasp becomes visible. We can see movements in formation, crystallization, factionalization, and institutionalization—as Tarrow (1988) has observed—only if we study the events in which they are manifested. But in order to account for the dynamics generating the cycle, the events produced by the interaction of challengers and authorities have to be connected to each other in a meaningful way. The sequences of interactions must be established; that is, social movements must be identified.

To do so, we need to turn to the other two dimensions involved—those concerning groups and the claims they articulate. In order to arrive at a coherent sequence, one could try to establish the "biography" of some group on the basis of all the events it has been engaged in. But there are many groups and the question then becomes which among the possible candidates we should choose. Webb et al. (1983, p. 327), for example, have chosen to follow the "biographies" of "a sample of 180 protest groups from different social sectors purposively sampled (ethnic, industrial, agricultural, environmental, and so on) from 6 European countries (Belgium, West Germany, Ireland, Switzerland, Italy, and the United Kingdom) for up to a 20-year period depending on the lifespan of the group (1960-1980)." Such a design obviously has some tremendous advantages with respect to the comparisons it makes possible. But questions remain: how is the sample of groups chosen and how are the groups defined? If by "groups" we mean social movement organizations and if we choose them at random from a list enumerating as completely as possible the "population" of SMOs in a given period of time—as Gamson (1975) has done— we place ourselves in a position in which it is still quite difficult to account for the dynamics of cycles of protest.

If, however, we do not choose at random but try to select a set of groups connected to each other in a meaningful way, the task of accounting for dynamics will be greatly facilitated. Suppose we choose all the SMOs involved in articulating the same underlying claims in a given period of time and try to trace their parallel "biographies" through the sequence of events produced by them all. These biographies are bound to be closely interrelated, and I would maintain that each one of the biographies becomes comprehensible only if we study them all at the same time. Such an endeavor, however, amounts to the (re-)constitution of a social movement, that is, the (re-)constitution of a series of interactions involving a cluster of groups (SMOs) articulating meaningfully related challenges over a given period of time.

II. NEW SOCIAL MOVEMENTS

The situation to be studied is, of course, even more complicated conceptually. In a given period of time, there may be more than one social movement mobilizing. Indeed, it is typical of the period in which the NSMs emerged that a plurality of movements were developing simultaneously (Nedelmann 1984). A cycle of protest unfolds as a result of the mobilization of all the social movements co-present in a given period (Tarrow 1988). Instead of restricting our attention to a single movement, we may consider studying a cluster of related, contemporaneous movements forming a social movement industry (SMI) or even all the movements mobilizing contemporaneously, that is the entire social movement sector (SMS).

The term "new social movements" (NSMs), in fact, refers to a cluster of social movements forming an SMI. It is important to note that it does not refer to the entire sector of contemporary social movements but is designed to refer to a rather specific, although difficult to circumscribe, cluster of present-day movements. This specific application of the term becomes most explicit in Dieter Rucht's essay in this volume, even as Rucht takes pains to distinguish between different variants of NSMs. Although NSMs are the most important contributors to the cycle of protest that took off in the late 1960s and lasted until the beginning of the 1980s in Western European countries, they were not the only movements contributing to the development of the cycle. The pervasiveness of the cycle carried in the main by the NSMs is demonstrated, for example, by the case of the mobilization process within the Catholic Church in Florence which is described by Tarrow in his chapter. Although this case can be accounted for only if it is put in the context of the cycle shaped by NSMs, I would hesitate to include this movement under the generic term of the "new social movements" as the term has come to be used among European scholars.

To explain why some movements qualify as NSMs and others do not, we have to consider the context within which the notion of NSMs has developed. As Rucht makes clear, this notion is connected to very broad concepts of social change. Rucht links the NSMs to complex and encompassing processes of modernization which imply, as Habermas puts it, an increasing differentiation of "life world" and "system" and a concomittant "colonization" of the former by the latter. For those not familiar with Habermas's imagery, it may be useful to point out the similarity between his distinction and the well-worn conceptual twins of Gemeinschaft versus Gesellschaft and mechanical versus organic solidarity. The colonization of the life world by systemic imperatives implies, among other things, the shift of control from the local, parochial level to the national, state level, as well as the shift of control from individual to corporate actors in general. These processes have, of course, been going on for quite a while, with the corresponding shifts in the repertoire of collective action that took place in the nineteenth century described by Tilly (1986). What the authors writing about NSMs, in fact, maintain is that these processes reached a new stage in Western Europe in the postwar period (see Beck 1983, 1986; Brand 1985). Only in the postwar years have the old, traditional bonds tying people to their immediate social environment been severed completely; only quite recently have people really been freed from traditional ties of class, religion, and family. The result has been an unprecedented degree of individualization which, paradoxically, has not increased individual freedom from control. On the contrary, individuals now find they are dependent on new kinds of structurally given circumstances. They find themselves free only to choose among alternatives prestructured by large, anonymous corporate actors, and they slowly discover that they are threatened by new types of unintended consequences of the decisions made by those anonymous corporate actors. Threats to individual autonomy by corporate actors articulating systemic imperatives (the "iron cage" of Max Weber) and new, invisible risks affecting people in more or less the same way irrespective of their social position (radioactivity or AIDS, for example) have replaced the dependence on traditional bonds and the deprivation stemming from inequality of resource distribution.

It is these double-edged consequences of large-scale processes of social change which, as I interpret the authors writing on NSMs, lie at the heart of the development of the new challenges we have witnessed over the last two decades. The ambivalence implied in these processes of social change is manifested in the claims articulated by the NSMs that are at the same time offensive (proactive) and defensive (reactive). On the one hand, the liberation from traditional bonds has opened up new opportunities for the realization of individual autonomy, and, with these new opportunities, new aspirations for the realization of individual lifestyles have arisen which are articulated (offensively) by the so-called NSMs. On the other hand, the awareness of new kinds of intrusions into the newly acquired action-spaces and the precariousness of the recently granted autonomy have grown as well, and this growing awareness is articulated (defensively) by the very same movements. The balance between offensive and defensive articulation is in some movements tipped more in favor of offensive claims than it is in others, and even in the same movement the emphasis may change, depending on conjunctural circumstances, as the movement develops.

The challenge of all NSMs implies a critique of the way the process of modernization has developed, but as Offe (1985) points out, this critique is articulated from the point of view of modernity, not from that of a romanticized past. There are, of course, reactionary tendencies in many NSMs. There are tendencies within these movements which are guided by the idea of restoring the bonds that have been severed by the modernization process and which envisage a return to the "world we have lost." To present these tendencies as typical of the NSMs would, however, be highly misleading. To get at the idealtypical core of these movements we have to note that they are above all constituted by members of the new middle class and in particular in social and cultural services. It is these groups of people which have especially high aspirations for realizing individually autonomous lifestyles (witness, for example, their well-documented postmaterialism), and it is these groups, too, which, given their high average level of education, have the greatest insight into the threats implied by the course the modernization process has taken. As I have tried to argue elsewhere, the postmaterialism of these new challenging groups is to be viewed neither as an indication of the particularistic interests of a new elite nor as a luxury these people can afford. It is better viewed as an indication of their insight that the pursuit of nonmaterial goals (individual lifestyles) is not only no longer assured by material well-being and economic growth but, on the contrary, is ever more constrained by the material conditions of production and by the institutional framework of the welfare state. New aspirations and need defense are in fact linked in a paradoxical manner in the claims of NSMs. In order to realize new aspirations these movements must follow a rather defensive strategy. This paradox is very well formulated by Beck (1986, p. 157): "Put in a general way, the spark triggering social conflicts and movements today (in contrast to the life-worlds determined by class-cultures) lies in the experience that the self-consciously perceived and expansively interpreted action- and decision-spaces are endangered."

In order to distinguish NSMs systematically from other types of contemporary movements, I propose a classification based on two distinctions referring to the claims articulated. The first distinction is that between movements and counter-movements, that is, between movements challenging the established authorities and movements defending established rights and privileges against these challenges. Counter-movements are always defensive, but challenging movements can, as we have just seen, be defensive too—for example, if their challenge is directed against the intervention of authorities in their life world. The second distinction I take from Raschke (1980, 1985), who uses it to describe the shift in the focus of political conflict which has taken place since the second half of the nineteenth century. Raschke distinguishes three types of political paradigms, subdividing the second of the two broad phases of popular struggle distinguished by Tilly (1986, p. 397). According to the first paradigm, the authority paradigm, political conflict involves questions of fundamental rights, such as voting rights, or basic human rights such as freedom of speech, and freedom of the press. According to the distribution paradigm, it is social rights which are at issue in political conflict. The main questions involve the stimulation and distribution of economic growth. Finally, according to the paradigm of lifestyles, what one may call cultural rights form the crucial objects of contention, rights such as the right to one's own lifestyle, the right to be different, the protection of the individual against entirely new kinds of risks. Although these distinctions were introduced to describe a chronological sequence, they can also be used to classify contemporary movements without any reference to historical development.

Combining the two distinctions leaves us with six categories of social movements. The idealtypical NSM represents those movements articulating claims to a right to a new lifestyle. As such it is distinctly different from five other types of contemporary movements:

Figure 1.   Classification of Social Movements

Paradigm	Movements	Counter-movements
authority-paradigm	ethnic movements regional movements	racist movements regional counter-movements
distribution-paradigm	labor movement	anti-tax movement
lifestyle-paradigm	new social movements	movements defending traditional lifestyles

The first one of these other types concerns movements articulating claims to fundamental political and human rights. The struggle of the civil rights movement dealt with by the essay of Doug McAdam in Chapter 2 is the most obvious case of such a movement in the United States. Given its primary concern with fundamental political and human rights I would not count this movement among the NSMs. The civil rights movement has, however, been an important precursor of the NSMs in the United States. For the first time, it developed elements of an action repertoire that has subsequently been elaborated by NSMs. In Western Europe, it is regional movements that typically have been articulating claims to fundamental citizens' rights, asking either for more regional autonomy or for the right to a separate state for a group of people with an ethno-regional identity rooted in the more or less distant past (Ganguillet 1985; Gerdes 1985; Esman 1977): examples are movements from the "celtic fringe" in the United Kingdom (Northern Ireland, Scotland and Wales), the movement of the Basques in Spain and movements from different parts of the French periphery (from Britanny, Corsica, the Basque provinces and the Southern provinces in general). Italy has known its separatists, too (in Sardinia, in Southern Tyrol, Friuli, and Val d'Aosta); the Belgians are perpetually ridden by conflicts between their two national communities giving rise to autonomist movements, and even the Swiss polity, known for its multi-ethnic integration, has experienced a severe ethno-regional struggle in the recent past. Fundamental political and human rights have also been at stake in many struggles within traditional institutions, the one within the Florentine church described by Tarrow in this volume being a case in point.

In contrast to this type of struggle, the challenge of the NSMs presupposes the demise of precisely those traditional institutions and the liberation of people from traditional ties and identities. The anti-authoritarian revolt of which the Florentine struggle was part marked the beginning of the cycle that brought forth the NSMs in Europe. This was a revolt against the vestiges of authoritarian institutions that had become anachronistic in a time when their functional authority had disappeared because of the dissolution of traditional social relations. But by clearing away the old rubble, this anti-authoritarian revolt that was led by the student movement in particular, prepared the ground for things to come.

Second, NSMs struggling for a new lifestyle are to be distinguished from movements claiming social rights, such as the labor movement. Not only the granting of fundamental human rights and the liberation of traditional authorities seem to be preconditions for the development of NSMs, the same seems to be true of the assurance that fundamental material needs are taken care of. More recent mobilization attempts of those marginalized by the labor market—welfare recipients and those unemployed—who organize to claim their social rights endangered by neoliberal politics should, therefore, be distinguished from NSMs. Although NSMs have to be distinguished from movements claiming social rights, their development in Western Europe has—as is already pointed out in the Introduction—to an important extent occurred in interaction with the movement of the traditional left. NSMs activists and sympathizers typically are supporting unions and parties on the political left (Müller-Rommel 1985). The specific nature of the interaction between NSMs and the "old" labor movement depends, among other things, on the characteristics of a country's cleavage structure, on the degree to which the traditional class conflict has been pacified, on the specific configuration of the leftist parties, and on the prevailing strategies of the members of the political system with regard to challengers in general (Brand 1985; Kriesi 1987a). In the case of the Netherlands, where the salience of class conflicts has been greatly reduced because of the cooperative posture of a relatively weak and moderate left, a rather strong NSM-sector with close ties to the organizations of the labor movement developed, transforming the traditional labor movement in the process (Kriesi/van Praag 1987; Kriesi 1987a). In the case of Italy, to name a contrasting example where class conflicts have remained much more salient in the accelerated and chaotic industrialization of the postwar period, the development of NSMs was slower and more dependent on the vagaries of the development of the labor movement. In combination with the prevailing repressive strategy of the system, the new attempts to challenge the system decomposed in the course of the 1970s as described by Donatella della Porta in Chapter 5.

To return to the general typology presented, NSMs are distinctly different from all types of counter-movements. They are not defending traditional privileges by denying fundamental political rights to others, as white suprematist movements have done in the United States, or as regional counter-movements have attempted to do in Western Europe (Ganguillet 1985; Kriesi 1985). NSMs are not denying access to social rights either, nor are they defending traditional material privileges. Antitax movements à la Glistrup in Denmark or farmers' movements defending their economic position in the face of the fiscal crisis of the Common Market are to be distinguished from NSMs as well. If professional groups are defending their privileged position by mobilizing for collective action, as physicians, for example, increasingly do, their movements are not to be considered "new" ones either. Although, in such cases, the constituency may overlap to a nonnegligible extent with the one of the NSMs, the particularistic claims of such movements are very different from the ones articulated by what should be considered NSMs. Finally, counter-movements defending traditional lifestyles, such as the antiabortion movement and the Moral Majority movement linked to it in the United States, are typically mobilizing against these NSMs and the impact they increasingly have on Western societies (Petchesky 1981).

III.   STRUCTURE AND ACTION

The distinction Bert Klandermans and Sidney Tarrow make between the two major new paradigms in social movement research—the resource mobilization approach and the new social movement approach—is related to another distinction, introduced by Coleman (1973, pp. 2ff.): the distinction between purposive and causal explanations. We are all familiar with causal explanations: some action is explained in terms of the outcome of prior actions or of a state of the actor or his environment that does not change. In the case of purposive explanations, the action no longer directly depends upon the outcome of prior actions nor upon attributes of the actor and his environment. There is the interposition of a conscious, rational actor whose choice determines the action to be taken and its outcomes: "In purposive theories, there is an implicit or explicit 'look-ahead' feature, in which the actor 'looks ahead' at the expected consequences of different outcomes for him, and adjusts his action to these possible consequences. This gives rise to the essential behavior principle of purposive action theories, the principle of utility-maximization."

European scholars studying new social movements often point to the structural developments that lie at the origin of these movements. They give causal explanations for the rise of these movements without much concern for the actual mobilizing strategies that the movements apply. In a way, the structural approaches of European scholars are still in the tradition of the "classic model" of conceptualizing collective behavior (McAdam 1982) and its emphasis on "structural conduciveness," precisely the model against which the "resource mobilization" people react so violently. These structural approaches cannot explain how structure is transformed into action.

Purposive explanations, on the other hand, generally suffer from what Berger and Offe (1982) have observed is true for game theory: "The game starts only after the actors have been constituted, and their order of preferences has been formed as a result of processes that cannot themselves be considered as being part of the game." Similarly, resource mobilization theorists tend to take preference structures and distributions of resources for granted. Melucci, as I read him, criticizes precisely this shortcoming, when he points out that models based on expectations and the resource mobilization tradition presuppose a theory of identity: "To elaborate expectations and to evaluate the possibilities and the limits of the action presupposes the capacity of an actor to define himself and his environment." Or, to put it somewhat differently, the estimated costs and benefits involved for a specific type of action are not the same for actors with different types of identities. The terrorists described by della Porta evaluate the costs and benefits involved in their activities much differently than do those who are not associated with them. A purposive theory that cannot explain such differences also fails to account for the transformation of structure into action.

"Why not try a synthesis?" Tilly (1978, p. 6) asks, but he immediately adds that such an endeavor turns out to be surprisingly difficult. A modest way to tackle the problem may be to rely on some division of labor: causal explanations would be employed to account for the development of structural opportunities and constraints of the mobilization process; purposive explanations would be used to account for the collective choices and strategic interactions taking place within the structurally determined action space. Goldstone (1986, p. 312), for example, suggests that separate theoretical models be used for explaining the different phases of a revolution—its origins, the revolutionary process, and its outcomes. The problem with this suggestion is that structural conditions and strategic interaction cannot be separated so neatly from each other. As Giddens (1984) points out, the structural conditions that make action possible are constantly reproduced in and through the activities of human actors. The structural properties of the system are at the same time medium and outcome of the practices they recursively organize.

The interdependence of structure and action suggests in the first place that we emphasize the continuity of collective action with the ongoing activities of daily life. Collective action emerges from the ongoing reproduction of structural conditions in society. Just as there is always enough discontent to form a basis for a mobilization process, so, one could say, there is always enough organization to start with in articulating discontent. "Organization" in this context does not necessarily imply "formal organization," rather, it refers to the way Tilly (1978, p. 63) uses the term: the more extensive the common identity and internal networks of a group, the more organized it is. Mobilization processes do not have to start from scratch. They can build on preexisting networks of informal relations as well as on preexisting networks of formal organizations, political or otherwise. They build on ongoing everyday activities producing and reproducing the structure of the group to be mobilized. The concept of the "micromobilization context" introduced by McAdam in this volume nicely captures this notion of insertion of mobilization into everyday life. Several essays in this volume document the usefulness of the concept of networks to capture processes of mobilization. What these essays indicate is that different types of ties are relevant for different types of mobilization processes. Mobilization involving high risk, such as that for the 1964 Mississippi Freedom Summer project studied by McAdam or the one for terrorist groups in the Italy of the 1970s studied by della Porta, rely primarily on strong preexisting ties (kinship ties, close friendship ties, or ties based on membership in the same political organizations), while mobilization involving little or no risks, such as the one for the Dutch people's petition, rely heavily on weak ties as well to be successful. High-risk mobilization presupposes a measure of mutual trust that is assured only by strong preexisting ties, while low-risk mobilization in general aims at large numbers of participants and so presupposes the existence of elaborate diffusion channels provided precisely by weak ties.

People normally know how to go on within the routines of social life. If asked, they are ordinarily able to describe what they do and to explain why. Such questions, however, are not normally posed and only rarely do actors articulate discursively what they do and why (Giddens 1984). "Settled" daily life is usually governed by common sense—a set of assumptions that has become so unself-conscious as to seem a natural, transparent, undeniable part of the structure of the world—and by traditions—articulated cultural beliefs and practices that are taken for granted. But this is not the case with "unsettled lives," as Swidler (1986), from whom I take these distinctions, points out. If daily life becomes disrupted in ways unpredicted by their accumulated knowledgeability, people will require new interpretations, which may be provided by ideologies, highly articulated self-conscious belief and ritual systems aspiring to offer a unified answer to problems of social action. It is in such a situation of crisis that the "framing" and "packaging" activities of movement actors become particularly relevant. Social movements may not be able to create grievances, but, as Klandermans points out in his chapter on consensus mobilization, they may be able to interpret grievances and in doing so they may contribute to the formation of mobilization potentials and prepare the grounds for their activation. The ideologies or "packages" that make an impact in a situation of crisis may have been around for quite a while but may not have made an impact up to that moment, as is shown by the case of nuclear power discussed by William Gamson. How a given ideology becomes relevant at a specific moment of crisis is still a largely open question. On the one hand, the "infrastructural" and "phenomeno-logical" constraints discussed by David Snow and Robert Benford, or the "cultural resonances" introduced by Gamson may be such that any attempt to interpret grievances in accord with the values and beliefs articulated by the movement turns out to be futile. The small leftist group that developed in the aftermath of the "cultural revolution" of the late sixties in many European countries, for example, had to make this painful discovery: the proletariat simply could not care less for their message. On the other hand, even if collective action does seem to have played a role in shaping interpretations of grievances—as in the case of nuclear power presented by Gamson—it was just one (admittedly "crucial catalytic") factor among others: media practices and the activities of other sponsors were other important elements that shaped the nuclear power discourse in a direction favorable for the movement.

Moments of crisis provide the chance for a "transvaluation of grievances" (Piven and Cloward 1977) or a "cognitive liberation" (McAdam 1982). It is in such situations of "transparent conflictuality" (Tarrow 1988) that ongoing activities and preexisting structures may be reoriented toward mobilization. Under the impact of the "unsettling" of everyday lives, grievances may be sharpened and geared to explicit articulation. A most impressive example of how a group reorients its internal organization to articulate its grievances on the basis of a reinterpretation of quite traditional beliefs and values is provided by Morris's (1984) account of the development of the civil rights movement. What Morris's reconstruction does not show is how a situation of structural crisis developed that gave rise to an "unsettling" of everyday lives which in turn triggered the reorientation of internal organization. This part of the reconstruction story of the civil rights movement is provided by the equally impressive work of McAdam (1982). My point is this: we cannot simply discard the insight of the classical "breakdown" theories that mobilization processes originate from crisis situations and that these situations are to some extent structurally determined by long-term developments not under the control of the political actors involved in the specific contests we are examining. Movements are unusual phenomena, people do not routinely become involved in mobilization processes. To acknowledge this fact is not to assume a sharp division between the routine of everyday life and the nonroutine of political mobilization, as has been assumed by the adherents of the classical models. To acknowledge this fact means trying to link mobilization processes to more encompassing theories of social and political change which account for the development of crisis situations that can reorient everyday life to mobilization activities.

In their sharp reaction against the classical model, students of contemporary movements in the United States—with some notable exceptions, such as Piven and Cloward (1977) and McAdam (1982)—have tended to neglect this broader view of the context of mobilization processes. American students of revolutionary processes of the more distant past such as Skocpol, Barrington Moore, Tilly, Wolfe, Wallerstein, Markoff, or Goldstone, on the other hand, have not suffered from such restricted views but have, indeed, heavily emphasized structural developments. To take but a more recent example, Goldstone (1986), to explain the English revolution in the seventeenth century, develops a structural model in which demographic change plays a crucial role. State fiscal distress, elite divisions, and popular disorders, all driven by the underlying force of population growth in the preceding century and a half, combined in mid-seventeenth century England to cause a state breakdown creating a revolutionary situation. I would suggest that the variables Goldstone uses could be applied with some success to contemporary movements as well. Take demographic change as a case in point: Easterlin (1980), an economist focusing on the question of the implications of the size of generations for very different phenomena ranging from age of marriage to divorce and suicide rates to political protest, links the unusual size of the postwar baby boom generation with the cycle of protest that developed in the 1960s in the United States. He does not develop this idea thoroughly, but one could follow his lead.

Changes in size and make-up of mobilization potentials, changes in the political opportunity structure and in political culture should, I believe, be linked to large-scale processes of social change to account for the development of critical situations providing the catalytic movement at the origin of social movements. "Mobilization potentials" form the conceptual link between the indigenous structural conditions of the group to be mobilized and collective action; "political opportunity structure" and "political culture" refer to the link between the external conditions of mobilization. In his essay, Gamson introduces the concept of "cultural conduciveness" to be added to the one of "structural conduciveness." I think this is a valuable idea to pursue, for the relative degree of "openness" of a political system is also a result of a more deeply rooted political culture. In employing the concept of "political culture," one must, of course, make sure not to label "cultural element" everything one simply cannot specify more concretely. If this concept is to be useful, it must be linked to the institutional setting and to the historical experience of a polity. In his comparison of English and French working-class consciousness, Gallie (1983) shows in an exemplary way how this connection can be made. The notion of political culture in general, or issue cultures in particular, can give us a handle on answering why certain framing efforts fall on fertile ground while others do not. With Klandermans, I would think that traditional mobilization is often as easy to get off the ground, and as radical as it turns out to be (Calhoun 1983), because it has a high experimental commensurability and narrative fidelity. Mobilization aiming at the implementation of new values and beliefs, on the other hand, has to rely, as Gramsci would put it, on the little critical "good sense" that is buried in the common sense of the everyday philosopher. Much more consensus mobilization, that is educational and consciousness raising, seems to be required in such a case.

The observation that structural properties of the system are at the same time the medium for, and outcome of, the practices they recursively organize has a second implication for the study of collective action which has not yet been considered: the conditions for collective action are shaped and reproduced by collective action itself. In other words, collective action directly affects the organization and opportunity of the actors involved (Tilly 1986, p. 397), but it may also have a considerable impact on the most basic structural conditions. There are, of course, revolutions that have changed the basic structural properties of societies. But even short of revolutions, basic structural changes can result from the aggregate effects of entire cycles of protest (Tarrow 1983). Most obviously, as Tarrow has discussed, cycles of protest are usually also associated with changes in the repertoire of collective action. As Sidney Tarrow (1983, p. 37) observes, it may indeed be their most distinctive trait that "they are crucibles out of which new weapons of social protest are fashioned." The cycle of protest that started with the students' movement in most Western European countries in the late sixties and reached its peak with the development of several NSMs in the seventies had particularly far-reaching consequences in this respect. It gave rise to what I would call the "quasi-institutionalization" of the social movement sector as a third arena of politics competing with the already established parliamentary party politics and neocorporatist interest-intermediation. The recognition in theory that movement politics are not very different from ordinary politics, just politics employing other means, reflects to some extent a development in the way collective action in social movements is viewed in Western European societies at large.

Most significantly, cycles of protest also leave behind a large potential of activists and sympathizers who can be mobilized by future movements. Different studies have shown that political protest is in general not the result of youthful idealism that subsides with aging but that young activists become permanently socialized by their experiences in the mobilization processes in which they participate early in their lives (DeMartini 1984). The conjunctural nature of the cycles of protest contrasts with the more continuous development of mobilization potentials. The latter do not disappear as cycles of protest subside, they only become less visible. Cycles of protest that fall short of a revolution may, nevertheless give rise to the development of a more or less extended counterculture—a way of life institutionalizing an alternative set of institutions that compete in many ways with the dominant culture. As I have tried to show in my essay, such a counterculture may form the core of the mobilization potential for subsequent movements. Complementing Schennink, who emphasizes the effects of the consensus mobilization efforts of the most important of the Dutch peace movement organizations, I have stressed the impact of the development of a much broader mobilization potential for NSMs in general as a consequence of the entire cycle of protest in the 1970s. Although the results of the consensus mobilization of the IKV were not negligible, the remarkable mobilization campaigns of the Dutch peace movement would not have been possible without the parallel mobilization of such other NSMs as the ecological movement, the women's movement, the squatters' movement, and especially the antinuclear movement, on whose potential the peace movement could draw as well.

Even if all the elements described here come together, it is still impossible to predict the development of a movement. All that is possible is to specify a certain probability that a mobilization potential will turn into an active challenger under given contextual circumstances in a given historical situation. The occasion that sparks the mobilization usually comes at unpredicted moments, and sometimes it does not come at all. The occasion may be more or less accidental and so give the impression that movements develop spontaneously and erupt like volcanos. Resource mobilization theorists have done well to attack the volcanic imagery of classic theorists. Nevertheless, I think there is a factor of unexpected spontaneity at the origin of movements which cannot be captured by resource mobilization theorists (Killan 1984). At a given moment, all the assembled elements seem to fall into place. It is often a first, unexpected collective action which constitutes the movement and the interaction system between challengers and authorities at the same time. In my analysis of the movement of Zurich (Kriesi 1984), nothing struck me more than the unexpectedness of its formation—elements that had all been present for some time, but had not earlier fallen into place, suddenly became a coherent movement.

REFERENCES

Beck, Ulrich. 1986. Risikogesellschaft. Auf dem Weg in Eine Andere Moderne. Frankfurt: Suhrkamp.

Beck, Ulrich. 1983. "Jenseits von Klase und Stand?" Pages 35-74 in Kreckel, R. (ed.), *Soziale Ungleichheiten. Soziale Welt.* Sonderband 2. Göttingen.

Berger, Johannes and Klaus Offe. 1982. "Functionalism vs. rational choice?" *Theory and Society* 11:521-26.

Brand, Karl-Werner (ed.). 1985. *Neue Soziale Bewegungen in Westeuropa und den USA. Ein Internationaler Vergleich.* Frankfurt: Campus.

Calhoun, Craig Jackson. 1983. "The radicalism of tradition: Community strength or venerable disguise and borrowed language?" *American Journal of Sociology* 88:886-914.

Coleman, James C. 1973. *Mathematics of Collective Action.* Chicago: Aldine.

Coleman, James S. 1986. "Social theory, social research, and a theory of action." *American Journal of Sociology* 91:1309-35.

DeMartini, J.R., 1984. "Social movement participation: Political socialization, generational consciousness and lasting effects." *Youth and Society* 15:195-223.

Easterlin, Richard A. 1980. *Birth and Fortune.* New York: Basic Books.

Esman, Milton J. (ed.). 1975. *Ethnic Conflict in the Western World.* Ithaca, N.Y.: Cornell University Press.

Gamson, William A. 1975. *The Strategy of Social Protest.* Homewood, Ill.: Dorsey Press.

Ganguillet, Gilbert. 1985. *Le Conflit Jurassien: Un Cas de Mobilisation Ethno-Régionale en Suisse.* Projet de recherche: *Le citoyen actif.* No. 2. Zurich: Institut de sociologie.

Gerdes, Dirk. 1985. *Regionalismus als Soziale Bewegung. Westeuropa, Frankreich, Korsika: Vom Vergleich zur Kontextanalyse.* Frankfurt: Campus.

Giddens, Anthony. 1984. *The Constitution of Society.* Cambridge, Eng.: Polity Press.

Goldstone, Jack A. 1986. "State breakdown in the English revolution: A new synthesis." *American Journal of Sociology* 92:257-322.

Killian, Lewis M. 1984. "Organization, rationality and spontaneity in the civil rights movement." *American Sociological Review* 49:770-83.

Kriesi, Hanspeter. 1984. *Die Zürcher Bewegung. Bilder, Interaktionen, Zusammenhänge.* Frankfurt: Campus.

Kriesi, Hanspeter. 1986. *Nieuwe Social Bewegingen: Op Zoek Naar Hun Gemeenschappelijke Noemer.* Inaugural lecture delivered at the University of Amsterdam, June 16.

Kriesi, Hanspeter. 1987a. "Neue Soziale Bewegungen: Auf der Suche Nach Ihrem Gemeinsamen Nenner." *Politische Vierteljahresschrift* (forthcoming).

Kriesi, Hanspeter. 1987b. "The Alliance Structure of the Dutch Peace Movement." Paper presented at the workshop New Social Movements and the Political System. ECPR International Joint Workshops, Amsterdam, April 11-15.

Kriesi, Hanspeter (ed.) 1985. *Bewegung in der Schweizer Politik. Fallstudien zu politischen Mobilisierungsprozessen in der Schweiz.* Frankfurt: Campus.

Kriesi, Hanspeter and Philip van Praag, Jr. 1987. "Old and new politics: The Dutch peace movement and the traditional political organizations." *European Journal of Political Science* 15:319-46.

McAdam, Doug. 1982. *Political Process and the Development of Black Insurgency, 1930-1970.* Chicago: University of Chicago Press.

Morris, Aldon D. 1984. *The Origins of the Civil Rights Movement: Black Communities Organizing for Change.* New York: Free Press.

Müller-Rommel, Ferdinand. 1985. "New social movements and smaller parties: A comparative perspective." *West European Politics* 8:41-54.

Nedelmann, Brigitta. 1984. "New political movements and changes in processes of intermediation." *Social Science Information* 23:1029-48.

Petchesky, R. Pollack. 1981. "Antiabortion, antifeminism, and the rise of the new right." *Feminist Studies* 7:206-46.

Piven, Frances Fox and Richard A. Cloward. 1977. *Poor People's Movements: Why They Succeed, How They Fail.* New York: Pantheon.

Raschke, Joachim. 1980. "Politik und Wertwandel in den westlichen Demokratien." *Aus Politik und Zietgeschichte* 36:23-46.

Raschke, Joachim. 1985. *Soziale Bewegungen. Ein Historisch-systematischer Grundriss.* Frankfurt: Campus.

Rucht, Dieter. 1982. "Neue Soziale Bewegungen Oder: Die Grenzen Bürokratischer Modernisierung." *Politische Verteiljahresschrift,* Sonderheft 13:272-92.

Swidler, Ann. 1986. "Culture in action." *American Sociological Review* 51:273-86.

Tarrow, Sidney. 1983. *Struggling to Reform: Social Movements and Policy Change during Cycles of Protest.* Western Societies Paper No. 15. Ithaca, N.Y.: Cornell University.

Tarrow, Sidney. 1988. *Democracy and Disorder: Society and Politics in Italy, 1965-1975.* Oxford: Oxford University Press (forthcoming).

Tilly, Charles. 1978. *From Mobilization to Revolution.* Reading, Mass.: Addison-Wesley.

Tilly, Charles. 1984. *"Social Movements and National Politics."* Pages 297-317 in Charles Bright and Susan Harding (eds.), *Statemaking and Social Movements.* Ann Arbor: University of Michigan Press.

Tilly, Charles. 1986. *The Contentious French.* Cambridge: Belknap Press, Harvard University Press.

Tilly, Charles, Louise Tilly, and Richard Tilly. 1975. *The Rebellious Century: 1830-1930.* Cambridge: Harvard University Press.

Touraine, Alain. 1978. *La Voix et le Regard.* Paris: Seuil.

Webb, Keith et al. 1983. "Etiology and outcomes of protest: New European perspectives." *American Behavioral Scientist* 26:311-31.

Young, Nigel. 1986. "The peace movement: A comparative and analytical survey." *Alternatives* 11:185-217.

Zald, Mayer N. and Robert Ash. 1966. "Social movement organizations: Growth, decay and change," *Social Forces* 44:327-340.

International Social Movement Research

Edited by **Bert Klandermans**
Vrije University, The Netherlands

Volume 2. Organizing For Change:
Social Movement Organizations in Europe and the United States

In preparation, Spring 1989

ISBN 0-89232-964-5   Institutions: Approx. $58.50
                       Individuals: Approx. $29.25

Social movements have traditionally been distinguished from other types of collective behavior by their high levels of organization. Nevertheless, it took until 1976, when McCarthy and Zaid introduced the distinction between social movements and social movement organizations, before social movement literature directed its attention more to social movement organizations than to social movements as objects of study. Despite this concentration on social movement organizations over the last decade, literature on social movement organizations as organizations is still scarce. In particular, empirical studies of the organizational characteristics of social movement organizations are lacking. This anthology, however, brings together papers that examine social movement organizations as organizations. Contributors from such different countries as Denmark, Germany, the Netherlands, Great Britain and the United States draw upon research into such varied movements as the civil rights movement, the labor movement, the environmental movement, the peace movement, the women's movement, and the anti-nuclear power movement. In the introductions to each section of the book a theoretical framework for the study of social movement organizations as organizations is developed.

DATE DUE

DATE DUE			
DEC 07 2009			
FEB 15 2016			
OCT 03 2016			
GAYLORD			PRINTED IN U.S.A.